HOLLAND REAL ESTATE
YEAR
BOOK
2006

EDITORIAL

LOCATIONS

DECISION MAKERS

INDUSTRY TRENDS

CORPORATE

WHO'S WHO

MAPS & INDEX

Rabo Vastgoed is giving a new allure to the historic town centre

Focus on the entire neighbourhood. With an eye for detail, we consider not only the surrounding buildings and the historic context, but also the various interests of all those making use of the area. In today's city and town centres space is scarce and individual interests are complex, so we at Rabo Vastgoed carefully listen to, and look at life in the entire area. We focus on who lives and works in the neighbourhood, and combine this with a clear appreciation of the existing everyday environment. Bringing all these factors together, our final aim is to involve all members of the surrounding community in enriching the area both visually and functionally.

Rabobank

ALL ABOUT REAL ESTATE IN THE NETHERLANDS

Holland
REAL ESTATE
CITIES ● REGIONS ● PROJECTS ● INDUSTRY TRENDS ● COMPANIES ● PEOPLE

COUNTRY BOOK
EUROPE REAL ESTATE
PUBLISHERS B.V.
North Sea Building,
Gevers Deynootweg 93,
2586 BK The Hague
P.O. Box 84416,
2508 AK The Hague,
The Netherlands
Tel.: +31 70 352 86 00
Fax: +31 70 352 86 60
E-mail: info@holland-re.com
www.holland-re.com

JEANNETTE BLOKSMA, *Publisher*

MARINUS DIJKMAN, *Editor-in-Chief*

MANAGEMENT TEAM
DRS. JACQUELINE LAUREY-MAASLAND,
Senior Editor
ELLEN BEKKER, *Head of Production*
PETER SCHREUTER, *Sales Manager*
ERIK GOOSEN, *Creative Director*

EDITORS
MICHIEL VAN DEN BROEK
DICK GROENENDIJK
KEES HAAK
BEN MAANDAG
FLEMMING DE MOLL
DRS. OLA SINOO

PRODUCTION
INGRID HOEVENAGEL, *Traffic*
YVONNE FERNHOUT, *Traffic*
CAROLINE SONNEVELD, *Research*
LEN 'T HOEN, *Illustrations / Lay-out*
MAREK MOGGRÉ, *Illustrations / Lay-out*
MARCEL VAN DEN BERG, *Lay-out*
LENNARD KRUITHOF, *Lay-out*
MARCO REIJKEN, *Lay-out*
ANDRÉ SNOEI, *Lay-out*
HANS MOGGRÉ, *Lay-out*

TRANSLATIONS
SUSHY MANGAT, *Proofreading*
KELLY ATKINSON, *Proofreading*
WILLEM KRAMER, *Translations*
BART PLANTENGA, *Translations*
RAY PABLA, *Translations*

INTERNET & DATABASE PUBLISHING
JEROEN SCHELLEKENS, *ICT Programs*

ADVERTISING
Europe Real Estate Publishers B.V.
Sales Department
PETER SCHREUTER, *Sales Manager*
MICHIEL FOEKENS, *Sales Executive*
P.O. Box 84416, 2508 AK The Hague
The Netherlands
Tel.: +31 70 352 86 00
Fax: +31 70 352 86 60
E-mail: sales@holland-re.com

SUBSCRIPTIONS
Europe Real Estate Publishers B.V.
Administration Department
E-mail: subscribe@holland-re.com

PRODUCTION SERVICES
HAASBEEK PRINTING
(Alphen aan den Rijn) *Print/Binder*

ISBN 9077997059 / 9789077997055 (paper)
9077997075 / 9789077997079 (bound)
ISSN 1572-820X

FROM THE EDITOR

Small country with big ambitions

'Good things come in small packages' is an expression that can surely be said to apply to the Netherlands. With a total size of only 35,000 km² and a population of 16.5 million the Netherlands is small in comparison to other European countries. But its strategic location on the European mainland, its fine labor force, and its internationally orientated business community make this small country great.

The Netherlands has always been known as a 'water country'. And there is good news with respect to this – the Dutch water policy is changing. Water is being seen less as a competitive enemy and more, according to our State Secretary Melanie Schultz van Haegen, as an essential element and starting point for town and country planning. With regard to the real estate industry, this is a positive shift.

The importance of providing more room for water storage runs parallel with the increased appreciation of bodies of water in public spaces, as can be seen in this year's edition of the Holland Real Estate Yearbook. Living along the water has always been popular in the Netherlands, but nowadays homes are being increasingly built on and in the water. Project developers, urban planners and architects are eagerly taking advantage of this trend.

In addition, the editorial staff of the Holland Real Estate Yearbook 2006 has picked up on another ambitious project – the participation of the Netherlands on the European high-speed railroad (HSL) network. When the new trains and railroad come into service in 2007, travel time between Amsterdam and Paris will be reduced by approximately 1.5 hours.

The Dutch government designated six of the most important railway stations in the Netherlands as New Key Projects. These stations, connected to the HSL network and parts of the cities, have to develop into metropolitan areas with a favorable climate for living and working. In the article 'HSL and New Key Projects' we asked the opinion of the parties involved.

This seventh annual Holland Real Estate Yearbook includes the annual Holland Real Estate Housing Debate, where the management of major real estate developers in the Netherlands came together in the country's political press center Nieuwspoort. Besides this topic you will find a review of real estate developments in all major cities and regions, as well as an alphabetical list of Decision Makers in Dutch real estate.

I hope you will enjoy reading it.

Marinus Dijkman
Editor-in-Chief

March 2006

www.holland-re.com

EDITORIAL

LOCATIONS

DECISION MAKERS

INDUSTRY TRENDS

CORPORATE

WHO'S WHO

MAPS & INDEX

Skyline or horizon?

At FGH Bank, we provide the horizon for great ideas. This is why investors and developers rely on our in-house expertise and solid, flexible finance solutions. No other bank is better equipped to realize their vision. Offices in eight Dutch cities and our association with the Rabobank Group give access to local market know-how and an extensive network. So broaden your perspective and give us a call. Your idea may soon be part of the skyline. *www.fghbank.nl*

HOLLAND REAL ESTATE

THE PEOPLE

Marinus Dijkman,
Editor-in-Chief

Jeannette Bloksma,
Publisher

Jacqueline Laurey,
Senior Editor

Erik Goosen,
Creative Director

Ellen Bekker,
Head of Production

Peter Schreuter,
Sales Manager

Michiel Foekens,
Sales Executive

Sushy Mangat,
Proofreading

Jeroen Schellekens,
ICT Programs

Caroline Sonneveld,
Research

Ola Sinoo,
Senior Editor

Flemming de Moll,
Editor

Dick Groenendijk,
Editor

Ingrid Hoevenagel,
Traffic

Yvonne Fernhout,
Traffic

YEARBOOKS AND INTERNET

Holland Real Estate, one of the Country Books of Europe Real Estate Publishers, forms a gateway to Dutch real estate by publishing a yearbook about the Dutch market and by serving as a portal to the industry via Internet. The Europe Real Estate Yearbook, together with a daily newsletter and website, aims to create a more transparent European real estate market. The Real Estate City Books promote major European cities as the place to be. More information about the yearbooks can be found on www.europe-re.com, www.holland-re.com and www.amsterdam-re.com.

EUROPE REAL ESTATE   COUNTRY BOOKS   CITY BOOKS   INTERNET

Some of the photographic material has been supplied by third parties. Every care and consideration has been taken to verify if any copyright was due. In case of omissions please contact the publisher.

Europe Real Estate Publishers B.V., P.O. Box 84416, 2508 AK The Hague, the Netherlands, Tel.: +31 70 352 86 00, Fax: +31 70 352 86 60, E-mail: info@holland-re.com, Website: www.holland-re.com

PUBLISHER

EUROPE REAL ESTATE PUBLISHERS B.V. *is chartered in The Hague, the Netherlands. It is a privately owned company based on a shareholders construction.*

MARINUS DIJKMAN, *President and CEO*

Senior Vice Presidents
JEANNETTE BLOKSMA, ERIK GOOSEN

Management Team
DRS. JACQUELINE LAUREY-MAASLAND, ELLEN BEKKER, PETER SCHREUTER

ADVISORY BOARD
PROF. DR. PIET M.A. EICHHOLTZ
Maastricht University

PROF. DR. KEES KOEDIJK
University of Rotterdam and Maastricht

PROF. IR. HANS DE JONGE
Delft University of Technology
Chairman of the Brink Groep

PROF. DR. ED F. NOZEMAN
University of Groningen/ Amsterdam School of Real Estate Independant Consultant

PROF. DRS. ING. HENK J. GIANOTTEN
University of Tilburg
President of the EIM Groep

ONNO BREUR
Member of the Board of Vesteda

RENÉ BUCK
President of Buck Consultants International

IR. CEES HAKSTEGE MSC
Director of Cristel Vastgoed

DRS. RENÉ J.M. HOGENBOOM
CEO Altera Vastgoed

DR. AART C. HORDIJK MRICS
Director ROZ/IPD Property Index
Visiting Associate Professor
Delft University of Technology

PETER C. KEUR
Chairman of the Board of FGH Bank N.V.

IR. KARIN LAGLAS
Managing Director of Rodamco Europe in the Netherlands

AD A. MAST, MSC., FRICS
Managing Director of Schiphol Real Estate

BERTUS L.H. PIJPER
Former CEO of Bouwfonds Property Finance

MR. HENK R. PORTE MBA MRICS MRE
Interim Manager/Advisor

IR. CAREL E.C. DE REUS
Managing Director Johan Matser Projectontwikkeling

MR. RONALD W.M. SMEETS
Director Fortis Vastgoed Beleggingen

IR. RUDY F.C. STROINK
CEO of TCN Property Projects

DRS. PAUL TRIP MRE
Director IPMMC Vastgoed

IR. PAUL A.R.J. VISMANS
CEO of KFN

ING. PIETER WETSELAAR
CEO Rabo Vastgoed

COEN VAN OOSTROM
CEO OVG Projectontwikkeling

DRS. ING. HENK J.M. VAN ZANDVOORT
Chairman of the Executive Board Bouwfonds Property Development

DRS. IR. KEES C.A.M. DE BOO
CEO NS Vastgoed

DRS. J.A.M. MEUWISSEN MRE
General Manager ING Real Estate Development

www.holland-re.com

FOR DAILY NEWS ON THE DUTCH REAL ESTATE MARKET

Direct access to locations, projects or companies via windows structure

News search engine
Daily news and archive

Quick search

Upcoming events

Daily news

CITY BOOKS

COUNTRY BOOKS

YEARBOOK

DAILY MAIL LETTER

WWW.ROTTERDAM-RE.COM

WWW.HOLLAND-RE .COM

WWW.EUROPE-RE.COM

HOLLAND REAL ESTATE YEARBOOK 2006

ROOM FOR WATER AND LIVING **58**

DEBATE IN NIEUWSPOORT **64**

JAAP BLOKHUIS, MAN OF THE YEAR **46**

ARCHITECTURE: FRANCINE HOUBEN **94**

With a total size of 35,000 km² and a population of 16.5 million, the Netherlands is small in comparison to its neighbors. A strategic location on the European mainland; a labor force with a good knowledge of languages and a flexible work mentality; an internationally orientated business community and quality facilities are the basis of the Netherlands' good reputation for enterprise.

With the motto 'Return or Retail' Rodamco Europe focuses its investments on dominant retail locations. What does this mean for the Netherlands, one of Rodamco's four home markets? How do you play the investment funds market effectively? And what do you do with the eternally important office property? We discussed all of this with Karin Laglas, Managing Director of Rodamco Europe in the Netherlands.

With total assets that run into the hundreds of billions of euros, of which some 10% or so is invested in real estate, Dutch pension funds don't just make their mark on the international investment market, but on the Dutch real estate market as well. In conversation with four dominant trendsetters: Patrick Kanters (ABP), Werner Sohier (PGGM), Dick van Hal (Achmea Vastgoed) and René Hogenboom (Altera Vastgoed).

DEPARTMENTS

THE COVER

Viñoly, one of the landmarks of the prestigious Zuidas in Amsterdam, is designed by the world-known architect Rafael Viñoly. Ontwerpgroep Trude Hooykaas is responsible for the interior design. Developers are Fortis Vastgoed, G&S Vastgoed and ING Real Estate. See page 54. Photo: Trude Hooykaas/Luuk Kramer.

Sidebar tabs: EDITORIAL · LOCATIONS · DECISION MAKERS · INDUSTRY TRENDS · CORPORATE · WHO'S WHO · MAPS & INDEX

OVERVIEW EDITORIAL

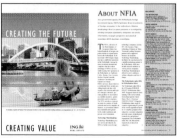

40. *Stadiums, lynchpin of real estate.*

64. *Debate in Nieuwspoort.*

94. *Francine Houben, Mecanoo.*

298. *IPD.*

263. *Decision Makers.* **333.** *Who's Who.*

Western Region.

Famous tulips.

Royal family.

Amsterdam.

391. *Index & Maps.*

TABLE OF EDITORIAL CONTENTS:

TABLE OF COMMERCIAL PAGES:

WHO'S WHO

CORPORATE PAGES

TABLE OF ADVERTISEMENTS

OVERVIEW LOCATIONS

100. *Amsterdam Airport Area.*

116. *Amsterdam.*

142. *The Hague.*

182. *Utrecht.*

196. *Western Region.*

216. *Central Region.*

238. *Eastern Region.*

248. *Southern Region.*

130. *Mahler4, Amsterdam.*

156. *Spuimarkt, The Hague.*

158. *New Babylon, The Hague.*

176. *Montevideo, Rotterdam.*

194. *Galgenwaard, Utrecht.*

208. *Spazio, Zoetermeer.*

226. *Stadshart, Almere.*

Amsterdam.

160. *Rotterdam.*

The Hague.

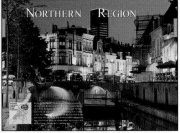

228. *Northern Region.*

138. *Oosterburgereiland, Amsterdam.*

Rotterdam.

Utrecht.

178. *Linea Nova, Rotterdam.*

260. *Piazza Center, Eindhoven.*

99. *Locations.*

EDITORIAL

LOCATIONS

DECISION MAKERS

INDUSTRY TRENDS

CORPORATE

WHO'S WHO

MAPS & INDEX

Quality Accommodation

vesteda

The Vesteda Tower in Eindhoven, the Netherlands, is one of the symbols of Vesteda's strategy: the higher rent sector, a top location, urban inspiration, residential quality, and architecture. The design of the tower, by former chief government architect Jo Coenen, deviates from traditional Dutch style. The tower is 90 metres high, offering 44 luxury apartments with a flexible layout. There is a well-equipped gym as well as guest accommodation. And no concession whatsoever is made in terms of quality.

www.vesteda.com

In Brief

BAM and MSREF takeover AM

Terra Amstel, a joint venture of BAM and ING, has taken over Dutch project developer AM together with the Morgan Stanley Real Estate Fund (MSREF). BAM is a Dutch real estate developer and contractor and the MSREF is a part of the American investment bank Morgan Stanley. AM withdrew from the stock market towards the end of the first quarter of 2006.

The takeover has cost both parties more than €1.4 billion (enterprise value). At the end of December 2005, BAM Group made an offer of €10.15 per AM share (with dividend and other payouts).

As a result AM was valued at €952 million, together with the outstanding warranty rights. Immediately following the acceptance of the offer for AM, on January 25, 2006 Terra Amstel sold AM Development to MSREF for €479 million.

This means that BAM paid €473 million for the company shares AM Wonen, AM Grondbedrijf and for AM Holding. Continuing amounts do not include the debt positions taken over by both companies.

In the coming years, AM Wonen will be put forward as an independent entity within the BAM concern. In the early phase, ING Investments Participaties will act as financier through a 50%-interest participation in Terra Amstel. NIB Capital will act on behalf of AM Development and Kempen & Co on behalf of AM Wonen during the realization of the deal.

Multi Development

A condition of MSREF is that AM Development's current management will go with them to the new entity. In the meantime, the name has been changed to Multi Development. A one-tier Board construction has been chosen; the Chairman's seat will be filled by Hans van Veggel and Arnold de Haan will fulfill the role of CEO.

BAM/AM

The Board of Directors of BAM/AM Wonen and BAM/AM Grondbedrijf will include Peter Noordanus and Peter Ruigrok, who will both share the role of Chairman. Furthermore, agreements have been made that AM Wonen will provide 35 to 40% of the construction production at BAM's construction company.

Pipeline

AM Wonen/Grondbedrijf has approximately €10 billion in the pipeline on the basis of more than 40,000 residences and €9 billion for Multi Development. The takeover has very few repercussions for personnel. At AM Holding seven people will have to be relocated and seven people will be made redundant.

MULTI DEVELOPMENT

- HQ Gouda, the Netherlands
- MSREF (financial partner)
- Pipeline €9 bln (Retail Projects)

Arnold de Haan
CEO

Hans van Veggel
Chairman
of the Board

BAM/AM WONEN AND BAM/AM GRONDBEDRIJF

- HQ Nieuwegein, the Netherlands
- Royal BAM Group (97,1%)
- Pipeline €10 bln (40.000 houses)

Peter Noordanus
Chairman
of the Board

Peter Ruigrok
Chairman
of the Board

Holland Real Estate
www.holland-re.com The B-to-B connector in global real estate. Your company profile delivered to the Real Estate Professional worldwide.

EDITORIAL ▼ LOCATIONS ▼ BUILDINGS ▼ INDUSTRY TRENDS ▼ CORPORATE ▼ WHO IS WHO ▼

EDITORIAL · LOCATIONS · DECISION MAKERS · INDUSTRY TRENDS · CORPORATE · WHO'S WHO · MAPS & INDEX

THE NETHERLANDS: GATEWAY TO EUROPE
A SMALL COUNTRY

A strategic location on the European mainland; a labor force with
a good knowledge of languages and a flexible work mentality;
an internationally orientated business community and quality
facilities - these factors are the basis of the Netherlands' longstanding
reputation for enterprise. What makes a small country great. *By Ola Sinoo*

AMSTERDAM AIRPORT AREA   MAINPORT ROTTERDAM   THE HAGUE, SEAT OF GOVERNMENT   UTRECHT CENTRAL STATION

WITH BIG AMBITIONS

World renowned architects are responsible for the skyline of Rotterdam, a virtual 'Manhattan on the Maas'.

PHOTO: MARCO DE NOOD

The expression 'good things come in small packages' can surely be said to apply to the Netherlands. With a total size of 35,000 km² and a population of 16.5 million, the country is small in comparison to many of its neighbors. Indeed, even its main cities are modest in size. Amsterdam, the largest city in the Netherlands, has a population of 740,000 – peanuts compared to metropoles like Tokyo, Mexico City or NYC, or, closer to home, London (7.5 million), Berlin (3.4 million) and Paris (11 million). However, the Netherlands' four major cities are all located very close to one another in the Randstad, more or less fusing into a single urban agglomeration. Thus combined, the region's population easily passes the five million mark.

Quick connections

Its small dimensions provide the Netherlands with several important advantages. Distances are short, in part thanks to an extensive network of railways and roads. Starting at the North Sea, one can reach the German border in a mere two hours, and the whole country can be traversed from north to south in a matter of four. The four main cities – Amsterdam, Rotterdam, The Hague and Utrecht – are all located within a radius of less than 80 km, within an hour's travel of one another, and recreational and natural areas are at close hand. In addition, billions of euros are currently being invested in infrastructure projects aimed at maintaining the Netherlands' high level of accessibility. Well-known examples are the HSL high-speed rail link, the Betuwelijn railway line and RandstadRail. Other plans include the Zuiderzeelijn – a magnetic hover-train connection between the Randstad and the northern provinces – and further expansion of the railway network in order to intensify rail-based transport between the western region of the Netherlands and the large cities in the southern provinces.

Gateway to Europe

In addition to its strategic location within Europe, the Netherlands has two important mainports at its disposal in the form of Amsterdam Airport Schiphol and the Rotterdam harbor. The mainports have excellent connections with the European hinterland, be it by land, water or air. This combines to make the Netherlands a true gateway to Europe.   >>

PHOTO: HANNAH ANTHONYSZ

Schouwburgplein, Rotterdam.

PHOTO: FRANS LEMMENS

Each year on Prinsjesdag (Budget Day), the third Tuesday of September, Queen Beatrix opens the Parliament year. The Queen presents a summary of the most important plans of the government for the following year.

Amsterdam Airport Schiphol

Amsterdam Airport Schiphol provides the capital with a direct connection with all major cities in Europe, the United States and Asia. In 2004, the airport transferred over 42.5 million passengers and 1.4 million tons of cargo, making it one of the continent's major airports. Besides accommodating air transport, Amsterdam Airport Schiphol also serves as a top business location, offering a WTC, various hotels and excellent on-site facilities. The Amsterdam Airport area provides international companies with optimum international multimodal accessibility, a healthy labor market, an attractive price/quality ratio, a strong

local knowledge economy and opportunities to modify their corporate structure and outsource activities. Amsterdam Airport Schiphol's appeal is confirmed time and time again. Since 1990, the airport was awarded more than a hundred first prizes in a range of categories by various international publications and organizations.

The Rotterdam harbor

For years, the Rotterdam harbor was the largest in the world. It has relinquished this position, but with a transshipment volume of 352 million tons the harbor still holds a respectable third place on the list of major international ports (only outranked by

Singapore with 393.4 million tons and Shanghai with 379.7 million tons). And Rotterdam is still the largest harbor in Europe by far. In the first half of 2005, 185 million tons of cargo was handled in the port of Rotterdam, a 5% increase compared to the same period in 2004. Havenbedrijf Rotterdam (the Rotterdam Port Authority) will unfold several ambitious plans over the next few years. The organization is aiming for 397 million tons of transshipped cargo in 2009, according to the Business Plan 2006-2010 presented in October 2005. The development of Maasvlakte 2 is a prerequisite for this growth. For a long time, it remained uncertain whether the project would ever be realized, but in November 2005 the Dutch government gave the go-ahead for the large-scale expansion. Construction on Maasvlakte 2 is expected to kick off in 2008, with the first terminal becoming operational around 2012.

International orientation

With on average 484 people per square kilometer, the Netherlands is one of the most densely populated countries in

The WTC Schiphol Airport (owner KFN) has been extended and now has a total floor surface of 52,000 m², devided over four office towers.

...arrives in the Binnenhof of The Hague in the golden carriage to deliver the Speech from the Throne. In this speech the Queen

the world. It is a multicultural society –in the large cities in particular one can find dozens of nationalities and cultural backgrounds living side by side. On January 2005, the Netherlands had 3.1 million residents of foreign descent, of which a slight majority came from a non-Western background. This means that one fifth of the total Dutch population is presently of foreign descent. But the Dutch population's strong international orientation should not be merely attributed to the increased immigration of recent decades. International enterprise is an established Dutch tradition, in full swing as far back as the Golden Age of the 17th century thanks to the efforts of the Dutch East India Company (VOC). Apparently the Dutch are born to think and do business on an international scale. One can gather as much from the population's above-average knowledge of foreign languages, which has benefited the country for decades. In addition to English, a large percentage of the Dutch labor force speaks German or French, and increasing numbers are mastering Spanish or Italian.

Trade and economy

The Netherlands' strategic location, the good knowledge of languages and flexible mentality of its labor force, its internationally orientated business community and high-grade facilities combine to make the country an attractive business location for foreign companies. Various global ranking models measuring the competitiveness of business environments confirm that the Netherlands is an excellent place to do business. It comes as no surprise that dozens of foreign companies decide to establish their (European) head offices in the Netherlands each year. Business services provision,

including banks, insurance companies and other service providers, is the Netherlands' largest economic sector. The companies active in this field are concentrated in the Randstad, while outside the Randstad farming and manufacturing are more fully represented. The Netherlands features a strong and diverse manufacturing sector, led by the agro-industrial, chemical, electronics and metal industries. An indication of the importance of this sector is the fact that five of the world's leading multinationals – Philips, Unilever, Royal Dutch/Shell Group, DSM and Akzo Nobel – were founded in the Netherlands.   >>

PHOTO: AEROCAMERA

Rotterdam's entrance to the harbour area. In the years ahead Maasvlakte 2 (2,000 ha) will be realized.

Knowledge economy

Due to the Netherlands' lack of raw materials, the Dutch government has a long history of investment in the local knowledge economy. The Netherlands has 13 regular universities. In addition, there are some 50 polytechnics spread across the country, as well as several extramural research institutes that employ a large percentage of the some 50,000 researchers working in the Netherlands. A majority of the active R&D staff, however, is employed by private companies.

Office market

The economic recession that struck many European countries in the first years of the new millennium did not pass the Dutch office market by.

There was a sharp decline in the volume of used office space, and today's figure fluctuates around approx. 40 million m^2.

Increasing vacancy rates – some 5.8 m^2 of vacant office space at the end of 2004 – naturally had an effect on the demand for new construction. While in the recent past the annual growth in the office market reached 5%, a mere 625,000 m^2 of new office space was completed in 2004: a meager 1.4% increase. At the end of 2005, some 11 million m^2 of new office developments was in the pipeline. A major portion of this can be found in Amsterdam (with 1.7 million m^2 planned), followed by Haarlemmermeer (1.5 million m^2) and Rotterdam (over 1 million m^2). The demand for new construction will remain limited in the years ahead. New buildings will not be so much used to expand the existing range, as to replace old ones in order to maintain the quality of the office market.

Retail market

The biggest trend in today's retail market is increasing scale. The sector's traditional fine-meshed network of shopping facilities will gradually be replaced by large-scale retail complexes with ample parking facilities on the outskirts of town. Between 2000 and 2005, total retail space in the Netherlands increased from 20.5 million m^2 to 25.4 million m^2. At the start of 2005, some 764,000 m^2 of retail space was under construction, of which nearly 60% was large-scale, inner-city development projects and new retail projects on the edge of the core shopping areas. At the start of 2005, some 1.9 million m^2 (7.2% of the total market) stood vacant, and this figure is expected to continue to rise over the next few years. In the same period, over 3.5 million m^2 of new construction projects – including some 1.4 million m^2 at large-scale peripheral locations – were in the pipeline.

Urban developments

In terms of urban development, the Netherlands never stands still. New urban areas are primarily developed on the fringes of the Dutch cities. The emphasis is on multipurpose locations that provide space for homes, offices, stores and other facilities. Well-known examples include Amsterdam's Zuidas and IJ-Oevers, Fascinatio in Rotterdam or The Wall near Utrecht. Great care is taken to preserve the country's many historic city centers, but with the redevelopment of the Spuimarkt area in The Hague and the area surrounding Utrecht Central Station, the cities in question will gain a completely new face in the years ahead.   <<

Rankings

1st Most flexible labor market

According to the Knowledge Base compiled by British forecaster and analyst Cambridge Econometrics, Amsterdam is one of the top 20 European city-regions with respect to growth prospects in the period 2004-2009. Forecast output growth for the Amsterdam city-region is almost 2.5% per annum. Forecast employment growth for the Amsterdam city-region is almost 1.5% per annum, earning it a fifth position. According to Cambridge Econometrics, Amsterdam's presence in the top 10 is a reflection of the fact that the Netherlands has the most flexible labor market in the EU and the highest level of part-time employment.

1st Best airport worldwide

Amsterdam Airport Schiphol has been named the world's Best Airport by Buying Business Travel, one of the most prestigious travel trade magazines of the United Kingdom.

Amsterdam Airport Schiphol was praised by readers for its AirportCity facilities and services. The airport's one-terminal concept is also greatly appreciated by U.K. travellers. Other airports nominated for the award were Dubai, Singapore, Hong Kong and Chicago.

10th Most competitive economy

In the Global Competitiveness Report 2005-2006 released by the World Economic Forum (WEF), the Netherlands belongs to the top 10 most competitive economies worldwide.

The ranking reveals that the global business community (117 economies were assessed) has a favorable view of the Dutch government and the Dutch business community. In the Growth Competitiveness Index (GCI), the Netherlands moved up from 2004's 12th position, now tied with Australia on positions 10/11.

ONLINE: www.holland-re.com/dutch

PHOTO: NBTC

< Above: The water level is often higher than the grass land.
Below: Famous Dutch tulip fields.

Holland Real Estate

www.holland-re.com The B-to-B connector in global real estate. Your compa

| EDITORIAL ▼ | LOCATIONS ▼ | BUILDINGS ▼ | INDUST |

HOLLAND IN FACTS AND FIGURES

Economic Profile

After a sharp and protracted slowdown from 2001 to 2003 and a short-lived recovery in 2004, 2005 was another gloomy year for the Netherlands. In the first quarter of the year real GDP fell by 0.8% quarter-on-quarter but it strongly recovered in the second quarter (+1.2% quarter-on-quarter) and this recovery should continue in the second half of the year. Nevertheless, on average, real GDP growth in 2005 will probably not exceed 0.50%, down from 1.7% in 2004.

Private consumption, which declined in 2003 and stagnated in 2004, is expected to decrease again this year, by about 0.25%. The main reason was a further decline in households' disposable income, by nearly 1% in real terms, due to the continuing decline in employment, renewed wage moderation after the excessive wage increases of the late-1990s and early-2000s, and a fall in non-labor income. Public consumption stagnated and public investment declined by about 0.75%, reflecting the continuing

effort to further reduce the government deficit. Gross fixed capital formation by corporations was nearly flat but investment in dwellings still increased by 3%.

Prospects for 2006 and 2007

GDP growth is projected to reach about 2% in 2006 and about 2.50% in 2007, essentially because domestic demand should be significantly more dynamic than in recent years. Developments in both private and public consumption are blurred by the reform of the

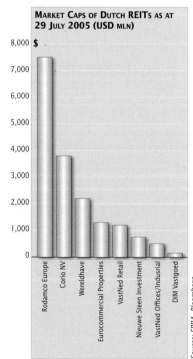

MARKET CAPS OF DUTCH REITS AS AT 29 JULY 2005 (USD MLN)

Source: EPRA, Bloomberg.

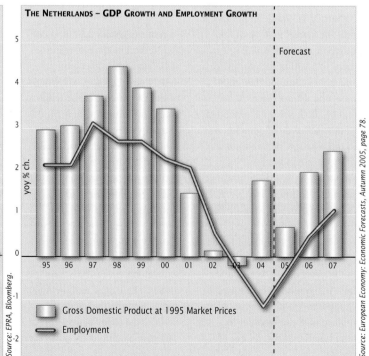

THE NETHERLANDS – GDP GROWTH AND EMPLOYMENT GROWTH

Forecast

yoy % ch.

□ Gross Domestic Product at 1995 Market Prices
— Employment

Source: European Economy: Economic Forecasts, Autumn 2005, page 78.

e delivered to the Real Estate Professional worldwide.

DS ▼ CORPORATE ▼ WHO IS WHO ▼

health care system on January 1, 2006, which will result in a shift from the former to the latter of about 1.7% of GDP. This institutional change is the main reason why private consumption is expected to decrease by about 3% in real terms and government consumption to rise by more than 9% next year. This shift apart, private consumption should rise by about 0.50% in 2006 as households' gross disposable income will broadly stabilize in real terms after several years of decline. In 2007, private con-

sumption is set to accelerate to around 2%: households' disposable income should rise significantly for the first time in years, essentially due to the recovery in employment; on the other hand, the saving's rate, which dropped considerably in recent years and thereby supported consumption, is expected to rise again.[1]

Footnotes
[1] European Commission:
European Economy, Economic Forecasts Autumn 2005.

STATISTICS

POPULATION (2005)	16,292,354
GDP GROWTH (2005)	0.90 %
CONSUMER SPENDING GROWTH	2.70 %
INFLATION (2005)	1.60 %
UNEMPLOYMENT	4.70 %
EMPLOYMENT (2004)	73.10 %
INTEREST RATES	2.25 %

MOST IMPORTANT CITIES — INHABITANTS

AMSTERDAM	739,295
ROTTERDAM	596,068
THE HAGUE	468,421
UTRECHT	275,797
EINDHOVEN	208,573

PRIME OFFICE RENT (Q4 2005)

LOCATION	RENT EURO/ SQ.M/YR	GROWTH % (PA COMPOUND) 5 YEARS	1 YEAR
AMSTERDAM SOUTH	300	-14.77	0.00
AMSTERDAM CENTRAL	250	-8.09	0.00
AMSTERDAM SOUTH-EAST	185	5.71	0.00
ROTTERDAM	182	11.66	0.00
THE HAGUE	195	4.84	0.00
UTRECHT	180	4.65	0.00

PRIME OFFICE YIELDS (Q4 2005)

LOCATION	YIELD % CURRENT	10 YEAR HIGH	RECORD LOW
AMSTERDAM SOUTH	6.00	6.50	6.00
AMSTERDAM CENTRAL	6.20	N/A	N/A
AMSTERDAM SOUTH-EAST	6.60	N/A	N/A
ROTTERDAM	6.25	6.75	6.25
THE HAGUE	6.25	6.50	6.25
UTRECHT	6.25	6.75	6.25

NATIONAL INDICES (2004)

BLN EURO	CURR. PRICES	%GDP
GDP AT PREVIOUS YEAR PRICES	488.6	100.0
PRIVATE CONSUMPTION	239.2	48.9
PUBLIC CONSUMPTION	118.5	24.3
GROSS FIXED CAPITAL FORMATION	94.6	19.4
OF WHICH : EQUIPMENT	28.3	5.8
CHANGE IN STOCKS AS % OF GDP	0.8	0.2
EXPORTS (GOODS AND SERVICES)	328.1	67.1
FINAL DEMAND	781.3	159.9
IMPORTS (GOODS AND SERVICES)	292.6	59.9
GNI AT PREV. YR. PRICES (GDP DEFL.)	489.8	100.2

MAIN FEATURES [1] bln Euro	Annual percentage change					
	81-01	2002	2003	2004	2005	2006	2007
GDP at previous year prices	2.5	0.1	-0.1	1.7	0.5	2.0	2.4
Private consumption	2.0	0.9	-0.7	0.0	-0.2	-3.0	1.8
Public consumption	2.6	3.3	2.4	0.0	0.1	9.5	3.0
Gross fixed capital formation	2.5	-4.5	-3.5	2.9	1.4	4.5	6.3
of which : equipment	3.8	-4.9	4.1	5.7	0.3	7.7	9.0
Change in stocks as % of GDP	0.3	-0.3	-0.1	0.2	0.0	0.0	0.0
Exports (goods and services)	5.4	0.9	2.0	8.5	3.3	4.8	5.3
Final demand	3.3	0.1	0.6	3.9	1.5	3.2	4.0
Imports (goods and services)	4.8	0.3	2.0	7.8	3.0	5.0	6.4
GNI at previous year prices (GDP deflator)	2.4	0.2	-0.9	1.8	0.5	2.0	2.4
Contrib. to GDP growth : Dom. demand	2.1	0.2	-0.5	0.6	0.2	1.7	2.9
Stockbuilding	-0.1	-0.6	0.2	0.2	-0.2	0.0	-0.1
Foreign balance	0.5	0.5	0.1	0.9	0.5	0.3	-0.4
Employment	1.2	-0.3	-0.9	-1.6	-0.6	0.5	1.0
Unemployment (a)	6.4	2.8	3.7	4.6	5.1	4.9	4.2
Compensation of employees/head	2.9	5.2	4.0	3.3	1.4	1.0	1.3
Unit labor costs	1.6	4.8	3.3	-0.1	0.3	-0.5	-0.1
Real unit labor costs	-0.6	1.0	0.7	-0.9	-0.6	-1.4	-1,7
Savings rate of households (b)	-	-	13.9	14.0	12.2	12.5	14.0
GDP deflator	2.2	3.8	2.5	0.9	0.9	0.9	1.6
Private consumption deflator	2.5	3.0	2.2	1.1	1.7	2.0	1.8
Harmonised index of consumer prices	-	3.9	2.2	1.4	1.7	2.0	1.9
Trade balance (c)	4.1	6.7	6.8	7.3	7.4	6.8	6.2
Current account balance (c)	4.0	6.0	5.8	6.1	6.0	5.4	4.8
Net lending(+) or borr.(-) v.-à-v. ROW (c)	3.6	5.9	5.6	5.9	3.8	3.3	4.8
General government balance (c)(d)	-3.2	-2.0	-3.2	-2.1	-1.8	-1.9	-1.5
General government gross debt (c)	66.5	51.3	52.6	53.1	54.0	54.2	53.8

(a) as % of civilian labor force; (b) gross saving divided by gross disposable income;
(c) as a percentage of GDP; (d) Including proceeds relative to UMTS licences
More info: www.europe.eu.int/comm/economy

ONLINE: www.holland-re.com/facts

CREATING THE FUTURE

New developments and concepts originate from a vision of the future in which places, functions and people play a central role. ING Real Estate combines this vision with experiences from the past and the client's requirements. A clear idea is developed of what is feasible and what has to be realised. It's an inspiring foundation to support the efforts for our future.

CREATING VALUE

About NFIA

As a government agency, the Netherlands Foreign Investment Agency (NFIA) facilitates direct investments of foreign companies in the Netherlands. Whether developing a first European presence or reconfiguring existing European operations, companies can obtain information, strategic perspective and practical assistance NFIA's business consultants.

The NFIA, a division of the Dutch ministry of Economic Affairs, has helped hundreds of foreign companies initiate or expand operations in the Netherlands. In all, more than 5,000 foreign companies have established operations in the Netherlands. Among the many prominent international companies that have taken advantage of NFIA's services while locating their operations in the Netherlands, are Starbucks Coffee, Boeing, Cisco Systems, Reebok, Boston Scientific, Archstone Consulting and GarrettCom Europe.
NFIA's services, all provided on a confidential basis, include providing insight and data with regard to site selection and logistics strategies; intensive, personal guidance on such matters as available incentives, permit procedures and tax structures. The NFIA introduces corporate investors to a variety of Dutch networks and service suppliers in business, to government authorities at national and regional levels, tand to academic and private sector consultants.

Technology Matchmaking

Technology Matchmaking is a new service provided by the NFIA to further assist foreign technology companies (sectors: ICT, Life Sciences, Nanotechnology, Polymers or Water Treatment) seeking European partners and a supportive business environment. Technology Matchmaking facilitates the search process for a suitable technology partner in the Netherlands, which may include research institutes as well as private enterprises. Technology Matchmaking is offered in strict confidence, without obligation and free of charge.

The Netherlands ranks fifth in Globalization Index

The Netherlands ranks fifth in the AT Kearney/FOREIGN POLICY Globalization Index 2005. Singapore heads the latest ranking, followed by Ireland, Switzerland and the United States. The A.T. Kearney/ FOREIGN POLICY Magazine Globalization Index ranks 62 countries representing 85 percent of the world's population, based on 12 variables grouped in four categories: economic integration, personal contact, technological connectivity, and political engagement. The Netherlands ranks 5th, 11th, 8th and 4th respectively in these four categories.

«

NFIA OFFICES:

THE NETHERLANDS
www.nfia.nl, e-mail: info@nfia.nl
● **NFIA The Hague (headquarters)**
P.O. Box 20101, 2500 EC The Hague
Tel.: +31 70 379 88 18, Fax: +31 70 379 63 22

UNITED KINGDOM
www.nfia.co.uk, e-mail: info@nfia.co.uk
● **NFIA London**
38, Hyde Park Gate, London SW7 5DP
Tel.: +44 20 7225 1074, Fax: +44 20 7584 3396

NORTH AMERICA
www.nfia.com, e-mail: info@nfia.com
● **NFIA New York** *e-mail: nfiany@nfia.com*
One Rockefeller Plaza, New York NY 10020
Tel.: +1 212 246 1434, Fax: +1 212 246 9769
● **NFIA Boston** *e-mail: nfiabos@nfia.com*
20 Park Plaza, Suite 524, Boston MA 02116-4399
Tel.: +1 617 426 9224, Fax: +1 617 426 8993
● **NFIA San Mateo** *e-mail: nfiasm@nfia.com*
San Mateo Bay Center, 901 Mariner's Island Boulevard, Suite 595, San Mateo CA 94404
Tel.: +1 650 349 8848, Fax: +1 650 349 8201
● **NFIA Chicago** *e-mail: nfiach@nfia.com*
303 East Wacker Drive, Suite 2610, Chicago IL 60601
Tel.: +1 312 616 8400, Fax: +1 312 616 8408
● **NFIA Atlanta** *e-mail: nfiaat@nfia.com*
3330 Cumberland Boulevard, Suite 500, Atlanta GA 30339
Tel.: +1 770 933 6275, Fax: +1 770 933 6276

JAPAN
www.nfia-japan.com
● **NFIA Tokyo** *e-mail: tokyo@nfia-japan.com*
3-6-3 Shibakoen, Minato-ku, Tokyo 105-0011
Tel.: +81 5401 0430, Fax: +81 5401 0429
● **NFIA Osaka** *osaka@nfia-japan.com*
Twin 21 MID Tower, 33rd floor, 2-1-61 Shiromi, Chuo-ku, Osaka 540-6133
Tel.: +81 6944 9234, Fax: +81 6944 3691

TAIWAN
www.nfia-taiwan.com, e-mail: info@nfia-taiwan.com
● **NFIA Taipei**
Room B, 5th Floor, Artist Construction Building, 133 Min Sheng East Road, Section 3, Taipei 10591
Tel.: +886 2713 5760 - ext. 170/180,
Fax: +886 2713 0194

KOREA
www.nfia-korea.com, e-mail: info@nfia-korea.com
● **NFIA Seoul**
Kyobo Building, 13th floor, 1, Chongno 1-ka, Chongno-ku, Seoul 110-714
Tel.: +82 732 1924, Fax: +82 732 1925

PR CHINA
www.nfia-china.com, e-mail: info@nfia-china.com
● **NFIA Hong Kong**
Consulate-General of the Netherlands.
Suite 5702, 57/F, Cheung Kong Center, 2 Queen's Road Central, Hong Kong
Tel.: +852 2523 5317, Fax: +852 2523 6440
● **NFIA Shanghai**
Consulate-General of the Netherlands.
Room 301D, West Tower, Sun Plaza
88 Xanxia Road, Shanghai 200336
Tel.: +86 21 6270 6220, Fax: +86 21 6270 6221

THE NETHERLANDS

If you search the web for information about the Netherlands, it won't be long before you arrive at the sites of various government agencies. These provide reliable information on doing business with and investing in the Netherlands.

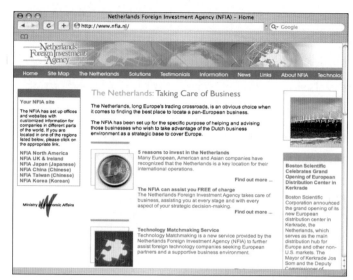

www.nfia.nl *Netherlands Foreign Investment Agency (NFIA).*
Quick access to relevant information about the Dutch investment climate.

I n addition to information provided by Dutch government bodies within the Netherlands, the number of Dutch embassies with websites is steadily increasing. As you might expect, these sites primarily contain information concerning bilateral business. Various sites, e.g. those of the Netherlands Foreign Investment Agency (NFIA), the Dutch Central Bank, Euronext and the Amsterdam Stock Exchange, give macroeconomic information about the Netherlands. The sites of the large banks, Rabobank, ING and ABN Amro also contain reliable information.
The highly comprehensive site of the Netherlands Bureau of Tourism www.holland.com could also prove very useful.

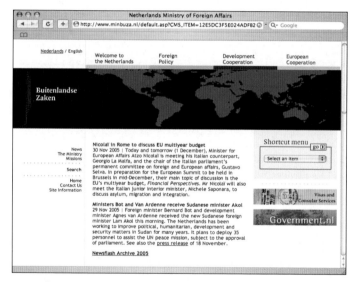

www.minbuza.nl *Site of the Dutch Ministry of Foreign Affairs.*
Internationally oriented site presenting clear information about the Netherlands.

Foreign Investments (NFIA)

The Netherlands Foreign Investment Agency (NFIA), which forms part of the Ministry of Economic Affairs, offers facilities for foreign companies interested in investing in the Netherlands. Via the site, NFIA experts supply information, strategic perspectives and practical support. The NFIA's free services are provided on a confidential basis. (www.nfia.nl)

Ministry of Foreign Affairs

The most extensive source of information on life in the Netherlands is to be found at the website of the Ministry of Foreign Affairs. Typical aspects of Dutch government policy are explained, and tourists and expats can obtain advice and keep abreast of the most important domestic news. (www.minbuza.nl)

Holland Real Estate

The web version of Holland Real Estate is a gateway to the Dutch real estate market. An extensive

ON THE WEB

www.holland-re.com *Holland Real Estate. The latest news and information about cities, projects and companies in the Netherlands.*

www.evd.nl *Information service of the Netherlands Foreign Trade Agency.*

www.minez.nl *Site of the Dutch Ministry of Economic Affairs.*

www.europe-re.com *In-depth analysis of the European real estate market.*

www.kvk.nl *Site of the Dutch Chamber of Commerce.*

www.government.nl *English news of Dutch government institutions.*

www.cbs.nl
Statistics of the Netherlands.

list of companies, projects, locations and decision-makers can be found, as well as daily financial and economic news in English. (www.holland-re.com)

Agency for International Business and Cooperation

The Agency for International Business and Cooperation (EVD) is part of the Dutch Ministry of Economic Affairs. Its mission is to promote and encourage international business and international cooperation. As a State agency and a partner to businesses and public-sector organizations, the EVD aims to help them achieve success in their international operations. (www.evd.nl) «

ONLINE: www.holland-re.com/internet

€80 BILLION FOR MOBILITY

HIGH SPEED TRAINS IN THE NETHERLANDS

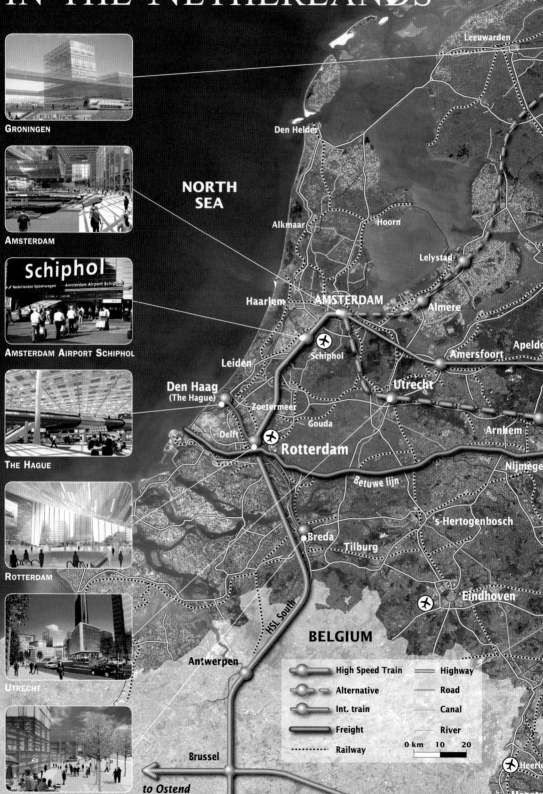

GRONINGEN

AMSTERDAM

AMSTERDAM AIRPORT SCHIPHOL

THE HAGUE

ROTTERDAM

UTRECHT

BREDA

NORTH SEA

Leeuwarden

Den Helder

Alkmaar

Hoorn

Lelystad

Haarlem

AMSTERDAM

Almere

Amersfoort

Apeldoorn

Leiden

Schiphol

Den Haag
(The Hague)

Utrecht

Zoetermeer

Gouda

Arnhem

Delft

Rotterdam

Nijmegen

Betuwe lijn

's-Hertogenbosch

Breda

Tilburg

Eindhoven

HSL South

BELGIUM

Antwerpen

Heerlen

Brussel

Maastricht

to Ostend

Luik

to Paris and London

		Legend	
High Speed Train	Highway		
Alternative	Road		
Int. train	Canal		
Freight	River		
Railway			

0 km   10   20

INVESTING IN MOBILITY

With the entry of the new Eastern European EU member states, good transport connections between the North Sea and the European hinterland have become even more important. As a gateway to Europe, the Netherlands is investing many billions of euros in the improvement of mobility, both within its borders and in the direction of the major European cities.

A well-functioning system for the transfer of people and goods is essential to the further development of the Netherlands' economy and international competitive position. In order to safeguard accessibility, the Dutch Ministry of Transport and Public Works has drawn up the Nota Mobiliteit (Mobility Memorandum), a traffic and transport plan charting all major infrastructure projects in the country. Between 2011 and 2020, some €80 billion will be reserved for further improvement of the Dutch infrastructure.

Prestigious projects

Some of the prestigious projects involved in this undertaking are the HSL high-speed rail link connecting Amsterdam and the Amsterdam Airport Area with Brussels (investment: €6.65 billion; operational in 2007), the Betuweroute railway line between the Rotterdam harbor and the German border (investment: approx. €4.68 billion; operational in early 2007) and RandstadRail, a light-rail connection between The Hague, Rotterdam and Zoetermeer (phased completion between 2007 and 2009).

Magnetic hover-train

In addition, plans are being developed for the construction of the Zuiderzeelijn, a magnetic hover-train connection between the northern provinces and the Randstad. A further expansion of the country's southern railway network is also under review, with the aim to considerably intensify railroad traffic between the Randstad and the BrabantStad region. ≪

ONLINE: www.holland-re.com/mobility

HSL AND NEW KEY

In 1997 the Dutch government designated six of the most important railroad station areas in the Netherlands as New Key Projects. With the approaching prospect of a high-speed railroad line, stations and parts of the city in their vicinity have to develop into metropolitan areas with a favorable climate for residential and business purposes. When the planning process got bogged down, the initial high expectations had to be adjusted, resulting in renewed optimism for the projects.

By Ben Maandag

PHOTO: ADAM KURDAHL

S ince the 90s, when it became clear that the Netherlands would be a part of a European high-speed railroad network, preparations began to provide a suitable infrastructure to accommodate these

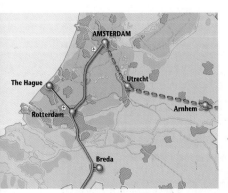

The six New Key Projects.

high-speed trains in the Netherlands. The results of these preparations are now discernable. Cutting through the Dutch landscape, this new railroad starts at the border with Belgium, crosses the Hollandsch Diep continuing to Rotterdam, and from there, the line cuts through the Groene Hart en route to Schiphol and Amsterdam. When the new trains and railroad come into service in 2007, travel time between Amsterdam and Paris will be reduced significantly. Some of the other changes being made in anticipation of the High Speed Line (HSL) are less apparent. It was expected that the HSL would come to play a significant

role, not only for the municipalities where the train would stop, such as Rotterdam and Amsterdam, but also for places like The Hague and Breda which would have an express connection with the HSL track, and for cities like Utrecht and Arnhem which would link up with the High Speed Line going east. For these cities, the arrival of the HSL is a stroke of good fortune. Connecting with a European network of high-speed trains that can compete with the advantages of air travel means new opportunities. Travel time to other European destinations will be reduced significantly, making these urban regions more attrac-

PROJECTS

tive. Consequently, they can anticipate serious economic growth.

Impulse

To further boost these expectations, the Dutch government announced the development of six of the most important railroad station areas in the Netherlands as New Key Projects, with the intention of providing a new impetus to these metropolitan areas. €1 billion was made available not only to optimize public transport facilities, but also to improve the quality of residential zones on the development site and create a climate that would be most favorable for the establishment of inter-

nationally oriented businesses. Development of the railroad station areas did not progress in keeping with the enthusiasm that initially greeted the project. With the exception of Arnhem, where construction had already com-

menced with the building of a prestigious new station district when the New Key Projects were announced, the other municipalities were slower than originally expected when it came to the planning process. >>

The bridge over the Hollandsch Diep has a total length of 1,975 m.

EDITORIAL

Parties involved

One of the most important reasons accounting for the delay in the development of the station areas was the fact that it involved the restructuring of local transport and buildings located downtown, involving a large number of concerned parties. Reaching consensus with so many parties is a difficult task.

The federal government is one of the parties involved, as are the municipalities where development is slated to begin. Private parties are also involved, such as investors and real estate developers. And then there's the NS (Dutch Railways), an organization that, since its privatization, has been divided into the separate rail management companies ProRail and NS. All of these parties often have different interests that aren't always in agreement with each other.

Budget

"It's complicated," explains Mr. Kees de Boo, chairman of the Board of NS Vastgoed (Real Estate). "There's much more involved than just new stations. You also have to consider how we Dutch do business.
This project involves an economic process between cities and the federal government and there is also a democratic process involved. Our common concern is always if there are sufficient funds."

"For the HSL station areas, the NS looks for distinctive facilities that aim for comfort," says De Boo. "Things like special-purpose waiting areas.
These facilities must meet high standards because we expect an increase in international passengers that will form the basis for our international operations. Real estate is one means of working on an area so that these operations thrive. Whatever the situation, the goal is to create a favorable environment."

Safety

De Boo explains that the district surrounding the new stations will be an area where residential, shopping and commercial interests converge.
"This combination has to work effectively both during peak hours and outside of peak hours. That means that you have to ensure that people feel safe there. NS Vastgoed is prepared to make a substantial investment in developing this property. We own property and we've agreed to plough our profits from this back

In 2007 the High Speed Train will stop in the

into station development. It's the government's job to build stations, but we will support that because it's also in our best interests. The NS also has an interest in stimulating travel by train," says De Boo.
"We believe that in any case, government agencies should provide an example for others by relocating to premises close to the railroad stations.
We've conferred with the government on this issue, but unfortunately we've seen that in practice, federal government agencies in the key project areas are not relocating to areas in the vicinity of the stations."
He immediately adds that it can be observed that municipal government is moving in that direc-

ABOUT NS VASTGOED

Drs. Ir. Kees de Boo
CEO NS Vastgoed

"NS Vastgoed wants to become known as a developer of locations and buildings in the vicinity of its train stations. There are fantastic opportunities there, but it's often a very complex undertaking. They can bring about significant changes such as ones to the infrastructure, and are generally very expensive to make. They also involve a number of interested players, whose needs all have to be taken into account. Building in city centers is something very different from building in farmland."

www.nsvastgoed.nl

city center of Rotterdam.

Collapse

At the moment the architecture firm is working on the key projects Rotterdam, The Hague Central Station and Utrecht and is busy with the renovation of Amsterdam Central Station. "We often see that we're not the first ones who have pondered over these plans," says Jan Benthem. "Plans had already been made for Amsterdam, Rotterdam and Utrecht. However, these plans were so complicated and ambitious that they collapsed when the recession hit. Still, plans for the development of the station areas have to be realized. "Benthem Crouwel distinguishes itself with its serious, pragmatic and business-like approach," explains Benthem. "And we make realistic plans. We indicate where the possibilities are and where the opportunities lie. Schiphol has turned out to be more than just a public transport machine and we created opportunities for all the developments surrounding it. At first it was an airport and a station until we transformed it into an integrated whole. Schiphol was our calling card." According to Benthem the station developments offer so many opportunities that the parties involved sometimes want too much. "Everyone >>

tion. "In Utrecht the municipality is building its offices next to the station. And in the municipalities of Gouda and Zaandam you can see that they are also considering doing the same, which demonstrates how Utrecht's decision is encouraging other cities. Meanwhile, in Delft, a tunnel is under construction and the municipality will establish its offices next to the station. But all these activities are taking place at a level below the large projects."

Architect Jan Benthem of Benthem Crouwel is also well informed regarding this subject. His firm made a name for itself by designing the station terminal at Schiphol Airport. Since then, Jan Benthem and Mels Crouwel

are welcome guests at many station sites where, with their sound designs, they often manage to get a bogged-down decision-making process moving again.

ABOUT BENTHEM CROUWEL

"Characterized as sober, practical and functional, our work is also acclaimed for its expressive and aesthetic qualities. Functionality and internal logistics are important priorities in our buildings. We continuously look for good, though not always obvious, solutions to design problems. We do not hesitate to apply modern technology in a user-friendly way. Our commissions are highly varied. Architecture, urban design, infrastructure and interior design are often interwoven. We love our work."

Ir. Jan Benthem
Benthem Crouwel
Architekten bv

www.benthemcrouwel.nl

PHOTO: MUNICIPALITY OF UTRECHT

In the next 15 to 20 years the Utrecht station area will completely be redeveloped into a sparkling new city center.

can see that you have to look further than just the station, but then the expectations and ambitions start piling up on each other so that in the end, even the smallest alteration is no longer possible. The decision making process is also more difficult. So many parties are involved that it's impossible to make any deci-

sions." Benthem envisions an increasingly important role for the architect in this process. "We're expected to dissect the project in such a way that all your decisions don't have to be made all at once, but in phases. We try to present the project in ordered, easily manageable pieces and at the same time we structure the plan so that you

can see the long-term results related to more than just the station itself. This way, all parts of the project can be realized in phases. We are the intermediary, the director and the surgeons who intervene at the right moment and make the programmatic decisions."

Risks

One of the questions that commonly arise related to these large-scale projects is: who will emerge as the driving force? Or as Kees de Boo says, "It's about looking for who is really providing the impetus for the project. Who has actually commissioned it?" The role of the government has also changed. Or rather according to De Boo, "It's more the case that government has consciously chosen to play another role so that the financial risks in such large-scale projects are more evenly distributed."

PHOTO: NS VASTGOED

Ambitious plan for Gouda's Central Station area (NS Vastgoed).

Dr. Peter Pol, an urban policy researcher at the Erasmus University in Rotterdam who received his doctorate degree in 2002 for his research on the economic effects of the arrival of the HSL on station areas, finds that an effective 'driving force' is essential in such large-scale projects. "You need an effective driving force to literally get everything on track and moving. Take a look at Lille in northern France. It was Pierre Mauroy who accelerated that process and got the Euralille project moving. He was an influential mayor with a good capacity for organization." Pol elaborates, "At the moment you can see that Breda and The Hague are reasonably resolute, even though they failed to obtain a direct connection with the HSL. They can still make this up and recover if they invest wisely. A city like Den Bosch, which was not designated as a key project, has also shown that it is independently capable of developing its station area."

Expertise

According to Pol, the task of directing lies with the city's administrators. "It's not the government or the railroad company that has the biggest interests, it's the municipality." He points out that Utrecht's municipal services lacked the expertise to supervise the transformation of the station. That, combined with a lack of public support, can lead to some difficult outcomes. According to Pol, "At the time, the construction of Hoog Catherijne was a sore point that still has negative repercussions for the city." "The key projects need visionary people," says Pol. "People with a broader vision who see things not only at the municipal level, but beyond that to the regional level as well. You can't limit the

station to being just a construction task. You need to put strategies in place so that the city and its surroundings can benefit from it as much as possible." Pol believes that the Zuidas is a good example of this. "That's going to be the most important station in Amsterdam and it will be the core of the region. When the municipality realized this, it took action immediately." The economic effects of the renovation of the station areas will certainly bring matters to completion; Peter Pol has no doubts about that. "But that will come at a later phase. For that you can again look at the example of Lille: investors had faith in the city and they saw a favorable climate for investment. That will also happen here, but it could have been realized at an earlier stage. At the moment investors are waiting to first see what the government is going to do, and then they'll try to step in and reap the benefits." Kees de Boo elaborates, "Progress has been made even though you have to acknowledge that there hasn't been any growth in the real estate market. The secret is to plan beyond economic cycles. This type of planning is something the

Amsterdam Airport Schiphol.

government could use to its advantage by being at the right place at the right time to obtain prime locations at low costs. If you're talking about competing on an international level, then more effort needs to be put into the Amsterdam Zuidas in particular. The other areas are more subject to national pressure. What I mean is that here in Utrecht we shouldn't get the idea that we have to compete with Paris. Nevertheless, where money and prestige are concerned, I believe that you should choose for prestige. Over time, that is the most important consideration.">>

PHOTO: PROJECT AGENCY ZUIDAS

The new HSL-station on the Zuidas, Amsterdam.

Amsterdam Zuidas

There is intensive development taking place in the area just to the north of Schiphol with the construction of numerous office buildings. There has been much discussion and research regarding the location and design of the new station, and many designs were considered. In the end, the most expensive version was chosen, the 'dokmodel', where the entire infrastructure will be built underground. "If that plan is to succeed anywhere, it will succeed here," states Peter Pol. "Above ground, pedestrians will regain what is their domain, and human proportions will be the norm. When this area develops further, everyone will benefit and that influence could extend as far as Rotterdam." Kees de Boo adds, "The Zuidas is the only location where they are building from scratch."

Central Station The Hague

The terminal will be renovated according to a new design from Benthem Crouwel. A new office complex will be built on the plaza in front of the station,

designed by Rem Koolhaas and his firm OMA. Jan Benthem explains, "The bundle of railroad tracks presents a barrier. We're trying to negate this obstruction by using a design that will elevate that part of the city above the railroad tracks. The station will be shifted around so that it no longer divides Bezuidenhout from the downtown area. The other connections will then be our point of departure instead of the terminal. A covered plaza

will be created and together with OMA's new construction and the renovation of Babylon by Meyer en Van Schooten, the station itself will form the core of a new transportation junction and of a completely renovated urban area."

Rotterdam

William Alsop had designed a master plan that was notable for its 'champagne glasses' that the architect referred to in order to indicate the shape of these extraordinary buildings. This plan however was too ambitious and too expensive. Peter Pol explains, "Of course Pim Fortuyn played a role in this when he referred to it as a megalomaniac plan. At that time his party had to oppose the plan." A new plan is now at an advanced stage of the planning process. While this plan calls for a more modest station building, it is not lacking in ambition. The design comes from Team CS, a joint venture that includes Benthem Crouwel, Meyer en Van Schooten, and West 8. Peter Pol adds, "I worry the most about Rotterdam because it has

PHOTO: BENTHEM CROUWEL

In 2020, the new The Hague Central Station will be completed.

The new Utrecht station terminal will be covered by a light undulating roof construction.

PHOTO: MUNICIPALTY OF UTRECHT

turned into a budget-driven project. This project is very important to Rotterdam in its bid to attract higher income residents to the city. This project in particular could have benefited from extra support from the federal government."

Utrecht

The idea that something has to be done with Hoog Catharijne has been floating about for some time now. The Utrecht Centrum Plan (UCP) succeeded in stirring up emotions but it ultimately proved to be so complicated that there was no public support for the plan. Starting again was the task at hand, and Benthem Crouwel began work on a new plan. Jan Benthem recounts, "This project was also extremely complex but our plan is more logical. The bus terminal will be placed on either side of the station and the express tram will be shifted to the other side of the station. Our point of departure is that the ground level is higher in the station area. You have a nice street at plus-eight meters where important buildings will be situated. A new boulevard will be constructed above the railroad tracks and then the station will again be recognizable for what it is - a train station."

Breda

Koen van Velsen and the studio Quadrat produced the design for a new station that will bridge the north and south sides of the city, negate the barrier created by the railroad tracks and provide a new boost to the surrounding areas.

Arnhem

Plans for the development of a new station arc at the most advanced stage in Arnhem, where Ben van Berkel's (UN Studio) design for an eye-catching new station development was already under construction when the decision for the New Key Projects were made. The plan is being executed in phases and is nearing completion. When the HSL East is realized, Arnhem will be ready. ≪

PHOTO: MUNICIPALITY OF ROTTERDAM

Rotterdam's Central Station, the city's most striking renovation.

ONLINE: www.holland-re.com/hsl

STADIUMS LYNCHPIN

A football stadium may once have served only one chief function – as a playing field for players with seating for the fans – but today's stadiums have become the heart of a multifunctional community. Modern stadiums are a place for sports, culture, leisure activities, shops, offices and housing, creating synergy with their fusion. The construction of a contemporary stadium project has become more interesting than ever for developers. It is, simply put, a powerful force in the world of commercial real estate.

By Michiel van den Broek

Euroborg stadium, centrally located in

In the city of Groningen in the north of Holland, the new FC Groningen stadium has become the dazzling centerpiece of the multifunctional district known as Europapark, that is currently under construction. Europapark consists of four sections: an office area measuring 200,000 m², the residential area De Linie, Helperpark, and the Euroborg stadium complex. Euroborg is a multifunctional complex that, besides the stadium, also contains a casino, movie theater, fitness center, cafes, restaurants and hotels, stores, offices and two tall residential towers. Meanwhile, just 50 km away in Heerenveen, SC Heerenveen's soccer stadium lies at the heart of the new development called Sportstad, a collaborative project of Sport Club Heerenveen, the city of Heerenveen, De Friesland Insurance Company, and the ROC Friesland College educational institute. The development plans for the area around the old football stadium consist of a multifunctional sports center, a 'health boulevard,' a 'lifestyle passage', a hotel with a convention center, an educational center, 60,000 m² of office space, 360 apartments, and a leisure center plus stores measuring a combined 20,000 m².

A fascinating stretch

J. Voorrips, Assistant Director of the Ballast Nedam Development Company, is closely associated with the development of

Euroborg. "It was a complex and fascinating stretch of some seven years. The soccer club was experiencing financial difficulties and the city didn't want to get burned with this project. That made it a bit more difficult to get all of the parties to agree on the plans. There were a lot of different designs that made the rounds."

PHOTO: EUROBORG

The new cinema near Euroborg.

OF REAL ESTATE

PHOTO: EUROBORG

Europapark Groningen, will be a multifunctional complex including a casino, cinemas, cafes, office space and apartments.

In the end, however, they found themselves in a development cooperative that included the business partners (Ballast Nedam ontwikkelingsmaatschappij, Volker Wessels Vastgoed and BAM Vastgoed) and the city, which managed to put up the non-profit portion of the €190 million total project costs. The commercial buildings were developed and sold separately, while FC Groningen rents the stadium from NV. "Coming up with an acceptable business plan required a lot of improvising," Voorrips notes. "You're constantly learning in this kind of environment. So, in this case, it became evident that a soccer club must focus on its core business: soccer-related activities. And because it is an important actor in the story, you have to try to work together with them. That worked out in the end, but it did take some doing. Project development is a very particular profession. That is what we need to concentrate on. A shoemaker should stick to his trade." >>

Sportstad Heerenveen comprises a multifunctional complex and the renovated Abe Lenstra Stadium.

Realism conveyed

Sportstad Heerenveen uses its soccer stadium as the driving force for further development. A. Hilbrink, the Director of Projectontwikkeling Noord at Van Wijnen, has really seen the project blossom since 1992. "We built and expanded the stadium in a series of steps. When we finally finish the last expansion, that of the northern stands, the stadium will seat 26,000. That is pretty amazing when you realize that Heerenveen only has a population of 40,000. The soccer club's popularity has provided us with these incredible possibilities for project development."

If Hilbrink is saying something like this, you know it must be true. He is not one to give the wildly ambitious forecasts that often characterize stadium development projects. "Clubs and cities often think that a new stadium pretty much automatically ensures profits and that it is a solution to their financial problems. I am always very clear in this regard - it only makes sense to invest in new accommodations if the club itself is ready for them. The sky's the limit when it comes to their expectations, but you have to remain realistic. When it comes to stadium construction, the developer's most important task is to convey a sense of realism."

Emotion

Stadium development is different from other projects because of the emotion factor. It's inherent to the nature of sports. Pride and overestimation often get in the way of a clear view of the situation. Local administrators are almost always overwhelmingly positive about the possibilities of a project like this. Build some skyboxes and they will be sold out in no time. Develop commercial space between the columns and under the grandstands and they will be rented out in no time. This is how club administrators - but also city councils - sometimes think. And then when things don't go according to plan, it is not uncommon for the city to end up taking over the stadium to prevent even worse consequences.

Nobody is ever prepared for a worst-case scenario, notes Hilbrink. "There has to be a sound development plan before the first stone is even laid. What do you expect to make your money with? How do you expect to earn back you initial investment? A new coat should be neither too loose nor too tight. The development process can

In addition to the stadium the entire ADO The Hague complex will offer 33,500 m² of retail space, leisure facilities and offices.

The Amsterdam ArenA possesses a magical attraction and gives an additional boost to Amsterdam Southeast.

easily eat up a period of four to six years. As a developer you have to look toward the long term, but that doesn't always count for the others involved."

Ambition

Voorrips, not unlike Hilbrink at Van Wijnen, believes that the task of a project developer is to link ambition to a sense of realism. But he further notes that, "We are also there to control the quality. The project can go wrong at the top, but just as easily at the bottom as well. A stadium can be too cheaply developed so that the eventual users of the stadium are actually adversely effected by it. Studies show that people behave better in a warm and friendly building. That is why most new stadiums have made increased use of glass. You also have to keep the commercial aspects of the stadium in mind because if a stadium ends up being an ugly gray colossus, the stores won't thrive either."

Internationally

Ballast Nedam has built up an international reputation with its

development of two soccer stadiums in Portugal for the 2004 European Championships. Both Sporting Lissabon's José Alvalade Stadium and FC Porto's Dragão Stadium have been highly praised. Voorrips observes that, "these stadiums were made possible via a combination of multifunctional design and inner city redevelopment. A new stadium in the Southern European countries is perceived quite differently than it is in the Netherlands. In the south it is considered quite prestigious to have your offices located in or near a stadium. The fame of a particular soccer club radiates outward and has a positive impact on area businesses. In the Netherlands, we mostly see the problems; here stadiums are often associated with potential vandalism. That makes it a lot more difficult to develop this type of real estate."

Driving force

In spite of the reservations of the Dutch, Ballast Nedam has successfully built stadiums for, among others, Sparta (Rotterdam), FC Twente

(Enschede), NAC (Breda), Willem II (Tilburg), Roda JC (Kerkrade), ADO (The Hague, under construction) and, of course, the home of Ajax, the Amsterdam ArenA. The ArenA has successfully served as the driving force behind a number of other projects in Amsterdam Zuid-Oost. The area has seen the development of a sizeable cluster of new office towers, as well as leisure and entertainment facilities and large retail trade outlets. Ballast Nedam is now involved in GETZ, a new entertainment center next to the ArenA, which will be the first of its kind in the Netherlands. >>

The GETZ Entertainment Center will become the center of the ArenA Boulevard.

Multifunctional usage

Stadium development has consequently grown to become one of the core sectors of this company that used to focus exclusively on construction. In 1981, it was responsible for the first stadium development project - Nieuw Galgenwaard in Utrecht - which also included commercial real estate as part of the plans. Since then the stadium and the surrounding area have undergone a new phase of renovations, but at the time the concept was considered to be very refreshing. Offices and business space were developed separately and the money that this generated made it possible to build the stadium. The city was also very happy with the multifunctional nature of the stadium. If a soccer stadium is only used for soccer matches on 25 days of the year, it's not an efficient use of the space. A large, expensive building that is seldom used ends up costing a great deal of money,

more than can be recouped on soccer match ticket sales alone. The development of commercial real estate is one solution to this problem, while another involves attempting to increase earnings via the stadium itself. Stadium buildings, with some extra facilities added, lend themselves well to events such as concerts, festivals, and other large-scale events. The Amsterdam ArenA and the Gelredome in Arnhem are good examples of this. The stadiums are used for other purposes just as often as for soccer matches. The Gelredome even features a removable playing field for events such as pop concerts.

Lucrative

What makes stadium construction so interesting for project developers? Hilbrink immediately mentions the PR aspect. "It places you center stage. Everyone wants to work on this kind of project. Developers, con-

struction companies, and advisors come to us. From a technical standpoint, a stadium is not really much more interesting than other projects. But what it does offer is lots of publicity. Construction workers stand in

PHOTO: ZWARTS & JANSMA

The area around the completely renovated

Stadiums in the Netherlands (new developments and renovations)								
Stadium	Location	Club	Inauguration	Renovation(s)	Capacity	Costs	Architect	Developer
Nieuw Galgenwaard	Utrecht	FC Utrecht	1981-1982	2002 - 2004	25,000 seats, 44 skyboxes, 2,100 business seats, 50 press seats		Zwarts & Jansma Architecten	Ballast Nedam
Sportstad / Abe Lenstra	Heerenveen	SC Heerenveen	August 20 1994	2003-2005	21,600 seats		Alynia Architecten Harlingen b.v. BNA, Harlingen	Van Wijnen Project- ontwikkeling
Oosterenk ❶	Zwolle	FC Zwolle	Summer 2006		10,000 seats	€35.4 million		SOZ (Stadion Ontwikkeling Zwolle), IPMMC
Euroborg	Groningen	FC Groningen	January 2006		20,000 seats	€190 million	Wiel Arets Architecten	Ballast-Nedam, Volker Wessels Vastgoed and BAM Vastgoed
Frisia ❷	Alkmaar	AZ Alkmaar	Summer 2006		16,000 seats	€80 million	Zwarts & Jansma Architecten	
ADO	The Hague	ADO Den Haag	Summer 2006		15,000 seats	€28 million	Zwarts & Jansma Architecten	Ballast Nedam
Amsterdam ArenA	Amsterdam	AFC Ajax	April 14 1996		51,100 seats, 1,564 business seats, 216 press seats			Ballast Nedam an BAM
Oostpoort	Haarlem	HFC Haarlem	2007-2008				Wiel Arets	Maeyveld
Gelredome	Arnhem	Vitesse	March 25 1998		30,000 seats			

Galgenwaard Stadium in Utrecht will be developed with new offices, homes and parking areas.

line to apply for these kind of jobs. In no other industry is absenteeism as low as in the construction industry. That is because there is a sense of pride here. This kind of project is important for everyone involved.

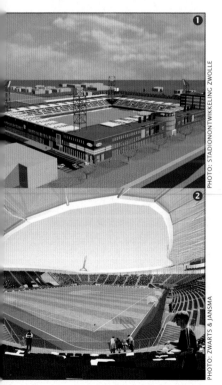

PHOTO: STADIONONTWIKKELING ZWOLLE

PHOTO: ZWARTS & JANSMA

In financial terms, these projects depend on the commercial development of the area surrounding the stadiums. Sometimes you receive a city grant. That allows you to develop the stadium with the idea of also developing the surrounding area. That can be very lucrative."

Sportstad Heerenveen is a good example of this. Van Wijnen was busy for years with the development and construction of this stadium, and now the company is also involved in related offshoot projects. Here a credible plan was developed that involved the logical synergy being applied between the various projects.

"There is going to be an educational establishment that will make use of the sports facilities," Hilbrink points out. "There will also be a 'health boulevard' that will be available to both the students and users of the sports facilities, while the soccer club will be able to make use of all of these establishments. The plans make sense and we are very happy with them." «

J. Voorrips
Assistant Director of the Ballast
Nedam Development Company

A. Hilbrink
Director of Projectontwikkeling
Noord at Van Wijnen

ONLINE: www.holland-re.com/stadiums

Man Of The Year

DRS. JAAP G. BLOKHUIS, CEO OF REDEVCO EUROPE

DRS. JAAP G. BLOKHUIS, CEO OF REDEVCO EUROPE

NOT JUST THE MAN, BUT THE TEAM

By a large majority of votes, the Holland Real Estate Advisory Board and 25 leading property figures have elected Jaap Blokhuis, CEO of Redevco Europe, Man of the Year 2006. Blokhuis is particularly appreciated for his passionate leadership and his strategic approach to the European property market. Under Blokhuis' management, in the last five years Redevco has developed into one of Europe's leading retail real estate companies. The company is active in 15 European countries and develops and manages a portfolio of top-location retail property in major cities throughout Europe. The Redevco portfolio, which also includes office buildings and logistics centers, currently comprises over 1,000 buildings worth an estimated €6.5 billion.

By Ola Sinoo

Redevco Europe was founded as a limited European Real Estate Investment Company in 1999. Redevco (Real Estate Development Company) is the Netherlands' number three investor and is also active in the European market as a property developer. Redevco is a modern, professional asset management organization with a long and rich history as a family company. As the private real estate fund of the Brenninkmeijer family – of the C&A clothing chain – the alternatively structured Redevco is one of the most important private funds in Europe. Under the guidance of Jaap Blokhuis (formerly employed by ING Real Estate), Redevco's initial targets have by and large been achieved. The organization is strong and well established in many national markets; the portfolios have been restructured and expanded; the geographical and sector spread has been improved; and the tenant mix is now more balanced.

Strength

Redevco is already active in 15 countries – Austria, Belgium, the Czech Republic, Denmark, Finland, France, Germany, Hungary, Italy, the Netherlands, Portugal, Spain, Sweden, Switzerland and the United Kingdom – and has built up substantial portfolios in several of these markets. The activities of Redevco are coordinated at the European level by Redevco Europe, based in Amsterdam, the Netherlands, and at the local level by regional offices. A small team of real estate   >>

Lumion, Geneva, Switzerland. Redevco development, completed in 2004. After being fully let, sold to KanAm early 2006.

PHOTO: REDEVCO

FITNESS
COMPANY
Peek&Cloppenburg
Peek&Cloppenburg
kant center
kant center
SALE

professionals coordinates the company's European activities. Redevco's strength lies in its ability to combine a European strategy with a profound know-how of national markets. Redevco attaches great importance to the cross-border exchange of know-how and experience. The success of Redevco is based on having an outstanding team of local real estate professionals, an excellent initial portfolio (C&A properties) and on its corporate values, such as integrity, professionalism, and honesty towards each other.

From downtown to the outskirts

In line with Redevco's origins as the real estate branch of the C&A fashion chain, the company strategy in the early years focused on retail property at A1 locations. After all, the C&A buildings have traditionally been located in the core shopping areas of the larger European cities. Since then, however, Redevco has considerably expanded its horizon, including projects at other locations – suburban shopping centers – and new areas. "Over the past few years, we have seen retailers' interest shifting from downtown to the outskirts of

Bershka store on the Kalverstraat, Amsterdam, the Netherlands.

PHOTO: REDEVCO

town," Blokhuis explains. "In the town center, suitable large buildings are scarce, while in the outer-lying districts there is ample space for development. Moreover, retail areas on the edge of town have an additional advantage: they generally have excellent accessibility. In the core shopping areas, the retail function will remain an important focus, but we also aim to provide a good response to developments on the side of the retailer – our customer. Shopping areas have

also become an investment target." The first acquisitions resulting from this strategy are now a fact: several small-scale shopping centers in France and Sweden have been acquired. In 2005, Redevco added two French retail developments (with a combined worth of €33 million) and two retail projects in Sweden (€50 million) to the portfolio.

Cross-border expansion

In addition, Redevco has increasingly sought new openings   >>

PHOTO: REDEVCO

PHOTO: REDEVCO

Praxis, Assen, the Netherlands. Acquired from IBI Real Estate in 2003.

< Kant Center, Berlin, Germany. Redevco development of previous C&A store plus adjacent P&C store.

PHOTO: REDEVCO

Princes Street, Edinburgh, United Kingdom. Previous C&A store, redeveloped in conjunction with adjacent store, completed in 2005.

outside its Dutch home market as part of a strategic policy of geographical diversification. Of the total property portfolio of €6.5 billion, a mere 7% is now invested in the Netherlands. The emphasis is on the German market (23%), Belgium and Luxembourg (21%) and the UK (19%). In addition to the 15 European markets in which the company is currently active, in the coming years Redevco will also keep a close eye on emerging markets such as Poland, Romania and Turkey.

Eventful year

2005 was an important year for Redevco. This is particularly true with regard to developments within the organization. The company head office moved from Amsterdam's Weesperstraat to the redeveloped location Wibautstraat 224 – the former Renault building located within a stone's throw of the Zuidas. In addition, a number of heavyweight executives were added to Redevco's ranks: Frank de Moes was appointed CFO, Luuk Lantinga (formerly Ahold) became the new Managing Director Netherlands and Jörg Bitzer (formerly Walmart and P&C) became Managing Director Central Europe. The portfolio was also subjected to a major review. In 2005, some €150 million was disinvested. Simultaneously, Redevco considerably strengthened its position in the European

market by initiating some €600 million worth of new projects. A retail building in the center of Palma de Mallorca (€20 million), the Parisian Uzan portfolio (€37.5 million), the Austrian Mid portfolio (€100 million), three retail parks in Switzerland (€35 million) and the former Ahold portfolio in Spain (over €210 million) were added to Redevco's assets. All in all, in 2005 the Redevco portfolio was enlarged to eventually comprise some 1,000 buildings, representing a total worth of more than €6.5 billion.

Loosening the ties with C&A

Through this extensive reshuffling of the portfolio, the Redevco team has managed to further loosen the fund's ties with C&A. "At the time of Redevco's establishment in 1999, C&A's share was no less than 95%. As we did not wish to be dependent on one chief tenant, we strove to gradually dismantle this dominant position," Blokhuis explains. By shifting the focus of the portfolio, C&A's share in the Redevco portfolio was reduced rapidly. When the fashion chain pulled out of Redevco's UK property holdings in 2005, the total number of C&A buildings was around 400. Blokhuis: "Once the planned sale of 34 prominent retail buildings from our German portfolio has been rounded off, the C&A share will have been brought back to 35%. We eventually intend to establish an interest of 25%."

European redevelopment area

Development will become an increasingly important part of Redevco's activities. Particularly in the area of redevelopment, Blokhuis foresees good perspectives in the European market in the years ahead. In Belgium, Redevco is currently involved in nine redevelopment projects – a result of the 2001 acquisition of the GIB Immo portfolio. The company is also developing and redeveloping projects in the UK and Germany. In 2005, for instance, Redevco completed the Kant Center, the extensive redevelopment of a retail complex in Berlin. Blokhuis: "Other parties' property has become prohibitively expensive, leading us to refocus on upgrading our own projects. This is what we intend to do throughout Europe. Creating a European redevelopment area is an important next step."

Ambitious long-term plan

Redevco has an ambitious growth objective. The main target for the company's tenth anniversary is to expand the portfolio to €10 billion by 2010. The intention is to cover all major cities in the European market, including future members of the European Union. In the next three years, Redevco will be paying particular attention to the markets of Poland, Romania and Turkey. Redevco is expecting particularly good investment opportunities in the retail property and logistics sector, but the company will also continue to monitor the main office markets in these countries. «

Drs. Jaap G. Blokhuis (47)

After graduating in Social Geography and City Planning at the Vrije Universiteit Amsterdam, Jaap Blokhuis joined ING Real Estate (formerly Nationale-Nederlanden) in 1983. During the first few years of his employment at ING, Blokhuis was responsible for market research, property and asset management. This was followed by two years working in the Netherlands, the UK, Germany, Spain and Greece. In 1990, Blokhuis was appointed General Manager of the London office, overseeing the set-up of this new branch. Two years later, Blokhuis moved to the United States, where he became Vice President of ING Real Estate in Washington DC. Upon returning to the Netherlands, from 1994 to 1999 Blokhuis worked as Director Real Estate Asset Management/Fund Management, and was responsible for establishing the first ING property funds.

At the end of 1999, Blokhuis left ING to become CEO of Redevco Europe. Heading the new organization, Blokhuis transformed the C&A corporate real estate holdings into a new asset management company. Under Blokhuis' management, the C&A rental share was brought back from 95% to 40%, and the portfolio expanded from €4 billion in 2000 to €6.5 billion in 2005.

MAN OF THE YEAR AWARD: AN OVERVIEW

2006 JAAP BLOKHUIS,
CEO OF REDEVCO EUROPE

2005 RUDY STROINK,
CEO OF TCN PROPERTY PROJECTS

2004 HANS VAN VEGGEL,
COO/CCO/VICE CHAIRMAN OF AM NV

2003 JAN DOETS,
CEO OF ING REAL ESTATE

2002 TON MEIJER,
CEO OF MAB GROUP

2001 CEES HAKSTEGE,
CEO OF BOUWFONDS HOLDING

Berlage, The Hague, the Netherlands acquired from Provast in 2005.

ONLINE: www.holland-re.com/manoftheyear

WE DO REALISE WHAT IT TAKES TO DEVELOP AND INVEST IN THE PLAYGROUNDS OF OUR FUTURE!

FORTIS
Vastgoed

Fortis Vastgoed Ontwikkeling ■Fortis Vastgoed Beleggingen ■Fortis Vastgoed Landelijk

Archimedeslaan 6, 3584 BA Utrecht, The Netherlands   www.fortisvastgoed.nl

Short News

Public officials sign Zuidas-Dok agreement

The State, the Amsterdam City Council, the province of Noord-Holland and the Regionaal Orgaan Amsterdam (a partnership of 16 Amsterdam councils) have ratified agreements made earlier about the procedures concerning the establishment of the Zuidas-Dok Initiative. It regards decisions pertaining to the financial contributions of the individual parties and the requirements of the plan for the Zuidas-Dok Initiative.

The State and the Amsterdam City Council selected five financial organizations in September 2005 for possible participation in the Zuidas-Dok Initiative: ABN AMRO Bank, Bank Nederlandse Gemeenten, Fortis Bank, ING Real Estate and Rabobank Nederland (listed here alphabetically). The final decision about the execution of the Zuidas-Dok

Impression of the Dock model. Above a frontal view, below a side view of the underground public transport and road network.

plan, which concerns the development of the underground infrastructure, is expected at the beginning of 2007.

The total investment for the Zuidas-Dok on the prestigious Zuidas in Amsterdam amounts to approximately €2 billion over a period of more than 20 years. The final investment that the various parties will make in addition to this initial amount, is approximately €3 to €4 billion for a real estate program comprising about 1 million m².

www.zuidas.nl

New Microsoft HQ at Schiphol Center

As of September 2007, Microsoft will establish offices at Schiphol Center. In 2006, construction of an 18,000-m2 office building and a parking garage for 450 cars will begin on the parking terrain located across from the headquarters of the Schiphol Group. Schiphol Real Estate is the developer of the new Dutch headquarters of Microsoft. Architect agency Cepezed in Delft is responsible for the design.

Cathedral for Rotterdam

The Rotterdam City Council and project developer Provast have reached an agreement concerning the construction of an enormous covered market on the Binnenrotte in Amsterdam. The Board of Mayor and Aldermen of Rotterdam have approved the sale of the land to Provast. The project will be constructed on the 1.5-hectare Grotemarkt location in the Laurenskwartier. Completion is scheduled for 2009. The covered market is important for the Laurenskwartier's transformation into an exciting district. The developer has referred to the building as an 'icon for the city, a cathedral for Rotterdam'.

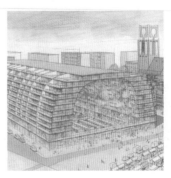

Market on the Binnenrotte.

EDITORIAL LOCATIONS DECISION MAKERS INDUSTRY TRENDS CORPORATE WHO'S WHO MAPS & INDEX

A STRIKING MIX OF ORIGINALITY AND FUNCTIONALITY

VIÑOLY SHINES ON THE ZUIDAS

The new office building on the Zuidas by world-renowned architect Rafael Viñoly – the first of his designs to be realized in Europe – is both a visual triumph and a solid design in terms of functionality.
The Viñoly building is one of the landmarks of the Netherlands' most prestigious office locations. A characteristic feature of the building, which is part of the Mahler4 complex, is the exterior stairway that has been 'carved' into the façade and runs in a spiral around the building. The projecting vertical profiles and the contrast between the dark glass of the façade and the clear glass of the layer behind further enhance this effect. These features have even earned the building its nicknames of 'the Split' and 'the Flash'.

By Flemming de Moll

The architect didn't conceive this remarkable exterior stairway for purely aesthetic reasons. Viñoly stresses that, with its broad iron stairs, the structure serves a definite function. "The lot in question was small, but the client desired a lot of square meters of office space. In order to save space inside, I placed the fire escapes on the exterior of the building – on the façade."
But there's more to this stairway, which Viñoly prefers to call an 'extended walkway'. "It is a continuation of the public area, snaking up towards the terrace on the roof of the first horizontal block and proceeding to the second terrace located in the middle of the tower." In the design, the fire escape – which is usually closed for reasons of security – has been made accessible to the public. But the stairway is also a creative elaboration of the initial requirements Viñoly had to comply with in his design. The urban master plan is based on straight walls at street level (reaching to the first 6 floors), with receding building blocks constructed overhead. This arrangement ensures a maximum amount of sunlight and open views for the building's various floors. A stairway that cuts through the Viñoly tower provides a very original solution to this problem.

Unique appearance

The Viñoly building consists of a 26-m-high base of six building layers, with a double-layered tower built on top of this. In accordance with building requirements, the tower recedes a few meters at the 17th floor, at a height of 62 m. The maximum height of the building is reached 10 floors higher, at 91 m. The structure's stability is ensured by the combination of a steel skeleton and a concrete center. The exterior stairway that loops in a spiral around the building connects the various receded levels and simultaneously defines the building's unique appearance. At night, special lighting enhances the building's resemblance to a 'lightning bolt'. Viñoly is enthusiastic about the execution of his design. "This building in Amsterdam has turned out exactly as I had intended. It is a great experience to see my building surrounded by all these other impressive structures on the Zuidas." >>

PHOTO: ANDREAS BRAUN

Viñoly, landmark of the prestigious Zuidas in Amsterdam.

PHOTO: TRUDE HOOYKAAS/LUUK KRAMER

The extended walkway snakes up to the terrace on the roof. >.

The stylish waiting room with deep-pile carpet and soft leather lounge chairs.

Eye-catching projects

Rafael Viñoly, an architect of international renown, was born in 1944 in Uruguay. He fled the country, which was then ruled by a dictatorial regime, in 1978, and moved to the United States. In 1982 he established the firm of Rafael Viñoly Architects PC, which today also has offices in London.

Viñoly's eye-catching projects include the Samsung Corporate Headquarters in Seoul and the Boston Convention Center. The architect earned worldwide acclaim with his design for the Tokyo International Forum, an almond-shaped building with a square that accommodates – among other things – five theaters covered by a spectacular undulating roof. In contrast with this complex, in his design for the Mahler4 tower Viñoly has emphasized the building's exterior. This distinctive feature is what actually marks it as a Viñoly design. "In the case of an office building, one can't waste valuable floor space in the interior. I am grateful to Boekel De Nerée that they agreed with the excellent proposal by their interior architect Ontwerpgroep Trude Hooykaas (OTH) to make floor space available for a light shaft that runs across four floors."

Daylight

The law firm and notary's office of Boekel De Nerée was the first tenant to move into the Viñoly building. In addition to the ground floor, the firm also rents the four stories above, which each have an impressive floor space of some 2,000 m². This gives the office an impressive entrance on Mahlerplein and a double-height ground floor featuring special facilities like an auditorium for debates and seminars, a company restaurant and a stylish waiting room with deep-pile carpet and soft leather lounge chairs.

OTH is responsible for the interior design of the 350-employee office. A significant contribution to its light and spacious appearance is made by a central open space that stretches across four

The mezzanine forms an ideal location for company get-togethers.

PHOTO: TRUDE HOOYKAAS/LUUK KRAMER

The open centerpiece of the Boekel De Nerée office (Trude Hooykaas).

FACT SHEET

Viñoly, Zuidas, Amsterdam

Program:
- Gross floor space: 32,260 m^2
- Surface area, commercial space: approx. 2,030 m^2
- Surface area, office space: approx. 26,160 m^2
- Number of floors: 25
- Height: approx. 95 m

Developers:
Fortis Vastgoed, G&S Vastgoed and ING Real Estate

Architect:
Exterior: Rafael Viñoly Architects, Christina Seilern
Interior: Ontwerpgroep Trude Hooykaas

Structural Engineer:
Van Rossum Raadgevende Ingenieurs

Contractor:
G&S Bouw

Building cost:
€40 million

Design and realization:
2003-2005

Tenants:
Boekel De Nerée (Ground-4th floors)

More information:
www.mahler4.nl
www.zuidas.nl

floors, allowing daylight to reach the building's interior. The various floors are connected by a staircase within this open space. The centerpiece of the office has to be the enormous bookcase in the open space. Spread out over four floors, it forms the firm's new library. "The library is the heart, the center of the organization," explains Ferdinand van Dam, interior architect at OTH, on the design of the interior. Its semi-transparent plastic components, tinted a soft jade-green and illuminated by a strip of light running along the top of the case, lend the enormous array of books a remarkably calm appearance. The bookcase forms a colorful object in a stylish interior dominated by steel, glass, wood and gray and white.

Open and transparent

More color can be found in the firm's art collection, which comprises some 200 works. The collection plays a prominent role in the interior design. The restaurant is decorated with large oil paintings, as is the seminar space. Most of the works, however, are given a more traditional setting in the office rooms that line the building walls. In principle, these spaces are of equal size. Meetings are not organized in boardrooms, but are rather held in the larger and smaller halls spread throughout the building. The design is a clever answer to the employees' wish to meet in corridors, on the staircase and in the intermediate areas that have been fitted with high iron tables. The bar located on the building's mezzanine forms an ideal location for company get-togethers, confirmation ceremonies and parties. Hans Nicaise, Chairman of the Board of Boekel De Nerée, is extremely pleased with the firm's new accommodation. "The appearance of the Viñoly building suits a firm like Boekel De Nerée perfectly – it is both open and transparent." ≪

PHOTO: TRUDE HOOYKAAS/LUUK KRAMER

Architects Ferdinand van Dam of OTH (l) and Rafael Viñoly (m).

ONLINE: www.holland-re.com/vinoly

ROOM FOR WATER

The Netherlands and water are inextricably linked: no country on earth has such an abundance of rivers, canals and dikes. To a considerable extent, the Dutch owe their current economic position to the water around them. After decades of holding back the waves, the government is now giving water more room, both in the rural landscape and in the cities. On the one hand this is a pure necessity for containing the water in the future, on the other it is an expression of the growing interest in waterside living, working and recreation.

By Kees Haak

The strong growth of the Dutch population and the Netherlands' ongoing urbanization has put water in an increasingly tight corner, particularly in the course of the last century.

Until recently, Dutch water management was more or less synonymous with pumping off water and raising dikes. In short: combating the water. This strategy has been overtaken by new concepts.

Living in harmony with the country's water parties has become a necessity in an era of climatic change, rising sea levels, increased melt-water and heavy rains. The country must literally create more room for water, as the land subsides and the sea level rises. While this may sound threatening, the situation does offer unique opportunities for developing new attractive living, working and recreational environments.

PHOTO: KAREL TOMEI

In the 90s the Goese Meer was built as the

PHOTO: KAREL TOMEI

The Brouwersdam, built in the Dutch Delta area.

Delta Works

In order to counter the menace of the water, the Netherlands has constructed no less than 3,500 km of primary dams: dunes; river, lake and sea dikes; storm surge barriers and dams. This is how 'the Dutch Miracle' came about: the former enemy was transformed into an ally that brought wealth and prosperity. The Dutch capital Amsterdam

AND LIVING

basis for the prestigious villa park in Goes which shares the same name. It is bordered by an 18-hole golf course with many water features.

also originated in such a dam. Over the centuries, the small medieval settlement near a dam on the Amstel river has developed into a colorful collection of canals, embankments and town houses that forms a truly successful mix of water and architecture. No less than a quarter of the Netherlands is located below sea level. Whether it is polder creation or dike construction, the Netherlands has always been at the forefront of innovative water technology. The best example of Dutch water engineering is the world-famous Delta Works. They are an amazing example of construction ingenuity, admired by specialists the world over. The Delta Works protect the hinterland from floods without endangering the environment or the fishing industry. >>

PHOTO: KAREL TOMEÏ

The Delta Works in the province of Zeeland.

PHOTO: PETRA APPELHC

Paleiskwartier, Den Bosch. Architect Tony McGuirk designed residential buildings like sailboats on the water.

Floating cities

The Dutch government has developed an integral approach to town planning that provides a harmonious mix of water, space and nature. Indeed, the policy centers on creating space: space for living, working and recreation. The new policy naturally requires innovative solutions. Dutch Docklands International, for instance, has conceived a combined Styrofoam-concrete structure that would enable the construction of entire floating cities. Other interesting examples include floating homes in Maasbommel or the possibility of building on mounds made of dredging residue.

Melanie Schultz van Haegen, State Secretary of Transport and Public Works, bears responsibility for the government's new urban development policy. As Schultz van Haegen explains in *Real Estate Magazine*, "We have to provide room for water, before it takes this space of its own accord. We need to broaden rivers and create more water storage in the areas surrounding the cities. This will be the foundation of our water policy in the 21st century. We have to take the increased possibility of floods and water shortages into account. By 2015, I aim to have realized the efficient distribution of water in the right areas and for a variety of functions. I intend to follow a policy based on initial containment of the water, followed by retention and finally draining of the water."

Water management

Over the years, Dutch companies have developed extensive know-how in the field of water management. They have a wealth of experience in dredging and land reclamation projects, both within the Netherlands and internationally. Furthermore, with organizations like the Netherlands Water Partnership (NWP) the Netherlands is an important link in the chain of global water management.

The Dutch are also renowned for other forms of water-related expertise. One can consider water construction for ports, water treatment – like the desalination of water resources – and groundwater storage. This expertise is put into practice across the globe.

Water retention

An important aspect of the new water policy is the drainage of rainwater. In most areas this is handled by the local sewer system. But old or small sewers tend to overflow in the event of heavy rainfall, something that can be avoided by allowing more rain to drain away directly into the soil or by guiding it towards a canal. This is often impossible due to asphalt and construction.

PHOTO: MIN. OF TRANSPORT, PUBLIC WORKS AND WATER MANAGEMENT

State Secretary Melanie Schultz van Haegen.

In various new developments, excess rainwater is led through a system of pipes to subterranean storage facilities, where it slowly seeps into the groundwater. At numerous sites throughout the country, construction has started on special water retention areas. The Dutch water system is now required to make more space available in crucial areas for the storage and draining away of excess water. In addition, it is also possible to temporarily store water in retention areas above ground.

Multipurpose space

Schultz van Haegen elaborates, "I do not simply see the water as a threat, I also acknowledge the opportunities it offers, for instance with regard to recreation and the construction of attractive living and working environments. More room for water doesn't necessarily mean less space for other functions. A good solution is to use space for a variety of purposes simultaneously – to develop intelligent, innovative ways to combine homes, enterprise and water storage. Developers and constructors can play a significant role in this development. Fortunately, they are already making work of this and are coming up with increasingly clever solutions."

"I expect the business community to take an innovative approach to these matters. It is necessary to develop new construction technology that enables large-scale floating projects. By employing such innovative technology on the city outskirts – where spatial and economic developments have slowed down due to the 'room for the river' policy – we can provide these areas with a new impulse," con-

Floating greenhouse

In the Westland area, one can find the world's first floating greenhouse. The demonstration model, officially opened in June 2005, is situated in the water retention area beside the Flora Holland flower auction in Naaldwijk. It is a revolutionary concept, as the entire structure is in direct contact with the water, rather than simply built over it. This technology makes it possible to create a platform of any size you should require. It could also be used for other floating structures, such as floating homes, offices and gardens. According to developers Dura Vermeer, a floating greenhouse is just one of the possible solutions to meet the growing demand for space for housing, employment and recreation. Over the next 50 years, 500,000 ha of land will have to be reserved for water retention. By developing floating structures, it becomes possible to combine different claims on the available space.

PHOTOS: DURA VERMEER

tinues Schultz van Haegen. "This is good for the water and good for the economy. Designs already exist for 15 test projects."

New canals

In the last few decades, the Dutch cities have made considerable efforts to drive water out of the city. Today, many of these decisions are somewhat regretted, and various new projects aim to let water reclaim its place in the urban environment. Even the construction of new canals is being considered. Furthermore, the Dutch riverbanks offer splendid opportunities for the development of spectacular waterfronts, and many old harbor >>

PHOTO: DURA VERMEER

Impression of a floating city.

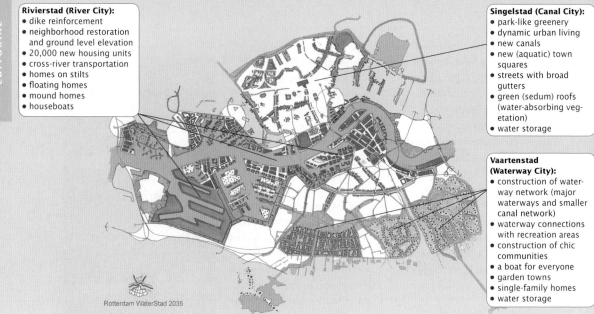

Rivierstad (River City):
- dike reinforcement
- neighborhood restoration and ground level elevation
- 20,000 new housing units
- cross-river transportation
- homes on stilts
- floating homes
- mound homes
- houseboats

Singelstad (Canal City):
- park-like greenery
- dynamic urban living
- new canals
- new (aquatic) town squares
- streets with broad gutters
- green (sedum) roofs (water-absorbing vegetation)
- water storage

Vaartenstad (Waterway City):
- construction of waterway network (major waterways and smaller canal network)
- waterway connections with recreation areas
- construction of chic communities
- a boat for everyone
- garden towns
- single-family homes
- water storage

Rotterdam WaterStad 2035

Impression of the Rotterdam Waterstad 2035 plans.

areas can be transformed to accommodate new urban functions. Rotterdam, Amsterdam, Leiden and The Hague have all currently developed attractive plans to this end.

Living on the water

The last few years have brought a growing interest in water dwellings. Such homes can be found in the districts of Almere-Buiten and IJburg and two harbors near Kortenhoef. The IJburg residential project, constructed on an artificial island

near Amsterdam, features a minimum of 250 homes on the water. A number of other water projects are also being prepared in the forelands of the Maas river near Maasbommel, to the south of the Frisian provincial capital of Leeuwarden and near Middelburg in the province of Zeeland. In 2000, construction started in Hoofddorp on the residential neighborhood Floriande, the largest VINEX location in the municipality of Haarlemmermeer. This neighborhood will be characterized by

an abundance of water and will feature 12 islands with 300 homes each. The islands can be accessed by bridges connected to an apartment building.

Rotterdam Waterstad 2035

Rotterdam Waterstad 2035, for instance, a plan developed by the City of Rotterdam, the Waterschap Hollandse Delta district water board and the Schieland en Krimpenerwaard polder board, offers an amazing range of opportunities for new water-themed residential environments, public

Dutch capital Amsterdam has developed from a medieval settlement near a dam into a colorful collection of canals,

Residential area near Rotterdam.

HRH Prince Willem-Alexander

In the field of water management, the Netherlands has a very prominent expert at its disposal, in the figure of HRH Prince Willem-Alexander, the country's future king. The prince is an honorary member of the World Commission on Water for the 21st Century and patron of the Global Water Partnership.

transport over water and a healthy water system.

"Bringing water back into the city center is a good approach to solving water issues," says State Secretary Schultz van Haegen. "Furthermore, its presence nearby raises our consciousness of actually living in a huge delta. Unfortunately, there isn't one solution that works in each case. We are required to develop tailored solutions, which necessitates good collaboration between the municipality, developers and the water board."

A fine example is the project Rotterdam Waterstad 2035, which offers a realistic view of a feasible and acceptable solution for water issues in this major international seaport. Schultz van Haegen explains, "What attracts me to Rotterdam Waterstad 2035, is the fact that water management organizations and spatial planners joined forces to investigate how the necessary large-scale construction can be combined with a further improvement of Rotterdam's urban development. They reached the interesting conclusion that Rotterdam's water issues form a 'trump card' in terms of town planning."

Taking water issues into consideration in inner-city redevelopment projects should become as natural as planning an area's parking facilities. This too was a very complicated affair a mere 20 years ago, and not always elaborated satisfactorily. It is now a standard element of a location's operation. «

Melanie Schultz van Haegen (VVD)
State Secretary of Transport, Public Works and Water Management.

- Member of the Leiden City Council, April 1994-May 2002
- Researcher and Advisor, B&A Groep, based in The Hague, 1995-1997
- Senior Advisor, B&A Groep, based in The Hague, 1997-1999
- Alderman for Economic Affairs, Land Issues, Tourism and Parking and Communication in the Leiden City Council, October 12, 1999-July 22, 2002
- State Secretary of Transport and Public Works (responsible for air traffic, water, shipping and environmental legislation pertaining to shipping and the Royal Dutch Meteorological Institute KNMI), as of July 22, 2002
- Member of the lower House of the Dutch Parliament, January 30, 2003-May 27, 2003

embankments and town houses.

With the kind collaboration of Real Estate Magazine/Eric Harms.

ONLINE: www.holland-re.com/water

DEBATE IN NIEUWSPOORT INTERNATIONAL PRESS CENTER THE HAGUE

ONE MILLION LOW-RENT

According to the participants in this year's Nieuwspoort debate, the housing market is only a market in name. This has everything to do with the dominant position of the Dutch government. The state regulates rent levels and keeps them artificially low, provides generous subsidies to low-income tenants, and furthermore demands a 6% 'conveyance tax' when tenants decide to move to an owner-occupied home. The results are extremely limited circulation, 'scheefwonen' low-building production and outrageous price levels. Newcomers to the housing market cannot afford to buy their own home and the waiting list for rental homes can be as much as eight years. What needs to be done and who needs to do it?

By Dick Groenendijk

Ten board members of various leading property developers, constructors and investment firms pulled up a chair to talk with prominent politician Adri Duivesteijn, main spokesman on this topic for the PvdA in the Dutch parliament. Chairman Kees Koedijk, Professor of Financial

Peter Ruigrok (AM) middle: "If you invest in neighborhoods, it usually results in dynamism."

Management at Erasmus University Rotterdam, sets the ball rolling: "Mr. Duivesteijn, what do you think about the idea of simply abolishing the conveyance tax, since no one really remembers why it was introduced in the first place? This would allow things to start moving again in the housing market, and would particularly benefit the newcomers to the market."

Statement 1: *Conveyance tax is not an unassailable institute. A macro-approach would be better than ad hoc policies.*
Adri Duivesteijn (PvdA): "The conveyance tax isn't sacred. We could abolish it, but this

HOMES ON THE MARKET

"Conveyance tax isn't sacred."

"Bring a million social homes on the market."

"Abolish the conveyance tax."

would have it's financial consequences for the government. The alternative of taxing 'scheefwonen' (the current situation where a large portion of social housing is occupied by high-income tenants – ed.) would be a risky venture in my opinion. It could well lead to the undesirable development that people >>

PARTICIPANTS IN THE NIEUWSPOORT DEBATE

1. Chairman: Professor Kees Koedijk, Erasmus University Rotterdam
2. Friso de Zeeuw, Bouwfonds MAB Ontwikkeling
3. Pieter Wetselaar, Rabo Vastgoed
4. Carel de Reus, Johan Matser Projectontwikkeling
5. Peter Ruigrok, AM
6. Lex Pouw, Ymere
7. Adri Duivesteijn, Partij van de Arbeid
8. René Scherpenisse, Stuurgroep Experimenten Volkshuisvesting
9. Dietmar Werner, Volker Wessels Vastgoed
10. Menno Maas, AMVEST
11. Huub Smeets, Vesteda
12. Jan Willem van den Bos, Meeùs
13. Marinus Dijkman, (initiator), Editor-in-Chief, Europe Real Estate Publishers

Huub Smeets (Vesteda) 3th from left: "New quality homes will eventually be subleased too. At double the original rent."

Adri Duivesteijn (PvdA) middle: "We could abolish the conveyance tax, but this would have financial consequences for the government. The alternative of taxing 'wrong use' (social housing occupied by high-income tenants) would be a risky venture."

decide to move out of certain neighborhoods. If you start taxing higher-income earners living in relatively cheap accommodation, they will move to other areas where they get a better standard of living for the same money. This undermines the social differentiation that is so important for the standard of living in the inner cities. By solving one problem, you create a new one. That is why I advocate a broader approach. Take a close look at conveyance tax, a possible taxation of rent/income discrepancy and the deduction of

Menno Maas (AMVEST): "No circulation, waiting lists and 'wrong use' all require a macro approach, rather than ad hoc policies."

mortgage interest, but also look at their interrelationship. You can do this within the context of a general revision of the tax system." Menno Maas (AMVEST): "We currently have a gridlock situation in the housing market. No circulation, waiting lists, 'wrong use', etc. These are all interrelated issues that cannot be addressed with ad hoc policies, but require a macro-approach. In the Netherlands, we have the absurd situation where higher-income groups are subsidized via the system of mortgage interest tax deduction, the middle-income earners benefit from 'wrong use', and low-income earners receive rent subsidy. These artificial constructions prevent the housing market from actually functioning as a market." Huub Smeets (Vesteda): "It is strange that newcomers are not served by the current housing market. The Netherlands has 2.5 million homes in the social housing sector. If one relates this figure to the number of people receiving rent subsidy – the people in the lowest income groups, for whom this type of home is ultimately intended – there are a million low-rent

homes too many. A million homes in the social sector that are occupied by people who are fully able to pay for something else. They initially started in one of these homes, have since built a career, but continue to live cheaply. As a result newcomers cannot find an affordable home. That can't be the intention! Simply taxing 'wrong use' is not the only solution to this situation; one needs to take additional measures. Crack down on illegal subletting for instance. This problem should not be underestimated.

In Amsterdam, in particular, people move, but keep their cheap rental home and rent it out for a considerably higher rent. And with regard to social differentiation - let's focus on creating a more varied range in the old city neighborhoods so that people can develop a housing career in their own neighborhood."

Statement 2: *Create a large-scale social housing market and prevent subsidized subletting!* René Scherpenisse (SEV): "We have approx. 2.5 million low-level rental homes in the

Netherlands, with an average rent of €350, and 3 million owner-occupied homes with an average price of €219,000. There is hardly anything available between these two extremes. This means that a large portion of the Dutch population, with a household income of some €30,000-€50,000, isn't really served by the current market. The solution to this problem is in the hands of the housing corporations. In my view, this surplus of a million social housing units is eligible for sale on the market. With a few extra measures you can put these homes within reach of people who can't buy a home on the regular market. This makes it possible to create a large-scale social housing market for prospective homeowners."

Friso de Zeeuw (Bouwfonds MAB Ontwikkeling): "In the Netherlands, we intensively stimulate the demand for homes with a system of subsidies and tax deductions, while little is done to improve the supply side. There has been tension in this situation for many years now. But I believe that people are now in the right frame of mind to

Carel de Reus (Johan Matser):
"An entrepreneurial government could easily give new impetus to the development of the housing market."

make a big move forwards. We shouldn't think up a whole new series of support measures, but rather address the underlying issue – supply. And this means production and comprehensive reform of the Dutch system of support measures and taxes."

Lex Pouw (Ymere): "A lot of the discussion surrounding the price-making process and demand support will evaporate if we were able to stimulate production. This is the pivotal issue, in my opinion. I don't see the point of targeting the 'wrong use' problem. This will only lead to complicated debates, without any systematic outcome. It is vital to disconnect this issue from the necessity to build. Because we need to build! And this also applies for the social sector, where the housing stock is relatively old – at least 30% of these homes are ripe for replacement. In order to execute our housing responsibilities as a corporation, we definitely need to focus on improving quality. And this can only be done by means of new construction."

Smeets: "It's impossible to maintain that you still need new construction with the enormous existing buffer of social rental housing. Mark my words – those new quality homes will eventually be subleased too, at double the original rent. And I also fail to understand why you apparently don't have a problem with the fact that people with a decent income can continue to stay on unhindered in a subsidized home."

Pouw: "What's wrong with someone opting for low living expenses and accepting lesser quality in the process?"

Carel de Reus (Johan Matser Projectontwikkeling): "Many people who live below their means wouldn't mind moving to

Pieter Wetselaar (Rabo Vastgoed):
"If you promote demand in a market with insufficient supply, it will have zero effect."

better-quality accommodation. But as builders we haven't developed these better homes. We will have to put a great deal of work into amending this situation. And it would be good if the government made another billion or so available to make moving up the housing ladder an attractive prospect from a financial point of view. This shouldn't be a problem, because the extra 30,000 homes that we should start building each year would result in some €3.5 billion in revenue. With a bit of persuasion, an entrepreneurial government could easily give new impetus to the development of the housing market."

Peter Ruigrok (AM): "We are currently involved in the restructuring of some 15 ageing postwar neighborhoods. The people living in these neighborhoods generally want to stay there or want to return after restructuring. Even if that means having to pay a realistic market price for their home. In my opinion, there's no reason to fear that people with more disposable income will move away from these neighborhoods. On the contrary, if you invest in these neighborhoods, it usually results in a great deal of dynamism." >>

Carel de Reus (Johan Matser) middle: "Continuing building is the only solution for getting out of the current deadlock. Otherwise you get the situation where parties who have the money to invest in the housing stock will start investing abroad."

Statement 3: *Stimulating demand in the current market has no effect. The housing corporations are sitting tight on their property. The answer is to focus on the supply side – more production.*

Pieter Wetselaar (Rabo Vastgoed): "At the moment, particularly in the sector targeting newcomers, it is really a case of increasing the offer rather than stimulating demand. If you promote demand in a market with insufficient supply, it will have zero effect. It will merely be a waste of taxpayers' money. And as far as the offer

Lex Pouw (Ymere): "Make work of production! We need to sell more, but trading privately-owned homes is still a different matter than producing them."

is concerned, it is definitely not the case that all newcomers in the housing market want a single-family home in the suburbs. A large percentage opts for small units in the city center. We will be realizing a number of projects geared towards this situation."

Jan-Willem van den Bos (Meeùs): "We recently commissioned a study of the demand for living accommodation in each of the Dutch regions. This survey showed that there is indeed a considerable demand for living space in and around the inner-city areas. Both in the rental and the privately-owned sectors. The offer will also have to be expanded in the middle and higher segments of the market."

Duivesteijn: "I am convinced that many people who are now living too cheaply would like to buy their social rental home. But in many cases this simply isn't possible, because the corporations are holding on to their property and are insufficiently prepared to dispose of these units. This situation must be addressed. By bringing a significant portion of these social homes to the owner-occupied market, you take the pressure off the

market and avoid the price being driven up further. And we need production – particularly by the corporations, and especially in a period of recession."

Scherpenisse: "If you really want to achieve results with such a transformation of the social housing stock, you need to offer the homes at an attractive price, in other words below what the market would ask. Taking account of the balance sheet value, this could be a fairly cost-neutral measure for the corporation involved. And make no mistake, the ethnic middle class in the cities would rather buy than rent. For them, buying a home is a value in itself because it allows you to build up capital."

Pouw: "The nice thing about property is that you are allowed to make your own decisions about it. After all, would you go around forcing a homeowner to sell his house? So why should a corporation? And – on top of that – for less than the market price? For 50 years, government policy has made a mess of the rental market. Should we now do the same thing to the owner-occupied market and the price-making process? Make work of

production! We need to sell more, but trading privately-owned homes is still a different matter than producing them."
Duivesteijn: "What is creating this tension in the housing market? And how can you achieve a breakthrough? These are issues that we need to give fundamental thought to. And corporations need to approach it on the basis of their social responsibility, which gives them a whole other perspective than a private owner or a commercial landlord."
De Zeeuw: "You are giving the buyers a little financial present, but what are the alternatives for the corporations to bring the housing market in the large cities back into balance?"
Pouw: "There is an intense debate going on in Amsterdam at the moment about the allocation system, which stifles development. The same applies to the rent level policy. What should you expect if you are in fact offering homes at too low a price? But the most important issue is new construction. This is something that we really have to work on."
Scherpenisse: "But what are you doing for the large group of people with an income between €25,000 and €50,000, who come just short of being able to buy a home? You let them stay put in social housing. That costs money, a lot of money in fact. After all, these are subsidized homes."
Pouw: "The government's rent level policy forces us to charge a low rent. This is where the fundamental problem lies."
Smeets: "Which doesn't dismiss the fact that we simply haven't built enough homes in the Netherlands. Even during the boom of the 1990s we didn't do enough. It isn't even so much a case of making anticyclical investments – we have to keep building

on a cyclical basis, even when we are going through a slump as we are at present."

Statement 4: *The key is to continue building (anti)cyclically. Housing production has to return to the level of 100,000 units per year.*
De Reus: "It's the only solution for getting out of the current deadlock. And then it could still take another 10 to 20 years. If we can't establish some sort of continuity, you will get the situation where parties who have the money to invest in the housing stock will start investing abroad. This is already going on."
De Zeeuw: "Let's not be too pessimistic. It's clear that building production is on the rise. It's a slow development, but it is taking place."
De Reus: "Even if we can step up the annual production to 100,000 homes – although we're currently way below this figure (70,000 in 2005 – ed.) – this still won't suffice to make up the difference. On the contrary – at that level the backlog will still continue to grow."
De Zeeuw: "What a load of non-

Friso de Zeeuw (Bouwfonds MAB): "Let's not get too grim. Building production is on the rise. It's a slow development, but it is taking place."

sense. Dutch contractors aren't even able to deal with these volumes. They could take on 80,000 at the most. And such a figure emphatically includes a portion of fairly simple, cheap homes for newcomers."
De Reus: "I recognize the problems faced by newcomers, but you can only solve the current problems by adopting a long-term policy. This means building selectively, and building homes of high-quality." >>

Huub Smeets (Vesteda) middle: "We have to keep building on a cyclical basis, even when we are going through a slump. Even during the boom of the 1990s we didn't do enough. We simply haven't built enough homes in the Netherlands."

Marinus Dijkman (Europe Real Estate Publishers) is the initiator of the yearly Holland Real Estate housing debate in Nieuwspoort, The Hague.

Dietmar Werner (Volker Wessels Vastgoed): "Even 100,000 new homes is a negligible figure when compared to the Netherlands' total housing stock. If you really want to get things moving in the housing market, you will need to focus on structural change: the large-scale sale of rental homes to people who want to buy them. And a policy that makes it possible to charge a cost-effective rent for a home."

Statement 5: The Dutch population is ageing. How should the construction community respond to this development? Will the future bring special locations for senior citizens or even complete cities geared towards this age group? Would this make sense?
Wetselaar: "I don't think so. One of the characteristic features of Dutch society is that people, whether they are old or not, prefer to stay close to their old neighborhood – within a radius of some 10 km or so. Relocating to a completely different region, as people do in the US for instance – Florida, California – is by no means common here. And we also don't believe that a Sun City would get off the ground.

A sunny neighborhood or a sunny street reserved for senior citizens – perhaps. But that's about it."
Koedijk: "But what are these senior citizens actually asking for?"
Wetselaar: "Senior citizens are very liberated, particularly in the owner-occupied market. They definitely do not want to be addressed on the basis of their age or care requirements. They want a normal living environment – perhaps an apartment – that offers the possibility of home automation. A lot can already be done in terms of technology. Even existing apartments can be equipped with home automation without too much effort. The location is another important factor: senior citizens prefer to be located close to facilities. This is something that municipalities should take more account of in their urban development policies. Affluent senior citizens would like to invest in their city, but they need to be provided with the opportunity to do so."
Smeets: "People do not want to live in a complex solely populated by senior citizens – let alone a city. 75% of the over-65 age group aims to live in the (inner)city in their golden years. In time, this will create a problem for the Vinex locations (large-scale residential developments in the periphery of existing urban centers – ed.). People will stay there after reaching 65, but it is highly unlikely that these locations will still suit the needs of the over-75 age group."
Scherpenisse: "When discussing senior citizens, they always seem to be presented as a homogeneous group. Obviously, they are not. There are definitely senior citizens that prefer to live in a special complex with a range of facilities at close hand. But such an environment would drive

other pensioners mad. As soon as the weather permits it, they take to the road and drive the camper to Spain for the winter… Such different lifestyles cannot be served by a single concept."
Maas: "We should also classify senior citizens in different age categories. At present, investors, developers, corporations and politicians primarily target the 55 to 70-year-olds, as they are easily served as a group. But the following age group – the over-75s – is often left to waste away in nursing homes and homes for the elderly that do not meet modern requirements. We also need to invest in these people. We have developed the Lekker Leven (Pleasant Living) concept for both age groups, which entails carefree living with regard to security, facilities and tailored care. Residents can choose from a range of convenience facilities, for instance a shopping service."
De Reus: "You are still offering these facilities within the context of hardware. I believe this will

Ten board members of various leading property talk with politician Adri Duivesteijn about the

no longer be necessary in the future. The market will establish the linkups with care systems and convenience facilities. Let's focus on providing differentiated, quality homes."

Smeets: "Providing custom solutions is the key issue. In the owner-occupied and higher-level rental sectors this won't pose that much of a problem. But I do worry about the senior citizens who depend on the housing corporations."

Pouw: "New construction is a very important issue for the housing corporations. A significant portion of our housing stock was built before the Second World War. They are generally apartments that are accessed by staircases – in other words without an elevator, so not suitable for senior citizens. This problem can only be solved by building new homes. And we are paying close attention to differentiation. Increasingly, we are focusing on developing accommodation for small-scale communities of senior citizens."

Statement 6: *Senior citizens are the newcomers of the future. How do you avoid the development of a catastrophe when this target group dominates the market in 10 to 15 years?*

Duivesteijn: "The problem currently faced by newcomers to the housing market – of not being able to find anything suitable – will also present itself in the near future to the elderly. And this will become particularly apparent in the case of senior citizens with limited financial resources. There are quite a few examples of successful housing projects that target the over-65 age group. But the problem is quantity – the numbers involved are formidable. We have definitely failed to develop an answer to this issue of mass volume."

De Zeeuw: "I expect the most good will come from stair lifts and other relatively simple solutions that make existing single-family units suitable for senior citizens with mobility problems."

Scherpenisse: "For years, SEV has been involved in adaptable con-

Dietmar Werner (Volker Wessels): "Take additional requirements into account, so that seniors can stay in their present homes longer."

struction. The blueprints are on the table. In order to realize adaptations, you will need to equip new homes from the outset with features like straight stairways, wide doorways, spacious toilets, etc. Unfortunately, many of these features fail to be realized in practice because such design features obviously take up more floor space."

Werner: "Yet this is where the challenge lies. To take additional requirements into account, so that senior citizens can stay on for longer in their present home."

Duivesteijn: "And in addition, work must be done on the entire surrounding infrastructure and the local service level. This is hardly given any structural thought in current government policy."

Scherpenisse: "In the case of the generation following the over-55 age group, this care issue plays a major role. The relation with care institutes is of prime importance. What we need to move towards, is a situation where both the housing corporations and commercial developers work in conjunction with the care institutes to deliver care in normal residential complexes that can replace nursing home care." <<

developers, constructors, housing corporations and investment firms pulled up a chair to Dutch housing market.

'WE'VE BECOME A LITTLE MORE INVOLVED AS INVESTORS'

With a portfolio of some €3 billion, Rodamco Europe in the Netherlands has assumed an important position within Rodamco Europe, which manages a total portfolio of €8.7 billion. With the motto 'Return or Retail' the company has decided to focus its investments on dominant retail locations. What does this mean for the Netherlands, one of Rodamco's four home markets, or indeed for Rodamco Europe itself? How do you play the investment funds market effectively, while simultaneously maintaining a sound long-term vision with regard to the ever-demanding consumer? And what do you do with the eternally important office property? We discussed all of this with Karin Laglas, Managing Director of Rodamco Europe in the Netherlands.

By Dick Groenendijk

Rodamco Europe, with its motto 'Return or Retail', has embarked on a new strategy, opting to only invest in 'dominant retail locations' and, wherever possible – and profitable – to divest its office holdings. Rodamco Europe in the Netherlands is now focusing on investment strategies in various types of retail properties, as Karin Laglas, its Managing Director since 1 July 2004, points out.

"In the local interpretation of our overall European strategy we distinguish between four categories of activity. First, city centers, which remain the place that Dutch people head for to make their special purchases. Second, urban district centers: large, popular shopping areas with excellent parking facilities and a large service area in an urban setting, just outside the traditional, historic downtown areas.

Winkelcentrum Leidsenhage in The Hague area is a good example of this, as is the Winkelcentrum Overvecht in the Utrecht area. Stadshart Amstelveen and Stadshart Zoetermeer, meanwhile, are two examples of this type of shopping center which, in this case, also serve as the city center's heart."

"A third category for us is the neighborhood shopping area, those places close to home where shoppers can do their daily shopping, with plenty of supermarkets, grocers and ordinary stores. And lastly we are also aiming at 'specialty retail', those properties with unusual offerings and/ or an obvious leisure activity quality. An example of this would be Batavia Stad, the first factory outlet center in the Netherlands, near Lelystad in the province of Flevoland." >>

Karin Laglas: "Rodamco Europe usually chooses to run its own properties in order to increase their value."

Well-equipped shopping centers

If you ask Laglas about the Stadshart Amstelveen shopping center, which Rodamco Europe in the Netherlands purchased from Commerz Grundbesitz Investmentgesellschaft mbH in May 2005, a broad smile begins to stretch across her face. "Stadshart Amstelveen is a well-equipped shopping center in a prestigious and prosperous suburb of Amsterdam," she says. "After La Part Dieu in Lyon and the recently acquired Donauzentrum in Vienna, the third-largest asset in Rodamco Europe's total investment portfolio. It is one of the top shopping centers in the Amsterdam region and includes approximately 48,000 m^2 of retail space, including restaurants, 1,591 parking spaces, and 2,800 m^2 of office space. Access to Stadshart Amstelveen is excellent, as it is located right next to the A9 highway and also has plenty of parking. It is located in the immediate vicinity of Amsterdam-Zuid, which includes the Zuidas area, currently the prime office location in the Netherlands, and it has an allure of its own. Plus the shopping center was realized by a fantastic developer, MAB." MAB is Laglas's former employer.

Batavia Stad in Lelystad was the first factory outlet center of the Netherlands. lies approximately 60 km from the cities of Amsterdam and Utrecht.

Fun shopping concepts

The typical fun shopping concept is something that Rodamco Europe in the Netherlands would gladly invest more money in. But because of strict government regulations, these options remain rather limited at this time. For example, that is why con-

struction of the NL.C Geldermalsen – a planned mega-mall with plenty of leisure activity elements, located in the Dutch heartland on the outskirts of the urban region – ultimately failed. That is something Laglas truly regrets. "This project, in a unique location for this country, truly won Rodamco Europe's enthusiastic support. We really would have liked to have invested in this kind of project, provided that all the conditions could be met. A project like this has to be unique and modern, not some mirror image of something that already exists elsewhere in another downtown area or other urban center. In other words, an innovative retail strategy where retailers can show an entirely different side of themselves. Something that offers 'try

Vier Meren shopping center in Hoofddorp (27,000m^2).

A succes from the start. Batavia Stad

and buy' and leisure and fun. I think there is room for this kind of project in the Netherlands, even though only to a limited degree. Because fun malls should not have to signal the death knell for similar types of shopping areas that already exist in various city centers."

The flywheel

When it comes to modernization and progress in the four home territories where Rodamco Europe is currently active, it always chooses to play an active role. "When it comes to retail property, Rodamco Europe usually chooses to run its own properties – we call it managing – in order to increase their value," Laglas points out. "We make the shopping-center area more pleasant, to attract more visitors who come and spend more. This can be facilitated by renovation of the building exteriors, improved parking facilities, the addition of related services such as creches, restaurants and cafes, perhaps an art lending library, a museum, and also by organizing events. But most of all, we aim for a good mix of tenants – tenants that will appeal to the shopping public. This set of instruments that ensures that people gladly come to do their shopping here is something we try to incorporate as much as possible. At the end of the day, this serves as our basis for rent increases, and with that comes a higher yield, and, of course, increased value. Investing in the good management of a particular project stimulates the flywheel effect."

Reshuffling the investment portfolio

Adding value via proper retail management only works with the right kind of focus. That is why Rodamco Europe in the Netherlands performed an analysis of its Dutch investment portfolio. "Our strategy of focusing on dominant locations has made us analyze our investment portfolio. If we own, say, just one or two stores in a smaller city, with no other property there, then we have to ask ourselves whether this fits in with our added-value philosophy through active management. Basically, these are fine investments on their own but the extended distribution of property requires an entirely different management approach. We are planning to selectively sell off these properties as necessary. In this way, we can limit the sheer number of properties in our portfolio and the number of cities where we own real estate. This enables us to focus more of our attention on adding value to the remaining properties via our self-management strategy." That is how Laglas describes the strategic reorientation. Besides retail space, Rodamco Europe in the Nederland's portfolio includes some €400 million worth of office space, which it intends to sell off as well.   >>

Spazio Zoetermeer

The shopping center Spazio opened its doors in Zoetermeer, close to The Hague, at the end of 2005. Spazio (15,500 m²) represents a dramatic expansion of the current Stadshart Zoetermeer shopping center. International retailers such as H&M, Zara and Media Markt already chose for Spazio. Total retail space in Stadshart Zoetermeer, including Spazio, is now roughly 70,000 m²

(68% of which is owned by Rodamco Europe). It will attract some 11 million visitors annually. The market value of Spazio, including retail space, parking facilities and offices, is €57 million and produces a net initial yield of 7.1% annually. The development of the new shopping center was realized in close cooperation with AMVEST (243 apartments).

Piazza shopping center in Eindhoven has four retail floors and high quality standards with a remarkable and transparent design (architect: Massimiliano Fuksas).

However, there is no hurry here. "You have to be sensible when it comes to your portfolio. You have to choose the right moment. Some very good rental properties, such as the Robeco House in Rotterdam, are not exactly the most exciting investments to have in your portfolio. In these cases you just have to wait for the right moment to trade them in for some attractive piece of retail space."

Expansion moves

Rodamco Europe is known as a Fiscale Beleggings Instelling (FBI, Fiscal Investment Institution) in the Netherlands. This basically means that Rodamco Europe in the Netherlands is not entitled to develop projects itself. But the organization can certainly improve its existing portfolio, as well as protect the value of its current investments. That is what it is currently doing, says Laglas. "Especially in the sense of expansion. Large chains are constantly urging us to expand current facilities in order to be able to offer them larger units and new possibilities. Today, retail people are requesting considerably larger spaces than they were some twenty or thirty years ago. Back then, a standard unit

Stadshart Amstelveen

Stadshart Amstelveen, acquired in May 2005 from CGI mbH for a sum of €296 million, represents the third-largest asset in Rodamco Europe's total investment portfolio. It is one of the top shopping centers in the Amsterdam region and includes approximately 48,000 m² of retail space, including restaurants, 1,591 parking spaces and 2,800 m² of office space. The tenant mix is strong and includes Dutch department ment stores like De Bijenkorf, an Albert Heijn supermarket, and roughly 170 specialty stores (Blokker, Claudia Sträter, Douglas, Esprit, H&M, MEXX, Timberland, and WE). Stadshart Amstelveen welcomes well over seven million visitors per year. Rodamco Europe acquired the shopping center at an average net running yield of 5.9% (years 1-3).

was basically 100 to 150 m². With new international concepts by such retailers as Zara and H&M, you are already quickly dealing with a considerably larger amount of space; 1000 m² is not that unusual these days. That is why we systematically re-examine our portfolio to see where we might find some room – physically as well as market-wise – to make our next expansion move."

Collaboration with a developer

The improvement of a shopping center usually requires working with a number of different developers. But unlike earlier times, Rodamco pretty much have free rein now. "As investors, we have clearly become more involved," notes Laglas. "Generally not in annoying manner, however. We enter into a collaboration agreement with the developer, and from the very beginning we gladly offer them all of our exploitation expertise. Contributing our own expertise is something we find essential. And after all, we want the project to be realized. It is, therefore, essential for us that we can contribute our long-term plans to the development prospectus." Recognizing the right place

Karin Laglas, who for years served in a leadership position at MAB, a leading developer in the Netherlands, has not really noticed any major differences in the ways that investors and developers think. "It's more about nuance. As an investor you look a bit more consciously at the long term and that's what guides you in your decisions regarding certain specifications. But, in general, we both pretty much practice the same profession. Recognizing the right place and what you have to do there – that is precisely what both the investor and developer do."

Shifting roles

It is not so surprising then that the distinctions of the old days have gradually begun to disappear. This development also has its negative side. "You see developers adding these projects into their own portfolios more and more often or just linking them directly to their own funds. For us investors it thus becomes increasingly difficult to find good properties. To compensate for this loss of market potential, we can only turn to improving our own portfolios. The more that developers begin to play an investor's role, the more they push investors the other way." «

Rodamco Europe

Rodamco Europe N.V. is the leading listed retail property company in Europe. With a €8.7 billion investment portfolio it owns and operates quality retail properties, especially shopping centers. Rodamco's home markets are the Netherlands, Belgium, Sweden, Denmark, Finland, France and Spain. Rodamco is also currently active in Central and Eastern Europe, in countries including Austria, the Czech Republic, Germany, Hungary and Poland.

Rodamco Europe is an independent investment company with variable capital, which qualifies as a Fiscal Investment Institution (FBI) under Dutch law. As long as all of the conditions of Dutch tax law have been adequately complied with, an FBI is not required to pay corporate income taxes in the Netherlands. Rodamco Europe also qualifies as a Société d'investissements immobiliers cotées (SIIC) under French law. When an SIIC meets all of the relevant legal conditions, it does not need to pay French corporate income taxes on current income from, and realized capital gains on, French real estate. Rodamco Europe is listed on the stock exchanges of Amsterdam, Paris, Frankfurt, and Brussels. The company has a 'single A with stable outlook' rating from Standard & Poor's in the US.

MORE INFORMATION
Rodamco Europe
P.O. Box 22816
1100 DH Amsterdam
The Netherlands
Tel.: +31 20 312 01 20
Fax: +31 20 312 02 41
Website: www.rodamco.com

A NEW GENERATION CHANGES THE FACE OF REAL ESTATE

A change is taking place in the Dutch real estate community. The last decade saw a new generation come to the fore, with an innovative view of the business of property development. People like Rudy Stroink (TCN Property Projects), Coen van Oostrom (OVG Projectontwikkeling) and Paul Trip (IPMMC Vastgoed) have each paved their own way in the industry, changing the face of the Dutch real estate market in the process.

By Marinus Dijkman & Ola Sinoo

In today's market, demographic developments such as the aging population and the resulting falling proportion of younger people threaten to create an excess supply of office space, and customers are becoming increasingly discerning and articulate about their needs. Even in this difficult climate, companies like OVG Projectontwikkeling, TCN Property Projects and IPMMC Vastgoed have successfully taken the lead in developments. The new generation of property developers who have taken over the top positions during the past few years has a different take on development processes, sending a breath of fresh air into the Dutch property market. For the innovators of the 21st century, the customer is the *leitmotiv*.

Tailored solutions

"There are two approaches to real estate development," says Paul Trip, former CEO of ING Real Estate Development and Director of IPMMC Vastgoed since November 2005. "Traditionally, a building is developed first and then the developer starts looking for a client. The new companies take a different approach: they develop a tailor-made building in close consultation with the client." For Coen van Oostrom, CEO of OVG Projectontwikkeling, the customer has been the focal point of operations since the establishment of the company. "Our ability to provide tailored solutions is a major added value of OVG as a developer. It is of crucial importance that you offer your client made-to-measure accommodation."

Purpose-orientated building

According to Rudy Stroink, CEO of TCN Property Projects, focusing on the client's needs has always been a rather neglected issue in the Netherlands, something that he finds regrettable. "Property development in the Netherlands is excessively geared towards construction. Developers take insufficient account of the client's needs," Stroink explains. "The client isn't just looking for 'a store', he needs a certain type of store. One should consider the project's final purpose and its end users right from the design phase. We also prefer to keep our projects in our portfolio. Only by operating a building yourself can you exploit its full potential – particularly in the long term." >>

The Wall, Utrecht (concept IPMMC, 60,000 m² of leisure and retail space, developer: Burgfonds).

Rudy Stroink
CEO of TCN Property Projects

Coen van Oostrom
CEO of OVG Projectontwikkeling

Paul Trip
Director of IPMMC Vastgoed

TCN Property Projects

Established over a decade ago, TCN Property Projects has since grown into one of the leading firms in Dutch real estate. Working from offices in the Netherlands, Germany, Portugal, Belgium and Hungary, the company develops innovative real estate concepts across the continent and strives to remain responsible for their subsequent operation. TCN Property Projects has 250 employees, all working in one of the following divisions: TCN Concepts, TCN Development, TCN Management and TCN Assets. These four divisions provide the perfect answer to the property life cycle. The company is set apart by its innovative concepts and creative approach towards the design, management and financing of real estate.

OVG Projectontwikkeling

OVG Projectontwikkeling was established in 1997, mainly working as a developer of apartments in stately town houses. From 2000 onwards, the emphasis shifted to larger retail and office development projects, with investment levels in excess of €10 million. At the start of 2006, OVG Projectontwikkeling has a staff of 30 and a turnover of €300 million. The company faces a strategic decision: will it remain a national player in commercial development and broaden its portfolio in different sectors such as housing, stores or hotels, or will it cross the Dutch border to become a international office property developer? CEO Coen van Oostrom is inclined towards the second option, as it creates more space for tailored developments, an OVG specialization that is one of the pillars of the company. OVG distinguishes itself in the market by its made-to-measure solutions and short construction periods.

IPMMC Vastgoed

IPMMC Vastgoed is an independent real estate organization, specializing in consultancy, management and the development of complex real estate assignments. The company was founded in January 1995. A fourth activity, concepts, has enabled the company to gain extensive expertise in the field of concept development. Working with 45 employees, IPMMC Vastgoed distinguishes itself with its integral knowledge of the property market and its unique approach to the 'art of construction'. Combining creativity with commercial clout and solid project management, IPMMC Vastgoed is able to both develop and implement its real estate solutions.

Urban Entertainment Center, Schiedam.   *UWV building, Rotterdam.*   *DaimlerChrysler, Utrecht.*

ING House, Amsterdam (management IPMMC, 20,000 m².).

Privileged position

The young developers didn't always have it easy in their early years with their unconventional ideas and solutions. Now that they have made names for themselves in the market, though, they have claimed privileged positions. After all, they can benefit from one of the main advantages of smaller-sized operations: the ability to respond quickly to developments. They have short lines of communication, can make relatively quick decisions and are able to maintain a large degree of flexibility. These are important assets in a market demanding new solutions.

Quality improvement

"Demographic stagnation is causing the demand for office space to decrease," says Stroink. "The office market is saturated. We are, to all intents and purposes, finished building. This is why in the next few years the emphasis will not be on new construction but on the redevelopment of buildings. Particularly those from the 50s, 60s and 70s. These buildings are extremely outdated. The floor sizes do not meet current and future needs and the level of facilities is a great deal poorer than that of recent developments. They simply do not meet today's

demands, which makes it impossible to rent them out. If, on the other hand, these buildings are redeveloped, it's possible to make a considerable improvement in the quality of the existing buildings and make them attractive for the market again. I expect that structural redevelopment will allow us to amply meet future market demand."

Keep things moving

Van Oostrom too considers redevelopment the best way to keep the market open. "But you do have to get to work straight away. All too often, a building is bought and the owner leaves it for a spell before finally getting to work on it. We have a different approach at OVG. Immediately after acquiring a property, we develop a tailor-made redevelopment plan in close consultation with the client, and we make a clear agreement regarding the project's short-term completion. We stick to this agreement, to ensure that we keep the project moving. For why would you take the maximum duration for, say, a building inspection, if it could also be done more quickly? With a short-term development or redevelopment you limit the construction period, and therefore you limit the costs. For our company, speed is the key to offering a very competitive price."

Still room in the office market

According to Trip, there's still a lot of room left in the office market. "Insofar as there is a problem with office developments, this is primarily limited to the low end of the market. Even though the office market may not be as easy as before, there is def-

Plein Westermaat, Hengelo (TCN, 80,000 m² of retail space).

initely still sufficient demand. The demand for quality office accommodation in particular will increase further. Take the new business park Papendorp, for instance, on the southern edge of Utrecht. Over the last few years, companies like OVG, Multi Development and IPMMC have developed tens of thousands of m² of new made-to-measure office space at this location."

A more efficient sector

One of the main objections made by the progressive developers regarding the 'traditional' Dutch real estate sector is its system of favoritism and 'like knows like', making it a market where a lot of business is conducted underhand. "It is not an open system," Stroink says. "This is an unhealthy situation in the sector." Although he does expect major changes in this area. "All too often right now, people break the rules - but this is going to change. A new type of government is developing that takes a firm line with the real estate community, providing clear, consistent rules that everyone is expected to adhere to. This will result in a more efficient, tougher sector and a more transparent market. I am an unreserved supporter of this development."

Optimum free market process

Van Oostrom agrees that the old opaque market is not an ideal system – particularly from a customer standpoint. "Although today, the market is more transparent than it was, say, five years ago," he says. "The advisors are more professional, resulting in increased competition and transparency. I view this as a positive development. Indeed, OVG prefers a competitive situation.

De Haagsche Zwaan, The Hague (OVG, 18,000 m² of office space).

Competition leads to optimum free market processes and allows you to respond optimally to the demands of the principal – the client for your building."

Price and quality

"We notice that today, companies – in other words, our clients – have a far more strategic approach to real estate," says Van Oostrom. "In this way, companies aim to realize reduced costs. I expect this trend to continue over the next few years. Market development will increasingly be determined by clients' cost considerations." Trip too expects clients to take a more cost-conscious view of accommodation. "And the demand for quality buildings – buildings that are comfortable, spacious and energy-efficient – will continue to grow." Stroink agrees. "The client is no longer merely asking for a building, but for values like space, flexibility and a pleasant atmosphere. You may have to outsource particular services, but as a developer you will increasingly be required to offer a total package that forms an all-in response to the client's requirements." ≪

MORE INFORMATION

TCN Property Projects

Symfonielaan 1
P.O. Box 7207
3430 JE Nieuwegein
The Netherlands
Tel.: +31 30 600 10 40
Fax: +31 30 630 01 22
E-mail: info@tcnpp.com
Website: www.tcnpp.com

OVG Projectontwikkeling

Montevideo
Otto Reuchlinweg 1132
3072 MD Rotterdam
The Netherlands
Tel.: +31 10 240 03 10
Fax: +31 10 240 03 12
E-mail: info@ovg.nl
Website: www.ovg.nl

IPMMC Vastgoed

Janssoniuslaan 80
P.O. Box 85457
3508 AL Utrecht
The Netherlands
Tel.: +31 30 281 73 00
Fax: +31 30 281 70 15
E-mail: info@ipmmc.nl
Website: www.ipmmc.nl

ONLINE: www.holland-re.com/developers

<small>ROUND TABLE REAL ESTATE FINANCIERS
ING REAL ESTATE FINANCE, BOUWFONDS PROPERTY FINANCE, FGH BANK</small>

REAL ESTATE EVOLVES INTO A FINANCIAL PRODUCT

The sustained strong position of real estate as an investment category means that investors in real estate will also continue to experience good times, even though the competition is fierce and more and more involvement is being demanded of them than ever before. The old traditional, passive role has been replaced by creative, cooperative thinking. This has resulted in refined 'demand-driven' financial structures or 'structured finance' in the technical jargon. But how do you in your daily routine maintain a grip on yields and risks, the two prime concerns of every financier? HRE talks with the CEOs of the market leaders in the Netherlands: Marcel Kokkeel from Bouwfonds Property Finance (ABN Amro), Hein Brand from ING Real Estate Finance (ING Group), and Peter Keur from FGH Bank (Rabobank Group).

By Marinus Dijkman & Dick Groenendijk

A quiet revolution is taking place in the world of real estate financing. The traditional supremacy of the bidders, the capital providers, has vanished. The investors, those on the demand-side of the market, increasingly determine the course of the financing of their own real estate projects. Top managers have concluded that real estate financiers have to offer more than just standard products and solutions. This is certainly the case for those market players who want to make their mark. *Marcel Kokkeel* of Bouwfonds Property Finance comments, "Real estate investors really appreciate a financier who presents himself as client-oriented. With someone who says, 'I understand your problem. I'm your man. Maybe I can't make all the arrangements myself, but I can figure out a solution for you.' Structured finance, for example, is about the dividing up of loans or an additional piece of equity. So you're no longer thinking just about loans traditionally, but are willing to step outside the limitations of your own product. How you do this is of secondary importance. It's not that important to the client; it's all about the fact that you are going to do it. An example? This was pretty clearly the case when we sold off a group of Vendex/KBB stores this past year." *Hein Brand* of ING Real Estate Finance joins in, "Well, for me, the Vendex/KBB-deal was still relatively traditional, especially because it was heavily leveraged. When you're talking about structured finance – a term with many facets – I found the takeover of Nagron Grondbezit and its subsequent withdrawal from the stock exchange a better example. Loans tailored to the level of holdings and businesses, with various structures and matching securities, all to make it possible tax-wise and legally." >>

Huize Hoevelaken.

PHOTO: IMRE CSANY

Three professionals in real estate financing in the park at Huize Hoevelaken.
L-R: Marcel Kokkeel, former Chairman of the Executive Board of Bouwfonds Property Finance, Peter Keur, Chairman
of the Board of FGH Bank and Hein Brand, Member of the Management Board/CEO Finance ING Real Estate.

PHOTO: IMRE CSANY

Over the years, the finance market has become increasingly international, also in the Netherlands.

Cross-border trend

Peter Keur of FGH Bank agrees, "The business is getting more and more complex, that's for sure. Over the last few years, the finance market has become increasingly international in nature, also in the Netherlands. It used to be that besides Dutch bidders, you would only see some German banks, but these days you also run across Americans, the British, and Australians. This cross-border trend forces you to go beyond your traditional product and to develop and offer other, more unique forms of financing. In any case, that's what you're being compelled to deliver. The times of supply-driven financing are a thing of the past now; it has really become demand-driven these days. This is a trend that has yet to reach its peak. You see that financiers from other countries like the United States and Australia are willing to go a lot further than European financiers."

Demand-side as driving force

Brand, however, warns against over-exaggeration. ING Real Estate Finance, he notes, still conducts most of its sales via "traditional lending products." And that goes for FGH Bank as well, finds *Keur*. "But if you want to see increased growth, it's pretty obvious that you have to start offering product combinations with the demand-side as the driving force in the form of a lending and equity assortment. We believe that this gives a clear indication that you trust your client and that you want to do business with him. However, it is essential here to apply the art of saying 'no' because sometimes developers really demand a lot. You have to know the market and your partners, including their track records – that's what's important. And you don't offer this kind of financing to just anyone."

"We see it a little bit differently," says *Brand*. "We don't provide equity. Never. But that is because of the way we divide the various

Bouwfonds Property Finance

Marcel Kokkeel
Former Chairman of the Executive Board of Bouwfonds Property Finance

Bouwfonds (ABN Amro), is one of the largest real estate concerns in the Netherlands and is also active in international markets. Development, Property Finance and Asset Management are its core activities. Bouwfonds Property Finance (210 employees in 2005), had in 2005 a portfolio of €10 billion, generated a turnover of €3.7 billion, of which more than €2 billion was generated in the Netherlands. The former Chairman of the Executive Board of Bouwfonds Property Finance is Marcel Kokkeel (47). During the production of this yearbook, it was announced that as of March 1, 2006, Marcel Kokkeel accepted a new job outside Bouwfonds.

branches within our organization. ING Real Estate consists of three business lines – Finance, Investment Management, and Development – that basically work in close cooperation with each other, but each with their own responsibilities. This means in most instances we call on our investment colleagues. And on balance, if we know the party well, then equity is certainly an option."

Real estate financing

In spite of the changing market climate, the general feeling of the gentlemen around the table is one of satisfaction. This is in part because the much talked-about malaise in the office sector has largely vanished. *Kokkeel* explains, "In our profession, we have relatively little trouble with the current situation of not much being invested in offices. After all, as a financier you are not that dependent on new developments. You will continue to see large transactions, but they usually involve existing buildings. These also need to be financed. Just think about all those real estate funds and smaller funds. Financing the acquisition, subdivision and resale of real estate has evolved into an important activity for us. Real estate in

PHOTO: IMRE CSANY

Keur, FGH Bank: "The art of saying 'no' is essential."

ING Real Estate Finance

The ING Group is a global financial services company of Dutch origin that provides a wide array of banking, insurance, and asset management services in over 50 countries. The Real Estate division has three business lines in which the three key competencies – development, investment management and finance – are carried out. ING Real Estate Finance, with headquarters in The Hague and a worldwide network of offices, generated a turnover of €6.5 billion in 2005, of which €2.5 billion was in the Netherlands. The total number of employees in the Netherlands is 230. The CEO at ING Real Estate Finance since 2002 has been Hein Brand (50).

Hein Brand
Member of the
Management Board/
CEO Finance ING
Real Estate

general, you could say, is evolving more and more toward a financial product. And we facilitate that. The liquidity of this market has grown immensely and we don't foresee this growth trend ending any time soon."

European Market

"The real estate market throughout Europe is highly variable, in the areas of investment and financing,"explains *Brand*. "In general, you can't really describe it as a real European market yet. It all varies greatly from country to country when it comes to development, size, degree of openness, and yields. There are also enormous differences among the countries located in the Central and Eastern European hot spots. Poland, for instance, has a much more mature real estate market than say the Czech Republic. That has a lot to do with the size of the market and the number of investment products available. Many of these markets are still not really that deep or large. In some countries, €50 million is considered a large transaction. And then you only have a couple of these per year. That pretty much determines the market structure and risk profile.

Yields under pressure

Brand continues "ING remains pretty reserved when it comes to Central and Eastern Europe. Many of these markets are simply not deep enough, and when something goes wrong, assurances are hard to find. And your legal position is not always equally as strong. In general, we only finance institutional parties. You could say, deptor and real estate has to be in balance." This is where the various parties differ. "That is something we would never do, acting from the debtor's angle as competing-colleague," says *Kokkeel*. "We focus specifically on the quality of the real estate – wherever it may be in the world. If the quality is high, then we'll participate; if not, we won't. No matter how good the debtor may be. That is because of our roots: Bouwfonds is a real estate player who engages in banking and not the other way around." *Keur* remains silent and that is understandable because FGH Bank – as a subsidiary of Rabobank – only does business inside the Netherlands. But that doesn't necessarily mean that he has turned his back on the eastward expansion of Europe. »

PHOTO: IMRE CSANY

Brand, ING: "ING likes to do business in the US."

After all, real estate remains real estate, regardless of the passports carried by the developers and users. All three agree that the yields in Central and Eastern Europe for both investors and financiers are under a lot of strain these days. This has to do with market conditions: tremendous high demand and a limited supply of real estate investment products. *Brand* continues, "Moreover, you also have to deal with a lot of financiers competing among themselves to the point where you have to ask yourself whether the relationship between risk and yield in this region really makes sense."

Risks have their price

When it comes to the issue of the obvious relation between yield and risk, these three financial investors have plenty to say. "ING Real Estate," *Brand* volunteers, "likes to do business in the US. It's a highly developed country, with a risk/yield relationship that is often quite a bit more agreeable than you might expect. More agreeable, in any case, than in Europe. Maybe this is because they know better than anyone else what the risks associated with real estate are – and then ask a fair price for it. In highly competitive markets this aspect is sometimes forgotten." *Keur* nods in agreement and brings up the example of the stormy arrival of the German mortgage companies on the Dutch market in the early 1990s. "They began financing to a great extent with low yield and with almost no margins, which led to a sizeable erosion of the overall market. It ended up being just a price war. Look, its not the real estate itself that determines the risks but its marketability. And those risks have their price." The man from FGH Bank sees a similar development happening these days, with margins that are

(too) tight, in building trade financial circles. "I just think we shouldn't participate in this area because building trade financing entails a certain amount of risk. As specialists we carefully weigh the risk in the commercial real estate sector, just like the large players like ING and Bouwfonds do elsewhere. It's based on assessment and research. We are able to do this because we have

Financiers will and should never be trendsetters

an extensive professional system at our disposal. And, of course, this has its price tag." *Brand* continues, "The client generally values this kind of professionalism. If we and then another large party of one sort or another says 'no,' then the client is really left wondering and must seriously ask himself whether this is really a sound investment for which he is seeking financing."

Increasingly broader scope

Risk evaluation has become increasingly important now that developers and investors in an up-till-now fairly conservative Netherlands have begun seeking

Peter Keur
Chairman of the Board of FGH Bank

FGH Bank

FGH Bank, with a history that goes back to 1890, has since the end of 2003 been a subsidiary of the Rabobank Group, one of the largest financial service providers in the Netherlands. Within the Rabobank organization, FGH Bank augments Rabobank with what has been its specialty for decades now, the financing of commercial real estate. The bank limits itself to the Dutch market, where in 2005, it realized a turnover of some € 2.7 billion. Its headquarters is located in Utrecht plus it counts seven regional offices. FGH Bank employs a total of 215 people. Peter Keur (52) has been FGH's Chairman of the Board since 1995.

out alternative forms of real estate. Like parking garages, for example. Or public sector buildings like hospitals and prisons. These three gentlemen, however, are not yet that impressed but are willing to approach it creatively and with open minds. *Kokkeel* says "Anything that more or less generates a steady stream of income, such as toll roads or airports, for instance, is potentially

interesting. If there's income, you have trade. That is what we like to look at. But in a critical way." *Brand* goes on, "The whole world is looking for secure real estate. Real estate is, in any case, hot. If you can't get your hands on secure real estate, then you start looking at other possibilities. As a result of which, the definition of real estate becomes broader and broader. The level of professionalism also affects this market."

Purchasing land

The trio also considers the purchase of land as something to potentially finance. Maybe more

so than before but still with some caution. "We have agreed to clear game rules at FGH Bank," says *Keur*, "which means rules concerning the form in which we do it, the percentage of our total balance, and who we are financing. No speculators, for instance."

The other two financiers have a similar policy of maintaining strict frameworks. "The period of time is also important," states *Brand*. "Take the financing of the property around Amsterdam Airport Schiphol, for instance. We were certainly looking at it from a different perspective than we were 10 years ago. The whole situation has become a lot less rosy since then. And you see that you never know what kinds of surprises might pop up. Plus the entire process of opening up an area can have an enormous impact on the eventual basic situation surrounding this area."

Zuidas as trendsetting project

Keur calls the Zuidas project a prime example of "difficult land component financing." New land is actually created by human hands, because all of the on-site infrastructure – the highway, train, and other public transport – disappears underground into an enormous tunnel. It's a costly and lengthy project, while the ultimate purpose of the new space as it was developed, is still surrounded by an air of uncertainty. Thus far, local government has claimed important parts of the space for, among other things, a sports center and green space. "These long-term perspectives and kinds of political decisions are irritating for us financiers to keep an eye on," sighs *Brand*. "But in the end we still ended up participating – yes, that's right – just like all the

Kokkeel: "Never act from the deptor's angle."

other big financiers in the Netherlands, in fact. It's a situation that involved having a lot of conversations with insiders and calculating the values and interests. But the financing of property remains a risky business. You can earn incredible yields, that is true. But also incur heavy losses." *Keur* continues, "The Zuidas was, in fact, probably the only area in the Netherlands where a tunnel project of this sort could ever have any chance of succeeding. It involves future access to Schiphol, an area with a European significance which will no doubt have enormous appeal. That's why we thought investing money here was justified." "This is a good example of real estate financiers' new demand- and finance-driven policies," *Kokkeel* adds. "But there are certainly limits. Financing a casino is certainly in order. But not financing it as a casino. Be a prophet in your own free time if you want. You can try to see 15 years into the future, but I don't think that's the job of a financier." *Keur* concludes, "Predicting trends, anticipating them and then acting upon them – that's fine. But financiers will and should never be trendsetters." «

DUTCH PENSION FUNDS

Dutch pension funds are among the largest institutional investors in the world. With total assets that easily run into the hundreds of billions of euros, of which some 10% or so is invested in real estate. These heavyweights don't just make their mark on the international investment market, but on the Dutch real estate market as well. How do they view recent real estate developments? What trends do they consider serious and how do they focus their investment strategies on these trends? HRE talks to four dominant trendsetters: Patrick Kanters, Managing Director Real Estate Europe Asia Pacific at ABP; Werner Sohier, Head of Real Estate North America at PGGM; Dick van Hal, Managing Director at Achmea Vastgoed; and René Hogenboom, CEO at Altera Vastgoed.

By Marinus Dijkman & Ola Sinoo

The World Port Center (l) by architect Norman

"Investing in real estate in 2006 is becoming an increasingly professional affair," says Dick van Hal, Managing Director at Achmea Vastgoed, with total managed assets of €7 billion which is invested in both its own and in external real estate funds. "Funds are increasingly becoming more transparent, they are using increasingly more modern investment techniques, making for both better organized cash flows and supervision."

Werner Sohier, Head of Real Estate North America at PGGM, is of the same opinion and admits that he would like to significantly increase their investments in real estate. "PGGM has a total portfolio of €71.5 billion, of which 11.5% (€8.5 billion) is invested in real estate. In the coming years, we'd like to expand our portfolio by several billion. But we are not the only ones who want to increase real estate investments. During the past few years, interest in real estate and investment in real estate products throughout the entire institutional market has boomed."

Some nuances are in order at this point, believes Patrick Kanters, who, since August 2005, has been Managing Director Real Estate

Office building in Utrecht (Altera, 22,000 m²).

CHANGE ACCENT

PHOTO: ING REAL ESTATE

Foster on Rotterdam's Kop van Zuid is a joined investment of Achmea Vastgoed, BPF and TPG.

Europe Asia Pacific at ABP, which, with invested assets of €190 billion, makes it the largest pension fund in Europe. "We are also strongly adding new investments in the area of real estate. But differences in transparency are not dependent solely on the fund manager, but also vary per region. There are vast differences worldwide. The US has by far the most transparent structure;

Europe is still in the development stage, and there are also differences between countries within Europe. In Asia, by contrast, transparency still leaves much to be desired."
René Hogenboom has been the CEO of Altera Vastgoed since 2000. Altera Vastgoed manages assets of €1.4 billion and is the only one of the four here that invests exclusively in the >>

PHOTO: JOOP VAN REEKEN

Braingate, Rotterdam (KFN/ABP).

WTC Schiphol Airport, Amsterdam owned by KFN (ABP is the 100% owner of KFN).

Netherlands. "Transparency in the Netherlands is pretty good. There is strict supervision and better yet; the level of knowledge of the real estate product among pension funds has increased dramatically. If you don't measure up to the international market standards, no professional is going to trust you with his assets."

Diversification

"As an investor you are constantly confronted by risks," notes Sohier. "It is our responsibility to recognize and manage those risks. In general, as a large organization we have some advantages. We are better at carrying risks and we have the capacity to diversify when it comes to products, sectors, and regions."

ABP has spread its risks across among various regions and it selects the best funds in each region. Its real estate portfolio is invested 46% in Europe, 44% in the US, and 10% in Asia-Pacific region. 65% is invested in listed funds, 35% in non-listed, although the organization now strives for a more balanced distribution. Kanters: "Diversification is the most important instrument. In Europe, we are heavily invested in non-listed funds, while in the US and Asia we are more heavily invested in listed funds. American and European funds are generally more transparent, there is more information available, and it is broadly covered by analysts. Non-listed funds and joint ventures provide us investment opportunities that are highly correlated to direct investments. You have to sudy these opportunities in-depth to be able to pick the best but also to shape them to allign them to our objectives."

"We want to take controlled risks within our portfolio. It is pension money which means it's the money of our participants," Van Hal points out. "But with good dispersal you can limit your risks. We have comprehensive histori-

Patrick Kanters
Managing Director Real Estate Europe Asia Pacific ABP

Stichting Pensioenfonds ABP

ABP is the pension fund for government and education employers and employees. With total invested assets of approximately €190 billion, ABP is the largest pension fund in Europe. The ABP investment managers, therefore, operate from facilities in the financial centers of Amsterdam and New York. The assignment for ABP's asset managers is simple: get as high a yield as possible, keeping the risks in mind. This is to ensure that the pension schemes remain affordable over the longer term. ABP has invested 11% of its total portfolio in real estate, including both listed and non-listed funds. **www.abp.nl**

cal information at our disposal where we can see what the yield-risk profile is. You have to try to stick to this line. Achmea Vastgoed invests directly in the Netherlands and via investment funds not-traded on the stock exchange in foreign countries – sound funds with sound management from a distance. We screen funds and managers very carefully before we invest in anything."

"You have to put all of the investment risks on the table, analytically speaking, to ensure a balanced diversification. In other words, don't put all your eggs in one basket," advises Hogenboom. "Altera offers separate sector portfolios for retail, residential, offices, and industrial/logistic space. Pension funds make up their own minds where they want to invest and in what manner. Despite the fact that the Netherlands is relatively small, our portfolio is still reasonably diversified. In the retail segment, for instance, we invest in inde-

PGGM

The PGGM pension fund manages the pensions of (former) employees in the health care and welfare sectors. PGGM manages pension assets totaling €71.5 billion (end 2005), which are comprised of pension premiums and investment yield, and serves as the source for the payment of pensions. 11.5% (€8.2 billion) of total assets are invested in real estate. The goal for the coming period is to expand this to 13% of total assets. The Investments division, which employs 140 people, is responsible for managing the pension assets. PGGM, with its headquarters in Zeist, has some 1,100 employees.

Werner Sohier
Head of Real
Estate North
America PGGM

www.pggm.nl

pendent buildings at high-street locations. This is how you instantly achieve good dispersal across a variety of cities, markets, and properties."

Internationalizing

Van Hal predicts that the market will continue to become more and more global. Dutch investors will increasingly go to foreign countries, and on balance foreign investors will become increas-

ingly more visible here. He sees this as a positive trend, "You receive more investment volume this way. Market growth increases competition. That often means you get more information and knowledge of the product, the region, and/or the country." We are seeing more cross-border action among institutional investors, namely from the British, Irish, and Scandinavian side," Hogenboom says. "But don't   >>

Avalon Columbia in Columbia, Maryland, USA (PGGM investment).

Dick van Hal
Managing
Director Achmea
Vastgoed

Achmea Vastgoed

Achmea Vastgoed finances and invests in housing, retail, offices, and business space for institutional investors and provides pensions for pensioners. Achmea Vastgoed manages 60 pension funds with total assets of €7 billion (€4 billion in real estate, €3 billion in mortgages). Achmea Vastgoed formulates, protects, and takes responsibility for the implementation of its investment and portfolio policies. An optimal investment policy and effective reporting and analysis allows institutional investors to maintain an overview of their portfolios. Achmea Vastgoed has a business mortgage fund and a housing mortgage fund and is active in Europe and North America. **www.achmeavastgoed.nl**

think that what you can do in the Netherlands, you can do elsewhere, because that just isn't so. The management of real estate is best left to representatives in the respective countries."

PGGM, which only invests via funds, will only invest in a private fund if it has a good fund manager. Sohier: "Real estate investing remains a local business. So you always need a manager who knows the local situation

down to the finest details."
Kanters says, "Because of our size, ABP sometimes ends up as co-investor in properties. We haven't forsaken the real estate market. But that can only happen if we co-operate with excellent local managers. To have the proper exposure we invest worldwide."

"The world is getting smaller," says Sohier. "Previous national investors are investing interna-

tionally and international investors are now investing worldwide. The Far East has always been far away for many, but seems to be getting a little closer."

Shifting to Asia

"PGGM wants to increase its worldwide exposure to the economic regions with strong economic growth such as Central Europe, Mexico, and Asia. China is growing at an explosive rate, but be careful," Sohier emphasizes, "investing in China is not easy. There is not much product, and there are few listed funds and the culture and way of doing business is very different. PGGM has a long history in the Far East, which has made us knowledgable on matters like ownership title structures, legal and tax, hedging of currencies and market parties. We can operate there thanks to our network."

Kanters continues, "There are markets where ABP would like to move into, especially in areas with difficult access such as the

PHOTO: EPPO NOTENBOOM

Mariënburg, shopping on two levels in the heart of Nijmegen (Achmea Vastgoed).

PHOTO: ALTERA VASTGOED

The Rijnplein shopping and leisure center of Alphen aan den Rijn is an Altera investment.

Japanese and Korean logistics markets. But we have noticed that these markets are slowly beginning to open up, which makes real estate increasingly more accessible." Many parties are currently looking at Asia, but only very few of them actually invest there. Asia implies risks, because governance is regulated differently there, transparency is lower, but also because the real estate market in some areas is still a lot less mature."

"Asia is certainly booming," Van Hal observes. "But you really have do your research there; there are certainly opportunities but all of them are not equally as good."

Opportunistic investments

In the meantime, pension funds have not only broadened their horizons to new regions, but also new (niche) segments. "Up till now, the universe was fairly limited," Sohier notes. "Now we would really like to further tap into these new sectors, such as assisted living, senior housing, or student accommodations. These niche products can potentially yield higher returns than the older sectors where investors have traditionally looked at."

Kanters adds, "We have invested most of it in core investments – retail, housing, offices, and logistics – but we are also pursuing more opportunistic investments, such as the hotel sector and parking garages. These are niche categories, but we are also looking to invest here. If the economy were to improve then a product like hotels suddenly becomes more interesting."

You have to look carefully at niche markets worldwide," Van Hal believes. "You have to keep an eye on, for instance, the aging population, which promises to be a new segment. Think about health care real estate or housing and facilities for seniors."   <<

Altera Vastgoed

Altera Vastgoed N.V. is a private and sectoral real estate fund working on behalf of pension funds. It manages assets totaling some €1.4 billion (January 2006). Under one legal and fiscal umbrella, and based on their own allocation desires, pension funds can participate in one or more of four administratively separated portfolios. These are devided into Dutch real estate sectors: residential, retail, offices and industrial/logistic. Pension funds have an optimal amount of freedom when it comes to allocation and flexibility: they can enter or exit on a quarterly basis and they can also switch between the various sectors. Pension funds can join by contributing Dutch real estate and or by depositing capital.

René Hogenboom
CEO Altera
Vastgoed

www.alteravastgoed.nl

ARCHITECT-DIRECTOR MECANOO ARCHITECTEN, FRANCINE HOUBEN

ARCHITECTURE WITH

The buildings designed by Mecanoo, the architectural firm headed by Francine Houben, appeal to people the world over. For Houben, intuition, experience and feeling for the location are important factors in developing the right composition for a new structure. The ongoing internationalization of architecture means that in more and more places, one can experience the 'Mecanoo feeling'.

By Ben Maandag

The wingshaped Learning Center in Lausanne rotates around its axis during the day

Francine Houben believes that architecture must stimulate the senses.

For Francine Houben, 2005 was a year to look back on with satisfaction. Not only did she celebrate her 50th birthday and her 25th anniversary as an architect, 2005 also brought the completion of the Montevideo building in Rotterdam. Stretching to over 152 m, Montevideo is a true 'city within a city' and the highest residential tower in the Netherlands. Houben's name is inextricably linked to Mecanoo Architecten, the Delft-based architectural firm of which she is the driving force. Soon after its founding, Mecanoo caught the attention of the architectural community with its winning entry for a competition for a youth housing complex on Kruisplein Square in central Rotterdam. The homes of the design combine spacious comfort with a beautiful appearance. A lot has changed in the 25 years following this acclaimed project. "Mecanoo's body of work has expanded enormously," says Houben. "It ranges from homes to schools to entire neighborhoods; theaters, scenery, libraries and skyscrapers; parks, squares and highways; the polder and the

ESPRIT

at the same speed as the earth: 15 degrees per hour.

Randstad; hotels, museums and even a chapel. Furthermore, our scope is becoming increasingly international. At present, our firm works all over the place: the UK, Poland, Albania, Spain, Italy, France, Denmark, Finland, Germany and Switzerland. This process of internationalization is a logical development."

Export commodity

More and more Dutch architectural firms are currently active across the border. Dutch architecture has become an attractive export commodity. This global-

ization is also taking place within the firm itself. "We are an international firm," explains Houben. "Most of the countries where we realize projects are represented in the firm. Many young architects join our team to learn the tricks of the trade. So in a way, we also serve as a kind of educational institute. Over the years we have gained a lot of international friends and contacts."

At present, Mecanoo's operations are mainly limited to the European market, and the reason is clear. "I don't like jetlag archi-

tecture," Houben states with emphasis. "The concept of flying in somewhere, doing your trick and leaving again doesn't appeal to me at all. This has everything to do with the location. In realizing an assignment, I want to collaborate with the people who actually come from the area. You need to familiarize yourself with a location and revisit it on a regular basis."

Driving force

Francine Houben holds the position of Architect-Director within the organization. The task of >>

PHOTO: JOOP VAN REEKEN

Montevideo, Rotterdam; a trend-setting mixed-use concept.

managing the firm has been delegated to the executive manager and the technical manager bears responsibility for the actual execution of Mecanoo's projects. "I guide the design process and head the team of architects, urban developers, landscape architects and researchers. I keep an eye on the development of the firm's company culture. I view myself as a driving force. I concern myself with our vision – what we stand for – but also with encouraging young designers. For international architects it's great to work in a firm where everything runs smoothly. We can focus on the design 100%." Working on an assignment, Houben generally relies on a combination of experience and intuition. "I always ask myself the question, what is the inspiration of the assignment? Who is commissioning? What is their ambition? This has to do with intuition, the experience you

have gained over the years. It is the broad international experience in particular that enables a good response to an assignment. Because I have lived in various cities in the Netherlands and lecture and design around the world, I feel I have developed a good sensibility with regard to the atmosphere of a particular location."

"I'm not someone who will make the same design over and over again," she continues. "In Spain, I will make a Spanish building – one that offers shade in the hot sun and responds to the Spanish light, which is entirely different from the famous skies over Holland. The new library for Delft Technical University, for instance, is an elevated grass landscape supporting a cone that pins the landscape to the site. The play of light, the enormous bookcase and the famous Mecanoo blue has created a beautiful, almost mystical atmosphere."

Palette

Houben explains, "I am sensitive to the specific atmosphere of a location. One of the first things I tend to do is look for material we might use. I have noticed that my palette of possibilities has become increasingly broad. After all, the job is similar to that of a

painter determining a composition."

Mecanoo's varied range of assignments, and the opportunity to constantly approach them with a fresh eye, is a source of satisfaction for the architect. "It may be difficult from a commercial point of view, but it is more fun and more rewarding. It also keeps you on your toes, and this acuity eventually becomes a trademark. This is Mecanoo's culture - this unique approach." A good example is the recently completed Montevideo complex on Rotterdam's Wilhelminapier, which combines living and working facilities. The project includes 192 homes, which are distinguished by the fact that they each have something special to offer. Overwhelming views of the Maas river; a porthole in the bedroom; unorthodox ceiling heights – the enormous variety even extends to the homes' individual dimensions and layouts.

Composition

"It is crucial to pay a great deal of attention to the composition," explains Houben. "This is particularly in the case of a high residential tower, which is a far greater challenge than an office tower. And we didn't want Montevideo to resemble a social housing project. The end result

The design for the prestigious Theatre and Congress Centre La Llotja Lleida appears from the Spanish earth. The concept is based on shadow (on hot summer days) and

The central library of Delft Technical University is linked by the latest electronic devices to libraries all over the world.

really breathes the atmosphere of the Holland-America Line. It stands next to Hotel New York on the Wilhelminapier, where the ocean steamers of the Holland-America Line debarked on their voyage to the US. At the same time, the building is in constant dialogue with the ever-changing Dutch heavens."

This emphasizes the importance of the materials used in the design. "The combination of red-orange stone with silver-black stone and aluminum is exactly right. This is one of the hardest decisions, because you have to reach it on the basis of a single cubic meter of stone. Are you making the right choice? A decision like this is irreversible, there's no way you can change it back."

Francine Houben wants her buildings to stand the test of time. "Take these chairs we're sitting on. They were designed 50 years ago by Charles and Ray Eames and still 'work'. This is what I wish to achieve with my buildings. They need to have a certain neutrality, because the program is always changing and architecture is required to cope with such developments. But at the same time it needs to emanate esprit, fun, *joie de vivre*. That is the 'Mecanoo feeling'. I'm proud of the fact that our work receives both serious critical attention and is popular with a broad audience. That it goes beyond academic circles and has an impact on people the world over.'≪

High-profile Mecanoo projects:
- **Montevideo, Rotterdam**
- **Delft Technical University Library**
- **La Llotja Lleida, Spain**
- **Chapel for the cemetary of St. Laurentius, Rotterdam**
- **Nieuw Terbregge, Rotterdam**
- **Bijlmer Park, Amsterdam**
- **Competition Palace of Justice, Trento, Italy**
- **Competition Learning Center EPFL, Lausanne**
- **Tirana Master Plan, Albania**

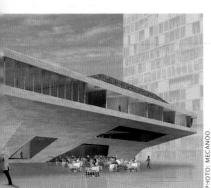

as a floating sand stone volume arising shelter (on rainy winter days).

Deck dwellings and water houses in the neighborhood Nieuw Terbregge in Rotterdam.

ONLINE: www.holland-re.com/mecanoo

SHOPPING, WORKING AND LIVING

KROONENBERG GROEP

Real Estate Investment & Development

LOCATIONS

NERVECENTER OF THE EUROPEAN BUSINESS WORLD

AMSTERDAM

Increasingly Amsterdam Airport Schiphol is turning into a center for high-quality business parks, which has a magic attraction for the international business community. The ultra fast connections with other parts of Europe give you the feeling that within Greater Schiphol you are part of a cosmopolitan, dynamic atmosphere of one of Europe's largest and most successful airports.

AIRPORT AREA

Amsterdam Airport Area is the leading international business location in the Netherlands.

Amsterdam Airport Area

Amsterdam Airport Area (AAA) consists of 11 public and private partners combining their strengths in international marketing, promotion and acquisition. All these partners are involved in planning, developing or selling industrial and office locations at and around Amsterdam Airport Schiphol including parts of the City of Amsterdam, like the Zuidas and Riekerpolder.

Amsterdam Airport Schiphol: best airport for business travellers.

AAA continues to dominate as a main logistics and business hub in Europe from where national and international companies direct their European headquarters, marketing & sales offices, training centers, (spare) parts centers, shared services and R&D to European logistics centers.

Awards

For many years Amsterdam Airport Schiphol has been voted the best airport for business travelers. In 2005 once again Schiphol has been honored as Best Airport in Europe by the leading British Travel Magazine Business Traveller. It is the 22nd time since 1980 that Europe's fourth-largest airport has received the award. The airport has won more than 100 prizes in a range of categories. The airport has also been honored with many awards as Europe's best cargo airport because of the quality of its cargo facilities and the efficiency of the cargo handling. Amsterdam

Airport Schiphol is the fourth largest passenger airport in Europe and the third largest cargo airport in Europe. 251 destinations in 90 countries are served.
AAA is the leading international business location in the Netherlands and its business community represents more than 1,200 international companies from around the world.
Every company has it owns reasons for choosing the Amsterdam Airport Area to set up their European business. Some of the reasons are: skilled, flexible and multi-lingual labor force, multi-modal hub, logistics expertise, excellent access to markets that matter, excellent ICT infrastructure, network of 1,200 international companies already present in AAA and space for future growth.

Werkstad A4

The north wing of the Randstad with a central position for mainport Schiphol is the most impor-

PHOTO: EPPO NOTENBOOM

tant motor for the Dutch economy. The area at and around the airport contains unique possibilities for innovation and new developments. One of the newest plans is the so-called Werkstad A4. This refers to an area south of the airport adjacent to Cargo World Schiphol and the area around the A4 highway. This area offers space for new logistics concepts, further expansion of Schiphol-related activities and an entirely new innovative greenhouse complex. With this development the gateway function of the Netherlands gets once again a strong booth. AAA is targeting clusters of companies for the Werkstad A4. The focus of this strategy is that clusters allow companies to be more innovative and productive than if they operate independently. In this way, AAA offers a more distinctive climate for establishing offices than other European regions.

A4 Zone West

This new 110 hectare logistics business park, which is part of Werkstad A4, is planned for 2009. The plan is to link the park directly to the cargo areas of Schiphol Airport via a dedicated cargo lane: a road for trucks only. In addition, a rail terminal is planned for the park, connected to the inter-city and high- speed rail networks. In this way, in the future it will be possible to transport air cargo from Amsterdam Airport Schiphol to Europe not only by air and road, but also by train. The A4 Zone is alongside the A4 motorway connecting Amsterdam and Rotterdam and will have its own motorway access. The park is designated for logistics service providers, European logistics centers, parts centers and training and repair facilities. A4 Zone is a development by Schiphol Real Estate, Schiphol Area Development Company, and the Municipality of Haarlemmermeer.

Responsible expansion

To maintain its international status, Amsterdam Airport Schiphol continues to renew and invest. For example, in 2003 a new runway – the Polderbaan – was taken into operation. This important expansion enables the airport to grow responsibly within the environmental limits and to remain competitive with other European main ports. This is far from simple for an airport in such a densely populated country as the Netherlands.

WTC Schiphol

A recent addition to office space has been the extension of the World Trade Center (WTC) Schiphol Airport by 28,000 m[2]. The development is divided over four office towers. This amounts to a doubling of the previous office space of the WTC which consisted of 24,000 m[2]. Under the eight towers, a five-floor parking garage has been built with space for 5,500 cars. The complex is linked by a traverse to the Sheraton Hotel, the Schiphol Plaza shopping mall and the airport terminal. As first lessees, project developer Schiphol Real Estate (SRE) has welcomed the pension fund ABP, ST Micro Electronics, Hiscox (a British insurance company) and Numico. The office complex is also easy to reach for visitors and employees arriving by car or train. The WTC Schiphol Airport also allows Numico the space to merge a number of offices in one building.   >>

PHOTO: EPPO NOTENBOOM

The WTC Schiphol Airport (52,000 m², owner: KFN).

$\mathsf{Λcre}$ *fund*

In December 2002, Schiphol Real Estate – the 100% real estate subsidiary of the Schiphol Group – created the Acre fund, a real-estate fund for institutional investors. Schiphol Real Estate retains a 50% interest in the fund. The structuring, marketing and share placement of the fund was a joint effort by Schiphol Real Estate and Dexia Securities. The Acre fund has a total worth of €193 million as of January 1, 2005. The plan is to grow to approximately €360 million within four years by extending the investment portfolio of Schiphol Real Estate in the Netherlands. The first tranche of seven buildings was placed when the fund was created (December 2002): Constellation (East); Avioport (Center); Kintetsu building (Southeast); Hankyu building (Southeast); Airfreight Center (South); International Mail Center (Southeast) and Northport (North). The second tranche of another four buildings was placed in December 2003: Caravelle (East); Skymaster (East); Expeditors (Southeast) and Freight Building 6 (South). The third tranche was placed in December 2004: 50% of the Schiphol Group Headquarters building. This total of twelve buildings (five with office facilities and seven with a mixed office and logistics function) is spread over the airport site of Amsterdam Airport Schiphol and was part of the investment portfolio of Schiphol Real Estate.

More information:
Schiphol Real Estate
Jan Krijnen
Manager Investments
Tel.: +31 20 601 32 97

Schiphol-Rijk, Vision Plaza, one of the three free-standing buildings constructed on a beautiful square.

Schiphol East

Schiphol East is increasingly developing into an industrial center with an entirely unique character. This historic area, where Schiphol airport was located until 1967 is being redeveloped in phases by Schiphol Real Estate into a contemporary business park with modern, pavilion-like office buildings in an attractive setting with views of the runways and the woodlands of the Amsterdamse Bos. The names of the buildings refer to aviation history: Constellation (6,800 m²), Caravelle (5,700 m²) and TriStar (12,000 m²). This last building, consisting of three towers of five floors, marks the entrance to this attractive business park. TriStar was developed by Schiphol Real Estate according to a design by Quist Wintermans Architects.

The German hotel chain Dorint-Sofitel has also opened its first Airport Business hotel at Schiphol East. This four-star hotel has 442 rooms, 15 conference rooms, restaurants, various bars, a fitness studio, Turkish baths and a sauna. In short, stylish accommodations that further strengthen the liveliness of Schiphol East. Previous to this, other public facilities also opened their doors including stores and lunchrooms.

Schiphol-Rijk

The office part of Schiphol-Rijk offers modern, multifunctional buildings set in a lush, green environment. The park offers an under-deck parking solution with the largest parking capacity in the region. A fiber optic telecommunications infrastructure and a high level security system make this a complete and attractive business park in the region. IT business represents most of the present activity but also a substantial number of auto-motive and aerospace companies are represented here.

Among the companies with large European operations in this office park one will find BMC Software, Unisys, Imation, QAD Software, UPC, EADS, Boeing, Hugo Boss, Eaton and Mitsubishi Motors Europe. IT company Network Appliance recently moved to Schiphol Rijk and leased over 5,000 m² for Vision Plaza Central. Although all land has been sold, Schiphol-Rijk still offers plenty of rental and development opportunities. An additional 70,000 m² of office space will come on line between 2005 and 2008, including a 35,000 m² campus facility existing of three independent buildings to be developed by Fortis Real Estate. Accessibility to Schiphol-Rijk by car and bus will be further improved when the Beech Avenue opens in 2007, completing the Airport Loop around Amsterdam Airport Schiphol. Furthermore the Provincial Road N201 and Kruisweg will be upgraded with two extra lanes in the short term to improve traffic flows to and from this business area.

Park Oude Meer, as part of Schiphol-Rijk, encompasses 55 hectares of land where more than 100 international companies are currently located. It is dedicated to large logistic projects and includes European Distribution Centres, VAL activities and spare parts centers.

Schiphol Logistics Park

Schiphol Logistics Park (SLP) is a new premier location for large airport-related logistic activities. SLP is adjacent to Schiphol-Rijk and the Cargo Areas of Amsterdam Airport Schiphol. The preparation of land and infrastructure will begin in 2007. Building activities are also planned for 2007. Plots are available from 13,000 m² up to several hectares. Building heights vary from nine to 27 meters. SLP is a joint venture between Schiphol

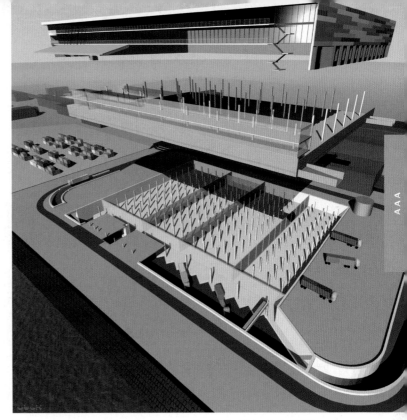

Building activities at the Schiphol Logistics Park will begin in 2007.

Area Development Company (SADC), KLM Royal Dutch Airlines and Schiphol Real Estate (SRE).

Since some land has been reserved for a possible sixth airport runway, land surrounding the business areas is presently devoted to greenscapes.

Architecturally abstract buildings form compact clusters with warehouses at ground level, offices, parking and other functions stacked above (multi-level facility). The infrastructure is specifically designed to accommodate trucks.

Cargo World Schiphol

One of the best locations for (air)freight traffic is Cargo World Schiphol South and Southeast with a host of possibilities for new collective business buildings, offices and warehousing. There are fast connections with the rest of the Netherlands thanks to the highways in the vicinity such as the A4, the A5 and the A9. The flagship here is the Columbus office building (4,800 m²), with its striking design and impressive appearance. The building affords a splendid view of the Kaagbaan – one of the busiest runways at Schiphol. >>

There are fast connections with the rest of the Netherlands thanks to the highways in the vicinity.

Business Park Beukenhorst, very easily reached by car, public transport and air.

Beukenhorst: a landscape of offices

The biggest and probably the most appealing office park in the Amsterdam Airport Area in terms of architecture and landscaping is Business Park Beukenhorst. It is located just to the south of Schiphol, right next to the A4 and A5 freeways. Apart from having its own railroad station, it also has a frequent ultra-fast bus connection with the airport terminal. More than 330 companies have already located here and many more are expected to come to the area. Considerable extensions to the east and south are envisaged, but for the time being the existing office area still offers adequate possibilities. Magnificent buildings or sections of them in every size are still immediately available. The literal and figurative high spot of Beukenhorst is the 75-meter high, 22-floor Zuidtoren. This building, created by the internationally renowned architects Kohn Pedersen Fox (KPF) is the final piece of South Point, a station area also designed by KPF, consisting of six beautiful office buildings. This is a project by Van den Bruele Kaufman, a developer that was previously responsible for building a splendid new head office for Thomas Cook Travel in Beukenhorst. The elegant Zuidtoren consisting of 16,540 m^2 is the physical entrance to the modern station building. The airport terminal is only one stop away. The back of the building has an aluminum skin, while the side facing the station is a veritable wall of glass. The entrance is especially alluring because of its double-height lobby and the protected

The Getronics office building in Business Park Beukenhorst.

The Spanish architect Calatrava designed the bridge to Business Park De President.

front driveway. The Zuidtoren has welcomed a number of new-comers including Abbott, Buena Vista Home Entertainment (Benelux), Burger King, CB Richard Ellis, and Nobilas. Other appealing and stylish complexes in which there is still office space available are the monumentally designed Gemini, Transpolis and Aquarius. Companies that have based themselves here or in the immediate vicinity include Canon, Bentley, Logica CMG, Chubb, TPG, Sanoma, Nortel Networks, and Plantronics.

De President

At the moment, not far from Beukenhorst, the Business Park De President (120 ha) is ready for construction. It is intended for companies that need office space as well as logistical func-tions. The entrance to De President is marked by an extraordinary bridge designed by the famous Spanish architect Santiago Calatrava. Another highlight is the Presidentshof, the central park with a large decorative lake. The first user of the new business park is Anglo Dutch, a German distributor of tires for motorbikes and scooters.

Schiphol Elzenhof

An equally new site still waiting to be developed is Schiphol Elzenhof to the north of the airport. This will be a top-level business park with roughly 180,000 m² of office space of international standing. The master plan provides for four large buildings with a powerful architectural presence airside. They are primarily intended for airport-linked companies, for example, international headquar-ters. The buildings will be located in a park-style environ-ment, surrounded by water and greenery. Furthermore, the spec-tacular view of the airport's runways will without a doubt soon give Schiphol Elzenhof a dynamic, cosmopolitan image. The Schiphol golf course – which is expected to be opened in 2006 – is located nearby. This means that it will be very easy for office workers and transit passengers to come here for a relaxing game of golf.   >>

Amsterdam Airport Area

Ruud Bergh joined Schiphol Area Development Company (SADC) on 1 March 2005 and succeeded Willem Trommels as Managing Director of SADC and Chairman of AAA. In his previous position Ruud Bergh was the Managing Director of the The Hague Development Corporation.

Bergh: "Amsterdam Airport Area has a lot to offer. The region has good accessibility, business exper-tise, international prestige and attractiveness. Together with the City of Amsterdam and Amsterdam Airport Schiphol, AAA is one of the most popular locations in Europe for international companies manag-ing their European activities from a

Ruud Bergh
Chairman Amsterdam Airport Area

central location. Over 1,200 foreign companies have already chosen to locate in the region. Amsterdam Airport Area comprises 11 public and private parties who are all involved in the planning, developing and sale of airport-related sites."

Many international companies, like IATA, have established at Airport Business Park Lijnden.

Lijnden

Airport Business Park Lijnden is a 35 hectare (net 20.5 ha.) high-quality, airport-related business park. After welcoming the first user in 2001, many international companies, like Nikon, IATA, Fiat, Biogen and NEC logistics

Mimex building.

have established at Lijnden. Companies choose Lijnden because of the high quality, the industrial image and its ideal accessibility.

Therefore, it is also no coincidence that Lijnden has acquired great popularity amongst fashion companies that combine show-room, office and logistics facilities. Lijnden is totally in fashion. Gerzon, Sixty, Paul Warmer and No Excess have already established offices here and currently The Sting is building a new facility with a warehouse and offices in the park. Early 2005 Schiphol Area Development Company (SADC) sold the last available plot at Airport Business Park Lijnden to Maeyveld. This 13,000 m² plot is situated along the A9. At this plot, six coherent buildings will be developed, providing business space for companies that need to create their own clear identity for a range of activities. Each of the six buildings will have office, industrial and showroom space, tailored to

the needs of the future user. With this latest sale and festive transfer of the last management tasks to the public space in October 2005, SADC has brought this successful project to an end. Furthermore, the development of a four-star on site hotel is almost ready.

Amsterdam-Osdorp

Airport Business Park Amsterdam-Osdorp is a new 45-hectare (first phase 20 hectares, second phase after 2009) business park for small and medium sized enterprises. Situated along the western boundary of Amsterdam in the urban district of Osdorp, it is directly adjacent to Airport Business Park Lijnden, thus creating a new airport-related business area on the north side of Amsterdam Airport Schiphol. The location can be reached easily from Amsterdam Airport Schiphol as well as the city of Amsterdam via the various motorways (A4, A5, A9 and

Airport Business Park Amsterdam-Osdorp (45 hectares).

A10), a new secondary road S106 and bus and tram lines. The site got prepared for building in 2004, and plots can now be obtained through long-term lease. Plot sizes vary from 2,500 m² to 3 hectares, of which 90% can be used for building activities. Building heights vary from 7 to 18 meters.

Ecological green zones and a rolling landscape punctuated by waterways make this an inspirational environment to work in and a new residential area is right around the corner. Subsidies are available for (clean) energy-saving measures such as solar energy panels. The development of this business park is based on a public/private partnership between Neighborhood Council Amsterdam-Osdorp and Schiphol Area Development Company (SADC).

Amsterdam Atlaspark

Atlaspark (110 hectares), which is to be developed, is 15 kilometers from the airport and is part of the Amsterdam port area. This business park is ideal for companies with large-scale logistical activities. It links together modes of transport that have traditional been seen as rivals (shipping and air freight). In the Atlaspark area a new high quality business park is under development: Business Park Greenport. This 'business resort' will focus on spatial quality, greenery, outstanding architecture and safety and is designated for logistics companies.   >>

Eighteen hectares of Atlaspark (near the harbors of Amsterdam) will be reserverd for airport related activities.

Riekerpolder

An extension of Amsterdam's prestigious Zuidas (South Axis) is the International Business Park Riekerpolder directly on the A4 and a less than 10 minute-drive from Amsterdam Airport Schiphol and Amsterdam Center. Riekerpolder is quickly revealing its future, final shape. This is because well over two-thirds of the planned construction volume in Riekerpolder has already been realized or is under construction. Consequently, only a few lots have already been developed. The plan to construct various high-quality office buildings has turned out to be right on the mark. The Dutch headquarters of IBM (Multi Development) has already been located here for some time. It has been greatly expanded with the addition of 31,000 m² of office space. Other projects that have been completed include the Adam Smith Building (20,000 m²), Westgate Building (Multi Development, 30,000 m², leased by PWC) and Tiara (11,000 m²). The former headquarters of Nissan Europe has been reassigned, with the owner Maeyveld selling the entire building (16,000 m²) to AXA. The clothing company Mexx, which, since 2001, has been part of the listed American fashion company Liz Claiborne,

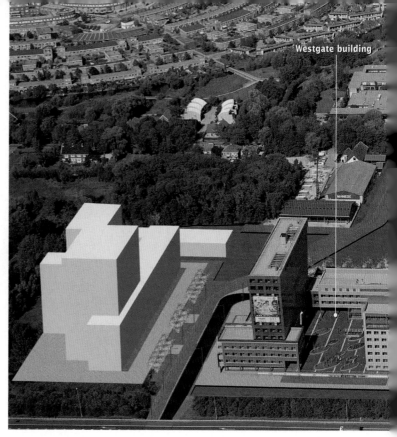

Westgate building

International Business Park Riekerpolder is quickly revealing its future, final shape.

has rented the complex and wants to expand it by a further 16,000 m² to include consumer-focused functions.

Riekerpolder is an attractive place of business, not only due to its location, but particularly because of its high-quality buildings and public spaces. The buildings are partially located around a square inner garden in which a pond will be constructed, guaran-

teeing a pleasant atmosphere for office workers and visitors alike.

Dutch Design Hotel Artemis

After completion of the Adam Smith Building, G&S Vastgoed is in the process of realizing two more eye-catching projects in Riekerpolder. Construction work of another 10,000 m² of office space in the Keynes building, adjacent to the Tiara Towers, is

The Keynes building is a development of G&S Vastgoed (10,000 m²).

Mexx occupies one of the eye-catchers of the

Tiara | Keynes building | Hotel Aeon Plaza | Adam Smith building | MEXX | IBM | AAA

Well over two-thirds of the planned construction volume has already been realized.

underway. Furthermore, on the north side of Riekerpolder next to the IBM headquarters, the new four-star hotel Dutch Design Hotel Artemis was opened in spring 2005. The hotel has a total floor area of approximately 12,000 m², including 256 rooms and a restaurant accommodating 175 guests. Moreover, the hotel has 500 m² of conference space, a spacious outside terrace mea-

business park.

suring no less than 700 m² and ample parking space, making the hotel a perfect venue for business meetings. The young, internationally renowned agency, Doos Arkitekter, succeeded in playfully incorporating themes such as Holland and Dutch Design in the minimalist interior design. The outside, with its striking asymmetric elements, has been designed by W.M. Zaaijer from Van den Oever en Zaaijer, the very same firm that restyled the Amsterdam World Trade Center (owned by one of the AAA partners, KFN). Their design, with high doors and porches, is a tribute to the Dutch master architect Dudok.

Living and working

The construction of the Dutch Design Hotel Artemis is in line with the plans to turn Riekerpolder not only into a high-quality working location,

but also to add other first-rate functions. Furthermore, the possibility of developing a congress center is being considered. Within the scope of the new structure plan 'Kiezen voor stedelijkheid' (Choosing for urbanity), further development of Riekerpolder will focus on 'metropolitan living and working' in the period leading up to 2030. As a result, the construction of temporary residences might be possible. Amsterdam's Dienst Ruimtelijke Ordening (Spatial Planning Office) has been commissioned by the Amsterdam Development Department to work on spatial development, in which the Ministry of Economic Affairs, the urban district Slotervaart/Overtoomse Veld and the Infrastructure and Traffic Department are also involved. Non-Amsterdam parties involved include DWR and the Schiphol Area Development Company. >>

Location	Project	AAA / Projects 2006 and beyond. Program ha. / m²	Development	Planning
Schiphol Center	Schiphol Center	Office location 110,000 m²	n.a.	n.a.
Schiphol	Schiphol Logistics Park	New logistics center 45 ha.	n.a.	n.a.
Schiphol East	Schiphol East	Business park, offices, parking 40,000 m²	n.a.	n.a.
Schiphol Southeast	Schiphol Southeast	Business location 35.5 ha.	n.a.	n.a.
Schiphol North	Schiphol North	Business location 13,000 m²	n.a.	n.a.
Schiphol Elzenhof	Schiphol Elzenhof	New business park 200,000 m²	n.a.	n.a.
Amsterdam	Zuidas	Office location 320,000 m²	n.a.	n.a.
Amsterdam	Riekerpolder	Office location 68,000 m²	n.a.	n.a.
Amsterdam	Atlaspark	Industrial location 110 ha.	n.a.	n.a.
Amsterdam	Oude Haagweg Zone	New office location	n.a.	After 2010
Hoofddorp	Graan voor Visch	Business location 20.7 ha.	n.a.	n.a.
Hoofddorp	De President	Business location 120 ha.	n.a.	n.a.
Hoofddorp	A4-Zone	New development 300 ha. Offices, logistics	SADC	After 2008
Hoofddorp	Business Garden Hoofddorp	Office location 60,000 m²	n.a.	n.a.
Hoofddorp	Business Park Beukenhorst	Office location 620,000 m²	n.a.	n.a.
Hoofddorp	De Hoek-Noord	New office location 22 ha.	n.a.	After 2010
Badhoevedorp	Badhoevedorp-Zuid	New office location 40 ha.	n.a.	After 2011
Aalsmeer	Schiphol Rijk	Office development 70,000 m²	n.a.	n.a.
ABP Oude Meer	ABP Oude Meer	Business location 10,000 m²	n.a.	n.a.
Nieuw Vennep	Nieuw Vennep Zuid	Business location 15,000 m²	n.a.	n.a.

More information: www.holland-re.com/projects

Amsterdam Airport Schiphol is used by 87 airlines flying to 210 cities in 83 countries throughout the world.

Almere Poort will become the fourth district in the southwest of Almere.

Almere Poort

Almere, situated 30 km from Amsterdam, and 45 km from Amsterdam Airport Area, has approximately 45 industrial plots and office locations. In Almere Poort, the locations Hogekant, Middenkant, Lagekant and Zakenpoort are in development. The ground was broken for Hogekant in the fall of 2004. This area offers space to logistics, and production companies and service providers. The area is about 16 hectares and the plots vary in size from 1,500 to 5,000 m². Lagekant and Middenkant collectively comprise 48 hectares. Lagekant is pre-eminently appropriate for companies with an office percentage of 30-70% of the total company development. Middenkant Zuid is a park like environment where clusters of small-scale companies are located. Lagekant leds itself best to high quality companies in small scale offices. The office location, Zakenpoort (600,000 m²), will mainly house companies in commercial services.

Stichtsekant

The Stichtsekant site, developed for top-level companies, lies in the southeast of Almere on the A27 highway. In the first phase, the sale of 47 hectares of logistics area has already begun. The plot sizes vary from 5,000 to 40,000 m². The second and third phases comprise 29 hectares of top-level companies and 54 hectares of mixed industrial companies. Durability is the focal point of Stichtsekant. The site has space for a wide range of services, including retail, catering, banking and child care. Together with an advanced ICT infrastructure, the location guarantees high quality. Stichtsekant has been recognized as a national example for landscape design by the Ministry of Economic Affairs and the Dutch Association of Garden and Landscape architecture. «

The Stichtsekant site, Almere, developed for top-level companies.

MORE INFORMATION

 Amsterdam Airport Area

P.O. Box 75700,
1118 ZT Schiphol
The Netherlands
Tel.: + 31 20 405 47 77
Fax: + 31 20 653 18 94
E-mail: info@aaarea.nl
Website: www.aaarea.nl

ONLINE: www.holland-re.com/aaa

Business locations Amsterdam Airport Area

Amsterdam Airport Area
Nerve center for your European business

N 208

N 202

ATLASPARK

A 9

POP

HAARLEM

A 200

A 205

ABP
AMSTERDA
OSDORP

N 205

ABP LIJNDEN

re-routed A9

N 208

A 5

BADHOEVEDORF
SOUTH

N 201

SC
ELZ

**AMSTERDAM
AIRPORT
SCHIPHOL**

A 4

HOOFDDORP

SCHIPHOL
CENTER

DE HOEK-NOORD

BUSINESS GARDEN
HOOFDDORP

SCHIPHOL SOUTH

GRAAN
VOOR VISCH

DE HOEK

SCHIPHOL
SOUTH-EAST

N 205

DE PRESIDENT

BEUKENHORST

Beechavenue

SKY

ABP OUDE MEEF

A4 ZONE

SCHIPHOL
LOGISTICS PARK

SCHIPHOL-RIJK

N 201

AALSM

NIEUW-VENNEP ZUID

Rotterdam/The Hague
(50 km)

Aalsm

ALMERE

CITY CENTER

ALMERE
POORT

A 6

A 27

STICHTSEKANT

A 1

AMSTERDAM

TELEPORT

A 10

AMSTERDAM
CITY CENTER

RIEKERPOLDER

ZUIDAS

RAI

OUDE HAAGSEWEGZONE

SCHIPHOL GOLF & BUSINESS
CENTER

SCHIPHOL NORTH

AMSTELVEEN

A 2

SCHIPHOL
EAST

ONY FOKKER
ESS PARK

	Amsterdam Airport Schiphol
	Existing office location
	Future office location
	Existing industrial location
	Future industrial location
	Residential location
	Recreational location

er Auction

re-rout

AAA partners:

 Schiphol Area Development Company (SADC)
SADC is responsible for the development of airport-related business parks in the Schiphol Area.

 Schiphol Real Estate
Schiphol Real Estate manages all commercial real estate activities at Schiphol Airport.

 City of Amsterdam
The City of Amsterdam is represented by the Foreign Investment Office. The FIO has also got contacts with planning and support management resources within Amsterdam's city management.

 **Port of Amsterdam**
The Port of Amsterdam exploits the area and also takes care of the construction, maintenance and renewal of real estate and infrastructure, and supports and supervizes companies which want to set up or expand.

 Municipality of Haarlemmermeer
The Economics Affairs Department of this municipality, where Schiphol Airport is located, manages development sites and business parks.

 City of Almere
The City of Almere is located in the Amsterdam Area and is the fastest-growing new town in Europe. New business parks and office locations with full ICT facilities are being allocated.

 Province of Noord-Holland
The responsible authority for long term urban development and economic planning in the region.

KLM Royal Dutch Airlines
KLM, one of Europe's leading global airlines, is a shareholder in one of the logistics parks.

KFN
KFN is a Dutch property investment company with €1.1 billion invested in offices in the Netherlands.

ING Real Estate
ING Real Estate is an international real estate company which is active in investment management, development and finance.

Multi Development
Multi Develoment is market leader in the Netherlands and holds a leading position in the commercial property development sector in Europe.

LARGEST OFFICE MARKET IN THE NETHERLANDS
AMSTERDAM

Amsterdam is continually developing modern new commercial and residential areas and expanding its infrastructure. The prestigious Zuidas takes up a prominent position in the region. Other major projects include the ongoing development on the banks of the IJ, where thousands of square meters of mixed-use working/living space will be completed in the near future.

Schiphol · Amsterdam · Utrecht · The Hague · Rotterdam

Former harbor and industrial areas along the IJ river have been assigned new functions, like popular residential

The Dutch capital's international appeal provides it with good perspectives, particularly in the case of the office market. Although recent years have shown a remarkably restrained development policy, a mega project like the Zuidas is sure to bear fruit in the long term. This new urban center will prove a major boost to office, retail and residential ventures. Its proximity to Schiphol Airport and excellent accessibility by train, subway and car make the Zuidas an attractive business location for people and companies alike.

With 5.8 million m², the Amsterdam office market is the largest in the Netherlands. Although supply exceeded demand by record levels in recent years, 2005 saw a cautious recovery. There still seems to be room for new developments, as there are shortages in the 3,000-4,000-m² segment and a demand for buildings with a historic appearance and status. Furthermore, there is little to no choice for small to medium-sized busi-

nesses wanting their own office. The total size of the planned retail developments is 400,000 m², with particular focus on the areas surrounding the Amstel and Sloterdijk railway stations. In the near future, obsolete harbor areas

PHOTO: EUROPE REAL ESTATE PUBLISHERS

Amsterdam has about 4,000 houseboats with access to electricity and water, sizes, colors and designs.

AMSTERDAM

neighborhoods, and business and culture areas.

like Houthavens, Westpoort, NDSM-werf and Oosterdokseiland will be transformed into residential areas, providing new opportunities for the retail sector. The former harbor and industrial areas along the IJ have also been assigned new functions. Oostelijk Havengebied is a popular residential neighborhood, and follow-up projects in Zeeburgereiland and IJburg will add another 20,000 homes to the housing stock. Plans for Oostelijke Handelskade and Zuidelijke IJ-oever include homes, cultural institutes and business accommodation. The former industrial zone of Noordelijke IJ-oever will be transformed into a lively city neighborhood. >>

The houseboats come in all shapes,

A boat trip through the canals is one of the main attractions for the 40 million people who visit the capital every year.

The IJ river from east to west. The city center is situated on the left, near Central Station.
On the right the northern embankment.

PHOTO: JEROEN MUSCH

Oostelijke Handelskade

The IJ and the harbors have always been areas of lively trade and activity, and this area can still be considered a natural habitat for commerce and creativity. Oostelijke Handelskade is situated on an island some two km long. An endless row of warehouses was erected here in the late 19th century, most of which have been renovated and assigned a new function. The Pakhuysen development encom-

DeLoodsen, Oostelijke Handelskade.

passes 20,000 m² of office space, showrooms and 150 homes. DeLoodsen is a joint venture by Hopman Interheem Groep, the City Housing Corporation and Moes Bouwbedrijf. It involves the construction of six 35-m high buildings, accommodating – among other things – 196 privately owned apartments and 121 rental apartments.
The tip of the Oostelijke Handelskade is the planned site of the new 380-room Mövenpick Hotel. The complex, which will reach some 65 m in height and will have a floor space of 26,000 m², is expected to be finished by the end of 2005.

Oostenburgereiland

Oostenburgereiland, a former location of the Dutch East India Company, is destined to become a new urban center, with some 11 ha of office space, studios and leisure facilities. The INIT busi-

ness complex is the most striking landmark on Oostenburgereiland. This glass-encased 'city within a city' offers 33,000 m² of office space and a communal car park used by various companies.

IJburg

IJburg is a new city district that combines a variety of urban functions in a natural setting. The plans for IJburg outline a total of 18,000 homes, 370,000 m² of commercial property and facilities including shopping centers, schools, daycare centers, marinas, a public library and sports facilities. The urban functions will primarily be concentrated in Centrumeiland, the heart of the district, which will be taken into use in 2007.

Oosterdokseiland

In the heart of Amsterdam, construction is underway on the Oosterdokseiland project (ODE).

A team of 12 renowned architects has been involved in the further elaboration of the 200,000-m² site. The plan consists of six plots, which have each been assigned their own function. Be it living, working, studying, shopping, leisure or going out: Oosterdokseiland represents a broad mix of all these activities. ODE is a development by Oosterdokseiland Ontwikkeling Amsterdam, a joint venture of Bouwfonds MAB Ontwikkeling, Meyer Bergman and Bouwfonds Property Finance, in collaboration with New Chinatown and the Municipality of Amsterdam. Completion of ODE is scheduled for 2009.

Stationseiland

Around 2010, the number of passengers passing through Stationseiland (the location of the major public transport hub Amsterdam Central Station) will have risen to 300,000. In order to cope with these increasing volumes, parties are currently improving both the infrastructure and the layout of Stationseiland. Construction activities will last until 2012. The new station hall located under the bus terminal will provide the station with an attractive waterfront façade. The concept for this ambitious enterprise was developed by Benthem Crouwel Architects. The Stationseiland redevelopment is a joint project of NS Real Estate and the municipal development company.

Westerdokseiland

On Westerdokseiland, living and working will go hand in hand with the planned construction of 900 new homes and no less than 50,000 m² of commercial space offering a splendid view of the IJ river. The island has been divided into three main areas: the City Side (La Grande Cour, 250 homes, Bouwfonds MAB Ontwikkeling), the Waterfront and the Head.
Westerdokseiland's marina and new square will be lined by 6,000 m² of facilities such as bars, restaurants and other small businesses.
Construction started in November 2004. The residential and commercial spaces are expected to become available in the course of 2007.

Centrum Amsterdam-Noord

A new district center is being developed for the district of Amsterdam-Noord, with some 3,500 homes, 50,000 m² of retail space, 150,000 m² of offices and various social and cultural facilities including a public library, a theater and a cinema.
The Centrum Amsterdam-Noord project (CAN) consists of 16 sub-areas that will be developed in phases. CAN is developed by Noordwaarts (a partnership of the City of Amsterdam and district Amsterdam-Noord) in collaboration with ING Real Estate and CZAN (a combination of Blauwhoed-Eurowoningen, Multi Development, Vesteda and Woningcorporatie Het Oosten). >>

Oosterdokseiland, a 200,000 m²-development very close to historic center and the Central Station.

The former Shell site (developer: ING Real Estate) will become an attractive residential and commercial area with 2,000 office, business and retail space, on the northern banks of the IJ river.

Shell site

The Shell site, a former industrial area located close to the city center on the Noordelijke IJ-oever, will be redeveloped into a new urban district. This area will become a mixed residential and business district with some 2,200 homes, 70,000 m² of offices and commercial space and 60,000 m² of urban facilities. Shell will bring all its research and office functions together under one roof in a New Technology Center (NTC). Construction started on this center July 1, 2005. The redevelopment of the Shell site is one of the first large-scale projects to be realized on the northern shores of the IJ.

Kraanspoor

At the former site of the Nederlandse Dok en Scheepsbouw Maatschappij (NDSM), ING Real Estate is currently developing the ultra-modern 10,000-m² office complex Kraanspoor. The three-story building was designed by Ontwerpgroep Trude Hooykaas. One of Kraanspoor's most remarkable features is a completely transparent climate façade with double glazing. The building offer a magnificent view of the IJ.

Teleport

In 2005, a new Stedenbouwkundig Programma van Eisen ('Urban Development Program of Requirements') was drawn up for the Teleport office and business park, ensuring cohesion between the various developments planned for the area. The facilities in the area surrounding the station will be expanded considerably between 2006 and 2008. The three squares near Sloterdijk station – Orlyplein, Piarcoplein and Carrascoplein – will be redeveloped in order to further strengthen their public transport function. In addition, the center's facilities will be developed con-

Kraanspoor office building on the northern banks (10,000 m², ING Real Estate).

homes and no less than 200,000 m² of

siderably. New hotel, retail and sports facilities and entertainment venues are designed to liven things up in the evening. Basic amenities will be increased by at least 5,000 m². There are also plans for the development of a Meeting Point (approx. 20,000 m²), which will offer hotel accommodation, small meeting halls and catering facilities. Construction on the Teleport center is expected to take place in the period 2009–2015.

Until 2015, however, the emphasis in terms of volume will be on the development of office space. Within this period, office space in the Teleport area could increase from today's 437,500 m² to approx. 700,000 m². For the moment, this development is concentrated in the area surrounding the station.

The Stadstuinen

In collaboration with the Ymere Housing Corporation, Bouwfonds Property Development is developing the Stadstuinen (City Gardens) area in the district of Osdorp. The Stadstuinen is part of the Westelijke Tuinsteden project, one of the largest renovation operations taking place in Europe today. In the Stadstuinen, everything revolves around space and green surroundings. A total of 415 homes, designed by DP 6 Architectuurstudio, will be realized in the Stadstuinen, of which 100 will be in the social housing sector and 30 in the free rental sector. Another 285 will be privately owned homes in the medium and high price ranges. The homes have been divided over eight blocks of alternating height, the tallest of which is 12 stories high. The homes will have their own parking space in a secure underground parking

space and large, well-situated outdoor areas in the form of balconies, terraces or jetties. The future residents will have a wide range of facilities nearby, including a neighborhood center, a theater, a public library, restaurants and sidewalk cafés, a shopping center near De Meervaart and a new covered shopping center at Plein '40-'45. Building of the homes started at the end of 2004.

Westpoort

Westpoort is an expanding harbor and industrial area located in the eastern part of Amsterdam's Sloterdijk III district. It accommodates 1,500 – for the most part small – companies. In collaboration with Van Wijnen Projectontwikkeling Noord, Maeyveld is developing the Woon- en Bouwcentrum Westpoort (Living and Building Center Westpoort) here. It is a striking complex that incorporates showrooms, catering facilities and retail and commercial space, with a joint rentable floor space of some 44,000 m² divided across two to three stories. The development consists of four blocks, with ample parking facilities for approx. 840 cars. The project is set for completion by mid-2006. >>

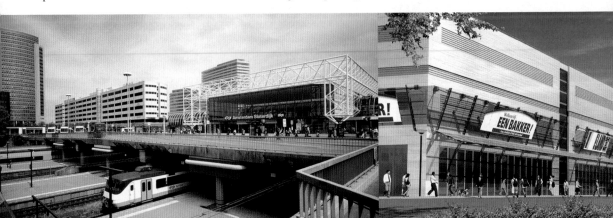

Teleport station at the heart of the area (Western Amsterdam).

Westpoort (44,000 m², Maeyveld).

Gershwin Symphony   Mahler 4

Ito   ABN AMRO   Viñoly

AMSTERDAM

The fact that the entire infrastructure is located underground makes ZuidasDok a unique project. The station Amsterdam Zui
will offer a mix of office buildings, homes, facilities, public spaces and parks.

ZuidasDok

Along the Zuidas, a 1,200-m
stretch of the A10 Zuid highway
and the adjacent railway tracks
will be led through a tunnel. In
terms of size, Amsterdam Zuid/
WTC will become the fifth-
largest station in the Netherlands.
A variety of public transport connections will make a stop here:
HSL, train, tram, subway, and
local and regional bus lines. The
urban development above ground
has been given the name

Amsterdam Symphony®.

Composer. A total of one million
m² of homes, offices and facilities will be built over this structure. Besides the so-called
ZuidasDok, another one million m²
will be developed in the surrounding area. Construction is
expected to start in 2008, and the
project is set for completion by
2030.

Vivaldi

The Vivaldi development consti-
tutes a completely new urban
area. The London-based firm of
Kohn Pedersen Fox Associates
(KPF) developed an outlook for
this park zone. It will feature five
elevated sports fields at a height
of some 10 m, built on top of a
park building that houses sports
facilities, a sports medical center
and a parking garage. A selection
of office buildings will be built
along the A10 highway. The first
to be built here is the new office
of Ernst & Young, designed by
Foster and Partners. This 87-m
high building will be completed
in early 2007.
The Zuidas' first 81 apartments

will be developed by Bouwfonds
MAB Ontwikkeling in the
Eurocenter complex. Also
Eurocenter will offer two office
towers with small-scale retail
facilities, catering facilities and a
500-space parking garage.
Eurocenter was designed by
architect René Steevenzs (PPKS)
and is set for completion by the
end of 2006.

Gershwin

The four construction consortia
participating in the prestigious
Gershwin living/working project
will each be responsible for a
variety of sub-projects.
Amsterdam Symphony® will be
developed by Bouwfonds MAB
Ontwikkeling; De Complete Stad
by BPF Bouwinvest, Het Oosten,
ING Real Estate and Ymere;
Royaal Zuid by Era Bouw, Prospect
and RaboVastgoed; and ZuidSchans
by Multi Development, AMVEST
and Bouwfonds MAB
Ontwikkeling. The striking
Amsterdam Symphony® complex
consists of three buildings: a residential tower that stretches to

Zuidas Dok
WTC

PHOTO: PROJECT AGENCY ZUIDAS

WTC will become the fifth-largest station in the Netherlands. Composer, the name of the developments above ground,

over 100 m, an equally high office building with a total floor space of some 40,000 m², and a 12-story five-star luxury hotel.

Mahler4

In addition to 166,500 m² of office space, the Mahler4 area will offer 193 loft-like apartments and 26,563 m² of facilities that include a parking garage with some 1,900 spaces, stores and catering facilities. Mahler4 will be developed by VOF Mahler4, (Fortis Vastgoed, ING Real Estate and G&S Vastgoed). The project is expected to be fully realized by the end of 2007.

VU-Kwartier

VU-Kwartier is the location of both the Vrije Universiteit (VU) and the VU Medical Center (VUMC). Working in collaboration with the City of Amsterdam, these organizations intend to make this area a livelier environment, by various means: renovation, new construction, expanding facilities and possibly even building new homes.

Kop Rivierenbuurt

Kop Rivierenbuurt is located on the eastern side of the Zuidas. Some 400 homes (50,000 m²) will be built here, as well as 50,000 m² of offices. Some 70,000 m² of facilities will also be realized, including a musical theater, accommodation for education, a hotel, stores and catering facilities. The area will be dominated by low-rise architecture. According to plans, the entire project will be completed around 2012.

RAI

The forecourt of the RAI conference center will feature an Expofoyer: an elevated building that can accommodate large parties and small exhibitions, parties and fairs. The Expofoyer was designed by the architectural firm of Benthem Crouwel. At the rear of the building one finds the planned site of a new Marriot hotel. The building, which will offer some 600 to 800 rooms, is set for completion by 2010.   >>

The Zuidas: 460,000 m² of office space, 10,000 homes and 250,000 m² of facilities.

ArenA Boulevard

The construction of Amsterdam ArenA has led to the development of a new urban hotspot in Amsterdam Zuidoost: ArenA Boulevard. This is destined to become the capital's second large urban center: a place to live, work, shop and enjoy oneself.

The ArenA Boulevard and the nearby Amsterdamse Poort shopping center are being developed into one big central area that provides space for a variety of facilities. The development of this area is a joint venture of the City of Amsterdam, the district council of Amsterdam Zuidoost and Ontwikkelingsmaatschappij Centrumgebied (OMC). The OMC development corporation was initiated by Ballast Nedam Ontwikkelingsmaatschappij, BAM Vastgoed and ING Real Estate. The Amsterdamse Poort area will be redeveloped first. Besides the enormous Shopperhal mall, in 2006 the shopping center will gain a new building for the district council, a sports center and new cultural facilities.

The new eight tracks and platforms of the new Bijlmer Station near the ArenA will be and connections to the Metro will sit below with clearly expressed orientation to the

ArenA Park

Five new 30-m tall residential blocks, housing a total of 273 apartments (privately owned and rental), will be erected in the area called ArenA Park. 282 covered parking spots will be laid out in closed-off sections in between the buildings. The five building blocks were designed by a.o. teams of the Amsterdam firms Claus & Kaan Architecten, and Van Sambeek & Van Veen Architecten. The ArenA Park project can be considered something of a first: these are the first residential projects to be realized in the ArenA area. Building officially commenced in November 2005, when the new homes were put on the market. The first building where construction started was De Aetsvelder.

ArenA Park, five residential building blocks housing 273 apartments.

Handelshuis

Handelshuis, a project by Leidschendam-based developer Bohemen BV, was initiated in mid-2005. The project in question involves the development of

raised on concrete viaducts with a total length of 325 metres. The concourse, bus station central station hall, connected with glass lifts, stairs and escalators to the upper level.

with a total rentable space of some 220,000 m², incorporating stores, offices, a theater, a hotel, a casino, restaurants, cafés and cultural facilities. Furthermore, a rooftop park with some 200 homes will be realized on top of the complex. Underground one finds approx. 1,100 parking spots. GETZ is expected to open its doors in 2007.

Station Bijlmer ArenA

The new Bijlmer ArenA railway, bus and subway station, located at a central point between Amsterdamse Poort and ArenA Boulevard, will become one of the most important public transport junctions in the Amsterdam area, offering a direct rail connection to Schiphol Airport. With its new status of Intercity station, and a projected capacity of 60,000 passengers a day, Bijlmer ArenA will be one of the top five stations in the country. Thanks to its transparency and wide range of retail facilities, the station will seamlessly connect the ArenA and Amsterdamse Poort locations with one another. Bijlmer ArenA is a design of Nicholas Grimshaw & Partners and is set for completion in 2007.   >>

a lively merchant area of some 70,000 m² (not including the 550-space parking garage), located to the northwest of the ArenA. The Handelshuis will include a 6,500-m² trade/conference center, a 3/4-star hotel with 150 rooms, office units ranging from 750 m² custom (tailor) made, catering facilities, fitness facilities, daycare facilities and small-scale showrooms. The project will be developed in four phases. Building starts in 2006.

GETZ

The development of the GETZ Entertainment Center will start in mid-2006. GETZ – an acronym of 'Gezondheid, Entertainment, Theater en Zaken' (Health, Entertainment, Theater and Business) will be situated in the new central area between the Heineken Music Hall and the Villa ArenA furniture mall. It will be a multi-purpose complex

Handelshuis, a 70,000-m² merchant area northwest of the ArenA (Bohemen).

Location	Project	Amsterdam / Projects 2006 and beyond. Program	Development	Planning
Amsterdam	Amstelstation	New development, offices 38,000 m² shops 2,000 m², residential 200 units	BAM Vastgoed	2014
Amsterdam	Amsterdam New China Town	Office development 152,000 m²	Rabo Vastgoed Bouwfonds MAB Ontwikkeling	2010
Amsterdam	DCG	Office development 126,000 m²	Maeyveld	n.a.
Amsterdam	IJburg	New residential development shops 8,200 m², residential 18,000 units	ING Real Estate Development IJ-delta, Waterstad	2012
Amsterdam	IJ Dock	New development, shops 3,000 m², offices 30,000 m², residential 65 units, parking 500 cars, hotel 280 rooms, investment €130 mln	William Properties B.V. Mun. of Amsterdam Rijksgebouwendienst	n.a.
Amsterdam	Parool Triangle	Office development, offices 62,200 m²	Multi Development	2007-2009
Amsterdam	Trivium 2	New office building, offices 7,500 m² residential 300 units	n.a.	2012
Amsterdam	Westerdokseiland	New development, offices and companies 50,000 m², shops 3,000 m² residential 900 units, leisure 6,000 m²	William Properties B.V. AMVEST Woningbedrijf Amsterdam	2007
Amsterdam	Westpoort	Shopping development, offices 5,000 m² shops and commercial space 45,000 m², parking 900 cars	Maeyveld, Van Wijnen	2006
Amsterdam	XXL (NDSM Werf Zuid)	Office and business development 300,000 m²	Johan Matser Projectontwikk. TRS, Lockhorst Bouw en Ontwikkeling	n.a.
Amsterdam Northeast	Buikslotermeerplein-Boven 't IJ	Expansion office building shops 10,000 m²	Blauwhoed B.V.	2006
Amsterdam Southeast	Arena Boulevard	New shopping center, shops 7,300 m²	BAM Vastgoed ING Real Estate Development	2007
Amsterdam Southeast	GETZ-project	New entertainment center, offices 9,280 m² parking 1,100 cars, hotel 300 rooms, total 200,000 m², investment €453,8 mln	Municipality of Amsterdam ING Real Estate Development Ballast Nedam, BAM Vastgoed	2009
Amsterdam Southeast	GETZ	Office development 23,667 m²	ING Real Estate Development Ballast Nedam, BAM Vastgoed	n.a.
Amsterdam Southeast	GETZ	Shopping development shops 47,334 m²	BAM Vastgoed, Ballast Nedam ING Real Estate Development	n.a.
Amsterdam Southeast	Science Park Amsterdam	New industrial area, offices 208,000 m² residential 600 units, 145,800 m²	Municipality of Amsterdam Universiteit Amsterdam	n.a.
Amsterdam Center	EastSite	New office area 200,000 m²	Heijmans IBC Vastgoedontwikkeling B.V.	2007
Amsterdam Center	Oosterdokseiland	New city center, offices 79,300 m² shops 15,500 m², residential 300 units parking 1,540 cars, leisure 7,000 m² culture 42,000 m², hotel 25,000 m² total 200,000 m²	Bouwfonds MAB Ontwikkeling. 2006-Bouwfonds Property Finance B.V 2009 Nieuw Chinatown Amsterdam CV Municipality of Amsterdam	2006-2009
Amsterdam Center	Stationseiland	New city center shops 6,000 m²	NS Real Estate Ontwikkelingsbedrijf Gemeente Amsterdam	2013
Amsterdam Center	Zuidelijke IJ-oever	Redevelopment area offices and companies 340,000 m² residential 3,500 units, 140,000 m²	n.a.	2019
Amsterdam East	Polderweggebied	New development, offices 12,500 m² shops 9,800 m², companies 13,500 m² residential 500 units, sports and leisure 11,500 m²	Bouwfonds MAB Ontwikkeling Woningbedrijf Amsterdam Woningcorporatie Het Oosten Gemeentelijk Grondbedrijf Amsterdam	2008
Amsterdam North	Centrum Amsterdam Noord	New development, offices 150,000 m² shops 28,000 m², residential 3,300 units mixed-use 6,000 m²	Multi Development, BAM Vastgoed Blauwhoed B.V, Ballast Nedam, ING Real Estate Development Vesteda, Woningcorporatie Het Oosten, OMC, Stadsdeel Amsterdam Noord, CZAN	2020
Amsterdam North	Shell Site	New development, offices, companies and shops 200,000 m², residential 2,000 units	ING Real Estate Development	2015
Amsterdam West	Opus 10	Office development 67,000 m²	Maarsen Groep, Aedes Vastgoed	n.a.
Amsterdam Zuidas	Atrium	Expansion office building 25,000 m²	Projectbureau Amsterdam Zuidas	2006
Amsterdam Zuidas	Gershwin	New development, offices 10,000 m² residential 1,200 units, facilities 10,000 m² hotel etc., 29,500 m²	Multi Development, Rabo Vastgoed, ING Real Estate Development, Mun. of A'dam, AMVEST, Bouwfonds MAB Ontwikk.	2009
Amsterdam Zuidas	Mahler4	New office area, offices 160,000 m² shops 15,000 m², residential 200 units 30,000 m², parking 1,950 cars, 10,000 m²	ING Real Estate Development 2005-Fortis Vastgoed Ontwikkeling 2007 G&S Vastgoed, Mun. of Amsterdam	2005-2007
Amsterdam Zuidas	Vivaldi	Redevelopment area, offices 100,000 m² residential 700 units, 93,000 m²	Mun. of Amsterdam Bouwfonds MAB Ontwikkeling	2006

More information: www.holland-re.com/projects

The Amstel Business Park and the Overamstel area lie south of De Omval (approx. 92 hectares).

De Omval

With the construction of the Rembrandt Tower (1994) and Breitner Tower (2001) and the completion of the Mondriaan Tower in 2002, Amsterdam has developed a small 'Manhattan on the Amstel', situated in the area called De Omval.

Amstelstation

Located close to De Omval is the busy Amstelstation railway station. Current plans for this area include new developments and a restructuring of the Julianaplein and Prins Bernhardplein squares. The remarkable Renault Building on the north side of the square will be restored and given a new function. At least 200 new homes will be built near Julianaplein. Plans exist to build a tower to the north of the station (max. 105 m). It will provide a visual link between this area and the towers of De Omval, and offer some 30,000 m^2 of floor space (28,000 m^2 of offices and 2,000 m^2 of

facilities). A new building to the south of the station will feature six office layers and another tower. This structure will offer 49,500 m^2 of floor space (38,000 m^2 of offices, a 10,000-m^2 hotel and 1,500 m^2 of facilities).

Amstel Business Park

At present, the Weespertrekvaart-Noord, Weespertrekvaart-Zuid and Amstel I and II plan areas have been incorporated within a single area: Amstel Business Park. In the next 10 to 15 years, Amstel Business Park, situated to the south of De Omval, will be transformed into a mixed living/working area with a range of facilities including catering, daycare and green space. A number of quality office buildings have been erected along the A10, serving as an indication of what to expect.

Amsterdam Science Park

Over the next ten years the City of Amsterdam, the Netherlands Organisation for Scientific

Research and the Universiteit van Amsterdam plan to turn the science park into an international center of knowledge. It is eventually going to provide a total of 500,000 square metres of office space, laboratories and educational buildings, a hotel, conference facilities, sports and cultural provisions, hundreds of homes, childcare and a railway station. Blauwhoed Eurowoningen will be responsible for the development of approx. 400 of the homes, concentrated in two plots: De Driehoek and Het Middensegment.   ≪

MORE INFORMATION

**City of Amsterdam
Real Estate Department**

P.O. Box 1104
1000 BC Amsterdam
The Netherlands
Tel.: +31 20 552 61 11
E-mail: p.cohen@oga.amsterdam.nl
Website: www.oga.amsterdam.nl

ONLINE: **www.holland-re.com/amsterdam**

THE URBAN LIFESTYLE

Inspired by space, architecture, and busy city life, Mahler4 is taking in a central position on the Amsterdam Zuidas. It's an urban complex of nine buildings linked by an underground parking garage and facilities at street level. With buildings designed by architects from four continents, the project gives Amsterdam a taste of global architecture. Innovative and with an eye for quality detailing, it is a dynamic and ambitious project.

Pursuing a broad approach, all functions of urban development have been integrated in full. The location justifies this extra attention and is a valuable addition to Amsterdam. Mahler4 shows an agreeable balance between living and working, a new impetus for urban Holland. Mahler4 is the first project on the Amsterdam Zuidas to be realized entirely in the spirit of the master plan for this area. Zuidas is situated along the higway A10, between the Old

South, designed by the architect Berlage, and the Van Eesteren post-war development of Buitenveldert. The Zuidas is commonly recognized as one of the most promising urban development areas for both offices and residences in the Netherlands.

Optimal location

Mahler4 is situated at the best site on the A10 ring road, with easy access from two exits (S108 and S109). There are optimal traffic

OF MAHLER4

FACT SHEET

Mahler4, Amsterdam

Program:
Retail: 5,000 m² and 5,000 m² services
Offices: 160,000 m²
Residential: 30,000 m²
(220 apartments)
Parking spaces: 2,100

Project developers:
VOF Mahler4, containing:
ING Real Estate Development,
Fortis Vastgoed Ontwikkeling,
G&S Vastgoed

Architects:
Hilberink Bosch Architecten (Den Bosch),
Erick van Egeraat Associated Architects
(EAA), FOA (London), Rafael Viñoly
Architects P.C. (New York), Toyo Ito &
Associates (Tokyo), Nicholas Jacobs of
Skidmore Owings & Merill (London),
Michael Graves & Associates (Princeton),
Medic & Puljiz of de Architekten Cie.
(Amsterdam), UN Studio (Amsterdam),
Van den Oever, Zaaijer & Partners
(Amsterdam), ZZDP Architecten
(Amsterdam)

Start of construction:
Mid-2002

Completion:
2005 – 2008

More information:
VOF Mahler4
Mahlerlaan 14,
1082 LS Amsterdam
P.O. Box 7887,
1008 AB Amsterdam
The Netherlands
Tel.: +31 20 661 48 28
Fax: +31 20 661 48 29
E-mail: info@mahler4.nl
Website: www.mahler4.nl

AMSTERDAM

facilities, most of which will be at underground level in future. It is in close proximity to Amsterdam Airport Schiphol, with the high speed train at its doorstep. By tram it's only a short ride to the Dam or Amstelveen. The complex is entirely built on an underground parking garage.

Phased construction

The nine buildings of Mahler4 are being built in three phases. The construction of the first and second phases began in mid-2002.

This phase consists of four office buildings, Viñoly, Graves, Som and Ito, the apartment tower, and the first and second phase of the parking garage. The first phase was completed in early 2005. Phase 2 is currently under construction and will be completed in 2006-2007. Phase 3 was started up mid-2004. This phase consists of four buildings, designed by Foreign Office Architects, Van Egeraat, UN Studio (Ben van Berkel) and Bosch. These buildings will be completed in 2008. ≪

ONLINE: www.holland-re.com/mahler

AMSTERDAM SYMPHONY®

SHOWPIECE OF THE ZUIDAS

On one of the Zuidas' prime locations, at the head of the Minerva axis in the heart of the new city district, Bouwfonds MAB Ontwikkeling is developing the new multi-purpose Amsterdam Symphony® building. It will combine a variety of complementary functions, ranging from offices, homes, a hotel and retail accommodation to public space and culture.

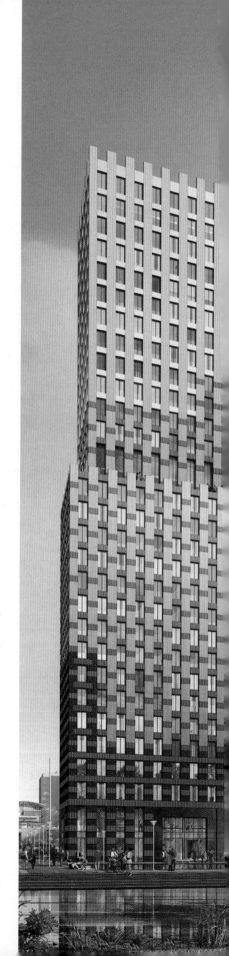

The striking Amsterdam Symphony® consists of three buildings: a tower that stretches to over 100 meters, housing around 100 apartments, an equally high office building of some 40,000 m², and a 12-story five star luxury hotel with approximately 210 rooms. This remarkable development also offers conference facilities. In the office tower, 3,000 m² have been allocated for a museum, art gallery and other cultural functions.

Meeting point

Some 2,500 m² on the ground floor have been reserved for catering and retail facilities. Amsterdam Symphony®'s underground parking garage will offer room for about 500 cars. The hotel's top of the range catering facilities can serve as a meeting place for both the local population and people from the surrounding office buildings and apartments. The design is based on the concept of voluntary mutual support, although each function can naturally support itself in its own right. This way, the users of the building can experience the joys of being multifunctional without the burdens.

Ideal location

Amsterdam Symphony® is located in the heart of the prestigious Gershwin living/working project, at the end of the Minerva axis, which runs until the Hilton hotel. The Gershwin project will feature an aquatic square to the south of Amsterdam Symphony® that offers various utilities, including catering. The wide range of functions incorporated in the complex make the Amsterdam Symphony® project an excellent example of the city's ambition to develop multifunctional areas that offer a balance between living and working facilities. «

Amsterdam Symphony®, Amsterdam

Program:
- Offices: 35,500 m^2
- Hotel: 12,500 m^2
- Art center: 3,000 m^2
- Retail: 2,500 m^2
- Apartments: 100
- Parking spaces: 500

Developer:
Bouwfonds MAB Ontwikkeling

Architect:
De Architecten Cie. (Pi de Bruijn)

Building commences:
2005

Completion:
2008

More information:
Bouwfonds MAB Ontwikkeling CVG B.V.
Wijnhaven 60
2511 GA The Hague
The Netherlands
Tel.: +31 70 306 85 00
Fax: +31 70 354 36 18
www.bouwfonds.nl

AMSTERDAM

www.holland-re.com/symphony

OOSTERDOKSEILAND IN

Right next to the Central Station, between the IJ river and the city center, the Oosterdokseiland (ODE) is being built. The master plan for this architectonic tour de force was drawn up by Erick van Egeraat Associated Architects. A team of twelve nationally and internationally celebrated architects has been involved in further elaboration of the 200,000-m² site. The plan consists of six plots, with a variety of different functions, making Oosterdokseiland an excellent location for (inter)national companies.

Living, working, studying, shopping, having fun and going out are all part of big-city life. And a broad mix of these activities is represented on Oosterdokseiland in Amsterdam, the section of the south bank of the IJ river where redevelopment will be the most radical and ambitious. In the plinth on the island's southern waterfront are the entrances to the public and commercial facilities that are

spread over the entire island at three levels (from level -1 to +1). The entrances to the offices are on the Oosterdoksstraat that borders the island on the northern side.

The six sites that make up Oosterdokseiland each have their own special function. For example, site 1 with its luxury hotel and congress center is a reflection of hospitality. Site 2 has a Far East theme with its

AMSTERDAM

F A C T   S H E E T

ODE, Amsterdam

Program: Oosterdokseiland total: 213,750 m² (not including 53,000 m² of parking space)

Developer: ODE is being developed by Oosterdokseiland Ontwikkeling Amsterdam (O.O.A. C.V.): a joint venture of Bouwfonds MAB Ontwikkeling and Meyer Bergman, in cooperation with New Chinatown (NCT C.V.) and the Municipality of Amsterdam

Architects: Master plan: Erick van Egeraat Associated Architects (EEA, Rotterdam)

Architekturbüro Baumschlager-Eberle-Grassman (Lochau); Future Systems (London); Jo Crepain (Antwerp); HVDN architecten (Amsterdam); Maccreanor Lavington (Rotterdam); David Chipperfield Architects (London); Jo Coenen & Co (Maastricht); Meyer en Van Schooten (Amsterdam); Zwarts & Jansma (Amsterdam), Agence Ter (Paris/ Karlsruhe); De Architecten Cie. (Amsterdam)

Investment: €800 million

Construction starts: 2004

Completion: Phased: 2006-2009

More information:
www.oosterdokseiland.nl
www.bouwfonds.com

Network Facility Centre (NFC, a European-Asian trade center) and wide variety of Asian shops and restaurants. Site 3 comprises the biggest Oosterdokseiland housing area. It is divided over three apartment blocks (one-third rental and two-thirds privately owned). There is also a big media store and a mega book-store located on this site.
In addition to the mega bookstore there will also be a public library on site 4. With an area of 29,420 m², this will be one of the biggest libraries in Europe. The big attraction on site 5 is the Amsterdam Conservatory. Under the Conservatory building and the adjacent office building, there will be a leisure center with bars, res-taurants, a casino, a family enter-tainment center and a concert hall. The leisure facilities extend to site 6 where the biggest office build-ing on the island is located. ≪

LIVING BETWEEN THE IJ

Westerdokseiland – at the head of Amsterdam's ring of canals – is a marvelous place to live. City Cour Combination, a cooperation of Bouwfonds MAB Ontwikkeling and Smits Bouwbedrijf, is developing a modern apartment complex called La Grande Cour. La Grande Cour promises a convergence of architecture, a magnificent view over the IJ and the warmth of Amsterdam's historical city center. This unique location guarantees a truly enjoyable living experience.

La Grande Cour's design is based on a vision. The design of the building with its 'arched towers' is by the Dutch architect Jeroen van Schooten of Meyer & Van Schooten, in cooperation with the architectural firms Heren 5 and De Architecten Cie. In his design, urban housing density adjusts itself to the panoramic view of the IJ river. Thus, the apartments combine the attraction of water, the romance of shipping and the big-city culture.

From cour to roof garden

On the ground level, the modern apartment building will comprise approximately 250 homes in various categories and around 2,300 m² of business space. There will be roughly 80 government sponsored rental apartments which have been taken over by Olympus, 123 middle- and top-range rental apartments, 30 AMH (a mortgage for people on average incomes), private property apartments and approximately 20 owner-occupied homes. An investor has bought a great

AND THE CITY

F A C T   S H E E T

La Grande Cour, Amsterdam

Program:
Construction of apartment complex
with approximately 250 homes
(approx. 80 government-
sponsored rental homes, 123 middle-
and top-range rental homes, 30 AMH
private properties and approx. 20
owner-occupied homes) and around
2,300 m² of business space

Developer:
City Cour Combination (CCC), a joint
venture between Bouwfonds MAB
Ontwikkeling and Smits Bouwbedrijf

Architects:
- Meyer & Van Schooten
- Heren 5
- De Architecten Cie.

Investment:
€80 million

Building commences:
December 2003

Completion:
2007-2008

More information:
www.lagrandecour.nl
www.bouwfonds.nl

AMSTERDAM

number of houses, which are offered in the free sector. The apartments are accessible via central, secluded entrance ways, the so-called 'cours'. These entrances are also planned as meeting places for residents. Another special meeting place is the roof gardens, which are also destined for common use. The roof gardens are exclusively for residents and offer a breathtaking view. The complex also provides a parking garage, which, like the 'cours' and roof gardens, is only accessible to residents.

Ideal location

La Grande Cour is located on Westerdokseiland, an island that offers special and unique living. The municipality of Amsterdam has planned the Westerdokshaven on Westerdokseiland, which will allow residents to moor their boats right next to their homes. The mix of both activities and residences is sure to make La Grande Cour a lively place to live with a typical Amsterdam ambience. «

The front of La Grande Cour.

100,000-m² NEW INNER

Oostenburgereiland will become a new, bubbling part of Amsterdam's center with up to 100,000 m² on the old Stork site. As a former location of the VOC, it is a location with a rich history. The entrepreneurial spirit of those days will come back to life with the area offering space to companies with a strong creative, innovative and commercial character. It's for companies that are linked to urban culture and feel a need for accessibility, image, services and facilities. Oostenburgereiland offers all of this in a high-quality total concept.

Amsterdam Oostenburgereiland is being developed and arranged according to the core values of authenticity and freedom. This means respect for the history of the area in combination with optimal flexibility for users. This has been worked out into various concepts. One of these is the Loft concept, which stands for the powerful, industrial design of 'modern' warehouses. For public spaces, another concept is being followed: informal, even flooring, specific green areas and a clear relationship with the water. The lots are being built according to the Roof top concept, which involves two complete lower layers with smaller areas above, so that unique roof terraces are created. These design and layout concepts are supplemented with concepts for services and leisure, so that Oostenburgereiland becomes a pleasant place to work and relax. Exactly what you would expect from a bubbling city center.

CITY

FACT SHEET

Oostenburgereiland, Amsterdam

Program:
100,000-m² new inner city

Consisting of the following clusters:
- Media & Design
- High-Tech
- Public sector and education
- Leisure & Culture
- Business services
- Special facilities
- Urban living

Developer:
Heijmans Vastgoed

Delivery:
Phased until approx. 2010

More information:
www.oostenburgereiland.nl
www.init.nl

For additional information, please contact one of our real estate partners:
Fris Bedrijfsmakelaars
Tel.: +31 20 301 77 20

Cushman & Wakefield Healey & Baker
Tel.: +31 20 301 42 42

AMSTERDAM

INIT: the beating heart

INIT is the eye catcher of Oostenburgereiland. This glass-covered city is a beautifully designed space to be collectively used by different companies. As a result of the impressive design, the size and central location, INIT is literally and figuratively the center of Oostenburgereiland. The building breathes an atmosphere of inspiring activity. There is always something happening. And this is the way INIT feeds the bubbling energy on Oostenburgereiland.

Easy to reach

Thanks to its favorable location in Amsterdam, between the center and the Oostelijk havengebied area, Oostenburgereiland is easily accessible. By car it is a short distance from the S114 exit on the A10 Ring road. Public transport is also an excellent option as it's just minutes from Amsterdam Central Station and stops for both trams and buses are within walking distance. «

ONLINE: www.holland-re.com/oostenburgereiland

NEW FUTURE FOR ABN

Right in the center of Amsterdam, on the corner of the famous Rembrandtplein, at the junction of the Utrechtsestraat, Herengracht and the Amstelstraat, the former ABN AMRO building awaits redevelopment. After thorough renovation, the historic building will accommodate a hotel, offices, shops, multifunctional space, and a parking garage for 120 cars.

The ABN AMRO building, located on the east side of the Rembrandtplein was realized in part in the 1930s and 1960s. The historical office building was abandoned when ABN AMRO Bank decided to position its central management in its new office tower in Amsterdam Zuidas. Over the next few years, the building will be completely redeveloped into a multifunctional complex that will fit in seamlessly with its environment. Rembrandt Ontwikkeling, a joint venture between Kroonenberg Groep and Bouwfonds MAB Ontwikkeling, is responsible for the completion of this complex project.

Quality boost

The building will accommodate a wide range of functions including a mix of offices, a hotel, a restaurant and parking facilities all under one roof. In short, it is a multifunctional building in the

AMRO BUILDING

F A C T   S H E E T

Rembrandtplaza, Amsterdam

Program:
- Office space: 10,000 m²
- Shops: 8,000 m²
- Hotel: 18,500 m²
- Parking spaces: 120

Developer:
Rembrandt Ontwikkeling CV (joint venture between Kroonenberg Groep and Bouwfonds MAB Ontwikkeling)

Architect:
ir. K. Rijnboutt,
De Architectengroep (Amsterdam)

Building commences:
2007

Delivery:
2009

More information:
Rembrandt Ontwikkeling CV
Wijnhaven 60
2511 GA The Hague
The Netherlands
Tel.: +31 70 306 85 00
Fax: +31 70 354 36 18
www.rembrandtplaza.com

AMSTERDAM

broadest sense of the word. The facilities will be integrated and will literally create a continuation of the Rembrandtplein. The renovated building will give the Rembrandtplein and the Amstelstraat a major boost in allure. Moreover, the Utrechtsestraat and the Herengracht will equally profit from the building's appeal.

Central location

The main entrance to the building will be on the Rembrandtplein,

centrally located in the heart of Amsterdam and easily accessible. The building is in walking distance from Central Station and can be reached effortlessly by both car and public transport. The tram stops right in front of the building and a bus stop and subway station are just around the corner. There will be ample parking facilities located under the building. What's more, the Stadhuis (town hall) parking garage is only a five-minute walk away. «

A bird's eye view of the ABN AMRO building.

ONLINE: www.holland-re.com/rembrandtplaza

INTERNATIONAL CITY OF PEACE AND JUSTICE

THE HAGUE

The skyline of The Hague has gone through some impressive changes in recent years. The city's new office towers are a remarkable sight. Still, The Hague's inner-city redevelopment is only half finished. The core retail area is being transformed and the Central Station area will be subjected to an extensive overhaul. The Hague is steadily building its image as an international city of peace and justice.

W ith 5.5 million m² of floor space, the region of The Hague is the second largest office location in the Netherlands. It chiefly owes this position to the fact that the city is the Dutch seat of government. Government-related institutes play an important role in the local office market, particularly in The Hague's city center. However, the government is scaling down operations at present. A smaller civil service will lead to less demand for floor space, which in turn could well lead to difficulties for the local real estate market.

The Hague is working on its image as an international city of peace and justice. The concentration of the Yugoslavia Tribunal, OPCW and Europol in a metropolitan area with quality facilities has created an attractive setting for similar international institutes. The World Forum Convention Center (WFCC) offers a starting point for this development.

The situation of previous decades – when large office buildings were dispersed throughout the city – seems to be coming to an end. Many new large-scale projects are now concentrated on the Haagse As, which runs from Wijnhaven-

The weekly antique market at the Lange Voorhout.

kwartier to Beatrixkwartier, along and over the highway. There was a decline in new construction activity in 2005, with annual production only a fifth of the average level of the last ten years. However, the demand for office space by governmental and semi-governmental organizations still guarantees a certain stability in the market, which means that The Hague did not feel the pinch of the economic recession to the same degree as other large cities. With regard to office developments, the emphasis is on the central metropolitan area (Den Haag Nieuw-Centraal), as well as other centers like Laakhaven, Ypenburg, Rijswijk and

Zoetermeer-Centrum. Incidentally, of the four major Dutch cities, The Hague boasts the lowest vacancy rates.

The Hague's core retail area is currently seeing considerable improvement in terms of quality. The project De Baljurk was completed in the first half of 2005, and the redevelopment of the Haagse Passage shopping mall will further enhance the quality of the retail offer. Furthermore, the Spuimarkt district will be redeveloped into a modern, large-scale core retail area.

These developments ensure that the city center will have a remarkably large volume of new projects in the near future.   >>

Kite festival on the beach in Scheveningen with the famous Kurhaus building in the background.

< *Summer in the city.*

In 2020, The Hague Central Station (Benthem Crouwel) will be a meeting place for 350,000 travelers a day.

Den Haag Nieuw-Centraal

A completely refurbished station, a lively Anna van Buerenplein; modernization of the Babylon retail and office area; the covering of the bus platform and the construction of a landmark tower on Koningin Julianaplein

The Central Station will be transformed into an international public transport hub.

– this more or less sums up the project Den Haag Nieuw-Centraal. While the direct reason for this project was the arrival of the HSL high-speed rail link and RandstadRail, it will also form the tailpiece of the Den Haag Nieuw Centrum project. A total

of 120,000 m² of office space will be realized at this location, as well as 50,000 m² of housing – both rental and owner-occupied – in the higher segments. Construction in the 400x400-m plan area will be finished around 2011. The new station will have an open orientation on all four sides. The building will form an attractive gateway to the city behind it. The cost of the plan, which is intended to create a prime location for travel, work, living and shopping, is estimated at some €800 million. Market parties will invest over €500 million – with NS Vastgoed, Multi Development, Maeyveld BV and Bouwfonds Property Finance as the major contributors – the City will invest more than €100 million and the Dutch government will contribute €128 million.

Five sub-projects

Nieuw-Centraal consists of five sub-projects, which include work on the station building itself and the construction of offices over the bus platform adjacent to the station hall. This intensive use of space will create 65,000 m² of new office space and 5,000 m² of space for retail and facilities. The buildings are intended to form impressive landmarks. Another sub-project is Koningin Julianaplein, which is located to the front of the station. The square will be dominated by striking high-rise architecture that houses a mix of living, working and retail functions. OMA (Rem Koolhaas) is responsible for the designs. The maximum building height allowed in this area is 90 m. The new developments will add another 25,000 m² of residential space, 45,000 m² of office space and 5,100 m² of retail space to the location.

New Babylon

The Babylon mall is located next to the square. It offers stores, offices and a hotel; the last two of which will gain more space after the center's planned modernization has been completed. The complex will be bordered by two new residential towers of 140 and 100 m respectively. More than half of the 330 apartments have been bought by AMVEST. An investment of approximately €57 million. Maeyveld BV and Bouwfonds Property Finance will be developing 54,500 m² of office space and 16,500 m² of retail space here. Nearby Anna van Bueren-plein will feature various cultural facilities. A three-story parking garage will be constructed under the square that holds room for approximately 1,000 cars.   >>

New Babylon (Maeyveld) consists of the redevelopment and expansion (80,000 m²) of the Babylon retail and office complex.

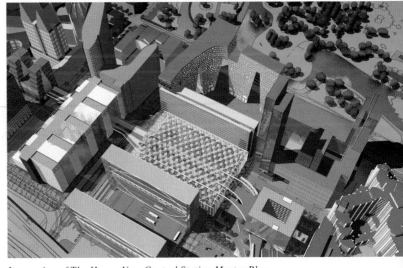

Impression of The Hague New Central Station Master Plan.

Wijnhavenkwartier

Walking from The Hague Central Station to the city center, one passes the district of Wijnhavenkwartier. The offices of the Ministries of Justice and Internal Affairs and the residential complex De Zwarte Madonna will be torn down in the near future. Wijnhavenkwartier will be an urban environment offering a range of entertainment, leisure, shopping, living and working facilities. The ministries will be relocated to the current site of De Zwarte Madonna. In addition, 520 homes and various urban facilities will be constructed in the area. The total cost of the project is estimated at €600 million.

In the plans for Spuiplein, the area's various theaters are joined by new retail, catering and cultural facilities and a fitness center. A second section will house a new hotel and conference facilities, and the third section will offer facilities for employees, residents and visitors to the area. A total of five towers will be constructed here. The ministry buildings will have a maximum height of 140 m, and the adjacent residential building will be up to 125 m. The other towers will stretch to approximately 70-90 m. Of the available floor space, 76,000 m² has been reserved for homes, 120,000 m² has been set aside for the ministerial departments and 45,000 m² for retail, catering and a hotel. The apartment blocks and the urban facilities are a joint development by local government, the Rijksgebouwendienst (which commissioned architect Hans Kollhoff for the ministry buildings), Bouwfonds MAB and Haag Wonen Kristal. The redevelopment of Wijnhavenkwartier will be completed in 2015 or 2016.

Spuimarkt

Spuimarkt, situated between Spui, Spuistraat, Wagenstraat and Veerkade, is currently being redeveloped into a modern core retail area. Market parties Multi Development, BAM Vastgoed and ING Real Estate are taking part in the project. More than 37,000 m² of retail space will be developed here for a variety of stores, including the major department chains C&A, HEMA, Bijenkorf and V&D. In addition, 25,000 m² of space for urban entertainment will be realized here – including a 10,000-m² cinema – as well as 320 homes. An L-shaped combined shopping arcade/residential complex is currently being realized at Rabbijn Maarsenplein (behind the Nieuwe Kerk). This sub-project, which will eventually house 14 retail units and 79 apartments, is scheduled for completion in mid-2006. A new retail and entertainment complex on the corner of Spui and Grote Marktstraat will house a Pathé multiplex with nine theaters and 2,300 seats, as well as a C&A outlet. 16,000 m² of floor space has been reserved for retail. The complex will be completed in the spring of 2007.

Architect Bernard Tschumi is currently working on the design for

The Spuimark project comprises a large-

the sector between Spuistraat and Grote Markstraat. Plans include the redevelopment of the former Marks & Spencer building (the temporary home of the C&A clothing store), the V&D building and the Asta building. Various stores will be realized at this location, on top of which

PHOTO: EUROPE REAL ESTATE PUBLISHERS

In this area three towers will be realized by Bouwfonds MAB Ontwikkeling.

scale restructuring and extension of The Hague's inner city shopping area.

one will find 80 homes and an elevated city square.

Two corridors connecting Spuistraat and Grote Marktstraat will be constructed at ground level, and there will be an underground connection to the nearby tram tunnel. The design will be presented in mid-2006.

Various homes and parking facilities are to be developed at a site along Gedempte Gracht behind the Bijenkorf department store. Further retail space will be developed at street level, to benefit from the many shoppers attracted to the area by the Bijenkorf. The location's present parking lot will be replaced by a parking garage. The adjacent Hema building will be fitted with a new façade.

Now that trams no longer run through Grote Marktstraat, it has become possible to turn the area into an attractive pedestrian zone. This will ensure a safe, relaxed shopping environment.

De Passage

Fortis Vastgoed has commissioned Provastgoed to develop De Passage, the Netherlands' oldest covered shopping street, originally built in 1885. The mon-

umental arcade will be completely modernized in order to utilize the vacant space in Hotel du Passage. The developer plans to attract more visitors to the mall by adding big retail attractions and catering facilities. The top stories will house a 10,000-m² hotel, 2,600 m² of offices and homes. >>

The oldest shopping arcade of the Netherlands, De Passage, renewed.

The RandstadRail runs through the Beatrixkwartier. On the right De Monarch (architect Mario Botta).

Beatrixkwartier

Beatrixkwartier, located directly adjacent to Utrechtsebaan, is presently undergoing a complete transformation. The project is a public-private collaboration between local government and six market parties: Fortis Vastgoed, ING Real Estate, KPN Telecom, Provastgoed, BPF Bouwinvest and Siemens. The development includes approximately 190,000 m² of new or renovated office space, a four-star hotel, over 460 apartments, retail, catering and various other facilities. The future RandstadRail railway line connecting The Hague with Rotterdam will run straight through the area. One of the largest projects on the Prinses Beatrixlaan is Prinsenhof. This building, which is already completed, effortlessly combines living, working and catering functions. Between three (semi-public) 'corporate gardens', one will find 65,000 m² of office space, 214 rental apartments, a

206-room hotel and 2,000 m² of stores and facilities. The large office complex De Monarch will also see phased completion in the course of this year. The building will be realized by developers Fortis Vastgoed Ontwikkeling and Provastgoed Nederland, who have attracted architect Mario Botta for the design. 73,000 m² of office space has been housed in a central building and four towers. De Monarch will also feature corporate gardens, as well as room for a grand café and stores on the ground floor.

Utrechtsebaan

Grotiusplaats is the collective name for six new structures planned over and along the Utrechtsebaan. One of these is the Grotiustoren on Juliana van Stolberglaan. The tower, a development by Multi Development, will lie parallel to the Palace of Justice. It consists of three building volumes and offers 26,000 m² of office space. Building is

expected to start in 2006. OVG Projectontwikkeling expects to finish De Haagsche Zwaan at the end of 2008. This 18,000-m² structure will resemble a swan's neck hovering over the Utrechtsebaan.

De Haagsche Zwaan (OVG, 18,000 m²).

Laakhaven

In the next few years, a new urban environment for living and working will be realized in Laakhaven West, an area bordering the Utrechtsebaan. In addition to 600 to 800 owner-occupied and rental homes, 28,000 m² of office space will be realized at this location, as well as 15,000 m² of business space and facilities. Building is planned to start in late 2006, and will last for about six years. At a location directly behind the railway station, TCN Property Projects is developing urban offices in the former KPN sorting office. The building's characteristic industrial architecture allows for the development of high-ceilinged loft offices. The Urban Offices project will offer 5,000 m² of traditional office space and 9,000 m² of loft-type office space. On the corner of Rijswijkseweg and Enthovenplein, Fortis Vastgoed Ontwikkeling is developing the office complex De Klok. 3,800 m² of floor space has been divided across five building layers. A prime example of the new Laakhaven development is Laakcenter, a multi-story complex that combines offices, commercial space, showrooms and homes. This project by Strabag Development houses over 59,000 m² of commercial space.

Binckhorst

The Binckhorst area will offer a mix of functions: living, working, leisure and retail. As envisioned in the area's structural plan, Binckhorstlaan will gain the allure of a big-city boulevard with a variety of tall building volumes that overlook the road. Two large office buildings have been developed on Binckhorstlaan. Snouckaert, a project by Multi Development and Delta Lloyd, accommodates 12,500 m² divided across two separate buildings. The formidable office complex Binck Elephant will be realized a bit further down by developer Haagse Olifant. The building's 30,000-m² floor space is distributed across four building units. The successful office project Haagse Veste 1 is nearing its completion. The development by Strabag and Ballast Nedam will offer over 13,000 m² of office space.

The City of The Hague is busily involved in the redevelopment of the former Caballero Factory and surrounding buildings into a center for innovative, cultural and creative businesses. The Caballero Factory is particularly well suited for companies working in the multimedia, graphic design, advertising, IT, communications, art distribution, events organization and architectural fields. The first phase of the project comprises a total of 15,000 m² of office and business space. This phase will be completed in January 2006. >>

The Flat-Iron

Public objection procedures led to some delay in the construction of a remarkable triangular residential tower on Rijswijkseplein. After halting altogether for a while, building recommenced in mid-2005 and the building is expected to be completed by early 2007. The 130-m tower, nicknamed The Flat-Iron, will house 300 studios for students and 48 apartments in the free sector. The Vestia housing corporation commissioned the development.

La Fenêtre

La Fenêtre (LATEI Projectontwikkeling) is one of the most remarkable new developments in the Central Station area: an enormous apartment building on steel fork-shaped supports, hovering some 20 m over the ground floor. Rudy Uytenhaak is responsible for the design. The building comprises 115 luxury apartments divided over 17 floors, which are being rented by Vesteda. A three story parking garage with some 150 spaces is located under the building.

Completion: end 2008

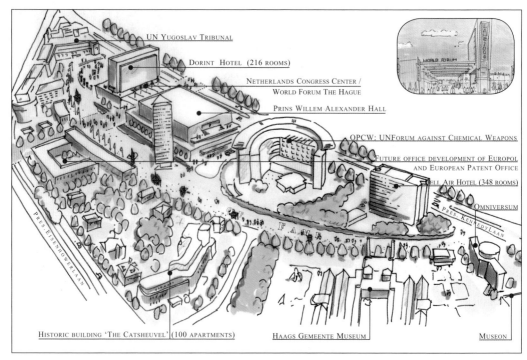

UN YUGOSLAV TRIBUNAL

DORINT HOTEL (216 ROOMS)

NETHERLANDS CONGRESS CENTER /
WORLD FORUM THE HAGUE

PRINS WILLEM ALEXANDER HALL

OPCW: UNFORUM AGAINST CHEMICAL WEAPONS

FUTURE OFFICE DEVELOPMENT OF EUROPOL
AND EUROPEAN PATENT OFFICE

BEL AIR HOTEL (348 ROOMS)

OMNIVERSUM

PRES. EISENHOWERLAAN

PRES. KENNEDYLAAN

F A M A

HISTORIC BUILDING 'THE CATSHEUVEL' (100 APARTMENTS)

HAAGS GEMEENTE MUSEUM

MUSEON

World Forum (95,000 m²) is the name of the redevelopment of the former Nederlands Congres Centrum by TCN.

World Forum

In September 2005, the Haagse Congrescentrum was renamed World Forum Convention Center (WFCC). Over 60,000 m² of meeting rooms and conference halls combine with the Netherlands' largest hall for conventions, meetings and theater productions to form an impressive new podium for international conventions and events. The center is part of The Hague World Forum – the district bordered by Johan de Wittlaan, President Kennedylaan, Stadhouderslaan and Eisenhowerlaan. This area houses, among others, the Yugoslavia Tribunal and OPCW. A 30,000-m² building is currently being designed for Europol at the HWF location. The different international organizations in this district all work in the areas of peace, justice and safety. The World Forum Convention Center, an initiative by TCN Property Projects, will be completed in the course of 2007. It will be followed in the near future by more developments that fit the theme.

De Monchyplein

The Burgemeester De Monchyplein project, on the former site of the old city hall, comprises both housing and office space. The location's three towers offer a total of 12,000 m² of floor space, and a small-scale office villa provide another 750 m². The villa forms a visual link between the existing architecture and the new office towers, which in turn attune with a large police station to the side of the square. The villa also forms a functional continuation of its surroundings, as the nearby old buildings often house offices. The first office tower will be occupied by the Belgian Embassy and various business services providers. The other two towers will be linked to form a single building.

The De Monchyplein project houses both housing and office space.

Scheveningen

Fortis Vastgoed Ontwikkeling has advanced plans for a nautical center in the harbor of Scheveningen. This will bring together a number of functions, including a hotel with 140 apartments, 1,200 m² of offices (most of it targeted at the maritime sector), 5,000 m² of commercial space, a 1,200-m² sailing center, and maritime retail and catering facilities. By 'flipping over' the marina, the complex will gain an attractive waterfront area on the side of the harbor. The accompanying boatyard will be completed by the end of 2006 and the nautical center a year later.

Due to the nearby commercial activity, permanent residence is not allowed in this area. This is why planners have opted for hotel suites, with a maximum stay of six months.

During the week, the center will be an attractive place to stay for business clients, and during the weekends it will accommodate water sports enthusiasts. The Center's catering facilities are meant to complement the present offer.

Developer Bouwfonds MAB Ontwikkeling and the KCAP architects & planners firm have developed a plan for the harbor area in Scheveningen: De Golfbreker.

Bouwfonds MAB Ontwikkeling is developing De Golfbreker on the northern harbourhead of the original fisherman's harbor in Scheveningen.

It outlines the development of a hotel, hotel-apartments, retail, leisure and storage facilities (total program 150,000 m²). At present, the area has two distinct functions: the local fishing-related industry is concentrated around the harbor, while recreational activities are mainly restricted to the boulevard, the beach and the sea. The plan for this area is based on the gradual hiving off of the old business architecture combined with the construction of new tourist/recreational functions, including temporary accommodation, leisure and parking facilities. Intensive use of the available space should allow these functions to be used simultaneously. The feasibility study for De Golfbreker is in an advanced stage. The Scheveningen fish market and the existing companies will be included in the redevelopment. The project will probably be completed in 2010. »

The Nautical Center Scheveningen is made up of 11 individual buildings.

Location	Project	Program	Offices / m²	Development	Planning
The Hague	ADO square	New development, offices 10,000 m², retail 8,000 m²		TCN Property Projects	2012
The Hague	Forepark	New development residential 125,000 m², leisure 100,000 m²	175,000	Mun. of The Hague Mun. of Leidschendam	2017
The Hague	Grotiustoren-Grotiusplaats	New office building parking 311 cars, miscellaneous 3,500 m²	26,000	Multi Development	n.a.
The Hague	's Gravendreef	Office development	65,000 m²	Heijmans IBC Vastgoedontwikkeling	a.o. 2006
The Hague	Schenkkade	New office building	16,000	OVG Projectontwikkeling	2006
The Hague	De Haagsche Zwaan	New office building	18,000 m²	OVG Vastgoedontwikkeling	2008
The Hague	Hoornwijck	New office area	200,000 m²	Multi Development, Heijmans IBC, Mainland, BAM Vastgoed	2008
The Hague	World Forum The Hague	Renovated/New office building shops 2,000-4,000 m², investment €55 mln	10,000	Provastgoed Nederland B.V. TCN Property Projects	2006
The Hague	World Forum Convention Center	New convention Center	60,000 m²	TCN Property Projects	2007
The Hague Beatrixkwartier	De Monarch	New office building parking 680 cars	73,000	Ontwikkelingsmaatschappij De Monarch CV	2006
The Hague Beatrixkwartier	Prinsenhof	New development shops 2,000 m², residential 214 units parking 1,070 cars, hotel 206 rooms	65,000	BPF Bouwinvest	2004-2006
The Hague Binckhorst	Snoeckaert	New development	14,000	Multi Development, Delta Lloyd	2006
The Hague Binckhorst	Caballero Facory	Redevelopment offices and business space 15,000 m2		Municipality of The Hague	2006
The Hague Center	New Babylon	Expansion shopping center shops 15,000 m²		Maeyveld	after 2005
The Hague Center	Den Haag Centraal	Office development	56,000	Maeyveld	2011-2020
The Hague Center	Nieuw Centraal	Redevelopment area residential 53,000 m², parking 1,853 cars facilities 37,500 m²	114,500	NS Real Estate Mun. of The Hague Multi Development	2011-2020
The Hague Center	Anna van Buerenplein-Nieuw Centraal	New development residential 10,000 units, facilities 10,000 m²	10,000	n.a.	2011-2020
The Hague Center	Kon. Julianaplein-Nieuw Centraal	Redevelopment area residential 59,000 m², shops 27,500 m², facilities 7,500 m²,	133,500	n.a.	2009
The Hague Center	Haagse Passage	Renovatie and expansion shopping center shops 2,000 m², hotel 100-125 rooms existing 4,300 m², total 6,300 m²		Fortis Vastgoed Beleggingen Provastgoed Nederland B.V.	2006
The Hague Center	Spuimarkt	Expansion city center shops 37,000 m2, residential 320 units parking 500 cars, leisure 4,000 m2, hotel 120 rooms		ING Real Estate Development Multi Development, BAM Vastgoed	2005-2007
The Hague Center	Wijnhaven-kwartier	Redevelopment city center shops 22,200 m², residential 580 units 75,000 m², parking 1,000 cars, 30,800 m² hotel and conference center 20,000 m²	147,000	Bouwfonds MAB Ontw. Mun. of The Hague Rijksgebouwendienst	2005-2014
The Hague Laakhaven	De Klok	New office building	3,800	Fortis Vastgoed Ontwikkeling Centacon B.V.	n.a.
The Hague Laakhaven	Laakhaven West	New shopping center	n.a	Johan Matser Projectontwikkeling B.V., Kristal Ballast Nedam	n.a.
The Hague Laakhaven	Strijkijzer-Rijswijkseplein	New residential area residential 350 units		Vestia Den Haag ZO	2007
The Hague Scheveningen	De Golfbreker	New development shops 5,000 m², parking 1,000 cars, 30,000 m² leisure 10,000 m², hotel 250 rooms, 16,000 m² sports 5,000 m², storage 16,000 m²		Bouwfonds MAB Ontw.	2006-2010
The Hague Scheveningen	Nautical Center	Hotel, offices 1,200 m², Commercial space 5,000 m², sailing center 1,200 m²		Fortis Vastgoed Ontwikkeling	2007
The Hague Southwest	Hoge Veld	New shopping center shops 6,700 m², residential 79 units		Bouwfonds MAB Ontwikkeling	2006
The Hague Ypenburg	Businesspark Ypenburg	New business park, 13 units	13,500	Kanters B.V.	n.a.
The Hague Ypenburg	Ypenburg	New residential development residential 11,000 units, total 6,000,000 m²		n.a.	2008
The Hague	Ypenburg-Centrumplan 4	New district center, parking 500 cars, residential 435 units, shops 11,000 m²		Rabo Vastgoed, Foruminvest	2006

More information: www.holland-re.com/projects

Ypenburg

Up until 2008, some 11,000 homes will be built on a 600-ha site in the district of Ypenburg, located between the municipalities of The Hague, Pijnacker-Nootdorp and Rijswijk. Future residents will be attracted to the neighborhood by its mix of space, natural surroundings and excellent array of facilities. The center of Ypenburg was developed by Foruminvest in collaboration with Rabo Vastgoed. The 15,000-m² shopping center will offer about 40 stores. Two beautifully designed parking garages have been realized under the building blocks.

Ypenburg Business Park comprises five quality business pavilions in a green park-like setting. All of the pavilions, developed by Kanters Projectontwikkeling, are equipped with an underground parking garage. The total floor space of the office buildings is 12,600 m². The individual buildings range from 1,900 to 3,400 m² and are very flexible in their arrangement. Depending on sales, construction can start as early as this year.

Leidschenveen

Forepark, located in The Hague along the A4 highway, will offer a mix of functions. The new stadium for ADO Den Haag soccer club (capacity 15,000

Hoge Veld: 2,050 homes to be finished in 2008.

The construction of the new ADO soccer stadium started in december 2005.

spectators) will be built here, as well as 20,000 m² of offices and 13,500 m² of retail/leisure. The project was commissioned by the City of The Hague, who will be contributing €33.5 million to its construction. Problems regarding the environmental permit have led to a slight delay in the plan's execution, and building only started at the end of 2005. For the long term (2017), the municipalities of The Hague and Leidschendam have plans to realize various large-scale office buildings (175,000 m²), housing (125,000 m²) and leisure facilities (100.000 m²) in the Forepark area.

The development area 's-Gravendreef borders Forepark. Heijmans IBC Vastgoed-ontwikkeling intends to realize seven office clusters at this location, the largest of which will have a floor space in excess of 16,000 m². The office buildings will be a few minutes' walk from the railway station and will each have their own underground parking garage. The design of the individual buildings has not yet been finalized. In total, the project comprises some 65,000 m² of office space. The first building might possibly be completed in early 2006.

Wateringse Veld

Wateringse Veld, a Vinex residential development located to the southwest of The Hague, is the planned site of 7,500 new homes for over 22,000 people. The largest sub-project still under construction is Hoge Veld (2,050 homes, to be finished in 2008). Bouwfonds MAB Ontwikkeling is developing a shopping center in the district. 't Hoge Veen will combine homes, shopping and various facilities including a daycare center, a library and a fitness center. The district center is marked by four towers that house 90 apartments and various other facilities. In addition, 't Hoge Veen will offer 23 city houses, two supermarkets, a department store and a number of specialist stores.　　《

MORE INFORMATION

Municipality of The Hague
City Planning Department

P.O. Box 12655
2500 DP The Hague
The Netherlands
Tel.: +31 70 353 46 11
Fax: +31 70 353 48 20
E-mail: so-econ@dso.denhaag,nl
Website: www.thehague.nl

ONLINE: www.holland-re.com/thehague

SPUIMARKT BECOMES

In recent years, the center of The Hague has been undergoing an overall transformation. The entire Spuimarkt project involves 53,000 m² of shops, hotels, restaurants and nightclubs, as well as 200 residences. The public areas will also undergo a full makeover. The new public transport brings nine million visitors to the center each year. As a result, The Hague will boast a core shopping area of international standing.

When the Spuimarkt area is complete, The Hague will boast a shopping boulevard, ranking internationally among thte best-known shopping streets. The Grote Marktstraat will be to The Hague what Las Ramblas is to Barcelona, the Meir to Antwerp and the Königsallee to Düsseldorf.

Retail chains

New retail formulas, the Pathé cinema, hotels, bars and restaurants, and the presence of major retail chains such as Bijenkorf, Hema, V&D and C&A should attract a large, diversified customer base. Zara has already opened a new shop in the former Marks & Spencer building. The first building complex of the Spuimarkt project will accommodate a nine-screen 2,300 seat Pathé multiplex theater, grand cafés and trend-setting shops. The multiplex cinema is entirely in keeping with the kind of entertainment facilities one expects to find in a modern urban center.

The Rabbijn Maarsenplein

The Rabbijn Maarsenplein will also feature a new apartment and

WORLD CLASS

shopping complex and become a social inner city magnet. When finished, the project as a whole will form a new dynamic entity.

New shopping area

The reknown architect Bernard Tschumi is working on plans to transform the buildings of Asta, V&D and the former building of Marks & Spencer into an entirely new shopping area. The redevelopment of this part of the Grote Marktstraat is well in line with the previously adopted urban plan. The aim is to increase the quality of the

shopping area by for instance attracting new retail formulas and integrating inviting entertainment facilities into the complex. The Spuimarkt will also accommodate two new arcades, one of which will be an H-shaped extension of the Haagsche Passage arcade to the Grote Marktstraat, and the other will be located near the Asta building. The arcades will be connected by a roofed passageway. There will be a direct connection to the new tram tunnel and apartments will be built on top of the shop. ≪

FACT SHEET

Spuimarkt, The Hague

Program:
- Retail: 40,000 m²
- Leisure: 13,000 m², of which 9,000 m² Pathé cinema
- Residential: 200 apartments
- Parking facilities: 500 parking places

Developer:
Ontwikkelingsmaatschappij Spuimarkt CV (Multi Development, BAM Vastgoed and ING Real Estate Development) in collaboration with the The Hague City Council.
Pathé Cinemas is developing the new multiplex theater.

Architects:
Bolles + Wilson, Claus en Kaan, Concrete, José Rafael Moneo & Alberto Nicolau and T+T Design

Investors:
ING Real Estate Investment Management, Fortis Vastgoed Beleggingen, Interpolis Vastgoed

Start construction:
November 2003

Completion:
Phased 2006 – 2010

More information:
ING Real Estate
P.O. Box 90463
2509 LL The Hague
The Netherlands
Tel.: +31 70 341 86 58
Fax: +31 70 341 87 00
Contact: Willem van der Ven
www.ingrealestate.com

Leasing agent for retail and leisure:
Cushman & Wakefield
www.cushmanwakefield.com
www.spuimarkt.nl

THE HAGUE

ONLINE: www.holland-re.com/spuimarkt

MULTI-PURPOSE COMPLEX IN STATION AREA

NEW BABYLON IN THE HAGUE

Bouwfonds Property Finance BV and Maeyveld BV have acquired the Babylon complex in The Hague. This complex is part of Den Haag Nieuw Centraal, an important development location in central The Hague.
Besides renovating the existing complex, the development of New Babylon involves expanding facilities with some 80,000 m² of new homes, offices, commercial spaces and parking facilities.

Plans include removing the current parking garage on the Anna van Buerenplein and replacing it with a new underground parking garage. The square will become an open pedestrian zone that gives access to the residential, retail, entertainment and professional facilities in New Babylon. The design by Amsterdam-based architectural firm Meyer en Van Schooten also outlines two residential towers of 140 m and 100 m respectively. New Babylon will be executed in phases. Construction on the underground parking garage below Anna van Buerenplein (960 spaces) will start the second half of 2006 and is scheduled for completion by the end of 2008. The first phase of New Babylon (approximately 14,000 m² of office space and 150 apartments) will kick off at the end of 2006

and will be completed by early 2009. The completion of the second phase is set for mid-2011. The arrival of the HSL high-speed rail link and RandstadRail will provide considerable impetus to the area around The Hague Central Station. The plan Den Haag Nieuw Centraal consists of five sub-projects, of which New Babylon and Anna van Buerenplein are two. New Babylon is located between The Hague Central Station, various ministry buildings, the Royal Library, the Rijksarchief national archive and the offices of KPN, NS and various other companies. The complex lies directly adjacent to the A12 highway. The renovated complex will have a strong presence in the area and transforms the current Babylon building's dark and closed-off environment into a light, open and airy complex. «

New Babylon, The Hague

Program:
- Renovation 21,000 m² of office space
- Renovation 12,000 m² of commercial space
- Accor-Sofitel five-star hotel
- New construction of 35,000 m² of office space
- New construction of 5,000 m² of retail
- New construction of approx. 330 apartments (50,000 m², divided over two residential towers of 140 m and 100 m respectively)
- Underground parking facilities (1,300 spaces)

Developer:
Babylon Den Haag BV (a joint venture of Maeyveld BV and Bouwfonds Property Finance BV)

Architect:
Meyer en Van Schooten Architecten BV

Completion:
- Construction of the underground parking garage (1,300 spaces): end of 2008
- First phase of New Babylon (14,000 m² of office space and 150 apartments): early 2009
- Second phase of New Babylon: mid-2011

More information:
Bouwfonds Property Finance B.V.
P.O. Box 15
3870 DA Hoevelaken
The Netherlands
Tel.: +31 33 253 91 10
Fax: +31 33 253 91 09
www.bouwfonds.nl

Maeyveld B.V.
Kingsfordsweg 201
1043 GR Amsterdam
The Netherlands
Tel.: +31 20 355 13 55
Fax: +31 20 355 13 33

THE HAGUE

ONLINE: www.holland-re.com/newbabylon

MANHATTAN ON THE MAAS
ROTTERDAM

Rotterdam is the Netherlands' preeminent high-rise city. Its bold and innovative architecture has earned the town international acclaim and given it its present modern and energetic image. In the tall buildings that dot Rotterdam's skyline, living and working are combined with a rich cultural offer located right in the heart of the city. Central Rotterdam now extends to both shores of the Maas river – the city's lifeline.

PHOTO: JAAP REIJNGOUD

Schouwburgplein in the center, surrounded by a multiplex cinema, theater, shops, bars and restaurants.

Rotterdam has developed to become a confident city with an international climate. For a long time, the city depended heavily on its world-famous seaport, but today commercial activity is dominated by business services. The Maas river is Rotterdam's lifeline. It offers an ideal backdrop for the luxury high-rise architecture that can be found at various locations along its shores.

Office space in Rotterdam totals some 3.6 million m². An important difference compared to other Dutch cities is that Rotterdam's office market can be characterized as a regionally orientated transfer market. A variety of large-scale new building plans are on the drawing board or currently under construction. This new construction is almost completely focused on the city center, with the exception of the new multifunctional district Fascinatio which is located on the A16 highway. In the short term, things don't appear too

bright for the office market. The older business parks in particular – with a mix of offices and businesses – are finding it difficult to compete with the new large-scale projects.

Indeed, the region has a sizeable planned reserve of over 1 million m². This may seem excessive, but with the correct planning and choice of location, disruption of the market can be avoided. In addition to Rotterdam's city

center, Brainpark III and, in the longer term, Rotterdam Airport are both promising office locations. As far as retail is concerned, there are no large projects in the pipeline for central Rotterdam. Attention has shifted to the redevelopment of old neighborhood centers in the surrounding districts. In addition, there are plans to build large-scale retail facilities on the edge of town, for example the Schieveste and Noordhelling projects. >>

PHOTO: BEN WIND FOTOGRAFIE

PHOTO: BEN WIND FOTOGRAFIE

Rotterdam expects 26 cruise ships to moor at the cruise terminal at the Kop van Zuid each year.

< *Hotel New York at the Kop van Zuid, the former HQ of the Holland-Amerika Lijn.*

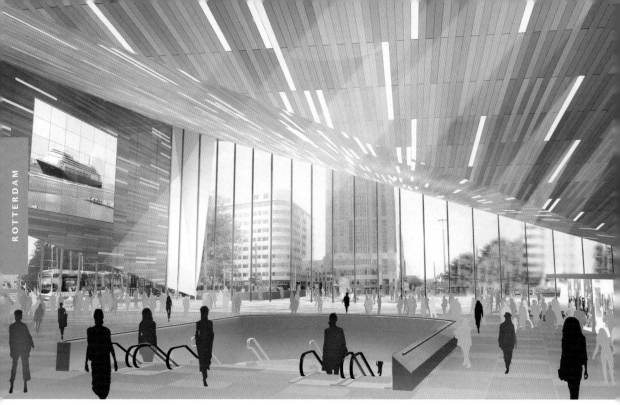

The new Central Station is probably the most striking renovation in the city center.

Rotterdam Central Station

Rotterdam Central Station, which was built in the 1950s, will undergo extensive renovations in the years ahead. Welcoming 140,000 visitors a day, Rotterdam Central Station processes as many passengers as the Schiphol mainport. The number of passengers that pass

Laurenshof by OVG Projectontwikkeling.

through Rotterdam Central Station is expected to virtually double within a period of 20 years, to 75 million per year. This has everything to do with the arrival of the HSL high-speed rail link in 2007 and RandstadRail, a light rail connection between Rotterdam and The Hague, in 2008. The station will gain a new station hall and a new subway station for RandstadRail, and the surrounding area will be subjected to a major overhaul. The redevelopment of Rotterdam Central has been commissioned by the Ministry for Housing, Regional Development and the Environment, the Ministry of Transport and Public Works, the NS railway company, Stadsregio Rotterdam and the City of Rotterdam. Together, the five parties have made a budget of €409 million available for the development of this ambitious project. The new Rotterdam Central Station building has

been designed by Team CS, a partnership of the famous Dutch firms of Benthem Crouwel Architecten, Meyer en Van Schooten Architecten and West 8 landscape architects. 2004 saw the start of preliminary operations. Construction of the new Rotterdam Central Station building started at the end of 2005/ the beginning of 2006.

The Rotterdam architect Wytze Patijn has drawn up a master plan for the areas to the south of the Hofplein. The skyscrapers (offices, apartments and leisure) will be placed in the second row behind the high street façades.

Laurenskwartier

By 2010, Rotterdam's oldest center, the Laurenskwartier – which is located in the eastern part of the city center – will be transformed into an attractive environment for living and business. It will offer lively squares with catering establishments and an abundance of green space.

PHOTO: ERASMUS MC

The new Erasmus Medical Center complex will have a total floor space of 300,000 m².

The Laurenskwartier is also the site of the BPF Bouwinvest project De Witte Keizer, a 70-meter-high tower that offers space for living, working and parking. The ground floor accommodates commercial space. De Witte Keizer has been designed by KCAP and was finished by the end of 2005.

One of the new projects in Laurenskwartier is the inner-city redevelopment Laurenshof, a project by OVG Project-ontwikkeling that includes 15,000 m² of offices, a 3,000 m² health center, 3,000 m² of stores and catering facilities, a residential tower with 115 apartments and a parking garage with approximately 250 spaces. Laurenshof has been designed by Kollhoff Architecten in collaboration with Rapp + Rapp. Construction on the Laurenshof started in the spring of 2005 and is an important step towards making the Laurenskwartier a lively central area.

Linea Nova

Linea Nova retail building, at the head of the Lijnbaan on Binnenwegplein, is being restored to its former glory by Janivo and Willemsen Minderman. Formerly occupied by the Ter Meulen department store, it originally consisted of three floors and has been repeatedly extended and modified over the last 50 years. The third floor and the roof will be transformed into a parking garage. Store space will be realized in the basement, first and second floor. The present fourth and fifth floors will be replaced by a 70-meter-high residential tower constructed on top of the third floor. The project will be completed in 2008.

Erasmus Medical Center

Over the next 15 years, the Erasmus Medical Center will be realizing a new medical center in the Rotterdam district of Hoboken. The complex will consist of seven building parts with a total floor space of 300,000 m². This will make the Erasmus Medical Center one of the largest buildings in the Netherlands. A large variety of medical and educational facilities will be housed here. Construction of the complex is expected to take some 10 years. >>

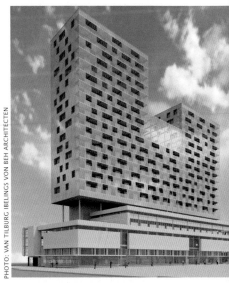

PHOTO: VAN TILBURG IBELINGS VON BEH ARCHITECTEN

Linea Nova (Janivo and Willemsen Minderman).

PHOTO: DAM&PARTNERS ARCHITECTEN AMSTERDAM

De Coopvaert residential tower, by Dura Bouw and Ballast Nedam.

Blaakhaven

Between 2005 and 2008, some 85 apartments, offices, stores, catering facilities, a hotel and parking garage will be realized in the Blaakhaven. The first project undertaken by NS Vastgoed is a 70-meter-high residential tower called Wijnhaeve. Construction started in 2005. Opposite Blaak railway station, developer Sterner Groep will be realizing the residential building The Red Apple. The building will offer 201 apartments and is set for completion by 2007.

De Coopvaert

The city square Plein 1940 is the site of a new development by Dura Bouw Rotterdam and Ballast Nedam called De Coopvaert. This luxury residential tower is based on a design by the firm of Dam & Partners. The first seven floors will hold

residential facilities, commercial units and offices (totaling 2,000 m^2). The top 20 floors have been reserved for the building's spacious apartments. According to plans, the residential tower will be completed by 2006.

Hoog aan de Maas

The development of the city's waterfront does not fail to amaze its inhabitants, as well as visitors to Rotterdam. The Hoog aan de Maas residential tower is currently being constructed over the former building of the Dutch central bank. It is a spectacular feat of architecture that will preserve the existing historically-listed bank building within its structure. The new office building of Ernst & Young is located adjacent to this tower. Both buildings will be approximately 75 meters high.

Wijnhaveneiland

Work on the continuing transformation of Wijnhaveneiland into a quality residential neighborhood is progressing. To date, three of the Waterstad Towers – developed by ING Real Estate Development and De Wilgen Vastgoed – have been completed. Another eye-catcher is the elegant Scheepmakerstoren. This slender luxury residential tower, completed in 2005, is 96 meters high and has 28 floors. The Scheepmakerstoren is a development by SOL Design & Development.

Hoog aan de Maas, constructed over the former Dutch Central Bank.

PHOTO: EPPO NOTENBOOM

The Wijnhaveneiland with the Waterstad Towers. The building site of Hoog aan de Maas is situated on the riverbank.

Baankwartier

The development of Baan-
kwartier – located behind the
Schiedamse Dijk – into a lively
urban environment involves the
construction of various independent residential towers. The
towers will be approximately
100 m in height. The plan was
developed by Fortis Vastgoed in
collaboration with 24H
Architecture and BBW Realtors
& Surveyors. A total of 1,100
homes will be realized in this
project, as well as 60,000 m²
of facilities.

The Red Apple

In December 2005, construction
of The Red Apple started at the
Wijnhaven. The project consists
of a 126-meter-high residential
tower, a car park and a mixed-
use building which seems to
hover above the other parts. >>

Residential towers to be constructed in the Baankwartier.   The Red Apple (KCAP Architects/Jan des Bouvrie).

PHOTO: JOOP VAN REIKEN

Montevideo, on the Kop van Zuid, was officially opened in December 2005 by the Mayor of Rotterdam, Ivo Opstelten.

Kop van Zuid

The Wilhelminapier plays a leading role in the developments at the Kop van Zuid. With Hotel New York, the Luxor Theater, the cruise terminal and the KPN building, the pier is one of the foremost locations to showcase the ambitions of city government. Furthermore, plans are at an advanced stage regarding the as yet undeveloped plots on the Wilhelminapier.

De Rotterdam, a development by Bouwfonds MAB Ontwikkeling, is perhaps the most remarkable

example of these projects. This multifunctional complex has been designed by architect Rem Koolhaas. He conceived a 'vertical city', stretching to a height of 135 m, where one will find shopping and leisure facilities (5,000 m²), offices (40,000 m²), homes (260 apartments) and a hotel (20,000 m², 260 rooms). A large public hall provides access to the building's various functions. Construction is expected to start by the end of 2005.

Another prominent building

on the Wilhelminapier, situated next to Hotel New York, is Montevideo. This trend-setting living, working and leisure concept is a development by ING Vastgoed. The 151-m-high building consists of 192 homes, 6,000 m² of offices and 2,000 m² of retail and catering facilities. One of the eye catchers of the Kop van Zuid will be the 227-meter-high Maastoren. This OVG project is still in an early stage of development. The building has mixed functions: 35,000 m² of office space, 125 homes and a parking garage.

Southern side developments

Vesteda Project will be developing five residential towers with a height between 70 and 155 meters on the southern side of the Wilhelminapier. These towers will provide space for around 900 luxury rental and privately-owned apartments with an average floor space of 175 m². There is also room for 950 parking spaces. One tower, named New Orleans (adjacent to Montevideo), has been designed by the Portuguese architect Àlvaro Siza; the other towers are named Boston, Chicago, Philadelphia and Havana (next to the Luxor Theater) and are designs of Spanish architects Cruz y Ortiz.

The first apartments will be ready by early 2008. The total project is expected to be completed in 2011.

Lloydkwartier

The demise of harbor activities in central Rotterdam created the opportunity to draw up a new plan for the former port areas of Parkhaven, Jobshaven and Schiehaven. This area, which was given the name Lloydkwartier, will be developed

Overview of new and already realized high-rise buildings on the Kop van Zuid.

mainly for living, working and leisure. It will feature 1,750 to 2,000 homes, a large proportion of which are fitted with work units. There will also be nearly 70,000 m² of facilities, including an area for sports and events and a large number of entertainment facilities. The Lloydkwartier has been divided into five sub-areas, each with its own distinctive character: the Entreegebied (living and working), the Müller-pier (living), the Lloydpier (living), the Lloyd Multiplein (leisure) and Schiehaven-Noord (living and working).

Katendrecht

In the near future, some 1,250 new homes will be constructed in the district of Katendrecht next to the Kop van Zuid. Some 13,000 m² will be made available for businesses, offices and other facilities. Real estate developer Volker Wessels Vastgoed, BOA Bouwmanagement en Strategie, the Dutch Chinese Foundation and the City of Rotterdam are working together on the realization of a European Chinese Center (ECC) in Katendrecht. This 80,000-m² complex, located near the entrance to the peninsula, is expected to be completed in 2006. The building will not only house businesses, homes and leisure facilities, but will also feature a Chinese roof garden and a reception hall. The project entails an investment of approx. €150 million.   >>

The Müllerpier in the Lloydkwartier.   *A total of more than 2,000 new homes will be built on Katendrecht.*

Plans for Rotterdam Airport now strive to offer an attractive mix of travel, accommodation and business (200,000 m² of offices

Rotterdam Airport

Rotterdam Airport is not only the western Netherlands' premier regional airport, it is also developing into a modern urban hub. In the coming years one of the most innovative business locations of the Netherlands will be realized here. More than was the case in the past, plans for Rotterdam Airport now strive to offer an attractive mix of travel, accommodation and business in the area. The airport is owned by the Netherlands' largest airport, Schiphol. Working in collaboration with airport management,

Schiphol Real Estate has formulated a comprehensive landscape and urban planning outlook that deals with the future development and arrangement of commercial real estate at Rotterdam Airport. The agencies of EGM Architecten and Paul van Beek Landschappen have been closely involved in the procedure.
The master plan outlines high-quality office and business accommodation, housed in striking modern architecture.
The range of business activity that will be found in these buildings is in line with the location's

image of business airport. The total development will comprise approximately 200,000 m² of office and commercial buildings, a hotel, 2,000 m² of catering facilities and ample parking space. Construction on the project will be carried out in phases.

Business park Rotterdam Airport

The plan defines three locations in the airport area, which will be developed in phases. Together, the Entrance Area, Airport Square and the Business Cluster form the business park. The site will be redeveloped into a remarkable area with a city-style entrance, a boulevard, a square, offices, a hotel, green space and parking facilities.
The Entrance Area will have a concentration of modern quality pavilion-like office buildings offering approximately 1,500 m² of space. This is the area where construction will start first. In addition to accommodating the surrounding office buildings, the

High quality business park at the Entrance Area and Airport Square.

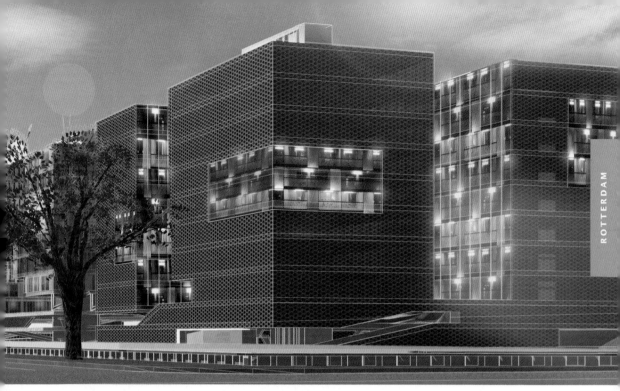

and commercial buildings), a hotel, 2,000 m² of catering facilities and ample parking.

central square will be laid out as a park & ride area. This includes short-term parking facilities and catering and commercial functions. Buildings on Airport Square will house 55,000 m² of office space, 30,000 m² of commercial space, a 400-room hotel and 2,000 m² of catering facilities. The buildings can range in size to a maximum of approximately 12,000 m².

The Business Cluster is located on the western and southern sides of the airport. The flexible office and commercial buildings located in this area will offer room for activities that require more space. The area is located at a short distance from the platforms, and will be fitted with a new infrastructure in order to provide modern and efficient accommodation for businesses with logistic and distribution functions. The Business Cluster comprises approximately 12,000 m² of office space, 80,000 m² of business space and ample parking space.

Park Zestienhoven

Living, working and relaxing in natural surroundings. The municipal master plan stipulates that the project is to be realized in phases. Building commences in 2006 and is set for completion by 2015. The first phase of Park Zestienhoven consists of some 600 predominantly low-rise homes in low-density arrangements. The second phase will offer a mixed residential environment, with approximately 900 apartments, ground-floor homes and single-family dwellings that are located along

canals and avenues. Some 43,000 m² of business space will be developed adjacent to Rotterdam Airport.
Hoog Zestienhoven will potentially be the site of various office and commercial buildings. However, this development depends on the construction of the RandstadRail station Meijersplein (completion in 2008), and the institution of an HSL shuttle. The realization of these transport junctions will have an effect on the future building density in this district. >>

PHOTO: EPPO NOTENBOOM

On the runway at Rotterdam Airport there is room for even the largest passenger aircraft.

Location	Project	Rotterdam / Projects 2006 and beyond. Program	Development	Planning
Rotterdam	Ahoy	New development, offices 20,000 m² hotel 174 rooms, parking 200-250 cars	BAM Vastgoed Ballast Nedam Bouw en Ontwikkeling B.V.	2006
Rotterdam	Brainpark III	New business park , offices 80,000 m²	Ontwikkelings Bedrijf Rotterdam William Properties B.V	2006
Rotterdam	De Veranda	New development, residential 1,200 units parking 2,500 cars, commercial facilities 40,000 m²	Multi Development	n.a.
Rotterdam	European Chinese Center	New development offices and residential 80,000 m² investment €150 mln	Volker Wessels Vastgoed City of Rotterdam BOA Bouwmanagement en Strategie The Dutch Chinese Foundation	2006
Rotterdam	Grote Beer	Office development 40,000 m²	OVG Projectontwikkeling Multi Development	2007
Rotterdam	Katendrecht	New development companies, offices and facilities 13,000 m² residential 1,250 units	n.a.	n.a.
Rotterdam	Kralingse Zoom	Redevelopment area, offices 117,000 m² parking 2,100 cars, 3,000 m²	City of Rotterdam Blauwhoed B.V.	2016
Rotterdam	Park Zestienhoven	New development residential 1,400-1,950 units, offices, companies and facilities 250,000 m²	City of Rotterdam	n.a.
Rotterdam	Lloydpier	New development, companies 65,000 m² residential 1,750 units, investment €180 mln	Van der Looy Projektmanagement B.V.	2006
Rotterdam	Parkhavengebied	New development, offices 55,000 m² residential 573 units, 105,000 m² parking 2,400 cars, leisure 45,000 m², facilities 14,000 m²	Merwede Groep Ballast Nedam Bouw en Ontwikkeling B.V.	n.a.
Rotterdam	Rotterdam Airport business park	New business park, offices 80,000 m²	Rotterdam Airport Vastgoed B.V. Schiphol Real Estate Rotterdam Airport	2010
Rotterdam	Stadskantoor	New office building 65,000 m²	OntwikkelingsBedrijf Rotterdam	2008
Rotterdam	Lloydkwartier	New residential development 1,175 units	Blauwhoed B.V Multi Development	2007
Rotterdam	Zuidplein	Shopping development 9,700 m²	ING Real Estate Development	n.a.
Rotterdam Center	Blaak-Haven	New development, offices 18,000 m² residential 100 units commercial space 3,000 m²	Blauwhoed B.V., NS Vastgoed	n.a.
Rotterdam Center	Central Station	Redevelopment city center, offices 200,000 m² residential 195,000 m², parking 5,000 cars leisure 121,000 m², total 641,000 m²	City of Rotterdam NS Vastgoed, Rodamco ING Real Estate Development	2013
Rotterdam Center	Coolsingel Tower	New office building 40,000 m² residential 106 units, parking 500 cars total 62,000 m², investment €220 mln	Bouwfonds MAB Ontwikkeling BPF Bouwinvest, Willemsen-Minderman Vastgoedontwikkeling B.V.	2006
Rotterdam Center	De Coopvaert	New residential complex residential 57 units, facilities 2,000 m²	Dura Bouw Ballast Nedam Bouw en Ontwikkeling B.V.	2006
Rotterdam Center	EuroBuilding	New office building, shops 10,000 m² residential 72 units, parking 400 cars offices 45,000 m²	Bouwfonds MAB Ontwikkeling Merwede Groep	2006
Rotterdam Center	Wijnhaveneiland	New development residential 140 units, parking 330 cars total 35,000 m², investment €70 mln	Sterner Groep B.V Woningcorporatie PWS	n.a.
Rotterdam-Kop van Zuid	De Rotterdam	New office building 40,000 m², shops 1,000 m² residential 260 units, 36,000 m², parking 600 cars 25,000 m², hotel 20,000 m², sports 4,000 m²	Bouwfonds MAB Ontwikkeling	2008
Rotterdam-Kop van Zuid	Kop van Zuid	New development, offices 400,000 m² companies 35,000 m², residential 5,300 units, leisure 30,000 m², education 30,000 m²	various	1990-2010
Rotterdam-Kop van Zuid	New Orleans & Havanna, Boston, Chicago, Philadelphia	New development residential 900 units, parking 950 cars facilities 18,000 m², total 200,000 m², investment €340 mln	Vesteda	2008-2012
Rotterdam-Kop van Zuid	Zuidplein	Shopping development 9,700 m²	ING Real Estate Development	n.a.
Rotterdam-Periphery	Nesselande	New district center, shops 7,000 m² residential 700 units, leisure 3,000 m², facilities 3,000 m²	Multi Development	2007
Rotterdam-Periphery	Nesselande	New residential development residential 4,750 units	Bouwfonds MAB Ontwikkeling	2007
Rotterdam-Periphery	Nesselande	New development residential 815 units	Bouwfonds MAB Ontwikkeling	n.a.
Rotterdam-Periphery	Noorderhelling	New development, offices 12,500 m² GDV 15,000 m², parking 1,500 cars mobility center 50,600 m², total 75,000 m²	Fortis Vastgoed Ontwikkeling BAM Vastgoed	2007

More information: www.holland-re.com/projects

Ahoy' offices

BAM Vastgoed and Ballast Nedam are developing two quality office buildings and a 174-room hotel in the close vicinity of the Ahoy' events center in Rotterdam Zuid. The buildings will offer 20,000 m² of office space. The project will be realized by the start of 2006.

Noorderhelling Mobiliteitscentrum

Fortis Vastgoedontwikkeling and HBG Vastgoed have joined forces to develop the Noorderhelling site in Rotterdam. Noorderhelling, which is located in the vicinity of De Kuip Stadium, covers an area of approximately 75,000 m². The total concept offers everything in the way of mobility and leisure activity. Building is expected to commence in the course of 2005, and the developers will most likely complete the center in 2007.

Brainpark III + Fascinatio

To the west of Fascinatio – a new 45-ha housing development on the edge of Rotterdam and Capelle aan den IJssel – the Rotterdam Development Corporation (OBR) is realizing the Brainpark III office site, a follow-up to the successes of Brainpark I and II. Brainpark III, which is approximately 10 hect-

The Ahoy' offices and hotel at the edge of the Zuiderpark (20,000 m² of office space and 174 rooms).

ares in size, comprises a total of some 80,000 m² of new office space. The completion of the final plans for Brainpark III is scheduled for 2006.

Vierhavensstrip

The former switchyard Vierhavensstrip, owned by the Rotterdam Development Corporation (OBR) and located in the West Rotterdam neighborhood of Delfshaven, will be redeveloped by Dura Vermeer Vastgoed, Fortis Vastgoed Ontwikkeling and OBR. The project involves the development of 45,000 m² of business space at ground level. An elevated city park of approximately three ha will be developed on top of this structure, at a height of some eight meters.

Nesselande

Multi Development is currently developing a district center for the new neighborhood of Nesselande in the northeast of Rotterdam, which will cover an area of 13,000 m². Nesselande will eventually offer 4,750 homes for 14,000 people, as well as a business park located on the edge of the A20 highway. The Nesselande business park will have a size of roughly 15 ha. Nesselande will also gain an entirely new shopping center of approximately 7,000 m², which will be developed by Multi Development. The shopping center is expected to open in the spring of 2007. Bouwfonds MAB Development is responsible for the development of 4,750 homes for 14,000 people.   ≪

Nesselande will eventually house 4,700 homes. Completion: 2007.

MORE INFORMATION

Rotterdam Development Corporation

P.O. Box 6575
3002 AN Rotterdam
The Netherlands
Tel.: +31 10 489 36 85
Fax: +31 10 489 71 49
E-mail: r.jongste@obr.rotterdam.nl
Website: www.obr.rotterdam.nl
Ms. M.J. Jongste

ONLINE: www.holland-re.com/rotterdam

ROTTERDAM IDENTITY

Pier 112 combines a maritime environment with big-city facilities. Five office buildings will be erected at a location on the western side of the Van Brienenoord Bridge – nearest Rotterdam – offering a fine view of the Nieuwe Maas waterway. Rotterdam city center and the Kralingse Zoom transport hub can both be reached from the location within 10 minutes. Pier 112's location and its conceptual architecture make it a unique project that provides users with a one-of-a-kind setting for their business.

Pier 112, the former site of the Schelde-Rademakers cog factory, consists of five three-story buildings and is a development by Beleggingsmaatschappij Schaardijk. The property, which offers an open view of the river, is characterized by the extensive use of glass, steel and wood. This, in combination with its location on the Nieuwe Maas, lends the project maritime distinctiveness. Users of the office buildings will have an impressive view of the busy Nieuwe Maas waterway. Decks constructed at various levels between the buildings allow the tenants to enjoy the atmosphere both indoors and outside.

Quality finish

Pier 112 has a quality finish: the multifunctional office building will be easily recognized from the Van Brienenoord Bridge, thanks to the use of polished ornamental concrete combined with steel and

OF PIER 112

FACT SHEET

Pier 112, Rotterdam

Program:
Pier 112, located between Rotterdam's western edge of the Van Brienenoord Bridge and the city's nature area De Esch, comprises five office buildings with a total floor space of 24,264 m².
- Building I (Dok I):   3,640 m²
- Building II (Dok II):   3,837 m²
- Building III (Dok III):   3,837 m²
- Building IV (Dok IV):   3,640 m²
- Building V (Dok V):   9,310 m²

A further expansion of the plan area by approx. 6,520 m² is possible. Another unique aspect of the location is its parking ratio of 1 to 40.

Developer:
D3M, Rotterdam

Commissioned by:
Beleggingsmaatschappij Schaardijk, Rotterdam

Architect:
Ir. R.B. Ligteringen bna, Rotterdam

More information:
Beleggingsmaatschappij Schaardijk bv
Weena 263
3013 AL Rotterdam
The Netherlands
Tel.: + 31 10 242 02 14
E-mail: info@pier112.nl
www.pier112.nl
Contact: Cees J.A. Helmons

ROTTERDAM

PIER 112

wood. In total some 24,000 m² of office space will become available, with four buildings offering 3,600 to 3,800 m² and the fifth having a floor space in excess of 9,000 m². The location's parking ratio of 1 to 40 further strengthens its unique character.

Accessibility

Pier 112 has excellent accessibility, both from the A16 highway and the Schaardijk/Maasboulevard. There is a direct connection with the Kralingse Zoom subway station via the automated People Mover. Furthermore, the Schaardijk has a five-minute bus connection with the Kralingse Zoom public transport hub.

The City of Rotterdam has committed itself to collaborating on a new, unique and innovative public transport plan. This plan includes amongst others the realization of a heliport and public transport over water. «

UNIQUE CONCEPT AT KOP VAN ZUID IN ROTTERDAM

MONTEVIDEO: CREATING HIGH RISE

The combination of residential, employment, leisure and entertainment facilities in one building had never before been adopted in the Netherlands. That is until now. ING Real Estate has developed a unique and highly ambitious project in both a conceptual and practical sense: Montevideo.

Montevideo is the centerpiece of Kop van Zuid, an atmospheric and evocative development area on the south bank of the Maas river. The building, rising up more than 150 meters from the Wilhelmina Pier, contains 192 exclusive apartments, a health club, and offices. There is room for restaurant facilities on the lower floors, with terraces along the water's edge. The transparent design, the choice of exclusive materials and the unique architecture of Mecanoo Architects, which uses playful and transformative façades, clearly demonstrate that this is a most unusual project.

More choice, better living

ING Real Estate was able to respond effectively to market changes with the Montevideo project. The variety of luxury apartments with names such as Sky, Loft, City and Water possess a range of features that include high ceilings and spacious sunrooms, balconies and loggias. The ING Optimal Living concept allows residents ultimate freedom to design the apartment layout themselves. This has been developed in response to the consumer's increasing need for flexibility. The apartments can also be equipped with domotica (home automation).

Complex high-rises

Multifaceted buildings are one of ING Real Estate's specialties. The Municipality of Rotterdam, ING Real Estate Development, Mecanoo Architects and Besix B.V. worked in close harmony to achieve this result. Throughout, ING Real Estate never compromised on the high level of ambition, examined all of the difficulties from a number of perspectives and then quite simply found a solution. In the near future, the development of the Baltimore office building and Chicago congress center and hotel will start on the Kop van Zuid. ≪

PHOTO: JOOP VAN REEKEN

Montevideo, Rotterdam

Program:

Residences:	192 apartments
Offices:	6,000 m²
Leisure facilities:	Fitness room, an Excellent Health Club and a swimming pool
Catering facilities:	1,800 m² catering establishments
Parking facilities:	273 spaces

Developer:
ING Real Estate Development

Investor:
Vesteda (rental apartments)

Partners:
Municipality of Rotterdam

Architects:
Mecanoo Architecten – Francine Houben

Contractor:
Besix B.V.

Start of construction:
Fall 2002

Completion:
Completion of first apartments in 2005

More information:
www.montevideorotterdam.nl

Residential:
www.atta.nl
(Tel.: +31 10 433 57 10)
www.ooms.com
(Tel.: +31 10 424 88 88)

Office:
www.demik.nl
(Tel.: +31 10 453 03 03)
www.joneslonglasalle.nl
(Tel.: +31 10 411 04 40)

Leisure:
www.adhoc-horecamakelaars.nl
(Tel.: +31 18 253 33 55)

ONLINE www.holland-re.com/montevideo

ROTTERDAM

MODERN RETAIL IN LEGENDARY DEPARTMENT STORE

LINEA NOVA IN

The retail building De Grote Lijn, the former home of the Ter Meulen department store at the corner of Rotterdam's Binnenwegplein and Lijnbaan, will be completely overhauled in the near future. This historic site will gain an attractive modern residential building and a new shopping center. The renovated building will house a range of separate retail units. An apartment complex of no fewer than 16 stories will be constructed on top of the original building. Linea Nova promises to become an impressive structure and a lively meeting point in the area.

Based on a plan by architectural firm Van Tilburg en partners, Willemsen Minderman Projectontwikkeling decided, together with the achitect, to restore the original design by Van den Broek and Bakema to its former glory.
This means tearing down approximately 4,400 m² of unprofitable retail space added in the 1970s, in order to reveal the 'monument of Dutch modernism' erected in 1948.
The construction, which was inspired by American examples,

was a revolutionary design in its day. The façade of the new retail building will be virtually identical to the original façade.

The stores on the first floor can be accessed from Binnenwegplein and the Lijnbaan shopping street. The interior arrangement of the building is designed to suit modern demands – smaller stores with their own entrances and an internal staircase leading to the second floor and the basement. Some 8,500 m² of retail space will be realized, divided among

ROTTERDAM

F A C T   S H E E T

Linea Nova, Rotterdam

Program:
- 8,500 m² of retail space
- 105 apartments
- parking garage (150 spaces)

Developer: Willemsen Minderman Projectontwikkeling, Capelle aan den IJssel

Project management: Objectum Bouwadvies & Procesmanagement, Capelle aan den IJssel

Owner: De Grote Lijn vastgoed bv, Zeist

Architect: Van Tilburg en partners, Rotterdam

Structural engineering: DHV Bouw en Industrie BV, Rotterdam

Building commences: second quarter of 2006

Completion:
- stores: second half of 2007
- homes: mid-2008

More information:
Willemsen Minderman
Projectontwikkeling bv
P.O. Box 5048
2900 EA Capelle aan den IJssel
The Netherlands
Tel.: +31 10 442 39 49
Fax: +31 10 451 52 31
E-mail: info@wilmin.nl
www.willemsenminderman.nl

the basement and the first and second floors. Several of the retail formulas currently located in the building will remain open throughout the renovation.

The plan also includes an apartment complex, which will be erected on top of the building's existing structure. This complex will have an open appearance. The exterior of the residential building will consist of a glass skin covering a wood-lined facade. The residents will also have access to a rooftop garden offering a splendid view of central Rotterdam. The homes, which will all feature a spacious loggia, can be reached via four central elevators and a walkway. The residential complex will house 105 apartments, with parking facilities for the residents located on the third floor of the original building. These can be reached via three car elevator systems. Linea Nova's retail units will be completed in the second half of 2007, with construction on the apartments lasting until mid-2008. ≪

ONLINE: www.holland-re.com/lineanova

THE TRANSFORMATION OF

ROTTERDAM

Katendrecht in Rotterdam is the scene of an extraordinary transformation. Over the next decades a total of more than 2,000 new homes will be built on this peninsula and supplemented with urban facilities. In 1997, the municipality selected Bouwfonds MAB Ontwikkeling as a partner for the first housing development on the Tweede Katendrechtse Haven. The project has now been completed and the parties involved look back on a successful collaboration with an extraordinary result.

A century ago, Katendrecht was a rural village for those financially well-off. This village disappeared as a result of the construction of the Rhine and Maas Ports. The well-to-do made way for dockworkers. Surrounded by harbor master's offices, the illustrious Katendrecht working-class area was born. The port subsequently moved towards the sea and this marked the district's decline, resulting in a bad image.

Master Plan

At the end of the nineties, the municipality of Rotterdam drew up a Master Plan for the peninsula. The Master Plan describes a combination of houses, recreational functions and a lot of greenery, parks, quays and a beach. In short, Katendrecht is undergoing a transformation into a new and modern residential environment as part of the Kop van Zuid. Accessibility has greatly improved due to the construction of the Erasmusbrug and

KATENDRECHT

F A C T S H E E T

Katendrecht, Rotterdam

Program:
244 owner-occupied housing,
consisting of:
- 63 affordable houses (€86,000)
- 91 non-subsidized owner-occupied
  houses on ground level
  (from €200,000 to €590,000)
- 90 non-subsidized apartments
  (from €200,000 to €590,000)
- 133 covered parking spaces

Developer:
Bouwfonds MAB Ontwikkeling in close
cooperation with the Nieuwe Unie
housing corporation and the municipality of Rotterdam

Architects:
Maccreanor-Lavington architects
(ground level houses) and Dobbelaar de
Kovel de Vroom architects (the block of
apartment buildings)

Investment: Approximately €42 mln

Start of construction: 2000

Completion: 2004

More information:
Bouwfonds MAB Ontwikkeling
P.O. Box 15
3870 DA Hoevelaken
The Netherlands
Tel.: +31 33 253 97 00
Fax: +31 33 253 96 85
E-mail: ontwikkeling@bouwfonds.nl
www.bouwfonds.nl

ROTTERDAM

the high-urban implementation of the Wilhelminapier.

Urban development

By completing the subproject Tweede Katendrechtse Haven, Bouwfonds MAB Ontwikkeling has demonstrated its great ambitions. The basic principles from the Master Plan have found their place: permanent urban development, efficient use of space, high density, a varied program and low-traffic streets. In total, 244 houses have been constructed.

The scale of the buildings fits within the urban context, respecting its cultural-historical basis. The transparency and visibility lines connect the inner area and the river. The houses have been designed to surround a square with greenery, ensuring the physical link between the existing and new houses. The plan contains a unique price-quality ratio and was awarded the highest recognition by the jury for the Rotterdam construction quality prize both in 2002 and 2004. ≪

ONLINE: www.holland-re.com/katendrecht

BUILDING NEW CITY CENTERS
UTRECHT

Utrecht is expanding, particularly towards the west of the city center. In time, the new district of Leidsche Rijn Centrum will increase the city's population by another 80,000. In the meantime, Utrecht's station area, which links up the old and new inner-city neighborhoods and the adjacent Hoog Catharijne shopping center, will be renovated on a grand scale.

BOOTJE VAREN
BIERTJE DRINKEN
0641-211606

The flower market on the Janskerkhof, one of the attractions in the historic city center of Utrecht.

PHOTO: UTRECHTS ARCHIEF

Utrecht

A characteristic feature of Utrecht's economic structure is the relatively large role played by the creative industries (media, art and design). This is good news, as employment in cities with a large proportion of creative professionals generally sees stronger growth than elsewhere. Furthermore, Utrecht is a very attractive place of residence, second only to Amsterdam. The city scores particularly well in the areas of higher education, culture and the close proximity of nature. Another of the town's merits is its relatively easy accessibility.

Within the Netherlands, you can hardly get any more central than Utrecht, making the town an attractive business location for companies. The supply of office space has expanded considerably in recent years. New construction is very popular. In Papendorp, Lage Weide and Kanaleneiland,

for instance, planned office developments have a total size of nearly 300,000 m², mainly situated in Leidsche Rijn Centrum, Papendorp and the Stationsgebied (the area surrounding the station). Moreover, satellite towns like Nieuwegein and Houten are feeling the impact of Utrecht's increased popularity.

The expansion of the renovated Hoog Catharijne shopping mall and the center of Leidsche Rijn will prove major impulses for future developments. The demand for shopping space in the core retail area shows no sign of relenting. Property rarely stays vacant for long. Two interestingly designed centers for large-scale retail trade are currently under construction along the A2 highway. Both buildings are elongated, futuristic structures that double as sound screens for the area behind them.

There is a considerable housing

shortage in Utrecht. Homes are usually only on the market for a short time. The portion of privately owned homes in the Utrecht housing stock, however, is steadily increasing. >>

PHOTO: UTRECHTS ARCHIEF

Well-maintained monastery gardens offer a quiet place for relaxation.

PHOTO: UTRECHTS ARCHIEF

< The Winkel van Sinkel is seated in a Neo-classical building from 1839. Nowadays the former shop is a very trendy cafe/restaurant.

In the next five years the area around the central station will become a new urban center.

Stationsgebied

After years of debate, in 2007 work will finally start on the area surrounding Utrecht's railway station. The number of passengers that go through Utrecht Central Station is expected to double in the next 20 years reaching a figure of some 100 million passengers per year. The present building cannot handle these volumes. The accommodation of central functions in the Stationsgebied will lead to the creation of a new urban center that relieves and complements the old town center. The 90,000 m²

New environment surrounding the Hoog Catharijne shopping mall.

Hoog Catharijne shopping center will be transformed into a modern connection between the old city and the new central functions on the west side of town (Jaarbeursterrein). City government will be responsible for coordinating affairs, with the most important partners being developer Corio (owner of Hoog Catharijne), NS Vastgoed and the Jaarbeurs convention center. The plan area covers no less than 90 ha. Developments include 204,000 m² of new office space, 63,000 m² of leisure, 45,000 m² of retail space, 33,500 m² of cultural facilities and 2,320 homes. Key elements in the new set up are the Stationsgebied's two main routes. The Centrumboulevard is an elevated thoroughfare connecting Vredenburg Square to Hoog Catharijne and the railway station. It descends to ground level at Jaarbeursplein and ends at the Merwedekanaal. The second route, the Stadscorridor, forms a traffic connection between the Vredenburg area

and the western side of central Utrecht. Sub-projects include Plein Vredenburg, Hoog Catharijne, the railway station and the Jaarbeursterrein. The plan area covers some 90 ha, with public investment totaling €1 billion (paid by the city of Utrecht – predominately – by the Dutch government), and private investment of some €2 to €3 billion. The City is expected to locate new council offices (57,500 m²) in the area, which will further speed up local development. Virtually all sub-projects will be completed by mid-2011, with only the construction of Westpleintunnel taking longer.

Public transport terminal

The new railway station will serve as a logical hub for a variety of public transport flows. The integrated station complex will process all incoming train, tram and bus traffic (both local, regional and international) within a single building. A light, spacious hall with an undulating

The public transport terminal will serve as a logical hub for a variety of public transport flows.

roof construction will be built over the platforms. The stores in the station hall will be situated in a long glass-walled strip along the northern side of the building. A number of new office developments are planned for the western side of the station. Construction on the new terminal is expected to start in 2008 and will be rounded off by 2011. The City of Utrecht will sign an agreement with NS Vastgoed (owner of the property) as soon as the design has been finalized. The Dutch government will provide the necessary funds – estimated at approx. €250 mln.

Muziekpaleis

At present, three cultural institutes in Utrecht are dealing with housing problems. Muziekcentrum Vredenburg lacks a decent hall for chamber music, the Tivoli music venue is responsible for noise pollution in the area and needs room to expand, and Stichting Jazz Utrecht (SJU) is facing the end of its current lease. Herman Hertzberger, architect of the present Vredenburg building, has been commissioned by the City of Utrecht to design a shared accommodation for the three institutes. It will be located on Vredenburgplein. The main hall of the music center will be retained and four new spaces will be built that provide another 20,000 m². In addition, 20,000 m² around Vredenburgplein have been reserved for retail. The square, which will still offer at least 6,000 m² of free space, will be surrounded on four sides by buildings. The compact design allows for the construction of retail space, as well as some 100 homes located above the stores. The Muziekpaleis has several external functions on the ground floor, including catering facilities and escalator connections. These will lead visitors to a square located within the building at a level of some 18 m. Renovation activities will last until the end of 2009.

Jaarbeursterrein

The planned construction on the premises of the Jaarbeurs convention center will involve building a luxury 250-room hotel (29,000 m²) with homes constructed overhead, a new Holland Casino, offices and a multiplex cinema. The 18 theaters of the present design will be elevated via a needle structure, freeing up space for meeting and catering functions and so on. Building commences in the first half of this year, and is set for completion by mid-2007. »

Herman Hertzberger has designed the Muziekpaleis on the Catharijnesingel.

The historic harbor of Parkhaven (opening spring 2006).

The Kanaleneiland Center Area Renovation

Parkhaven

The new residential neighborhood of Parkhaven will offer an abundance of space, greenery and car-free zones. The area is situated between Merwedekanaal and Croeselaan to the south of the Jaarbeurs and will feature homes in a style typical of the 1930s. The neighborhood's focal point will be its historic harbor with the berth of the Utrechtse Statenjacht. The project is a collaboration between the City of Utrecht, Bouwfonds MAB Ontwikkeling, Fortis and BPF-Bouwinvest. Some 1,000 homes will be built here in the period until 2008, as well as a harbor, commercial spaces, stores, catering and office facilities.

Kanaleneiland-Centrum

Local housing corporations, ROC Midden Nederland, the owner of the shopping center, Proper Stok and the City of Utrecht have drawn up a plan dealing with the spatial elaboration of Kanaleneiland-Centrum. The program will be executed in phases until after 2010, with Proper Stok responsible for the coordination of the development. Kanaleneiland is to become a new local center for living, shopping and education. Some 1,340 new homes will be built here, and some 500 demolished. The shopping center will be expanded by another 12,000 m². The educational institute ROC Midden Nederland will concentrate a share of its activities in this area, elaborating the expansion into a Community College concept. The southern section of Kanaleneiland, an inner-city industrial park on the corner of Beneluxlaan and Europaplein, will be the site of 1,000 new apartments for student housing. The three 70-m residential towers with student facilities at ground level will be developed by Rabo Vastgoed and SSH.

Galgenwaard

Since 2000, the City of Utrecht, the FC Utrecht soccer club and construction firm Midreth have been working on the redevelopment of Galgenwaard Stadium. This isn't merely a case of expanding the existing stadium: a sports complex has been built in the direct vicinity of the stadium and building has started on a residential tower and 30,000 m² of office space with parking facilities. Furthermore, the area's public space will receive an extensive overhaul. The project will be carried out in phases. A 30,000-m² office complex is currently under construction to the southwest of the stadium, a design by Cees Dam. The complex consists of four buildings, with an 80-m tall tower serving as the main building. The complex will have a campus-like appearance. The office blocks are characterized by vast expanses of glass, giving them a remarkably transparent character. A residential tower with 83 luxury apartments will be constructed nearby.

The Utrecht soccer stadium Galgenwaard (new

Plan consists of the construction of 1,300 homes, 12,000-m² expansion of the shopping center and 30,000 m² of educational facilities.

Oog in Al

In the popular residential neighborhood of Oog in Al, Heijmans IBC Vastgoedontwikkeling BV and Kanalenstaete Ontwikkeling CV will be redeveloping the Cereolterrein industrial site. The adjacent TPG site and the head office of KPN will also be included in the project. Kanalenstaete Ontwikkeling CV, a partnership between Blauwhoed/Eurowoningen BV and Van der Vorm Bouw BV, is the owner of the TPG building and site. Supported by this combination, Blauwhoed/Eurowoningen will be acting as developer and project manager.

Several valuable industrial landmarks will be preserved for future generations. Two themes have been given special attention in the urban development plan: the completion of the neighborhood Oog in Al and that of the nearby factory complex. In the case of Oog in Al, the new construction along the edge of the district consists of low-rise homes and an apartment building on the corner of Mozartlaan and Kanaalweg. On the industrial site, various interconnected buildings will be realized that include apartments, a library and catering facilities grouped around a center court. Building commences in 2007.

Westraven

For some time now, the Rijksgebouwendienst (Dutch Government Building Department, RGD) has had plans to build 23,000 m² of new office space, as well as renovate 27,000 m² of existing space on the Westraven site, located near the A12 highway. The future Westraven office building will offer an abundance of open spaces, court gardens, wind-free walkways and terraces. Two new wings will be built on opposite sides of the existing office tower, with glass and steel setting the tone. The building is set for completion in 2007. >>

residential tower, 30,000 m² of office space).

Westraven, 23,000 m² of office space for the RGD.

Leidsche Rijn Centrum

With 30,000 new homes, 720,000 m² of (gross) office space and 270 ha of business parks, Leidsche Rijn is the largest new construction site in the Netherlands. 10,000 homes have already been completed, and work has started on the district center Leidsche Rijn Centrum. Utrecht's second city center will be both urban in style and suited for a variety of purposes. A spectacular feature of the project is the structure built over the A2, which forms an 8-m high hill in the landscape. The master plan for the area was designed by urban planner Jo Coenen. Leidsche Rijn Centrum will measure approx. 800,000 m² of program, including 245,000 m² of office space, 45,000 m² of retail space, 8,500 m² of catering, 30,000 m² devoted to culture and leisure, 34,000 m² of non-commercial facilities and approximately 2,600 homes. The center will benefit from its excellent accessibility via the highway and the nearby railway line. In the heart of the center, one will find the so-called Stationsknoop – an area linking up the various locations and modes of transportation. Building will commence in 2008 or 2009, and the center will subsequently be developed

Birds eye view of the Leidsche Rijn area. In front, the Papendorp business park,

Atos Origin, Papendorp.

PHOTO: GERRY HURKMANS

in phases. A considerable proportion of the plans can only be realized after the structure over the A2 has been completed in 2011.

Papendorp

A large volume of Leidsche Rijn's 720,000 m² of office space will be developed in the office and business park of Papendorp. This estate is situated where the A2 and the A12 come together, and can be considered the leading location for head offices in the Netherlands today. Some 340,000 m² of office space has been planned in Papendorp, as well as approximately 160,000 m²

of quality commercial space with office facilities. The sites in question are distinguished by excellent accessibility, high-grade architecture and public space, and a park-like environment. A good example of these ongoing developments are the new headquarters of Daimler Chrysler Netherlands in the Nieuwe Rijn sub-area, which offers 16,000 m² of free space. The heart of the Papendorp area is De Taats, the district's elongated central location. This space has been reserved for the top segment of the Utrecht office market. The buildings in ques-

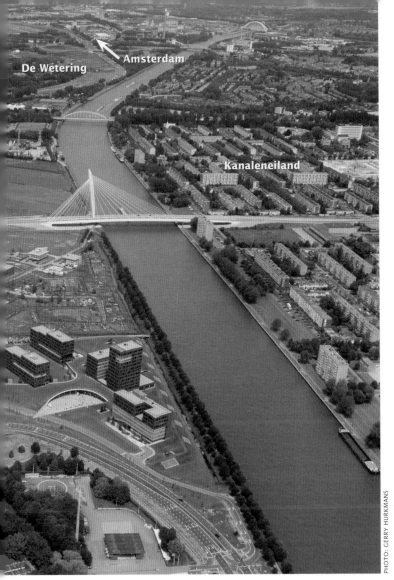

in the back, the residential sites.

suited for companies in the logistics and distribution sectors. Nearly all of De Wetering-Noord's sites have already been distributed. The size of the company lots varies between 0.2 ha and 2.5 ha. Along the A2, one can find an enormous sound barrier that houses the striking Cockpit building, designed by Kas Oosterhuis. The building houses a 6,300-m^2 showroom for the exclusive vehicles of the Hessing car dealership.

A completely different site, catering to another target group entirely, is De Wetering-Zuid. This park is eminently suited for high-quality, medical-technological and/or patient-orientated companies. Another remarkable building in De Wetering-Zuid is the multipurpose complex The Wall, which is being developed by Burgfonds. This 800-m tall structure serves as a sound barrier for the residential neighborhood Terwijde. The slender building has a floor space of some 60,000 m^2, of which 20,000 m^2 has been allocated for large-scale retail. It also houses catering (fast food) and leisure facilities and traditional business space. A new exit from the A2 has also been planned for De Wetering-Zuid. Completion is set for 2008.   >>

tion offer quality architecture in a remarkable setting. De Taats is particularly well suited for large-scale users who require at least 10,000-20,000 m^2 of space. In 2005, building started on Domus Medica. This building will soon house a number of the most prominent medical interest groups in the country.

De Wetering

The industrial area of De Wetering lies parallel to the A2 national highway, on the northern rim of Leidsche Rijn. It has a net size of 52.5 ha and is made up of two distinct parts: De Wetering-Noord and De Wetering-Zuid. Thanks to its excellent accessibility, De Wetering-Noord is exceptionally

The Cockpit building houses luxury car dealer Hessing.

Location	Project	Utrecht / Projects 2006 and beyond. Program	Development	Planning
Utrecht	Concorde Tower-Kanaleneiland	New office building 21,500 m²	Situs B.V.	2007
Utrecht	Croeselaan	Expansion office building 40,000 m²	n.a.	n.a.
Utrecht	GVU-terrein	New office building 15,000 m²	n.a.	n.a.
Utrecht	Stationsgebied	Renovation and expansion city center shops 40,000 m²	Corio ING Real Estate Development	after 2007.
Utrecht	UEC	New development shops 15,000 m²	Multi Development	2007
Utrecht	Utrecht woonboulevard	Shopping development 100,000 m²	Blauwhoed Vastgoed ING Real Estate Development	n.a.
Utrecht	Westentree	Office development 80,000 m²	NS Vastgoed	n.a.
Utrecht	Centrumkwadrant Overvecht	Redevelopment district center commercial space 11,000 m², residential 520 units	Johan Matser Projectontwikkeling AMVEST	2008
Utrecht	Rijnsweerd	New office building 28,000 m²	William Properties Achmea Vastgoed	2006
Utrecht	Merwede Park	New office park 25,000 m²	Maapron Vastgoed, Volker Wessels	n.a.
Utrecht	Stadscorridor	Redevelopment city center, offices 57,500 m² total 900,000 m²	n.a.	2011
Utrecht-Center	Centrumplan Utrecht	Renovation/expansion city center offices 204,000 m² shops 45,000 m², homes 2,320 units parking 2,500 cars, culture 33,500 m², leisure 63,000 m²	NS Vastgoed, Corio KFN Jaarbeurs Utrecht, Mun. of Utrecht	n.a.
Utrecht-Center	Parkhaven	New residential development apartments 900 units	Bouwfonds MAB Ontwikkeling Fortis Vastgoed Ontwikkeling	n.a.
Utrecht-Galgenwaard	Galgenwaard	Redevelopment, offices 30,000 m² shops 12,000 m², residential 83 units parking 1,254 cars, expansion soccer stadium	Bouwbedrijf Midreth B.V. Mun. of Utrecht, FC Utrecht	2006
Utrecht-Leidsche Rijn	Papendorp	New office park 340,000 m² Commercial space 160,000 m²	n.a.	2006
Utrecht-Leidsche Rijn	Papendorp	Office development 18,000 m²	OVG Projectontwikkeling	2006
Utrecht-Leidsche Rijn	De Cope Papendorp	New office building, offices 33,000 m² facilities 15,000 m²	Multi Development	n.a.
Utrecht-Leidsche Rijn	Cope-Noord Papendorp	New office building 50,000 m²	Multi Development	n.a.
Utrecht-Leidsche Rijn	De Taats Papendorp Kavel 3	New office building 40,000 m²	Bouwfonds MAB Ontwikkeling Multi Development Fortis Vastgoed Ontwikkeling	2004-2006
Utrecht-Leidsche Rijn	Hooggelegen	New regional center Shops 2,500 m²	Projectbureau Leidsche Rijn	2010
Utrecht-Leidsche Rijn	Leidsche Rijn Centrum	New development, offices 245,000 m² Shops 45,000 m², culture/leisure 38,500 m² Residential 2,600 units	Projectbureau Leidsche Rijn	after 2011
Utrecht-Leidsche Rijn	Leidsche Rijn vinex	New residential development Apartments 9,000 units	Bouwfonds MAB Ontwikkeling Fortis Vastgoed Ontwikkeling	n.a.
Utrecht-Leidsche Rijn	Strijkviertel	New business park Total 800,000 m²	n.a.	after 2007
Utrecht-Leidsche Rijn	Terwijde	New regional center, offices 10,000 m² Residential 550 units, shops 14,500 m²	Bouwfonds MAB Ontwikkeling Fortis Vastgoed Ontwikkeling	2008
Utrecht-Leidsche Rijn	Entreegebied Centrum-Wetering Zuid	New development total 56,000 m²	n.a.	after 2004
Utrecht-Leidsche Rijn	Poortgebouwen-Wetering Zuid	New office building 43,000 m²	n.a.	n.a.
Utrecht-Leidsche Rijn	The Wall-Wetering Zuid	New development, GDV/PDV investment €170 mln leisure and sports 50,000 m²,	Burgfonds B.V.	2008
Utrecht-Leidsche Rijn	Zorgboulevard-Wetering Zuid	New development Medical businesses 16,000 m²	n.a.	n.a.
Utrecht-Vleuten/De Meern	Vleuterweide	New regional center Shops 13,500 m² non-commercial facilities 20,000 m²	Ontwikkelingsbedrijf Mun. of Utrecht, Amnis, Fortis Vastgoed Ontwikkeling	2008
Utrecht-Vleuten/De Meern	De Boomgaarden-Vleuterweide	New development Apartments 127 units, business park	Fortis Vastgoed Ontwikkeling Bouwfonds MAB Ontwikkeling Multi Development	2008
Utrecht-Westraven	Westraven	Renovated/new office building 50,000 m² 23,000 m² new, 27,000 m² renovated	Rijksgebouwendienst	2007
Utrecht-Westraven	Woonmall Westraven	New shopping center Shops 60,000 m²	Mun. of Utrecht Blauwhoed B.V., Altera Vastgoed N.V.	2010

More information: www.holland-re.com/projects

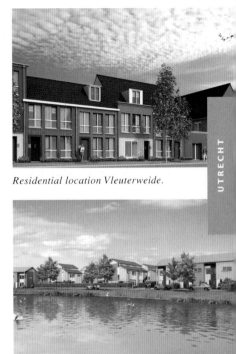

Residential location Vleuterweide.

Terwijde is one of the larger residential neighborhoods in Leidsche Rijn (Bouwfonds MAB Ontwikkeling).

Mesos Medical Center

Mesos will be building a new medical center in Leidsche Rijn. The Ministry of Health, Welfare and Sports has already approved the plans, and construction is intended to start in 2006. Mesos can move into its new accommodation in mid-2009.

Space has been reserved in the area surrounding the hospital for businesses working in the medical sector.

Strijkviertel

In a couple of years, the business park Strijkviertel will be developed on a site opposite Papendorp, to the northwest of the Oudenrijn traffic circle. This location borders both the A2 and the A12 highways and links up with the existing business park Oudenrijn. In terms of size, the site can be compared to De Wetering. It will mainly accommodate local and regional enterprise and light industry. Construction starts after 2007.

Terwijde

Bouwfonds MAB Onwikkeling is currently developing a shopping center in Terwijde, one of the larger residential neighborhoods in Leidsche Rijn with 4,000 homes. It will offer stores for practical shopping, but also for leisure shopping. Besides 14,500 m² of retail space, plans include 10,000 m² of offices and approximately 500 homes and apartments. The complex will be completed in 2008.

Vleuterweide

Another large new residential location in Leidsche Rijn is Vleuterweide, which is located between Vleuten and De Meern. In the period until 2010, some 6,000 homes will be built here, in six different neighborhoods. The first neighborhood, De Boomgaarden, with approximately 600 homes, has already been completed in the southwestern part of Vleuterweide. In the case of the second project, De Rietvelden, people have already

moved into some of the approximately 850 homes of the project's first phase. The second phase, with another 1,000 homes, is currently under construction. The homes range from affordable rentals to luxury privately owned homes. In central Vleuterweide, a shopping center with 13,500 m² of retail and catering, 20,000 m² of non-commercial facilities and 500 parking spaces will be added to the housing developments. The center is expected to be completed by the end of 2008. ≪

MORE INFORMATION

**Municipality of Utrecht
Department of
Economic Affairs**

P.O. Box 8406
3503 RK Utrecht
The Netherlands
Tel.: +31 30 286 40 73
Fax: +31 30 286 48 21
E-mail: ez@utrecht.nl
www.utrecht.nl/vestigingslocaties
www.leidscherijn.nl/werken-ondernemen

ONLINE: www.holland-re.com/utrecht

GALGENWAARD STADIUM

Having been thoroughly revamped, the capacity of the Galgenwaard Stadium in Utrecht, home of the FC Utrecht soccer club, has increased significantly. The number of seats in the stadium has almost doubled and a substantial amount of commercial space has been created. The area surrounding the stadium will be developed with new offices, homes and ample parking facilities, which underscores the functional character of the location. The large-scale renovation of the stadium and the upcoming development of the surrounding area are financed by Bouwfonds Property Finance.

The Utrecht soccer stadium redevelopment consisted of the renovation of the existing structure as well as new construction, and was carried out in four building phases. Seating capacity was increased from 13,500 to almost 25,000 seats. The business grandstand was expanded with business seats, business boxes and sky boxes. The South Grandstand now features a covered parking garage with approximately 400 parking spaces. Under each side of the stadium new commercial space has been created. The office spaces inside the stadium have been completely renovated. The development plan for the stadium's surrounding area provides 30,000 m^2 of office space and a parking garage with space for approximately 700 vehicles. In addition, a residential tower will be built with about 83 luxurious condominiums. The residential tower will have an underground garage with 91 parking spaces. Thanks to the

IN UTRECHT

FACT SHEET

Galgenwaard, Utrecht

Program:
Expansion of stadium capacity to 25,000 seats, commercial space (15,000 m²), office space (30,000 m² gross floor area), stadium (10,900 m²), residential tower (83 luxurious apartments), parking facilities (1,254 spaces) and renovation of the infrastructure and ecological zone

Principal: FC Utrecht, DMO and Memid Galgenwaard

Developer: Memid Galgenwaard B.V., a joint venture of Memid Investments and Bouwfonds Property Finance

Architects: Zwarts & Jansma Architects (Amsterdam), C. Dam & Partners (Amsterdam) and FBU (Utrecht)

Constructor: Midreth Construction Company

Investor: Eurocommerce, and others

Investment: €181 million

Completion: Stadium: August 2004
Area development: end 2007

More information:
Bouwfonds Property Finance B.V.
P.O. Box 15
3870 DA Hoevelaken
The Netherlands
Tel.: +31 33 253 91 10
Fax: +31 33 253 91 09
www.bouwfonds.nl

Midreth Construction Company B.V.
P.O. Box 112
3640 AC Mijdrecht
The Netherlands
Tel.: +31 297 233 733
Fax: +31 297 233 799
E-mail: info@midreth.nl
www.midreth.nl

UTRECHT

area development, Galgenwaard Stadium will not only be equipped with every modern facility available to soccer players and the public, but it will be further developed into a multifunctional location with wide appeal.

Realization and financing

A joint venture was formed between Memid Investments and Bouwfonds Property Finance for the redevelopment of Galgenwaard Stadium and the surrounding area.

The Midreth Construction Company has been doing all the building work, and Bouwfonds Property Finance is financing the entire development.
The stadium redevelopment took about three and a half years. Galgenwaard Stadium was officially reopened in August 2004. Memid and Bouwfonds started the building work in the surrounding area in May 2005. Completion of offices, residences and parking facilities is expected by the end of 2007. ≪

ONLINE: www.holland-re.com/galgenwaard

INTERNATIONAL ALLURE
WESTERN

① ALKMAAR	⑤ DELFT
② ZAANSTAD	⑥ LEIDEN
③ HOOFDDORP	⑦ ZOETERMEER
④ HAARLEM	⑧ SCHIEDAM

Traditionally, the western part of the Netherlands is the region with the strongest economy and the largest market for office and retail space. The leading Dutch cities of Amsterdam, Rotterdam and The Hague appeal to people's imagination the world over. But smaller towns like Haarlem, Leiden and Zoetermeer also benefit from large-scale developments in and around their city centers.

REGION

The cheese market of Alkmaar (North Holland).

Mr. H.C.J.L. Borghouts
Queen's Commissioner, North Holland

Prior positions include: Secretary General of the Ministry of Justice and Director General for Public Order and Safety at the Ministry of the Interior.

J. Franssen
Queen's Commissioner, South Holland

Prior positions include: Regional Police Force Manager in IJsselland, Chairman of the IJssel-Vecht Region, Mayor of Zwolle, member of the Lower House of the States General, and a member of the Executive Board of the Gooi and Vecht area Regional Authority.

I n the wake of their large neighbors Amsterdam, The Hague and Rotterdam, a number of smaller towns in the Western region have also embarked on large-scale development projects. Haarlem, for instance, is working hard to catch up in the office market. Some 240,000 m² of office space will be realized in the city in the period until 2020. The Spoorzone project stands out among these developments, with a total size of no less than 200,000 m². In addition, plans exist to develop another 50,000 m² of retail space in the Schalkwijk shopping center, among other locations. The Western region of the Netherlands is undoubtedly the country's most dynamic area with regard to the development of the retail market. The largest volume of retail space currently being built is in the province of South Holland, followed closely by North Holland. Approximately 270,000 m² of retail space are under construction in South Holland. In North Holland, some 185,000 m² of new space are being developed, and no less than 700,000 m² are on the drawing board – of which over half is planned for Amsterdam.

Besides the shopping capital of Amsterdam and the city of Haarlem nearby, the town of Alkmaar is also making considerable progress with its plans to construct some 40,000 m² of stores. Space for 20,000 m² of large-scale thematic retail has been reserved around the new AZ stadium. The fourth city of North Holland, Purmerend, is also extending its retail facilities, with an emphasis on neighborhood centers.

In terms of planned capacity, South Holland closely follows North Holland, with approximately 676,000 m² of retail space. The renovation and expansion of existing shopping centers plays an important role, with a focus on both the centers of small towns and neighborhood shopping centers in medium-sized cities. One of the new developments planned is the multipurpose location Schieveste to the north of Rotterdam and Schiedam. The Cadenza plan for the Centrum Oost area in Zoetermeer includes the construction of some 15,000 m² of retail. The Ikea outlet in Delft, situated on the A13 highway, will be expanded by no less than 15,000 m².   >>

A beach in North Holland.

< The Western region of the Netherlands is famous for its bulb fields.

The former site of the Mariastichting hospital in Haarlem (10,000 m²), will be developed by Bouwfonds MAB Ontwikkeling

Purmerend

The multipurpose shopping center Weidevenne is located in the center of the new residential district of Weidevenne on the southwestern edge of Purmerend. The neighborhood consists of some 6,500 homes for approximately 18,000 people. The shopping center, a development by Bouwfonds MAB Ontwikkeling, will have a total size of some 8,000 m² and rooftop parking facilities for 370 cars.

The DSB Stadium for the Alkmaar soccer club AZ.

Alkmaar

From 2006 onwards, the Alkmaar station area will undergo an extensive overhaul. Plans include a new tunnel connecting the platforms and underground parking facilities. On the northern side of the station, NS Vastgoed intends to realize some 37,000 m² of offices and/or homes.

The southern edge of Alkmaar, along the A9 national highway, is the future site of the new stadium for the AZ soccer club. The DSB Stadium will hold some 13,500 spectators and offer business rooms, lounges, restaurants and sky boxes.

Zaanstad

The Inverdan project in Zaandam will provide the city with a new modern town center. A number of projects will be realized at locations in the center and around Zaandam railway station, including 2,500 new homes, 140,000 m² of office space, a new 25,000-m² city hall, a public library, 18,000 m² of new stores and countless other facilities. Multi Development, NS Vastgoed, Saenwonen, de Woonmij and BAM are all involved in the development.

Haarlem

Plans for Haarlem's Spoorzone include 400,000 m² of space for commercial activities, 3,000 homes and 60,000 m² of recreational facilities. The Spoorzone Master Plan, with a construction

PHOTO: ZWARTS & JANSMA

and AMVEST. A striking feature are the urban villas along the Spaarne river.

WESTERN REGION

period planned to last through the year 2020, focuses on the quality of living and working. The accessible eastern section of the Oostpoort will form the gateway to the city. Eventually, 75,000 m² of commercial accommodation will be realized here, including 10,000 m² for offices and companies, a 10,000-seat stadium, conference and meeting facilities and park & ride services.

On the western edge of the city, Bouwfonds MAB Ontwikkeling is developing Raaks, a new district where modern new buildings are mixed in with the historic architecture. The plan entails a 6,000-m² shopping area, 200 homes, 1,000 m² for catering establishments and service-oriented companies, and 1,200 parking spaces.

An area of some 10,000 m² is being developed by Bouwfonds MAB Ontwikkeling and AMVEST along the Spaarne river, at the former site of the Mariastichting hospital.

Approximately 380 new homes, 10,000 m² of quality office space and more than 18,000 m² of covered parking space will be developed here. A green city square forms the heart of the plan. A 66-m tower will provide a new landmark in the South Haarlem area. Building will commence in 2006, with completion planned between 2007 and mid-2008.

In the period until 2008, five new buildings with approximately 220 owner-occupied homes will be erected at the historic Droste site, also situated on the banks of the Spaarne. The old factory silo and the national landmark featuring the well-known 'cocoa lady' will be preserved and assigned a new use. Some 12,000 m² of commercial facilities, 13,000 m² of office space and 3,600 m² of cultural facilities are being developed on the former site of Haarlem's Gemeentelijk Energie Bedrijf.

In 2006, Maeyveld BV intends to start with the construction of a

new stadium in the Zuiderpolder area. The project will include 50,000 m² of office space, a hotel, an exhibition area and a 1,500 space-parking garage. ING Real Estate has been selected to develop the new heart of the post-war district of Schalkwijk. This project comprises 12,000 m² of additional shopping space, 24,000 m² of office space, 850 homes, 2,700 parking spaces and 21,000 m² of cultural and recreational facilities.　　　　>>

Raaks, Haarlem, by Bouwfonds MAB.

Cultuurplein, a design of Kraaijvanger-Urbis, is the new cultural center of Hoofddorp.

Hoofddorp

The architectural firm of Kraaijvanger-Urbis is responsible for the winning design for a new cultural district in the center of Hoofddorp, Cultuurplein.
The existing De Meerse theater building, the Pier K center for arts and culture, the Hoofddorp public library and the town's pop/rock venue will all be brought together under a single undulating roof.

Halfweg

The Master Plan by Cobraspen Vastgoedontwikkeling for the old CSM sugar refinery entails the preservation of the two sugar silos, which will be converted into office high-rise buildings, each with a floor space of 12,000 m². The project is set for completion by the end of 2006. The former water building will house a restaurant. Plans are also in the works for a yacht basin, conference center and hotel.

Zoetermeer

Developer Johan Matser and the municipality of Zoetermeer are collaborating on the plan Cadenza for the Zoetermeer district of Centrum Oost. Plans include 15,000 m² of retail, 6,000 m² of office space, 2,000 m² of catering facilities and 700 parking spaces. A major section of the center will be covered over by a single glass roof.
As part of sub-plan 1 of the Oosterheem residential development, Dura Vermeer Leidschendam and Fortis Vastgoed Ontwikkeling are developing the Woontorens Willem Dreeslaan project.
The two residential buildings, offering a total of 98 apartments, are nearing completion.
Bouwfonds MAB Ontwikkeling

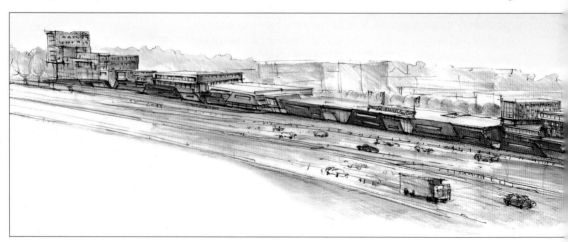

The Vierzicht area in Leiderdorp will offer 45,000 m² of office, retail and business space.

and Willemsen-Minderman Vastgoed Ontwikkeling are working together on the construction of De Hollandse Meester, a 163-m high office tower. Delivery is scheduled for the second half of 2006.
The Prisma Business Park, (municipalities of Zoetermeer and Bleiswijk) at a site along the A12 highway, will provide space for quality IT companies, transport and distribution firms and various other businesses.

Leiden

The municipality of Leiden, Bouwfonds MAB Ontwikkeling and Fortis Vastgoed Ontwikkeling intend to develop the area surrounding Aalmarkt. Some 5,000 to 6,000 m² of extra shopping space and an underground parking garage will be constructed here. The plan will be executed throughout 2007 and 2008. Bouwfonds MAB Ontwikkeling is in charge of the expansion and redevelopment of the De Luifelsbaan shopping center. Working in collaboration with Ahold Vastgoed, they will expand the surface area of the shopping area by 14,400 m², construct a residential high-rise with 92 homes and realize 700 parking places in the area.

The 163-m high De Hollandse Meester in Zoetermeer (total: 42,000 m²).

Leiderdorp

The W4 project: Wonen, Werken, Water & Wegen (Living, Working, Water & Roads) includes the recessed construction of the A4 highway, which means that in the future, Leiderdorp will no longer be split into two by the traffic artery. The plan is financed in part by the development of sub-areas adjacent to the new A4. Responsibility for the development lies with Ontwikkelingsbdrijf W4 Leiderdorp (OWB), a joint venture of the municipality and Behemen BV. The Vierzicht sub-area will offer 45,000 m² of office, retail and business space. This area will also house a new Healthcare Boulevard near the Rijnland hospital. A new furniture strip will also be realized near Meubelplein Leiderdorp.

Leidschendam

The Sijtwende plan consists of a city beltway, an underground corridor for buses or trams, around 700 homes, office buildings, a fire station and a police station. It is a joint project by Sijtwende BV, Bohemen and Volker Wessels Vastgoed.
More than 7,000 homes, 40,000 m² of office and business space, and a shopping center are planned for the Leidschenveen VINEX location, to be constructed over a period of seven to 10 years. A public-private partnership made up of Bouw Projekt Leizo B.V. (BPL), Bouwfonds MAB Ontwikkeling, AM Wonen, BAM Vastgoed and the municipality of Leidschendam is responsible for the development. >>

Delft University Technopolis Business Campus (ING Real Estate, Bouwfonds MAB Ontwikkeling).

PHOTO: BOUWFONDS MAB ONTWIKKELING

Rijswijk

At the site of Rijswijk's old town hall, Multi Development is currently collaborating with the local government on the development of 207 apartments and a cultural and leisure center, housed in two towers of 110 and 75 m respectively. 370 underground parking spaces are also included in the plan. The complex will be named Huis Ter Nieuburch. The developers intend to finish the two skyscrapers in 2008.

Delft

The Ikea furniture branch in Delft, located on the A13 highway, will be expanded by an

additional 15,000 m². This extra space will allow for the testing of new retail concepts in the enormous home furnishings store. At a 70,000-m² site on the Delft University Technopolis Business Campus, ING Real Estate Development and Bouwfonds MAB Ontwikkeling are developing a Research & Development center with international allure.

Capelle aan den IJssel

Located on the edge of Rotterdam and Capelle aan den IJssel is the site of the new residential district of Fascinatio, which features homes, shopping centers and business parks. Developers

involved in the project include Rotterdam Development Corporation, Bouwfonds MAB Ontwikkeling, Blauwhoed/ Eurowoningen, Johan Matser Projectontwikkeling, BAM Vastgoed and Vesteda. A number of office locations have been planned along the edge of the new district. 18 office buildings will be realized in the southern section. OVG has developed the 10-story Braingate office building at this site. Fascinatio will be fully realized by the end of 2008.

Schiedam

The period until 2018 will see the phased completion of the new urban center Schieveste, located between Rotterdam and the nearby town of Schiedam. Schieveste will offer 420,000 m² of office, business, and residential space, as well as various recreational facilities. The municipality of Schiedam is closely collaborating on the development with various market parties including NS Vastgoed and Blauwhoed.
Schieveste, covering an area of approximately 16 ha, is located

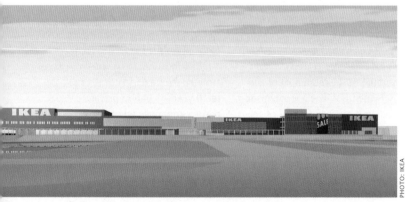

PHOTO: IKEA

The Ikea premises in Delft will be expanded by an additional 15,000 m².

to the north of the Schiedam-Centrum railway station. The estate is partially within Rotterdam city limits and partially in Schiedam.

To the north of the Schiedam-Centrum station, the municipality of Schiedam intends to develop a new Urban Entertainment Center (UEC) in collaboration with TCN Property Projects. The new center will address many of the local leisure needs, housing a variety of leisure formulas complemented by thematic catering establishments and retail outlets.

Dordrecht

Heijmans IBC is developing the 200,000-m^2 Amstelwijck Business Resort together with Multi Development.

The 74-ha Dordtse Kil 3 Business Park has attracted considerable interest, and part of the available ground has already been sold.

The Stadswerven development will offer 65,000 m^2 of business space, 1,600 homes and 1,000 parking spaces. The area, which links up with Dordrecht's city center, will also feature a new theater. ≪

MORE INFORMATION

Websites

www.noord-holland.nl
www.zuid-holland.nl
www.holland-re.com

PHOTO: MUNICIPALITY OF DORDRECHT

WESTERN REGION

Western Region / Projects 2006 and beyond.				
Zuid-Holland	**Project**	**Program**	**Development**	**Planning**
Alphen a/d Rijn	Central Station area	Redevelopment area, offices 94,000 m^2 shops 14,000 m^2	NS Real Estate Municipality Alphen a/d Rijn	2018
Barendrecht	Carnisseveste	Shopping development shops 15,600 m^2	Rodamco	n.a.
Delft	Spoorzone	Redevelopment area, offices 50,000 m^2 apartments 1,600 units, train tunnel new station, parking 3,000 cars	NS Real Estate Ballast Nedam Bouw en Ontwikkeling B.V.	2015
Delft	Zuidpoort	New city center, shops 18,000 m^2 apartments 58 units, 10,500 m^2, parking 900 cars, 27,000 m^2, culture 5,000 m^2	Bouwfonds MAB Ontwikkeling	2005
Dordrecht	Business Resort Amstelwijck	New business park, offices 200,000 m^2 hotel 180 rooms	Multi Development Heijmans IBC, Municipality Dordrecht	2012
Leiden	Aalmarkt	New city center, shops 6,000 m^2 apartments 80 units, parking 375 cars	Bouwfonds MAB Ontw.	2007-2009
Leidschendam	Leidschenveen	New development, offices and companies 40,000 m^2, shops 14,000 m^2 apartments 7,000 units	Municipality Leidschendam BPL, BAM Vastgoed, Wilma Bouw	2005-2014
Rijswijk	De Curie	New office building, 50,000 m^2	Bouwfonds MAB Ontwikkeling	2008
Rijswijk	Hways, Hoornwijck	Office development 80,000 m^2	BAM Vastgoed, Gemini Vastgoed	n.a.
Schiedam	Business Park Schieveste	New development, offices 160,000 m^2 facilities and a transferium 420,000 m^2	Municipality Schiedam NS Real Estate, Blauwhoed B.V.	2015
Vlaardingen	Stadskantoor	Office development 15,000 m^2	NS Real Estate	2010
Zoetermeer	De Hollandse Meester	New office building 42,000 m^2	Bouwfonds MAB Ontwikkeling Willemsen Minderman	2006
Zoetermeer-Center	Spazio	New shopping center, offices 6,400 m^2 shops 17,000 m^2, apartments 243 units parking 710 cars, health club 1,400 m^2	Rodamco Europe N.V. AMVEST	2005-2006
Zoetermeer-Center	City Center East	Redevelopment city center, offices 6,000 m^2 shops and leisure 17,000 m^2 parking 700 cars, restaurants 2,000 m^2	Johan Matser Projectontwikkeling B.V. Bouwfonds Property Finance	n.a.
Noord-Holland	**Projects**	**Program**	**Development**	**Planning**
Haarlem	023 Haarlem	Office development 40,000 m^2	Bouwfonds MAB Ontwikkeling BAM Vastgoed, Slokker Vastgoed Woonmaatschappij	2015
Haarlem	Raaks	Shopping development, shops 6,000 m^2 residential 200 units, parking 1,200 cars	Bouwfonds MAB Ontwikkeling Rodamco Europe N.V.	2008
Haarlem	Schalkwijk	Expansion regional center, offices 24,000 m^2 shops 12,000 m^2, apartments 850 units parking 2,700 cars, facilities 21,000 m^2	ING Real Estate Development	2005-2010
Haarlem	Spoorzone	Redevelopment area offices 186,000-201,500 m^2 companies 154,000-188,500 m^2, apartments 3,000 units, facilities 60,000 m^2, comm. activities 400,000 m^2	Municipality of Haarlem	2020
Hoofddorp	Floriande	Shopping development shops 10,000 m^2	Bouwfonds MAB Ontwikkeling	2007

More information: www.holland-re.com/projects

SHOPPING CENTER

Rodamco Europe, the largest publicly listed property investment and management company in the European retail sector, opened the €97 million-shopping center Vier Meren in Hoofddorp in September of last year. Hoofddorp is the central city of the rapidly expanding Haarlemmermeer area, part of the greater Amsterdam region. The shopping center has been (re)developed, adding nearly 27,000 m² of new retail space to Hoofddorp's city center. With 4.9 million visitors each year, Vier Meren establishes itself as a prime shopping location for Haarlemmermeer.

Situated above a large parking garage, Vier Meren covers 27,000 m² of retail floor space, effectively doubling the original retail space. A covered passageway connects to the existing Dela shopping center that runs along the Hema towards Polderplein. Polderplein has also been thoroughly renovated, thus creating a new downtown shopping circuit. There are 153 apartments situated above Vier Meren and this center will be expanded in the direction of the Nieuweweg to include a high-rise apartment building, stores and a movie theater/hotel complex.

A dominant position

The market value of Vier Meren amounts to about €97 million, generating a net initial return of around 6.4% while the return on Total Development Costs (TDC) is 8.1%. The property portfolio of Rodamco Europe in the Netherlands is valued at around €2.9 billion, of which 86% is in the retail sector. CEO Maarten Hulshoff states, "Vier Meren strengthens Rodamco Europe's position in the greater

VIER MEREN

Amsterdam region. We have worked very closely with local authorities that share our ambition. This shopping center reflects our firm commitment to expand our dominant position in healthy, growing urban areas."

Diverse design and tenant mix

The total surface area of Vier Meren is around 27,000 m², distributed over various floors (basement, ground floor, first floor) and small and large scale units (49 units in total) as well as an underground parking garage for 1,037 vehicles. There is a strong, viable mix of tenants, including retailers like Albert Heijn, Esprit, Sting, Free Record Shop, Blokker and C&A. The center consists of three buildings, each designed by a different architect, namely Lucas Ellerman van Vught, Rudy Uytenhaak and KCAP. AMVEST is the owner responsible for the development of a total of 153 apartments for rent in and adjacent to the shopping center. The catchment area of the shopping center encompasses 110,000 inhabitants with 4.9 million visitors expected annually. «

FACT SHEET

Vier Meren, Hoofddorp

Program:
- 27,000 m² of retail space (49 units)
- 153 apartments
- 1,037 parking spaces

Investors:
Rodamco Europe in the Netherlands and AMVEST

Tenants:
Including Albert Heijn XL, BCC, Blokker, Bruna, Burger King, C&A, Douglas, E-Plaza, Esprit, Etos, Free Record Shop, Forecast, Gall & Gall, Hessels, Het Huis, ING Bank, Kinki Kappers, Kippie, Lindessa, Miss Etam, Multi-vlaai, Oil & Vinegar, Ici Paris XL, Pliable, Primera, Setpoint, Sogno, Specsavers, The Sting, T-Mobile, Toys 'r Us, Van Haaren, WE Stores, Xenos

Management:
CBT Vastgoedmanagers bv
info@cbtvastgoedmanagers.nl

Architects:
Kees Rijnboutt: master plan
KCAP, Lucas Ellerman van Vught and Rudy Uytenhaak: three main buildings
GDA International: interior design of the shopping center

Completion:
2005

More information:
Rodamco Europe in the Netherlands
P.O. Box 22816
1100 DH Amsterdam ZO
The Netherlands
E-mail: info.nl@rodamco.com
www.rodamco.com

WESTERN REGION

ONLINE: www.holland-re.com/viermeren

SPAZIO ENHANCES

WESTERN REGION

Rodamco Europe completed work in 2005 on the Spazio shopping center in Zoetermeer. This development provides Stadshart Zoetermeer with approximately 15,000 m² of leasable new retail space. The market value of Spazio, including shops, parking space, and offices, is €57 million and generates an initial return of 7.1%. The total leasable area is approximately 15,000 m² of retail space distributed over 16 predominately large scale units, with about 6,400 m² in business space and an underground parking garage that can house more than 700 vehicles.

Spazio contributes to the upgrading of the downtown area and attracts national and international chains to Zoetermeer, including retailers such as H&M and Media Markt. Spazio derives its name from the different facilities that can converge in the shopping center. Here, 'space' is a recurrent theme as are 'patio' and 'courtyard'; or it can mean space in the sense of providing relaxation. The word 'spazier' is also another word for strolling. All of these elements are brought together in Spazio and situated at an ideal location close to the highways going to Utrecht and The Hague. The location is also in close proximity to a range of public transit services. Railway and bus stations are within walking distance and while vehicles can be conveniently parked in the surrounding area, Spazio itself also has more than 700 parking spaces.

Regional attraction

The total amount of retail space in Stadshart Zoetermeer, including Spazio, amounts to 70,000 m² and is expected to attract 11 million visitors annually.

ZOETERMEER

F A C T   S H E E T

Spazio, Zoetermeer

Program:
- Approximatley 15,000 m² retail space distributed over 16 predominantly large scale units
- 6,400 m² office and business space
- 1,380 m² leisure
- Underground parking for more than 700 vehicles

Investor/Owner:
Rodamco Europe in the Netherlands

Investment:
€57 million

Tenants:
- International: H&M, Esprit, Fitness First, MEXX, Media Markt, Jackpot and Burger King
- National: The Sting, Kruidvat, Man at Work, Jack&Jones and Brandstore

Completion:
2005

More information:
Rodamco Europe in the Netherlands
P.O. Box 22816
1100 DH Amsterdam
The Netherlands
Tel.: +31 20 312 01 20
Fax: +31 20 312 02 40
info.nl@rodamco.com
www.rodamco.com
www.spaziozoetermeer.nl

Rodamco Europe owns 68% of this retail space, which including parking areas and offices is worth €184 million.

Stadshart Zoetermeer has a strong regional attraction and that's why Spazio offers a long desired addition to the currently available retail, business and residential space. The space for relaxation and recreation has been increased and refined, giving a positive boost to the downtown core. This boost is amplified by renovations that took place on the east side, linking the existing Stadshart area to Spazio Shopping Space.

Spazio space

Spazio offers no less than approximately 15,000 m² of retail space. About 200 m² of that is destined for restaurant and catering venues while Spazio Officespace offers 6,400 m² of business space for rent. Rodamco Europe's total investment portfolio in the Netherlands amounts to €2.9 billion, 86% of which is in the retail sector. Spazio's development was carried out in close co-operation with AMVEST, which is building 243 apartments in three high-rise buildings bordering Spazio. «

ONLINE: www.europe-re.com/spazio

SAWA COMPLEX IN

In the Rokkeveen Office Park in Zoetermeer (near The Hague), the last SAWA plot is being filled in. The size and the scale of the new complex fits its surroundings perfectly. The convenient location, next to the A12 highway and the Zoetermeer train station, makes it very suitable for the new tenant Getronics PinkRoccade. The complex consists of several small-scale buildings.

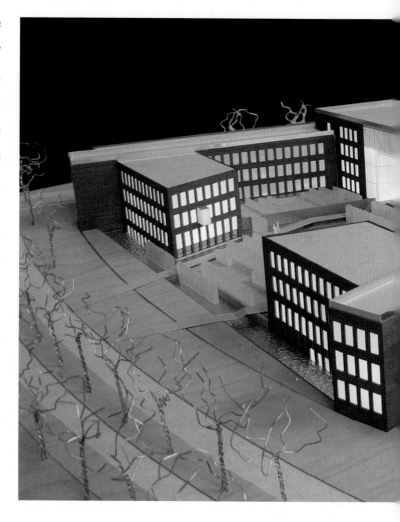

The small-scale buildings on the plot are merged to provide suitable premises for a single tenant. There are two main volumes which converge according to the urban plan. Three wings have been placed perpendicular to each main volume. The result is that each wing lies directly opposite its counterpart at the other main building. This way the separate building elements are united. The wings form three courtyards, each of a different size, layout and character. The separate buildings are connected on the upper levels, creating a series of archways on the first floor.

A specific consideration is the height difference of three meters between the Röntgenlaan and the Mahatma Gandhisingel at first floor level. The main volumes are centrally connected by a double-level glass entrance hall on the sunken ground level and by a bridge on the top level. On the sunken ground level a plaza

ZOETERMEER

F A C T   S H E E T

SAWA, Rokkeveen, Zoetermeer

Program:
18,200 m²
320 parking places in a basement parking area

Developer:
LSI Project Investment N.V.

Financier:
Bouwfonds Property Finance B.V.

Construction started:
Q3 2005

Completion:
Q1 2007

Tenant:
Getronics PinkRoccade

More information:
LSI Project Investment N.V.
P.O. Box 30065
3001 DB Rotterdam
The Netherlands
Tel.: +31 10 412 12 39
Fax: +31 10 412 14 36
www.lsi-nv.nl

Bouwfonds Property Finance B.V.
P.O. Box 15
3870 DA Hoevelaken
The Netherlands
Tel.: +31 33 253 91 10
Fax: +31 33 253 91 09
www.bouwfonds.nl

WESTERN REGION

has been created, and all primary entrances to the building are situated here – not only the central entrance hall, but also the two entrances to the parking garage, which is located underneath the building.

Over the sunken plaza a public space has been created, which facilitates a walkway over bridges and ponds in between greenery. It also features a bicycle path connecting Rokkeveen to the train station.

This has become an intrinsic part of the low-speed traffic route between the building elements.

The SAWA area, in which the project is developed, is part of the Rokkeveen Office Park, a prime location with nearly 45,000 m² of office space. SAWA consists of three courtyard-style office estates with a very pleasant atmosphere, further enhanced by the fact that all parking areas are hidden from view in the underground parking lots. ≪

ONLINE: www.holland-re.com/sawa

SPOORZONE GOUDA

The plans developed by local government and NS Vastgoed for Spoorzone Gouda have guts, vision and ambition. The relocation of a transit road that runs through the heart of the city will create an entirely new location on the northern side of the railway station. The area's gross floor space of 50,000 m² will accommodate a wide range of functions, making this modern new center the link between the old town and the other areas of the city.

The municipality of Gouda and NS Vastgoed worked in close consultation to draw up their ambitious plans for the development of the Spoorzone area. The plans combine investment in infrastructure with investment in real estate and public space. Many thousands of travelers, local residents, entrepreneurs and professionals will benefit from the changes taking shape in the new central area beside the tracks.

Huis van de Stad

A major booster of the project will be the new complex town hall 'Huis van de Stad'. This central accommodation for the Gouda city council is expected to open its doors in mid-2010. "Huis van de Stad will be a dynamic, customer-oriented center for municipal services and activities," explains Alderman Van Schelven, who is responsible for the project. "The Spoorzone area suits this purpose perfectly– it is a central location, near the heart of the city and very accessible, be it on foot, by bike, using public transport or by car." Huis van de Stad's new location is close to the railway station. It has a range of functions close at

FACT SHEET

Spoorzone Gouda

Program:
- Huis van de Stad: 19,000 m²
- Cinema: seven screens
- Homes: 16,000 m²
- Offices: 11,000 m²
- Hotel and commercial facilities: 3,000 m²
- Bus station: six stops + buffer
- Bike storage facility: 6,700 spaces
- Parking: 600 parking spaces including Park & Ride

Developer:
NS Vastgoed

Investment:
Approx. €130 million

Construction starts:
2008

Plan period:
2006-2010

More information:
NS Vastgoed B.V.
P.O. Box 2319
3500 GH Utrecht
The Netherlands
Tel.: + 31 30 300 43 00
Fax: +31 30 300 44 00
Website: www.nsvastgoed.nl

WESTERN REGION

hand, including a bus station, a cinema, stores, catering establishments, offices and homes. NS Vastgoed is responsible for the development of this area. The arrival of the RijnGouweLijn railway connection, which will have a station in Spoorzone Gouda, will further strengthen the area in terms of infrastructure.

Multifunctional location

KCAP architects and planners are responsible for the design of the station area. A characteristic feature of the selected design is the square dominated by the Huis van de Stad building. To the west there is a cinema and a new bus station, while on the eastern side the plans outline a number of residential buildings. The underlying idea is that the entire space forms a deck situated over the repositioned Burgemeester Jamessingel canal. Two parking garages will be built under the deck, as well as a large bike storage facility. A broad promenade for walking and cycling beside the railway tracks will connect this modern central area with the historic center. The ground preparations are expected to start in 2006, with construction on the new district starting in 2008. ≪

ONLINE: www.holland-re.com/spoorzonegouda

TECHNOPOLIS INNOVATIO

Knowledge and innovation will be the engines of the economy of the future. For this reason Technopolis is the ideal business location for both established and new companies in the high technology sectors. Technopolis is the joint 'statement for the future' of the government and TU Delft. It's the realization of a vigorous, modern Innovation Park, where government, business and science can optimally work together towards the world of tomorrow.

Technopolis Innovation Park is the prime location for international companies and knowledge-intensive organizations. Technopolis Innovation Park is an initiative of TU Delft, the City of Delft, Bouwfonds MAB Ontwikkeling and ING Real Estate Development.

Knowledge increase

Technopolis borders the campus of TU Delft, which has built up a solid international reputation as a technical university and technological innovator. The university has a pivotal function in one of the most powerful concentrations of technological activity and research in Western Europe. The result: an increase in knowledge through short lines of communication, a constant stream of information exchange and a supply of highly qualified talent. Part of Technopolis is already in use by R&D intensive institutions.

PARK DELFT

Advanced infrastructure

The road and ICT infrastructure in the region surrounding Technopolis is extensive and advanced. Its central location in the heart of West-Holland makes Technopolis an attractive European state-of-the-art site. With the two international airports of Amsterdam Airport Schiphol and Rotterdam Airport nearby and its connection to a sophisticated road and rail network, its continued accessibility is guaranteed.

Successful collaboration

Technopolis is, in short, the ideal breeding ground for successful collaboration between government, business and science. It's a unique concentration of knowledge and its application situated at the ultimate strategic location. In the exchange between science and business, knowledge and innovation gain momentum! «

FACT SHEET

Technopolis Innovation Park, Delft

WESTERN REGION

Program:
Phased development of 120 hectares (288 acres) with 600,000 m² of lettable space with high-quality commercial spaces, research facilities, catering, hotel, conference areas and extensive opportunities for relaxation. Aimed at companies with R&D components and research institutions with space available for back office functions and high-tech manufacturing.

Location:
Adjacent to the campus of the TU Delft Part of TU-district: advanced center of knowledge with university campus and a transitional zone with hotels and homes, site located next to A13 highway from Rotterdam to The Hague as a part of the A13 Kennisboulevard.

Developer:
Bouwfonds MAB Development
ING Real Estate Development
in co-operation with TU Delft
and the City of Delft.

Completion:
Phased

More information:
Technopolis Innovation Park
P.O. Box 110
2600 AC Delft
The Netherlands
Tel.: +31 15 261 09 06
Fax: +31 15 285 57 66
E-mail:
info@technopolisinnovationpark.com
www.technopolisinnovationpark.com

Technopolis Innovation Park
Powered by TU Delft

CENTRAL

① ALMERE
② LELYSTAD
③ DRONTEN
④ ZEIST
⑤ LEUSDEN
⑥ NIEUWEGEIN
⑦ AMERSFOORT

The Netherlands' central region forms an attractive business location for a variety of sectors. Scarce space in Amsterdam has led both people and businesses to the spacious city of Almere in the new polder to the north. Offices are finding room along the A2 highway, the Netherlands' most important traffic artery which runs straight through the country.

REGION

PHOTO: PROSPERO ALMERE

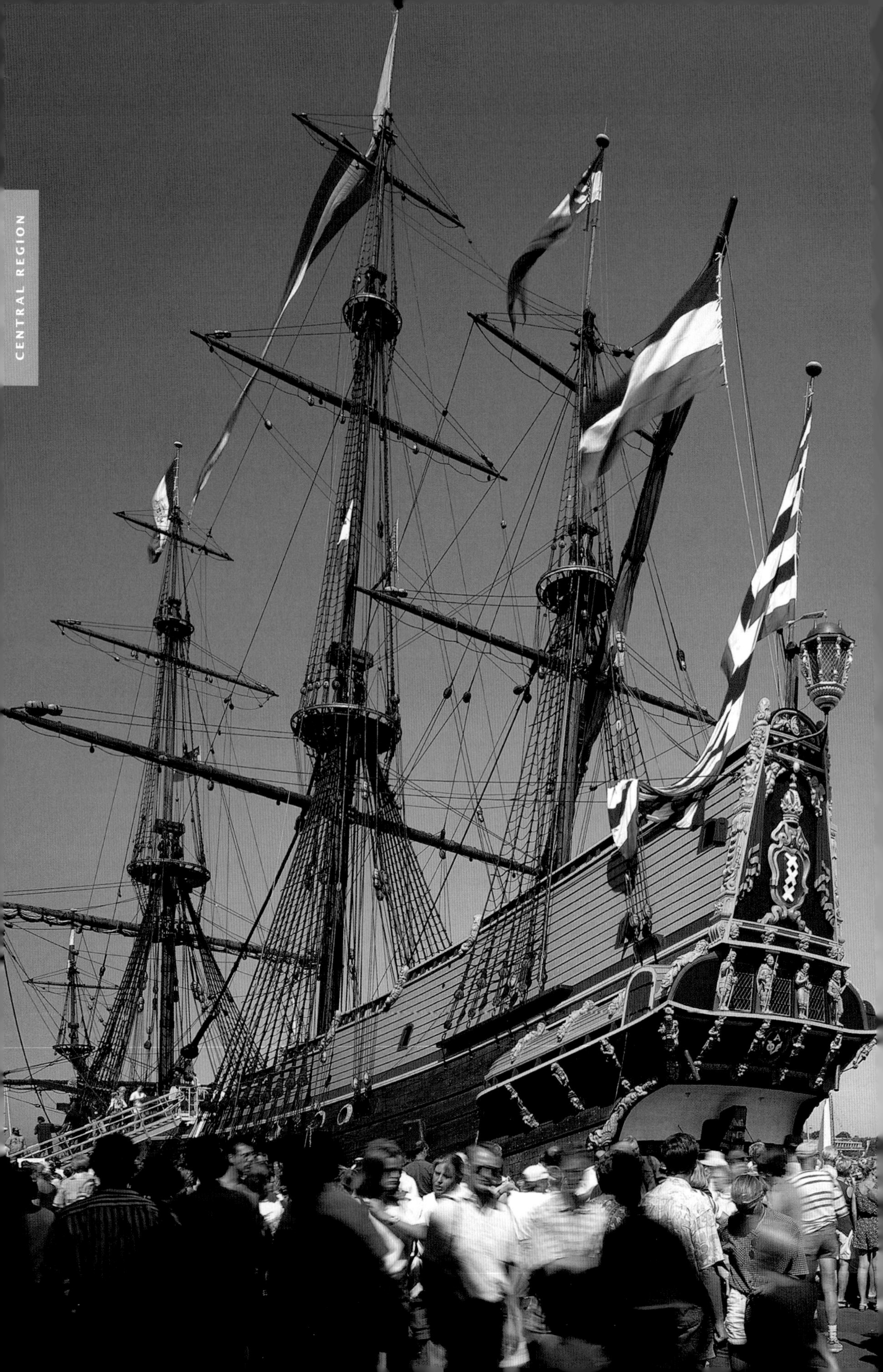

Amersfoort Central Station area.

Mr. B. Staal
Queen's Commissioner, Utrecht

Formerly: Partner and Board Member of BCG-Interim Management, Boer and Croon Group, Member of Parliament, General Manager of Randon Beveiliging, Commercial Manager of employment agency A.S.B. (Vendex), Police Commissioner in Almere.

Mr. M.J.E.M. Jager
Queen's Commissioner, Flevoland

Formerly: Mayor of Wageningen, Mayor of Culemborg, policy staff member for External Security, Ministry of Health, Welfare and Sports, city councilor in Heemstede.

Quite a few projects are on the drawing board in the greater Utrecht area, but substantial developments in the city itself are still underway. Nieuwegein, for example, has to deal with vacancy rates of 18%, mainly due to new construction in the city of Utrecht. Some 90,000 m^2 of new space is planned in the region around Utrecht, compared to 300,000 m^2 in the city itself. Thanks to a number of reasons, including a new connection with the A27 highway, Nieuwegein can still expand in the new business park Het Klooster.

Many municipalities are focusing on the redevelopment of their town centers. Nieuwegein in particular will be subjected to an extensive overhaul, involving the development of more than 28,000 m^2 of new retail. And the city of Amersfoort will gain a second city center with the construction of a new 10,000-m^2 theme center to the west of Amersfoort Central Station. Flevoland, the polder province that was only reclaimed some 30 years ago, has seen rapid expansion in recent years. Today, Almere already has a population of 200,000, and in due time this

is expected to double. A fifth city center, called Almere Poort (10,000 homes and 650,000 m^2 of offices), is currently being realized. The district of Almere Pampus will follow. Employment is steadily increasing. In order to provide work for the entire population, in the long term a production of 20,000 m^2 per year is required.

Almere presently has approximately 465,000 m^2 of office space. Part of this can be viewed as an overspill of the Amsterdam office market. This reason is becoming less prominent, however, with the leveling out of prices and an increased supply in Amsterdam itself. Some 150,000 m^2 have been added since 2000, but in 2004 construction came to a halt. Of all the Dutch provinces, Flevoland has the least amount of retail space. Supply lags somewhat behind the region's rapid population growth. A large-scale expansion of the Bataviastad outlet center is one of the measures currently being taken to get abreast of this development. This center, the largest inner-city retail project in the Netherlands, will add 85,000 m^2 to Almere's shopping facilities.   >>

PHOTO: PROSPERO

< Over 200 young people have built a reconstruction of the VOC-ship Batavia from 1628 at the Batavia Yard in Lelystad.

The Zakencentrum (Business Center) is located to the north of the existing Almere city center.

Almere

Almere is divided into districts, each with its own identity and center with shops and services. The districts are divided from each other by extensive green areas, which have become home to a large variety of living and business locations.

Currently, Almere consists of the districts Almere Stad (City), Almere Buiten (Outskirts) and Almere Haven (Harbor). Almere Buiten, in particular, has spaciously planned, green residential areas. Upon completion of the most recent new development in mid-2010, approximately 55,000 residents will live here. The oldest city district, Almere Haven on the Gooimeer, is also mainly made up of resi-

dential areas with a prominent marina with a lakeside beach, catering and retail facilities. Additionally, Almere is on the brink of realizing a fourth district, Almere Poort (Port) and has future plans to develop Almere Hout (Woods). In 2004 the population of Almere was 175,000. Within 15 years, Almere will grow to become the fourth-largest city in the Netherlands with 400,000 residents.

City Center Almere

The existing city center of Almere is going through considerable expansion. The so-called Zakencentrum (Business Center, approx. 190,000 m^2) will be located to the north of the center. New housing, shops, entertainment venues and other services will be realized on the south side. Architect Rem Koolhaas has designed a sloping grass field

Waterfront of the new City Center of Almere (Bouwfonds MAB Ontwikkeling).

that serves as a floor above the central section. This creates two levels, with infrastructure situated below and promenades above.

With the arrival of the Urban Entertainment Center (UEC), central Almere has gained a wide variety of entertainment and recreation options. The area will include space for health facili-ties, a restaurant, cafes and the entertainment center Doo World (4,000 m^2). The new city center is being developed by Bouwfonds MAB Ontwikkeling and Blauwhoed. In total, 90,000 m^2 of commercial facilities will be realized at the location, as well as 35,000 m^2 of entertainment.

Zakencentrum

A business center is being realized on the edge of the new City Center that will eventually comprise a total of 190,000 m^2 of office space. The first building in the complex that has been realized is the Alnovum, the location of the World Trade Center of Almere. The Institute for Information Engineering with its full-time program is also located here.

Almere Poort

Almere Poort will become the fourth city district. This area, located directly on the A6 highway, literally forms the gateway to Flevoland. The district will be home to 25,000 residents and a work location for 30,000. In the short term, 10,000 homes, 650,000 m^2 of office space, 60 ha of commercial space and 90,000 m^2 of sports and leisure facilities will be developed here. The center of Almere Poort is the future site of Omniworld, a 12,000-m^2 center for professional sports activity. Several locations for offices and logistic services are currently being developed: Hogekant, Middenkant, Lagekant and Zakenpoort. They will total some 600,000 m^2 and focus on the commercial services sector.

Other locations in Almere

Company location Sallandsekant is located in the east of Almere and has been especially developed for the logistics sector. It comprises spacious lots with sizes up to 50,000 m^2.

The Stichtsekant, developed for top-level companies, lies in the southeast on the A27 highway. The sale of 47 ha of logistics property developed in the first phase has already begun. The second and third phases comprise 29 ha of business space for top-level companies and 54 ha of space for mixed industrial companies. Stichtsekant has been recognized as a major example for landscape design in the Netherlands.

The large-scale industrial area of Vaart 1- 4 lies to the north of Almere. Durability and functionality are key focal points of the Vaart 4 development. >>

Almere Stad, the biggest development in Almere. The City Center (Bouwfonds MAB, Blauwhoed) will be completed around 2009.

Amersfoort

Amersfoort's new city district of Vathorst, which will be realized between 2001 and 2012, will offer some 11,000 new homes for 30,000 people. Participants in the development of Vathorst include the City of Amersfoort, Bouwfonds MAB Ontwikkeling, Heijmans IBC, De Alliantie, Thomasson Dura and Multi Development. Besides homes, the project offers health care facilities, education, sports, culture, shopping centers and the new Vathorst railway station. Bouwfonds MAB Ontwikkeling will realize the plan Centrumplan Vathorst, which totals some 17,500 m² and includes 500 parking spaces. Near the new station, Heilijgers is collaborating with INBO Architecten on the 11,000-m² office building Between. It will consist of two towers flanking a center structure.

Podium

A new office and business location is planned on the edge of Vathorst along the A1 and A28 highways: KantorenPark Podium Amersfoort. At this site, the City of Amersfoort, Heijmans IBC Vastgoedontwikkeling and ING Real Estate Development will work until 2014 on the realization of a total of 100,000 m²

of office space. Striking features of the plan are the characteristic campus concept and the area's park-like surroundings, which will accommodate an entire array of catering, leisure and various other facilities. At a location directly on the Amersfoort-Noord exit of the A1 highway, Heijmans IBC is developing the new Yris project. It will consist of seven office buildings with a total floor space of 21,000 m².

Eemkwartier

Central Amersfoort, to the north of Amersfoort Central Station, will be the site of the new Eemkwartier development. This new neighborhood, comprising some 500 homes, will be built in the heart of the city. Opposite Eempolis, NS Real Estate and Heilijgers will develop a variety of homes and apartments. The 65,000-m² office complex The Works will be subdivided into a number of smaller units. At a site on Amersfoort's Stationsstraat, Multi Development and Van Hoogevest Groep are presently developing a multifunctional complex. It will accommodate 15,000 m² of office space – including the new head offices of Akzo Nobel - plus a 100-room hotel and an underground parking garage.

To the north of Amersfoort Central Station th

Nieuwegein

Nieuwegein is currently preparing for an intensive renovation of its city center. Investor Corio will collaborate with developers ING and Multi Development to develop three city squares that

Office and business location Podium.

In the sound barrier of the A1, office building PrismA1.

Central Station Stationsplein

Eempolis Eemkwartier KPN AKZO/Agis/Philips

CENTRAL REGION

Eemkwartier is under development. Developers on this site are Multi Development, NS Real Estate, Van Hoogevest Groep and Heilijgers.

will be connected by a shopping route. A total of 28,000 m² of retail will be realized in the area, as well as 22,000 m² of large-scale retail, 80,000 m² of office space and 700 homes. This will double the amount of shopping space in and around City Plaza. The main attraction will be a new department store with seven residential towers built overhead. Most of the offices will be realized in the eastern part of the center. The building of a new culture square on the west side makes it necessary to tear down CityPlaza Plus. Theater De Kom will be refurbished and expanded. A new cinema with four to six theaters will also be realized on the edge of the square. The new

city hall building (approx. 16,000 m²) will be the center of attention on Stadhuisplein. The Admiraal II office complex, which comprises three office buildings on the Merwedekanaal (22,000 m²), is a development by Ballast Nedam Ontwikkelings-maatschappij. Completion is scheduled for 2006.
In the eastern part of Nieuwegein, one can find the site of the new business park Het Klooster, with a floor space of 730,000 m². To the north lies the new city district Blokhoeve Buiten, with some 700 homes, a large portion of green space and office buildings like The Cube (12,600 m²), developed by Multi Development; the project is in progress. The new 14-hectare

business park Galecopperzoom is being developed along the A2 highway. Multiplan Ontwikkeling is restructuring the former Auction Center into a 'working neighborhood' under the name Trinovium (80,000 m²). >>

The Admiraal II, Nieuwegein.

Architect Rob Krier is responsible for the urban construction of Batavia Haven, Lelystad.

Lelystad

Over the next 10 years, the City of Lelystad will be redeveloping the city center in collaboration with real estate developer William Properties. The plan includes the construction of a new parking garage, a so-called care strip (housing medical and social facilities) and 13 lots with an impressive array of striking architecture.

AMVEST, Rabo Vastgoed, Van Wijnen Projectontwikkeling and Stable International Development are working together on the development of the Batavia Haven housing project in the inner harbor of the Markermeer. Plans for the circular harbor include five apartment buildings and some 250 luxury apartments and penthouses. In addition, some 200 urban homes and smaller apartments will be built here. Space has been reserved under the new buildings for restaurants, boutiques, galleries and service facilities. The total project, which will be realized in five phases, is set for completion in 2007.

The Esplanade shopping center in Dronten, Foruminvest.

Dronten

Together with real estate developer Foruminvest, the municipality of Dronten has developed an ambitious plan for central Dronten. Known as the Esplanade, it will double the town's present retail offer. The catering function will also be expanded, particularly in the Redeplein and Havenplein areas. Besides adding new stores and catering facilities, the project also involves the redevelopment of public space. The center, the new shopping streets Kop van het Ruim and De Redepassage and a number of parking lots are expected to be completed by mid-2006. The renovated center will link up with the new cultural center De Meerpaal after completion.

Leusden

At a site adjacent to the existing office park Princenhof in Leusden, ING Real Estate intends to realize the Waterlane project: 29,000 m² of office space in a park-like setting. The new park's biggest tenants will be Interpay and ARAG. All space at this location has already been taken. Waterlane will be realized on both sides of the Interpay building, which is situated along Randweg. The precise details of the program were not yet determined when going to press.

Zeist

Pensioenfonds PGGM will be expanding its head office in Zeist. The additional 250,000 m² will be incorporated within the current building. Besides new office space, the project includes a new main entrance, a company restaurant that caters to 500 people and a conference center with a 200-seat auditorium. Furthermore, the new building will accommodate a call center, a dealing room and daycare facilities. A three-story parking garage with space for 1,000 vehicles is planned under the building. The project is set for completion by the end of 2006. «

MORE INFORMATION

Websites
www.provincie-utrecht.nl
www.flevoland.nl
www.wonenwerkenenwinnen.com
www.almere.nl
www.lelystad.nl

Central Region / Projects 2006 and beyond.				
Utrecht	**Project**	**Program** Offices / m²	**Development**	**Planning**
Amersfoort	Podium-Vathorst	New business park, offices 100,000 m²	ING Real Estate Development Heijmans IBC, Municipality of Amersfoort	2014
Amersfoort	Brouwershof	New development hotel 4,500 m², office space 4,500 m², parking 300 cars	Multi Development Van Hoogevest Ontwikkeling	2006
Diemen	Alpha Centauri III	Office development 26,341 m²	Bouwfonds MAB Ontwikkeling	n.a.
Ermelo	Ermelo	Office development 50,000 m²	Multi Development	n.a.
Hilversum	Arena Campus	Office development 40,000 m²	Delta Lloyd Vastgoed Phoenix Beheer, Multi Development	n.a.
Hilversum	De Twister	New office building 12,000 m²	Johan Matser Projectontwikkeling B.V.	n.a.
Hilversum	Media Park	Redevelopment area, offices 150,000 m²	TCN Property Projects	2004-2015
Nieuwegein	City Plaza	Expansion city center, offices 80,000 m² shops 50,000 m², residential 700 units	Multi Development, ING Real Estate Development, Corio Municipality of Nieuwegein	2004-2012
Nieuwegein	Admiraal II	New office building 22,000 m²	Ballast Nedam B.V.	2006
Woerden	Center	New shopping center shops 10,000 m², apartments 80-100 units parking 520 cars, leisure 700 m², investment €45 mln	Multi Development	sept. 2006
Flevoland	**Projects**	**Program** Offices / m²	**Development**	**Planning**
Almere	Almere Bad	Office development 75,000 m²	Maeyveld	n.a.
Almere Center	Almere Stad	Redevelopment city center, offices 2,000 m² shops 90,000 m², apartments 800 units parking 2,500 cars, entertainment 35,000 m², hotel 2,000 m²	Bouwfonds MAB Ontwikkeling Blauwhoed B.V.	2008-2009
Almere Center	Station area	New business park 80,000-105,000 m²	Municipality of Almere Van Wijnen Groep N.V.	2008
Almere Center	Zakencentrum centraal-Zakenpoort	New office building 65,000 m²	Bouwfonds MAB Ontwikkeling BPF Bouwinvest	n.a.
Almere Poort	Omniworld	New development, offices 85,000 m² shops 20,000 m², apartments 400 units	BAM Vastgoed Ballast Nedam B.V.	2015
Dronten	Esplanade	Shopping development shops 16,000 m²	Foruminvest	2006
Lelystad	Batavia Stad, ph.II	Shopping development shops 12,000 m²	Stable International Foruminvest	2006
Lelystad	Bioscience Park	New business park total 500,000 m², investment €100 mln	Heijmans IBC ARCADIS ID-Lelystad	n.a.
Lelystad	Lelystad Airport business park	Business park, offices 20,000 m²	Schiphol Real Estate Dura Vermeer	2015-2020
Lelystad	Bataviahaven	New development shops 3,500 m², leisure 5,000 m², residential 430 units, parking 800 cars	AMVEST, Rabo Vastgoed Stable International Van Wijnen Projectontwikkeling	2006-2010
Lelystad Center	Center	Renovation and expansion city center shops 17,200 m², leisure 6,700 m²	William Properties B.V. Municipality Lelystad, KPMG Metrum	2006-2009

More information: www.holland-re.com/projects

ONLINE: www.holland-re.com/centralregion

A NEW CITY WITH A PULSE

STADSHART ALMERE IN

If the Netherlands is known for anything outside of its borders, it is probably the polder landscape. Conquering land from the sea is one of the national merits. For example, the entire province of Flevoland was formed after closing the Zuiderzee by the Afsluitdijk. The largest city in Flevoland is Almere. This city was founded in 1975 and has grown from a village into a city with more than 160,000 inhabitants. The city is expected to have 220,000 inhabitants by 2010.

It goes without saying that a city of this size has a modern and well-equipped center. Internationally acclaimed architect Rem Koolhaas of the Rotterdam Office for Metropolitan Architecture (OMA) is responsible for the master plan of the Almere city center. Almere Hart CV – a limited partnership between Bouwfonds MAB Ontwikkeling and Blauwhoed Eurowoningen – and the munici-

pality of Almere are carrying out the Stadshart Almere development. It is owned by Rodamco Europe. Bouwfonds MAB Ontwikkeling is primarily responsible for the development and sale of commercial properties within the project. Blauwhoed Eurowoningen is responsible for the development and sale of approximately 950 homes that will be built in the center. The designers of the different partial

THE POLDER

FACT SHEET

Stadshart Almere

Program: Redevelopment city center
Approximately 70,000 m² net sales
area of retail and daytime catering.
Approximately 7,000 m² net sales area
of leisure and evening catering.
- A 2,400-seat cinema
- A live music venue/discotheque and
  dance café with approximately
  2,400 m²
- Approximately 2,050 m² of offices
- A three-star hotel with 120 rooms
- A fitness center
- 950 houses
- Parking area for approximately 2,500
  cars

Architect offices involved:
- Atelier Christian de Portzamparc, Paris
- David Chipperfield Architects, London
- Meyer & van Schooten Architecten,
  Amsterdam
- Gigon & Guyer Architekten, Zürich
- SeArch, Amsterdam
- OMA, Rotterdam
- Van Sambeek & Van Veen Architecten,
  Amsterdam
- S333, Jay Woodruff, Amsterdam
- De Architectengroep, Amsterdam
- Alsop and Störmer Architects,
  London
- De Architecten Cie., Amsterdam
- René van Zuuk Architecten, Almere
- Gunnar Daan Doeke van Wieren
  Architecten, Oosternijkerk
- Claus en Kaan Architecten, Almere

Development:
- Almere Hart CV (Bouwfonds MAB
  Ontwikkeling, Blauwhoed
  Eurowoningen)
- Municipality of Almere

Owner: Rodamco Europe
Investment: €225 million

More information:
www.stadscentrum-almere.nl
www.bouwfonds.nl
www.eurowoningen.nl

CENTRAL REGION

projects of the master plan are all renowned architects. For example, former National Building Master Kees Rijnboutt designed the premises on Blekerstraat. It houses the City Center Department, the Blauwhoed Eurowoningen sales center, and the Almere Hart's project office. Rem Koolhaas is personally responsible for designing a mega-cinema with approximately 2,400 seats. Christian de Portzamparc has done the main retail block in the city center of Almere. It provides 50 retail units on approximately 30,000 m².

British architect William Alsop has designed several buildings located around Waterplein, also known as the Urban Entertainment Center. This center includes a music hall/discotheque, a hotel and a family entertainment center (with a bowling alley and bars and restaurants). «

A NEW SUBURBAN LIFESTYLE

NORTHERN

❶ GRONINGEN
❷ LEEUWARDEN
❸ MEPPEL
❹ ASSEN
❺ HEERENVEEN

In the Netherlands' northern provinces, a number of cities are busily redeveloping their city centers, as well as formulating innovative concepts for the outskirts of town. Living in the country will acquire a new flavor with projects like De Blauwe Stad in the province of Groningen. But innovative developments are also taking place in Leeuwarden, Groningen and Heerenveen. The North is catching up.

REGION

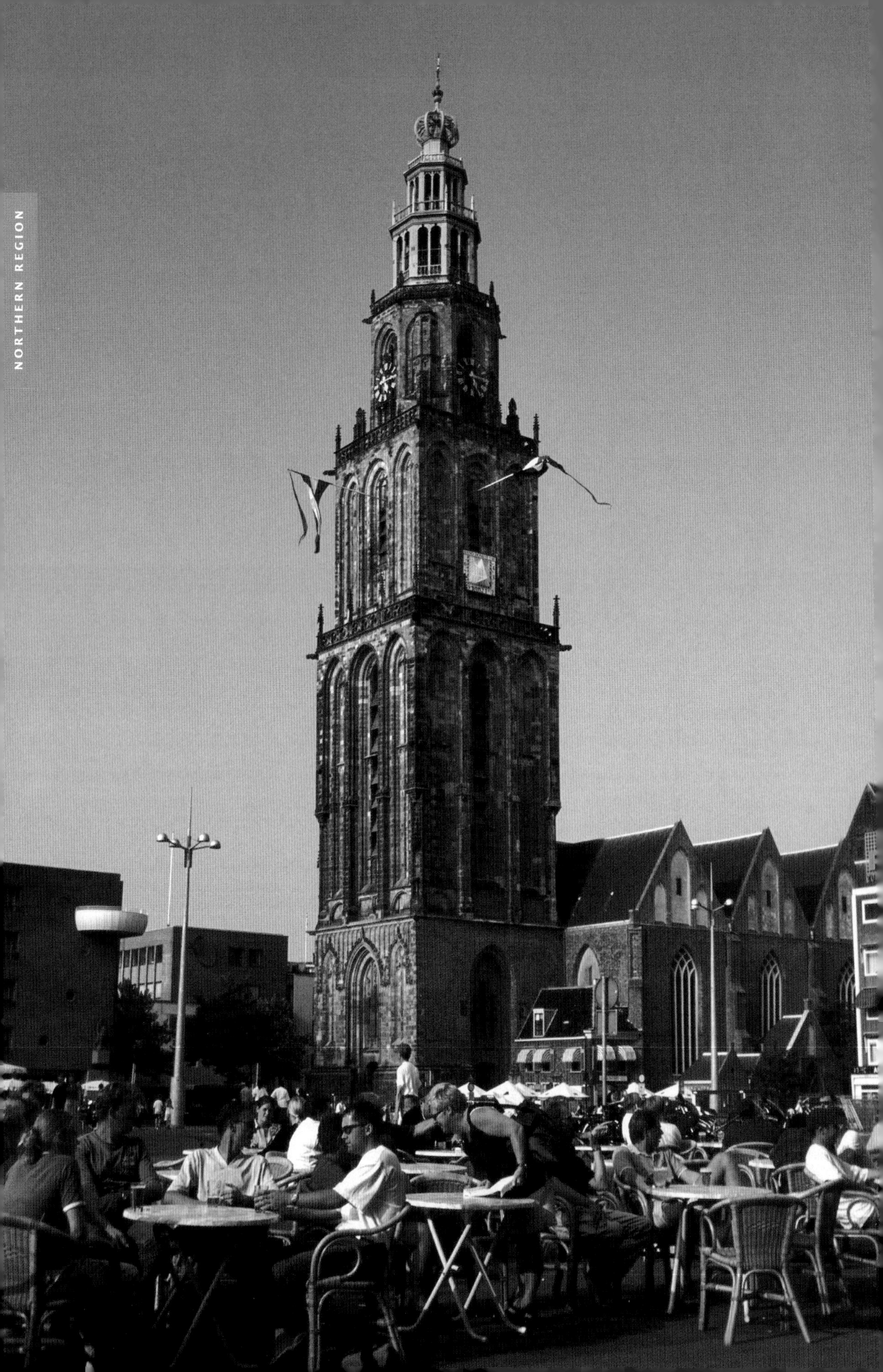

PHOTO: EPPO NOTENBOOM

Water recreation enthusiasts have come to the right place when they come to Friesland. They can take their boat to friendly villages, busy cities or quiet little spots.

J.G.M. Alders
Queen's Commissioner, Groningen

Prior positions include: Dutch Minister of Spatial Planning, Housing and the Environment; director of the European branch of UNEP (UN Environment Program) in Geneva.

The city of Groningen holds a prominent position in the North Netherlands. Combined with the city of Assen, Groningen offers over a million m² of office space. The main tenants can be found in the business services sector, government and education. That Groningen is a major city in the region can also be deduced from the development of the town's Europapark area. A wide range of functions will be realized around the new stadium of FC Groningen soccer club, giving the location a metropolitan atmosphere at all hours of the day.

Vacancy in Groningen is remarkably low: at 6% it barely exceeds friction vacancy rates. The future of the regional office market is defined by Groningen's ambition to develop the city into an economic area that can compete on a national and international level. In the North Netherlands, the main competitor in the office market is Zwolle.

Considerable amounts of retail space have been realized in the province of Groningen in recent years, including the construction of a new Ikea outlet. All of the current new developments are taking place in its capital, Groningen city, which is also the site of most of the new retail projects. The general overhaul of the central square Grote Markt was in the pipeline for a long while, but looks to be executed in the short term. This project will add 10,000 m² of retail space to the area. The total planned capacity of the province is 60,000 m², most of which involves redevelopments. New locations include De Blauwe Stad and the new Groningen neighborhood of Reitdiep.

Friesland is making particular work of the development of large-scale retail accommodation near Leeuwarden. The city intends to strengthen its position as a regional capital. The most important undertaking in this respect is Nieuw Zaailand, an inner-city restructuring project that will expand the core retail area. Leeuwarden-Zuid is the planned location of a large new residential area with 6,500 homes. >>

Drs. E.H.T.M. Nijpels
Queen's Commissioner, Friesland

Prior positions include: Dutch Minister of Spatial Planning, Housing and the Environment; chairman of the VVD party in Parliament, Mayor of Breda and chairman of the WWF in the Netherlands.

A.L. ter Beek
Queen's Commissioner, Drenthe

Prior positions include: Dutch Minister of Defense, member of the Dutch Lower House of Parliament, member of the PvdA party executive committee.

PHOTO: FRANS LEMMENS

< View of the Martini tower in Groningen.

The multifunctional and impressive Euroborg complex will accommodate the new FC Groningen stadium.

Europapark Groningen

Groningen is the largest city in the northern part of the Netherlands. The development of the new district of Europapark is in keeping with the city's ambition to strengthen this position. Construction of this big-city neighborhood in the southeastern part of Groningen started in 2001. The Europark district is defined by four quadrants: an office area Europawijk, the Euroborg stadium complex, the residential neighborhood De Linie and Helperpark. The new railway station Europark, located in the heart of the district, will be completed by the end of 2006. The office park Europawijk will offer a total of some 200,000 m² of office space. The district is particularly well suited for a mix of functions. The multipurpose complex Euroborg will be a central feature of Europapark. It will house the new stadium of

soccer club FC Groningen, a casino, a movie theater, catering facilities, offices and two tall residential towers. The center's developers are Ballast Nedam, Volker Wessels Vastgoed and BAM Vastgoed, working in collaboration with city government. Investment totals some €190 mln. Much attention was devoted to the architecture of the Euroborg by architect Wiel Arets. The small new development of De Linie (Bouwfonds MAB and Geveke) connects the neighborhood of Oosterpoort and Helpman via Europapark. De Linie is expected to be completed by the end of 2007.

CiBoGa

A new green residential neighborhood, CiBoGa, has been planned on the edge of Groningen's city center. The district's dense building volumes will spread out over the location, with plenty of room

for green space and water in between.
IMA Ontwikkelingscombinatie (ING Real Estate, Moes Projectontwikkeling and Multi Development) has planned 10,000 m² of retail, 45,000 m² of office space and 900 homes in this area. Completion: 2010.

CiBoGa, 10,000 m² of retail, 45,000 m² of

The Euroborg will also comprise offices, apartments, catering facilities, a 10-screen cinema, a casino, and a mega-supermarket.

De Blauwe Stad

De Blauwe Stad is a residential and landscape project in Oldamt, Oost-Groningen, of extraordinary proportions: 1,500 homes will be set in splendid natural surroundings, in an area the size of an entire city (with a circumference of some 23 km). The homes will

office space and 900 homes.

be concentrated in five residential areas. Nearly all the individual lots are directly connected to a new 8-km² lake. This development by Ballast Nedam, Bouwborg, BAM Vastgoed and Geveke Bouw will be in progress until 2013.

Meerstad

The innovative combined living/working/recreational area Meerstad has been planned within the triangle Groningen, Engelbert and Harkstede. Besides various government bodies, Multi Development, Koop Holding, Heijmans IBC Vastgoedontwikkeling and BPF Bouwinvest will also be participating in the project. Over the next 20 years, 10,000 homes, a 600-ha lake, quality landscape elements and a rugged natural environment will be realized in this area. The contsruction of Meerstad will cost an estimated €3 billion.

Westpoort

A prominent location with a direct connection to the A7 highway is the future site of the Westpoort industrial park. The first lots will be made available this year, and the entire 150-ha estate should be finished by 2014. When the A7 is completed in 2009 it will feature a direct exit to Westpoort.

Fivelpoort

The Fivelpoort business park will be developed on the southern edge of the town of Appingedam. With the harbor and industrial complexes of Delfzijl and Eemshaven nearby, the park has access to good international connections and transport facilities. Participants in the project are the municipalities of Appingedam, Delfzijl and Groningen Seaports. The park is set for completion by the end of 2006. >>

PHOTO: ING REAL ESTATE

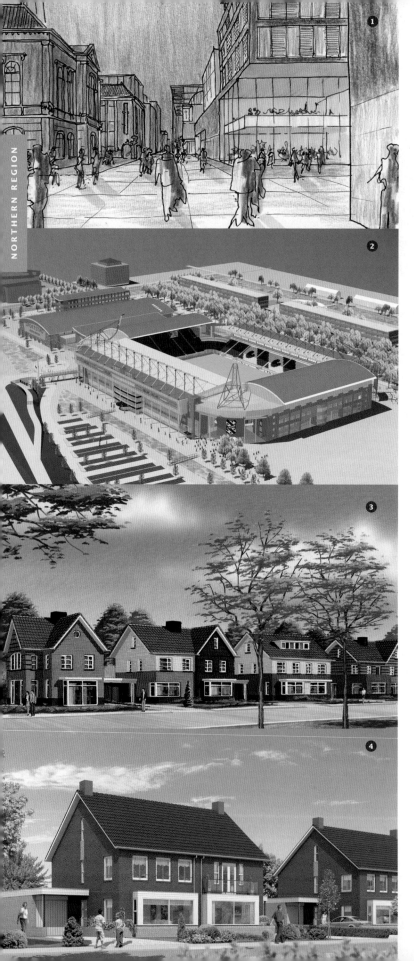

Leeuwarden

In Leeuwarden, the capital of the province of Friesland, a completely new district is currently being developed: De Zuidlanden. 6,500 homes, 55,000 m² of commercial facilities, 73,000 m² of public facilities and in due time 150,000 m² of office space will be developed here in the period until 2020. The district may even gain its own railway station. Investment in De Zuidlanden totals €350 million. The market parties participating in the project are Bouwfonds MAB Ontwikkeling, Heijmans IBC Vastgoedontwikkeling and BAM Vastgoed. The first buildings are already completed.

Business Park Leeuwarden

NS Vastgoed is the developer of Business Park Leeuwarden (23 ha), the intended location of the company's own 10,000 m² office building. The developer BAM Vastgoed also plan to realize World Trade Center Leeuwarden on this site. This project will include a conference center, a hotel and four office buildings with a total floor space of 13,000 m². The WTC is expected to open its doors in 2010.

Nieuw Zaailand

In central Leeuwarden, the province of Friesland, the City of Leeuwarden, the Fries Museum, ING Real Estate and Achmea will be collaborating on the renovation of Wilhelminaplein Square and the Zaailand shopping center. The project ❶ will create an attractive residential environment and a varied shopping experience, as well as enhance the cultural significance of the city's historic center. The retail space is expected to increase by 7,000 m² by 2010, and 13,150 m² by 2020.

Heerenveen

Sport, leisure, education, living and shopping come together in the innovative concept Sportstad Heerenveen ❷. This project is a partnership between Heerenveen sports club, the City of Heerenveen, De Friesland Zorgverzekeraar insurance company and the educational institute ROC Friesland College. Various projects will be developed around the existing soccer stadium: a multipurpose sports center, a health boulevard, 60,000 m² of offices, 360 apartments, leisure facilities and stores (with a total floor space of 20,000 m²) and parking spaces for 7,000 cars.

Assen

The new residential neighborhood of Het Palet ❸ is the future site of 300 new homes and apartments and a 10,000-m² office building. Developers Geveke, Ter Steege and Berg Projecten completed the first of these homes at the end of 2005. BAM Vastgoed is developing a new center for the district of Kloosterveen, a 244 hectares new area on the west side of Assen.

The Kloosterveste project involves the construction of 700 homes, approximately 11,000 m² of retail space, 11,000 m² of non-commercial facilities and 650 parking spaces.

Meppel

In Meppel, AM Wonen is developing the new neighborhood of Berggierslanden ❹, which involves the construction of some 1,100 homes over the next five years. The attractively arranged district will be distinguished by its abundant water features. Plans are already being developed for local canoeing, biking and walking routes. ≪

MORE INFORMATION

Websites

www.groningen.nl
www.europark.nl
www.assen.nl

Northern Region: Groningen, Friesland, Drenthe / Projects 2006 and beyond.				
Groningen	**Project**	**Program**	**Development**	**Planning**
Appingedam	Fivelpoort	New business park, businesses 450,000 m²	Seaports Groningen Mun. of Appingedam/Delfzijl	2006
Groningen	Europapark	New development, total 200,000 m² shops 6,000 m², residential 180 units parking 1,000 cars, leisure 8,000 m² facilities 10,000 m², investment €183 mln	Volker Wessels Vastgoed Van Wijnen Groep N.V. Geveke Bouw B.V. BAM Vastgoed	2005-2017
Groningen	Europapark	Residential development 9,500 m²	Bouwfonds MAB Ontwikkeling	2008
Groningen	Phoenix	Office development 13,500 m²	Volker Wessel Vastgoed	2011
Groningen	Meerstad	New development businesses and leisure 1,400,000 m² residential 10,000 units	Multi Development Heijmans IBC, Koop Holding B.V. BPF Bouwinvest	2004-2014
Groningen-Center	CiBoGa	New development, offices 45,000 m² shops 10,000 m², residential 900 units parking 1,500 cars	ING Real Estate Development Moes bouwbedrijf B.V. Multi Development	1998-2010
Oldambt	De Blauwe Stad	New housing development residential 1,500 units	Geveke Bouw B.V. Ballast Nedam, BAM Vastgoed Bouwborg	2005-2013
Friesland	**Projects**	**Program**	**Development**	**Planning**
Heerenveen	Sportstad Heerenveen	New development, offices 35,000 m² (Sports City Heerenveen)businesses 6,000 m², residential 300 units, sports leisure, parking 2,800 cars, education and healthcare 15,000 m²	Mun. of Heerenveen	2011
Leeuwarden	Business Park Leeuwarden	New business park total 230,000 m²	NS Vastgoed	n.a.
Leeuwarden	Zuidlanden	New development, offices 150,000 m² shops 55,000 m², residential 6,500 units facilities 73,000 m²	BAM Vastgoed Bouwfonds MAB Ontwikkeling Heijmans IBC	2005-2020
Leeuwarden	Nieuw Zaailand	Redevelopment district center shops 13,800 m², residential 104 units, culture 4,950 m², parking 720 cars	ING Real Estate, Achmea	2020
Drenthe	**Projects**	**Program**	**Development**	**Planning**
Emmen	Centrum Bargeres	Redevelopment district center shops 5,000 m², residential 200 units, healthcare 1,000 m²	Johan Matser Projectontwikkeling	n.a.
Assen	Kloosterveste	New district center, shops 11,000 m², non-commercial facilities 11,000 m² residential 700 units, parking 650 cars	BAM Vastgoed	2008

More information: www.holland-re.com/projects

HOLLAND 59 PROPERTY

In 2005, Bouwfonds Property Finance Netherlands successfully concluded a transaction – involving a total sum of €51.5 million – with German company MPC AG. MPC's activities include the formation of property funds with Dutch real estate for the Dutch and German markets. The company has extensive experience in this area. MPC has already placed 194 funds, with a total value of €10 billion. The current financing involves a mixed property portfolio that comprises offices and logistics real estate.

The transaction, involving a total sum of €51.5 million, was made possible thanks to a fine partnership between the Project Financing and Investment Financing divisions of Bouwfonds Property Finance Netherlands.
This led to the development of a flexible financing product that forms an excellent solution to the relation's needs: to have a flexible pre-financing facility at one's disposal in the preliminary phase, which, after introduction in a limited partnership construction in the second phase, serves as a long-term investment financing of the real estate fund. The portfolio, which was built

FUND

Holland 59 property fund

Program:
(Pre)financing of the MPC Immobilien-fonds Holland 59 property fund

Investment:
Investment totals €89.8 mln.
of which €51.5 mln. has been
financed by Bouwfonds Property
Finance.

Portfolio:
Two office buildings in Utrecht and
Gouda, four combined office/commer-
cial spaces in Eindhoven, Hoogeveen,
Nieuwegein and Haarlem.

Features of the deal:
- Bouwfonds Property Finance provides
  a flexible solution via a pre-financing
  construction involving a combination
  of Sales Kort (project financing) and
  Sales Lang (investment financing)
  arrangements
- Borrower has a strong financial
  position
- High-quality real estate (recently
  completed with high-grade materials)
- Long-term lease agreements (11.4
  years on average)
- Very strong tenancy (good rating)

More information:
Bouwfonds Property Finance B.V.
P.O. Box 15
3870 DA Hoevelaken
The Netherlands
Tel.: +31 33 253 91 10
Fax: +31 33 253 91 09
www.bouwfonds.nl

over the preceding year, was ultimately formalized in a property CV (limited partnership) construction. The property involved in the transaction comprises various recently completed, up-to-date buildings that have been rented out to quality tenants on a long-term basis. The portfolio includes two office buildings in Utrecht and Gouda and four combined office/commercial spaces in Eindhoven, Hoogeveen, Nieuwegein and Haarlem.

The investment product, which is geared towards private investors in Germany and Austria, has a term of nine years and three months. ≪

ONLINE: www.holland-re.com/holland59

CAPITALIZING ON ITS STRENGTHS

EASTERN

H. MARTENS

MOUNTAIN BIKES

① ENSCHEDE
② HENGELO
③ ZWOLLE
④ ARNHEM
⑤ NIJMEGEN
⑥ APELDOORN
⑦ DOETINCHEM
⑧ GELDERMALSEN

The eastern region of the Netherlands has developed to become the link between the Randstad and the Ruhrgebiet. The region is well suited for spacious business parks with a rural atmosphere. In the meantime, the larger cities are putting a great deal of work into inner-city development. Old neighborhoods are being transformed into modern districts. In short: the east is strengthening its position.

REGION

The Grote Markt in the historic city center of Nijmegen.

J. Kamminga
Queen's Commissioner, Gelderland

Prior positions include: Chairman of
the Employers' Organization for
Small and medium-sized Enterprise
(SME), member of Groningen's city
council, member of the Clingendael
council, Chairman of MDC.

Mr. G.J. Jansen
Queen's Commissioner, Overijssel

Prior positions include: Chairman of
the Arnhem-Nijmegen urban node,
Director-General to the Ministry of
Foreign Affairs and lecturer in
constitutional and administrative law.

The economic heart of the eastern part of the Netherlands lies in the so-called KAN area, the result of collaboration between Arnhem, Nijmegen and the surrounding municipalities. Over the past year, the area has made a modest recovery after recent setbacks. After a strong decline in demand for office space in the last few years, we are now seeing growth in the market, although it has not yet reached the level of the year 2000. This increased activity can mainly be attributed to Arnhem, as the Nijmegen market is still declining. In Arnhem, a number of large companies in the business services sector have moved into new buildings. But the vacancy in the area's office market is still a considerable 15%. In Arnhem's retail market, demand fell by some 4.5% in 2004, while supply increased by an impressive 64%. Vacancy in this market was 3.7%. After a strong decline in 2003, the demand for retail space in Nijmegen increased by 15% in 2004. Supply rose by 40%. Traditional sectors like business services, manufacturing and logistics play a dominant role in the economy of the KAN area. KAN also presents itself as the region's Health Valley. The knowledge centers that have developed around the universities of Nijmegen, Wageningen and Twente form important hubs for the development of expertise and productivity.

The eastern region of the Netherlands has positioned itself as a link between the Randstad urban conglomeration and the German Rheinland-Ruhrgebiet. In the near future, more and more spacious business parks will be constructed on the outskirts of the region's cities, offering a variety of quality office accommodation in a rural setting.

>>

A shepperd in the Veluwezoom nature reserve.

< The current shopping center of Arnhem will be extended
with the Musiskwartier.

Arnhem

A good example of the innovative developments in the KAN area is the IJsseloord 2 business park. Ballast Nedam and the Giesbers Group will be developing a total of 350,000 m² of commercial and office property. Over 40% of the total premises will be green space. Although the project is still under construction, a number of lots have already been taken into use.

The development of Musiskwartier in the center of Arnhem is currently nearing its completion. The new shopping area to be realized at this location will form an extension of Arnhem's existing retail center. Working in collaboration with city government, Multi Development and Vendex KBB are realizing 32,000 m² of retail space, 65 luxury apartments and an expansion of the present parking garage. Included in the plans is the redevelopment of the existing V&D department store. Rijnboog, the Arnhem district located between Rijnkade and the city center, is certainly ready for an extensive overhaul. Working with Spanish architect De Sòla-Morales, the municipality, Bouwfonds MAB Ontwikkeling, Blauwhoed, Portaal, SFB Vastgoed

The KAN area, the economic heart of the Eastern region, will mainly cater companies seeking a presentable and efficient location between the Randstad

and Vesteda have drawn up a master plan for the area. The total development entails 33,000 m² of retail space, 30,000 m² of leisure facilities, 80,000 m² of offices, 1,150 homes and 28,500 m² of cultural facilities. Building will last until 2022.

The area surrounding Arnhem Central Station is currently undergoing extensive renova-

tions. Until 2010, the developers Eurocommerce and Program Invest will be working with local government to develop 80,000 m² of office and retail space. The station itself will be redeveloped into a quality public transport junction with a direct connection to the eastern HSL high-speed rail link. Project investment totals €555 million.

'The Musiskwartier enhances Arnhem's local color'

"The oldest documents on the Musiskwartier date back to before 1992. That's a long time, but as inner city redevelopments require, the entire city has been involved in

the entire renewing process. After all, the new structure we're building will last for 100 years. We're adding a new loop to the main shopping axis, which goes further than just building. The construction of the V&D department store is a large-scale undertaking, and we're also enhancing the local color by means of two narrow streets and a square. The Musiskwartier forms the link between the open structure on the V&D side and the closely-knit struc-

Hans de Jong
Deputy Director
Multi Development

ture on the center side. That's why we've involved multiple architects, including Robert Stern. His historic style will certainly appeal to Arnhemmers."

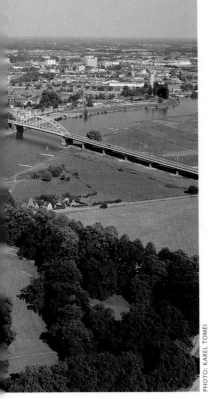

PHOTO: KAREL TOMEI

to larger regional and national
and the Rheinland Ruhrgebiet.

Owner Corio and developer
Bouwfonds MAB Ontwikkeling
plan to expand the Presikhaaf
shopping center with 10,000 m²
of stores and 1,400 homes. The
project, which is set for completion in 2008, is part of the redevelopment of the district. In
Schuytgraaf some 6,250 homes
in 25 different neighborhoods
will be built until 2012.

Nijmegen

Nijmegen is probably the oldest
city in the Netherlands, but has
some exciting new developments
occurring. Philips plans to expand
its office and laboratory facilities
in Nijmegen with a new knowledge center – part of a large-
scale master plan with offices
and retail, catering and entertainment venues, parking facilities
and a new network of roads. The
70,000-m² complex will house
offices, a conference center,
apartments, stores and sports
facilities. Stretching to 86 m,
the tower will be the tallest in
the city. The center will be
completed by the end of the year.
At the Vinex residential development of Waalsprong ❶, local
government, Multi Development,
Bouwfonds MAB Ontwikkeling,
BAM Vastgoed and Heijmans
IBC will be developing 12,000
homes in the period until 2015.
Waalsprong will be a complete
new city district located close to
Nijmegen's center. The City will
be realizing 2,000 apartments on
the center side of the Waal river,
including 40% in the social
housing sector. Plans include a
new bridge over the river. The
homes will be completed
between 2009 and 2020.

A popular referendum led to the
appointment of ING Real Estate
as developer of the city square
Plein 1944 ❷. The plan outlines
a conservative program with a
great deal of green space, homes,
a modest number of stores,
expansion of the existing cinema
and a four-star hotel. A remarkable feature of the project will be
a 16-m long 'town table'. The
square is set for completion in
2008. The ambitious urban
renewal project Koers West is
based on three main sub-projects: the rearrangement of
several existing business parks,
the development of the living/
working environment Waalfront
on the banks of the Waal (which
includes building some 2,000
apartments) and the construction
of a second city bridge. The
project will run until 2020.
On Nijmegen's southern rim, one
finds the future site of Lindenhof
Business Park, with a direct connection to the A73 highway. A
mere third of the 3.5-ha site has
been built over. The spacious
park will eventually accommodate 11 to 14 commercial buildings (1,000 - 4,000 m²), most of
which have been reserved for
offices. At present, three buildings have been completed.   >>

De Verbinding in Ermelo (5,000 m² of retail facilities and homes) is a project of Multi Development.

Ermelo/Ede

In Ermelo, Multi Development is developing De Verbinding, with 5,000 m² of retail facilities and homes. Besides a supermarket, the project will feature a number of first-floor commercial spaces and apartments. In addition, various small-scale low-rise homes and a multi-story apartment complex for senior citizens are included in the plans. De Verbinding will be completed in 2008.

At the end of 2005, ING Real Estate and Macéka Vastgoed finished work on Ede's Hof van Gelderland, which added 13,000 m² of retail and 57 homes to the city's core shopping area. Hof van Gelderland is a continuation of the Markt-Grote Straat shopping route. One of the main attractions is a new Media Markt electronics mega-store.

Apeldoorn

The City of Apeldoorn, BAM Vastgoed, 3W and Wieap Beheer will be redeveloping Van Gelderpark on the edge of Europaweg. The site will gain five office buildings with a total floor space of 45,000 m². Two of these have been reserved for the headquarters of the local police and fire departments. Van Gelderpark is part of the Zuidwestpoort project, which is intended to develop into a western gateway to the city. Some 200,000 m² of office space can be added to this in five stages. The ETV Group, initiator of Business Park Apeldoorn on the Arnhemseweg, has developed a new 10,000- m² office for the Kadaster land registry service. The park includes space for an additional six new office buildings.

At the end of 2005, city government approved plans for the construction of the Omnisportcentrum. It will be the first indoor athletics and cycling hall in the Netherlands. The complex will include a professional sports hall and a rollerblade track that can be used as a natural ice rink during the winter. Furthermore, 12,000 m² of office space and 10,000 m² of commercial functions will also be realized at this site. Libéma and Giesbers Groep are the developers of the project, which is set for completion in 2007.

Hof van Gelderland added 13,000 m² of retail and 57 homes to Ede's core shopping area.

The site of the Van Gelderpark will gain five office buildings with a total floor space of 45,000 m².

Geldermalsen

For some years now, there has been talk in Geldermalsen of the redevelopment of the area surrounding the city's railway station. Developers Ballast Nedam Ontwikkeling (BNO) and Dura Bouw Houten (DBH) might develop some 20,000 m² of offices, 500 parking spaces, stores and educational facilities. The municipality is still discussing the various plans.

Doetinchem

In collaboration with the City of Doetinchem, Kondor Wessels Projecten is developing the new residential neighborhood of Hamburgerbroek, which will have 1,200 homes, 30,000 m² of offices and 2,400 parking spaces. The City has not managed to acquire all the necessary property. However, the project will be realized in an altered form and is scheduled for completion in 2013.

Enschede

The Zuiderval project will be jointly developed on a 40-ha site by the City of Enschede and BAM Vastgoed. Six project subsectors will provide space for approximately 100,000 m² of office space, 20,000 m² of commercial space and company premises, 40,000 m² of mobility-related functions, 155 homes and 70 free lots for housing construction. Zuiderval, with a total investment of approximately €450 million, will be completed in the course of 2006.

The University of Twente is currently involved in a number of renovation and new construction projects on its campus. Plans include new research halls, an extensive overhaul of the existing sports halls and new accommodation for administrative and educational departments. The various projects should be rounded off by 2008.

Grolsch City is a mixture of living, working and shopping on the former site of the Grolsch brewery in the northern part of Enschede. The program, developed by local government and ING Real Estate, comprises a new shopping center (4,500-8,000 m²), 100 apartments, 50 homes and 20,000-25,000 m² of industrial space. Part of the factory complex is still to be redeveloped. 　　　　>>

ING Real Estate is developing Grolsch City, the former location of the Grolsch brewery.

Hart van Zuid in Hengelo. It involves the development of a totally new city district on the grounds of former factory complexes.

Hengelo

In Hengelo, TCN Property Projects is currently developing the third phase of the Plein Westermaat retail park, which will accommodate peripheral and large-scale retail businesses. The third phase, involving the development of some 18,000 m², offers room for leisure and retail. The location will have a total floor space of 75,000 m² and is scheduled for completion by mid-2007. Next to the park, one finds Westermaat Campus, a 150,000-m² office site. Developer Multi and the City of Hengelo are involved in the program's elaboration. The first offices have already been taken into use and the Campus Business

Center will be completed in 2006. Following the move of Stork and Dikkers to a location outside of Hengelo, 50 ha of inner-city space have been freed up for the Hart van Zuid project. Between 2015 and 2020, this area with its familiar collection of old factory complexes will be reintegrated in the city center. Hart van Zuid will consist of 75,000 m² of offices, 7,000 m² of industrial space, 2,000 residential units, 45,000 m² for educational facilities, 15,000 m² for culture and 18,000 m² of various other facilities. The total investment cost of the development by the municipality of Hengelo and the Van Wijnen Groep is €585 million.

Zwolle

The A28 national highway runs from east to west through the city of Zwolle. In the coming decades, a number of redevelopments will be initiated along a 500-m stretch of the road, including intensification of the area's zoning arrangements and the stacking of functions. In the Voorsterpoort area, ING Real Estate will develop 80,000 m² of office space and 40,000 m² of space for peripheral retail (completion in 2008). The nearby Kamperpoort will offer a mix of functions like offices and conference and events facilities. Holtenbroek I will be a high-density office district. Hanzeland, located to the south of the NS railway station, is a new inner-city combined living/working district. Construction is nearing completion in this area. Here, Eurocommerce and NS Vastgoed are developing 200,000 m² of office space, homes and facilities. Most of the homes have already been put on the market and many office buildings taken into use. Hessenpoort is a large-scale

Westermaat Campus, Hengelo (150,000 m² of office space).

business park of 112 ha located near the A28 highway. The project's first phase will be fully realized by 2008, and the municipality is currently preparing the second phase. IPMMC Akerpoort is involved in the development of a stadium complex for the FC Zwolle and Be Quick soccer clubs. Local government will contribute €8.4 million to the total investment. In addition to the 10,500-seat stadium, the area will gain a hotel/conference center and various retail/leisure facilities (with a total floor space of 10,000 m²). The project is set for completion in the course of 2006.

Nijverdal

In the center of Nijverdal, Johan Matser is redeveloping Dunantplein Square. With 4,500 m² of stores, 100 homes, cultural facilities and a 400-space parking garage, the square will serve as a renewed attraction in the core retail area. Completion is scheduled for 2006. ≪

MORE INFORMATION

Websites

www.enschede-stad.nl
www.hengelo.nl
www.hartvanzuid.nl
www.westermaatcampus.nl
www.multi-development.com
www.arnhem.nl
www.zwolle.nl
www.nijmegen.nl
www.apeldoorn.nl
www.tcnpp.com

EASTERN REGION

Eastern Region: Gelderland, Overijssel / Projects 2006 and beyond.				
Gelderland	**Project**	**Program**	**Development**	**Planning**
Apeldoorn	Omnisport Centrum	Apartment/office towers, offices 12,000 m² shops 12,000 m², cineplex, sports center 6,500 m²	Libéma, Giesbers Vastgoed	2007
Apeldoorn	Van Gelderpark	Shopping development, offices 45,000 m² shops 28,000 m²	BAM Vastgoed, 3W Wieap Beheer, Mun. of Amersfoort	n.a.
Arnhem	Businesspark Arnhem Kema-terrein	Business park, offices 25,000 m²	Giesbers Groep, KEMA BAM Vastgoed	2007
Arnhem	IJsseloord2	New office development 350.000 m²	Giesbers Groep Ballast Nedam	2015
Arnhem	Rijnboog	New development, offices 90,000 m² shops 33,000 m², leisure 30,000 m² residential 1,150 units, parking 3,900 cars hotel 8,000 m², culture 28,500 m²	Bouwfonds MAB Ontwikkeling BPF Bouwinvest, Vesteda Blauwhoed B.V., De Portaal	2006-2020
Arnhem Center	Arnhem Central	New development, offices 80,000 m² shops 5,000 m², homes 7,000 m² parking 1,000 cars, leisure 2,500 m² culture 1,000 m², investment €544.5 mln	ING Real Estate Development NS Real Estate, Eurocommerce Robex Groep	2005-2010
Arnhem Center	Musiskwartier	Renovation and extension of city center shops 32,000 m² residential 65 units parking 490 cars, other 1,000 m²	Multi Development Municipality of Arnhem, Koninklijke Vendex KBB N.V	2006
Nijmegen	KAN-gebied	Office development 30,800 m²	Rabo Vastgoed	2010
Nijmegen	Mercator Science Park	New office building 25,000 m²	Nijmegen N.V., Gelderse Ontwikkelingsmaatschappij	n.a.
Nijmegen North	Waalsprong	New neighborhood shops 20,000 m², residential 12,000 units education	BAM Vastgoed Bouwfonds MAB Ontwikkeling Heijmans IBC, Multi Development Municipality of Nijmegen	2010-2015
Veenendaal	Center	New city center shops 7,000 m²	BAM Vastgoed	2015
Overijsel	**Projects**	**Program**	**Development**	**Planning**
Enschede	Business & Science Valley	Business park, offices 6,000 m² business 12,500 m², parking 247 cars investment €32 mln	Multi Development	2006
Enschede	Stokhorst	Shopping development shops 70,000 m²	Multi Development	n.a.
Enschede	Zuiderval	New development shops 20,000 m² residential 155 units, 70 free lots mobility-related facilities 40,000 m² offices 100,000 m²	BAM Vastgoed Municipality of Enschede	2006
Hengelo	Oosterbos	Office development 30,000 m²	Dura Vermeer, Lammersen Droste Vastgoedontwikkeling	2010
Hengelo	Plein Westermaat phase III	Shopping development leisure and shops 18,000 m²	TCN Property Projects	2007
Zwolle	Westerlaan	Office development 40,000 m²	DC Vastgoedontwikkeling	n.a.
Zwolle	Stadion Zwolle	New development Shops, offices 48,000 m² and leisure	Multiplan	2008

More information: www.holland-re.com/projects

ONLINE: www.holland-re.com/easternregion

BENEFITING FROM HISTORY AND ACCESSIBILITY
SOUTHERN

❶ MAASTRICHT
❷ HEERLEN
❸ VENLO
❹ DEN BOSCH
❺ EINDHOVEN
❻ TILBURG
❼ BREDA
❽ MIDDELBURG

Many cities in the south of the Netherlands are graced with beautiful historical centers – making them attractive both as a tourist destination and as an international business location.
Modern redevelopments complement the authentic medieval hearts of towns like Maastricht, Den Bosch and Breda, giving the cities a more balanced structure.

REGION

PHOTO: FRANS LEMMENS

The Southern Region is famous for the yearly carnival festivities.

Mr. B.J.M. Baron van Voorst tot Voorst
Queen's Commissioner, Limburg

Prior positions included: State Secretary of Defense, State Secretary of Foreign Affairs, Dutch Ministry of Economic Affairs.

Maastricht is an old city that meets modern-day requirements. Over the past few years, the city has worked to improve its economic vitality and international appeal, leading to a boom in building activity. With the successful redevelopment of the neighborhoods Céramique, Randwyck and Annadal, Maastricht is making work of urban regeneration. Local government has positioned the city as a quality environment with a relaxed, bon-vivant atmosphere. And this approach has proven successful, because Maastricht's image is as solid as a rock – experience economy *avant la lettre!* In the office market, Maastricht competes with the nearby city of Heerlen. As a result, the two cities are focusing on specializations: Maastricht catering more to the commercial sector and Heerlen to (semi)-governmental organizations. As office locations, the cities in the southern region are slowly recovering from the slump of recent years. Demand is showing a slight increase while supply remains stable. Breda, a particularly positive example, is showing true recovery- more

transactions and more square meters. The West-Brabant area is mainly geared towards accommodating head offices for Benelux and European distribution centers. The region's excellent situation and accessibility are its main attractions as a business location. It has good connections both to the north and the south, and with the arrival of the HSL high-speed rail link, Breda's public transport facilities will improve considerably. As Brabant's second office center (900,000 m²), Den Bosch benefits from its location on the Amsterdam-Maastricht axis. Continuing development in Paleiskwartier, situated on the edge of Den Bosch's attractive city center, is sure to stimulate new developments. Eindhoven, finally, is the southern region's largest office city. Without the presence of major corporation Philips, however, it would be a whole other story. Most market developments depend on the electronics multinational in some form or another. However, this situation does have the advantage that – partially thanks to Philips – Eindhoven has developed into the country's leading knowledge center.   >>

J.R.H. Maij-Weggen
Queen's Commissioner, North Brabant

Prior positions included: member of European Parliament, Minister of Traffic, Waterways and Public Works, CDA party leader in European elections.

Drs. W.T. van Gelder
Queen's Commissioner, Zeeland

Prior positions included: Deputy Queen's Commissioner, member of the Provincial Executive of North Holland, member of the Provincial Council of North Holland.

PHOTO: OOG VOOR HOLLAND/RENÉ VAN DER MEER

< The historic city center of Maastricht is an attractive tourist location.

Entre Deux in Maastricht is a development of Multi Development and 3W (15,000 m² of retail space).

Maastricht

The direct surroundings of Maastricht Central Station will be redeveloped into an attractive area with small-scale retail and catering facilities. Plans include a parking garage located under the square that offers space for 280 vehicles. An 18,000-m² office complex - De Colonel - borders the square. This building, which also houses commercial spaces, leisure facilities and a parking garage, has been developed by 3W and NS Vastgoed. Mosae Forum (a development by the City of Maastricht and 3W) involves the intensive restructuring of the areas between Markt and the Maas river in the heart of the city. The project features a 1,150-space parking garage, 16,500 m² of council offices, a council hall (900 m²), retail space and 18,500 m² of catering, divided across two buildings and three building layers. Designed by architects Jo Coenen and Bruno Albert, Mosae Forum is expected to cost €162.5 million. It will be completed in the spring of 2006.

In the heart of Maastricht's core retail area, between Markt and Vrijthof, Multi Development and 3W are redeveloping the inner-city location Entre Deux. Owned by Fortis Vastgoed, Entre Deux will offer 12,000 m² of shopping facilities divided across three levels. A transparent covered shopping arcade will form a seamless connection with Maastricht's historic center. The project, which will also feature 19 apartments and parking facilities, will open its doors in the fall of 2006. The location concept was developed by T+T Design.

Belvédère

A fine example of Maastricht's drive to distinguish itself is the grand redevelopment of the central district of Belvédère, the largest and most ambitious project of its kind in the Netherlands. The plan area covers some 280 ha, with total investment reaching €1.3 billion. Working in collaboration with ING Real Estate and BPF Bouwinvest, the City of Maastricht will be involved in this project for the next 20 to 25 years. The Master Plan for Belvédère currently outlines

Hans Kolhoff is the architect of De Colonel (18,000 m² of office space).

The Avantis European Science and Business Park (100 hectares) is a joint venture of the cities of Heerlen and Aachen.

some 4,000 homes, 75,000-
100,000 m² of offices, 20,000 m²
of large-scale retail and 35,000 m²
of peripheral retail. The neighborhood will feature height differences and an abundance of
water and greenery.

Over the next decade, 1,000 new
homes will be built in the neighborhood of Malberg, as well as
various facilities. The project is a
collaboration between local government, the housing corporations Servatius and Woonpunt
and Multi Development. In 2009,
a new multipurpose center will
also be realized in the area.

Randwijck

Construction on the 70,000-m²
Campus Universiteit Maastricht
in Randwijck-Noord started at
the end of 2005. The project was
initiated by the Servatius housing
corporation and will cost approximately €100 million. Spanish
architect Santiago Calatrava is
responsible for the design. The
program includes student
housing, studios, apartments,
office space for start-up ventures,
a multipurpose sports center and
a parking garage. Campus
Universiteit Maastricht is set for
completion in 2008.

Heerlen

The Avantis European Science
and Business Park will be completed in 2009. The 700,000-m²
area has been divided into lots
ranging from 1,000 to 60,000 m².
Multi Development and 3W are
responsible for the development.
Business Park Coriopolis is the
spearhead of Heerlen's endeavor
to attract high-quality technological enterprise to the city. It has a
park-like design and offers some
125,000 m² of business space.
Stadspark Oranje Nassau (municipality, Multi Development and NS
Vastgoed), entails the development of 70,000 m² of office
space, 12,000 m² of large-scale
retail and 7,000 m² of station-
related retail, a 4,000-m² hotel,
26,000 m² of educational facilities, 510 homes and 1,775 parking
spaces. The project forms a virtual
bridge between the station's
northern and southern sides.
Opposite the station hall lies the
site of Telepark, a development
by Bouwfonds MAB
Ontwikkeling and the municipality of Heerlen. »

Maastricht University Campus will offer housing and facilities for students.

Sittard-Geleen

The city center of Geleen is currently undergoing partial redevelopment. At the end of this year, developers 3W and Van Kan-Jongen will have realized approximately 700 homes and 11,450 m² of retail space. In addition, local government oversaw the development of a 'culture cluster' with an underground parking garage. Total investment exceeds €10 million. The first sub-sector will be completed by mid-2008. The buildings of the C&A and V&D department stores in this area have already been torn down. A new local parking garage will open its doors in early 2007. The former MLK site – sub-sector 3 - will follow at a later stage.

Zitterd Revisited

The town of Sittard is also redeveloping its city center, under the motto 'Zitterd Revisited'. The master plan – developed by architect Jo Coenen – distinguishes five sub-sectors and outlines the construction of 1,500-2,000 homes, 10,000 m² of retail, 10,000 m² of office space and various cultural facilities over the next 20 years. The project is a partnership between the municipality, developers 3W, Heijmans IBC, Vesteda and the WVS housing corporation. The first homes will become available in 2007.

Roermond

In Roermond, the forecourt of the former Ernst Casimirkazerne barracks complex will be redeveloped by 3W and Van Pol Beheer. In future it will play a pivotal role in connecting Roermond's inner city, the previously realized Designer Outlet Center and the still to be developed Maashaven waterfront district. A mix of shops and leisure (including a cinema),

In 2005 an additional 10,000 m² of retail space opened at the Designer Outlet Center

bars and restaurants, offices (10,000 m²) and homes (150 apartments) will be built here in the years ahead, according to a master plan drawn up by Cees Dam.

Venlo

The Maasboulevard is an ambitious plan for central Venlo that provides an attractive mix of living, shopping, culture and rec-

The redevelopment of the city center of Geleen (3W and Van Kan-Jongen).

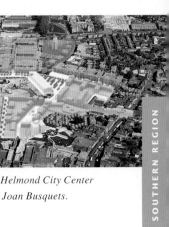

Masterplan Helmond City Center by architect Joan Busquets.

leisure, 155 luxury homes and a 9,000-m² city park. The floor space of the existing theater will be expanded by 3,800 m². Building starts in 2006 and the total project is scheduled for completion by 2008.

For years, the City of Venlo and market parties Multi Development, Janssen De Jong, Vesteda, 3W and Van Wijnen have been involved in the large-scale operation Venlo Centrum Zuid. This plan combines the reconstruction of local economic activity with urban renewal projects and housing construction. Up until 2009, 1,600 homes and 15,000 m² of office space will be built in this area. To date, over 1,100 homes have already been realized.

Trade Port Noord is a 140-ha industrial site that is being developed by 3W and Grontmij. It primarily accommodates companies in the logistics and trans-shipment sectors. The nearby Trade Port Oost follows the 'Trends & Trade' formula, which was conceived by developer TCN Property Projects. The area houses a 21,000-m² wholesale center for the business market.

Roermond. Owner: McArthurGlen.

reation. It is a joint development by local government and 3W. Divided into four sectors, the project will eventually add some 21,500 m² of retail, catering and

Helmond

The City of Helmond is working in close collaboration with ING Real Estate and Multi Development on the development of a plan for the city center, based on the partially revised master plan drawn up by Spanish urban developer Joan Busquets. Starting in 2006, central Helmond will be expanded with a range of new facilities, including 24,500 m² of retail and catering space, approximately 10,000 m² of office space, 800 homes, 2,500 m² of social facilities, a library, a hotel and 2,000 parking spaces. The total investment in the project, which is expected to take 10 to 15 years to complete, will amount to some €200 million. >>

The Maasboulevard will give Venlo an attractive mix of living, shopping, culture and recreation.

Nimbus Family Entertainment Center (TCN, 100,000 m².).

Eindhoven

On a site near the A2 highway close to Eindhoven, TCN Property Projects is developing the Nimbus Family Entertainment Center. This 100,000-m² complex will offer a combination of entertainment, culture, education and thematic retail. Plans furthermore include offices, a conference hall and a park & ride service. The project is scheduled for completion in mid-2007. Working in collaboration with Schiphol Real Estate, the municipality of Eindhoven is developing the Flight Forum business park in the vicinity of Eindhoven Airport. Its proximity

to the airport and the A2 arterial road makes Flight Forum an ideal home base for both airport-related and non-airport-related companies. The future location of Eindhoven's High Tech Campus, a development by Philips Vastgoed, will have a total size of no less than 910,000 m². The cost of the and landscaping and construction of 25 new buildings is estimated at €600 million. To enhance its campus character, the complex will include restaurants, shops and sports, recreation and daycare facilities, as well as five 'landscape zones'. The project will be completed in 2008.

Park Strijp

In the next few years, the departure of Philips will free up 27 ha of space for the realization of a new neighborhood near Eindhoven's city center. The Park Strijp master plan was drawn up by Bureau BVR, the City of Eindhoven and developer Volker Wessels. In the period until 2020, 3,000 homes will be built here, as well as 30,000 m² of commercial facilities and 30,000 m² of space to be filled in at a later date.

Den Bosch

The large-scale Paleiskwartier project in Brabant's main city of Den Bosch is now beginning to take shape. In 2008, the developers - the City of Den Bosch and Volker Wessels and their financial partners NIB Capital and Pensioenfonds Stork - will have realized 1,400 houses, 180,000 m² of office space and 30,000 m² of retail and restaurants in the area bordering Den Bosch Central Station. Cornelis Huygens Projectontwikkeling is currently preparing the Periphium office building at De Brand Business Park. It will have a total floor size of 24,000 m².

Flight Forum is a high-quality business park located in the dynamic surroundings of Eindhoven Airport.

Tilburg

Pieter Vreedeplein  in central Tilburg will be developed into a new city square with residential, retail and leisure functions. Bouwfonds MAB, Corio and local government are collaborating on the development of 23,000 m² of store space (with a Media Markt as a major attraction), a cinema (seven theaters, with a total of 1,800 chairs), a 9,800-car underground parking garage and 131 apartments. The project, which is based on a master plan by Jo Coenen, will be completed in mid-2007.

In Tilburg's Haestrecht Kwartier ❷ (Spoorzone), BAM Vastgoed is currently involved in the development of 24,000 m² of office space and a high-rise building with 65 apartments. Construction will be realized between 2012 and 2017. To the south of the city, Blauwhoed and Multi Development are developing the multipurpose project Kempenbaan (150,000 m² of office space, 70,000 m² of apartments and 20,000 m² of facilities for residents and businesses). Kempenbaan, devised by architect Jo Crepain, is scheduled for completion in 2006.

Breda

In the next quarter-century, the city of Breda will develop into a regional hub of European importance. The main objective of Breda's railway zone, a collaboration between local government and NS Vastgoed, is the development of a new city district with a balanced mix of functions. The ambitious plans for this area outline the realization of 400,000-500,000 m² of residential space, 250,000-350,000 m² of professional space and 150,000-200,000 m² of facilities. A key element of the plans is the development of a new public transport terminal ❸ that will provide the city with a shuttle connection to the Rotterdam and Antwerp HSL stations. The 13-ha quality business park Digit Parc – a development by the municipality and a business consortium – will offer 75,000 m² of commercial-type office buildings, office pavilions and business space. According to plans, construction will start in 2007 and the park will be completed between 2010 and 2012.

Bouwfonds MAB Ontwikkeling is expecting to finish the 25,000-m² Steenakker office park in mid-2006. The three office buildings near the NAC soccer stadium and the A16 highway will offer 5,500 m², 7,000 m² and 12,500 m² of floor space respectively.   >>

Rosada Factory Outlet on the crossroads of highways near Roosendaal.

Roosendaal

In the next two years, the Rosada Factory Outlet will be constructed along the A58 highway on the outskirts of Roosendaal. This large retail complex – a development by McMahon Development Group (MDG) – will offer 15,480 m² of fashion stores and catering and 1,200 parking spaces. The project entails an investment of €80 million. ING Real Estate Investment will take a 70% share in the project's financing, and MDG will be responsible for the operation of the complex. Rosada is expected to open its doors in the second half of 2006.

Bergen op Zoom

With the realization of the project De Parade, the West Brabant town of Bergen op Zoom will gain a new shopping axis in its city center. De Parade, a development by Bouwfonds MAB Ontwikkeling and local government, will connect various existing shopping streets with one another. The plan was designed by architects Rob Krier, Bob van Reeth, Sjoerd Soeters and Jan Weijts. It comprises 18,000 m² of retail space, 67 city homes and two parking garages with a total of 460 spaces. De Parade will be completed in the course of 2006.

De Parade in Bergen op Zoom will be completed in 2006.

The new residential neighborhood of Bergse Haven (85 ha) is intended to strengthen the ties between the Bergen op Zoom's historic center and the surrounding water. To this end, the City is collaborating with developer Multi Development and investor AMVEST to develop some 2,700 homes and various recreational facilities. The master plan for the area was developed by Soeters Van Eldonk Ponec Architecten. Investment will run to approximately €550 million. The project will be realized in the period 2005-2015.

On the site of the former Cort Heyligerskazerne barracks, Blauwhoed Eurowoningen is currently developing an exclusive green residential park on the Danish model, with 250 homes in a variety of housing types. The former barracks complex will be left more or less intact. Building commences in mid-2006.

Middelburg

The Mortiere plan outlines the construction of a shopping center, a residential neighborhood and a business park along the A58 highway in Middelburg, the capital of the southern province of Zeeland. Multi Development and Heijmans are collaborating on the development of 40,000 m² of office space, 300,000 m² of commercial space and 40,000 m² of retail. The plan area has a total size of over 230 ha. The shopping center will be developed into a large-scale furniture mall.

TCN Property Projects and concept developer RECC will work together to realize the ZEP Leisure Park in the Mortiere plan area. The 24,000-m² park will focus on all-weather leisure and

entertainment. Plans include a children's playground, an entertainment center, a spa & health center, a fitness center, thematic retail and catering. The park will open its doors in 2007.

Terneuzen

Handelspoort Zuid is a new business park located on the edge of Terneuzen, in the center of Scheldemond – a European region made up of both Belgian and Dutch territory. Here, Multi Development and Van der Poel are developing a total of 25 plots in three separate zones: Poort, Het Lint and Telepoort. The parcels range from 1,800 to 10,000 m². <<

MORE INFORMATION

Websites

www.brabant.nl
www.zeeland.nl
www.ingrealestate.com
www.multi-development.com
www.bouwfonds.nl
www.3winfo.nl
www.tcnpp.com
www.nsvastgoed.nl
www.heijmans.nl
www.bamvastgoed.nl
www.kfn.nl

SOUTHERN REGION

Southern Region: Limburg, Brabant, Zeeland / Projects 2006 and beyond.				
Limburg	**Project**	**Program**	**Development**	**Planning**
Heerlen	Stadpark Oranje Nassaupark	Office development, offices 70,000 m² shops 19,000 m², hotel 4,000 m², facilities 26,000 m², residential and parking	Multi Development, NS Vastgoed	n.a.
Heerlen	Telepark	New office building 33,000 m²	City of Heerlen Bouwfonds MAB Ontwikkeling	n.a.
Heerlen	Thema Centrum Wonen	New development, shops 14,000 m², parking 1,325 cars	3W	2008-2009
Maastricht	Mosae Forum	New development, offices 16,500 m² shops and catering 18,500 m², parking 1,100 cars	3W, NS Vastgoed	2006
Venlo	Maasboulevard	New development shops and leisure 21,500 m², residential 153 units	3W	2008
Brabant	**Projects**	**Program**	**Development**	**Planning**
Breda	Achter de Lange Stallen	New shopping center, shops 26,831 m² residential 70 units, 8,600 m², parking 740 cars	Bouwfonds MAB Ontwikkeling	2007
Breda	Railway zone	New development 250,000-350,000 m² residential 400,000-500,000 m², parking 3,000 cars, facilities 150,000-200,000 m²	City of Breda NS Vastgoed	2004-2025
Breda	Steenakker	New officepark 25,000 m²	Bouwfonds MAB Ontwikkeling	2006
Den Bosch	Paleiskwartier	New development, offices 180,000 m² shops 30,000 m², residential 1,400 units	Volker Wessels Vastgoed, NIB Stork, Municipality Den Bosch	2008
Eindhoven	Ekkersrijt	New shopping center shops 40,000 m²	ING Real Estate Development	2006
Eindhoven	Flight Forum business park	New business park, offices 85,000 m² businesses 175,000 m²	Municipality Eindhoven Schiphol Real Estate	2010
Eindhoven	Philips High Tech Campus	Office development, total 910,000 m²	Philips Vastgoed	2008
Eindhoven	Park Strijp	New development, offices 100,000 m² residential 1,600 units, facilities 60,000 m²	Volker Wessels Vastgoed Burgfonds	2006-2015
Eindhoven	Stationsgebied	Office development 40,000 m²	William Properties NS Real Estate	n.a
Eindhoven	Stationsdistrict	Shopping development shops 25,000 m², shops 16,000 m²	Hurks Bouw & Vastgoed NS Vastgoed, Heijmans IBC BAM Vastgoed, BVR	n.a.
Helmond	Suytkade	New city district, offices 15,000-42,000 m² businesses 25,000 m², residential 953 units leisure 34,000 m², education 7,000 m²	Van Wijnen Groep N.V. City of Helmond	2012
Son	Ekkersrijt	Shopping development shops 45,000 m²	ING Real Estate	n.a.
Tilburg	AaBe-Complex	Shopping development shops 40,000 m²	BPF Bouwinvest	2007
Tilburg	Kempenbaan	Office development 150,000 m² residential 70,000 m², business 20,000 m²	Blauwhoed B.V., Multi Development	2006
Middelburg	ZEP Leisure Park	Shopping development, leisure 24,000 m²	TCN Property Projects, RECC	2007

More information: www.holland-re.com/projects

A BOOST IN QUALITY FOR

The 37-year-old shopping center Piazza Center in Eindhoven has been drastically redeveloped. A distinctive feature of Rodamco Europe's new center is its 24-meter-high roof that ensures that the street retains its public character. This roof is an example of how the traditional design of the covered shopping mall with its roofed interior has been discarded, resulting in a more inviting shopping center where all the retail units on each floor are clearly visible. Piazza Center and Media Markt add 22,000 m² to Eindhoven's central shopping district.

Piazza Center was built in 1969, creating space for retail units, offices and a municipal library. For years it has served primarily as a low quality B-grade shopping center. The purpose of the redevelopment was to utilize an integrated vision encompassing the entire area to create an attractive (grade A1/A2) shopping environment. The center also makes an important contribution to how the public experiences Eindhoven's city center.

Increased synergy

The main attractions that form the pillars of this urban area are Piazza Center, Bijenkorf, C&A, Media Markt and three parking garages. The redevelopment has increased synergy between these points. One reason for this was the creation of a well-situated and versatile passageway between Piazza and Media Markt, by placing a foot bridge that gives access to the parking garage. The introduction into the project of a large scale catering and restaurant formula (La Place) increases the amount of time that consumers spend in the shopping center. Additionally, Piazza Center contains a number of prominent fashion retailers distributed on two levels. The project

PIAZZA CENTER

F A C T   S H E E T

Piazza Center, Eindhoven

Program:
- 15,000 m² Piazza Center
  (26 retail units and restaurant and
  catering facilities)
- 7,000 m² Media Markt
- 7,000 m² of office space

Developer:
William Properties b.v.
Rodamco Europe

Owner/investor:
Rodamco Europe

Architect:
Massimiliano Fuksas

Managment:
WPM Vastgoedmanagement,
Barendrecht

Tenants:
a.o. Media Markt, Perry Sport, Mexx,
Zara, Esprit, Society Shop,
Vero Moda, WE Stores, Men at Work,
Toys 'R Us, La Place

More information
Rodamco Europe
P.O. Box 22816
1100 DH Amsterdam
The Netherlands
Tel.: +31 20 312 01 20
Fax: +31 20 312 02 40
E-mail: info.nl@rodamco.com
www.rodamco.com

SOUTHERN REGION

has rented 100% of its units: all four retail levels and both levels of business units.

Illuminating ambience

This outgoing, lively shopping center offers an excellent line of sight to all retail levels and provides a good connection to the 18 Septemberplein and the main shopping street. Through the intelligent use of light and open spaces, the Italian architect Massimiliano Fuksas has created an ambience where visitors immediately feel at ease. The opulent escalators and glass elevators bring you to the four expansively arrayed levels.

Center of attraction

As part of the central retail system, Piazza has an anchoring role on the north side. Large-scale shops dominate both sides of the city center, complemented by a number of fashion retailers and specialty shops.
The existing premises of the Perry Sports shop have been integrated into the development. The center possesses enough critical mass to attract consumers on its own merits and is located in a primary catchment area containing 680,000 inhabitants within a radius of 20 kilometers. «

ONLINE: www.holland-re.com/piazzacenter

OPEN

refreshing

bam
vastgoed

living - working - shopping - multifunctional

Creating an open-access framework. A social context in which connections between existing and new, functionality and space can thrive. Time and again, no matter what the challenge. Continuously pursuing balance, based on communication with both participants and society. **www.bamvastgoed.nl**

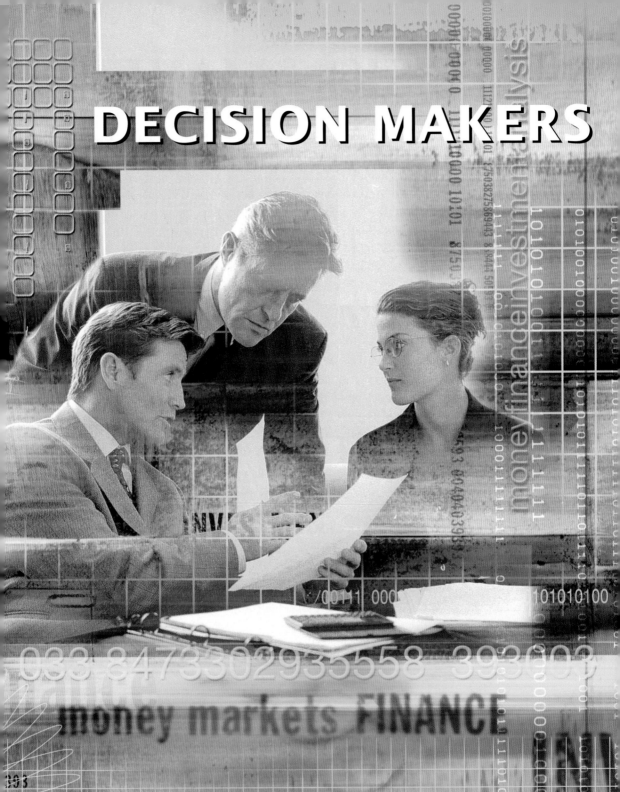

DECISION MAKERS

DECISION MAKERS
IN DUTCH REAL ESTATE

THE MEN IN CHARGE IN ALPHABETICAL ORDER:

A Arnoldussen, Edo – Amsterdam Development Corporation **265** **B** Bamberger, Lesley – Kroonenberg Groep **265** Bergh, Ruud – Schiphol Area Development Company (SADC) **265** ▪ Blight, David – ING Real Estate Investments **265** Blokhuis, Jaap – REDEVCO Europe **266** ▪ Bodzinga, Anne – BPF Bouwinvest **266** ▪ Boo, Kees de – NS Vastgoed **266** Brand, Hein – ING Real Estate Finance **266** ▪ Breur, Onno – Vesteda **267** **C** Cate, Hans ten – Rabobank **267** **E** Ernst, Erik – Interpolis Vastgoed **267** ▪ Eurlings, Nico – 3W **267** **G** Gerrevink, Reinier van – VastNed **268** ▪ Gongriep, Chris – G&S Vastgoed ▪ **268** Gool, Peter van – SPF Beheer **268** Groener, Gerard – Corio **268** **H** Haan, Arnold de – Multi Development **269** ▪ Hal, Dick van – Achmea Vastgoed **269** ▪ Hendrikse, Pieter – ING Real Estate Development **269** Hogenboom, René – Altera Vastgoed **269** ▪ Hooydonk, George van – Mn Services **270** ▪ Hoven, Jacques van – Heijmans Vastgoed **270** ▪ Hulshoff, Maarten – Rodamco Europe **270** ▪ Jautze, George – ING Real Estate **270** Jong, Rob de – TCN Property Projects **271** **K** Kalisvaart, Isaäc – Bouwfonds Property Development **271** ▪ Keur, Peter – FGH Bank **271** ▪ Kimmenade, Pieter van – Aareal Bank **271** Klijnen, Jean – Bouwfonds Asset Management **272** Kooistra, Foppe – Fortis Vastgoed Ontwikkeling **272** ▪ Kreij, Jan de – Corio **272** **L** Laglas, Karin – Rodamco Europe in the Netherlands **272** ▪ Lewis, Jeremy – Eurocommercial Properties **273** ▪ Liebe, Tie – William Properties **273** **M** Maas, Menno – AMVEST **273** ▪ Mast, Adriaan – Schiphol Real Estate **273** ▪ Meuwissen, Jaco – ING Real Estate Development **274** ▪ Munsters, Roderick – ABP **274** **N** Noordanus, Peter – AM **274** **O** Olland, Michiel – Bouwfonds Property Finance **274** ▪ Oosten, Joop van – Koninklijke BAM/AM **275** ▪ Oosten, Ton van – Maeyveld **275** ▪ Oostrom, Coen van – OVG Projectontwikkeling **275** **R** Reus, Carel de – Johan Matser Projectontwikkeling **275** ▪ Reijnen, Anka – Nieuwe Steen Investments **276** ▪ Riaskoff, Michel – Foruminvest **276** ▪ Roestenberg, Stan – Van Bohemen **276** Ruigrok, Peter – AM **276** ▪ Rutgers, Henk – Bouwfonds Holding **277** **S** Seelen, Jac – Ballast Nedam Ontwikkelingsmaatschappij **277** ▪ Smeets, Huub – Vesteda **277** ▪ Smeets, Ronald – Fortis Vastgoed Beleggingen **277** ▪ Stroink, Rudy – TCN Property Projects **278** **T** Tates, Nico – Aberdeen Property Investors Europe **278** ▪ Trip, Paul – IPMMC Vastgoed **278** **V** Verweij, Gijs – Wereldhave **278** ▪ Vismans, Paul – KFN **279** ▪ Visser, Adriaan – Development Corporation Rotterdam (OBR) **279** ▪ Vleugels, Ward – Q-Park **279** ▪ Vlimmeren, Ton van – Development Corporation Utrecht (OGU) **279** ▪ Vries, Anneke de – ING Real Estate Development Nederland **280** **W** Wattel, Jan Willem – Eurohypo **280** ▪ Werner, Dietmar – VolkerWessels Vastgoed **280** ▪ Wetselaar, Pieter – Rabo Vastgoed **280** ▪ Wolters, Jaap – Hanzevast **281** ▪ Worms, Cor – Achmea Vastgoed **281** **Z** Zandvoort, Henk van – Bouwfonds Property Development **281** ▪ Zwietering, Ted – Development Corporation The Hague (DSO) **281** ▪

COMPANIES IN ALPHABETICAL ORDER:

Edo Arnoldussen
CEO
Amsterdam Development Corporation

Edo Arnoldussen joined the Municipality of Amsterdam in 1975 as the coordinator for planning and coordination at the city's Department for Housing. In 1992, he was appointed general manager of the National Organization of Municipal Housing Departments in The Hague. In 1995, Arnoldussen returned to Amsterdam to head up local real estate affairs. In 1996, he was promoted to head the Department for City Development, Infrastructure and Municipal Management and in 1997, he became its General Manager. In 2000, Arnoldussen became CEO of the Amsterdam Development Corporation. The city's Development Corporation, combines the knowledge of neighborhood development, land exploitation, living and working. The chief task of the Ontwikkelingsbedrijf is to realize the goals set by the city for neighborhood and real estate development.

Lesley Bamberger
Director
Kroonenberg Groep

The Kroonenberg Groep is the largest private investment firm in the Netherlands and has many interests in the United States. Its most heroic feat is the redevelopment of the ABN-AMRO offices in the Leidseplein in Amsterdam. The Kroonenberg Groep rents out commercial real estate in the business real estate market in both the Netherlands and the United States. The majority of its stores are located in prime downtown locations, while a growing segment of its activities involve business buildings, offices, and stores in PDV/GDV locations. In December 2005, Bamberger purchased the De Barones shopping center in Breda for a sum of approximately €118 million from Commerz Grundbesitz Investmentgesellschaft (CGI).

Ruud Bergh
Managing Director
Schiphol Area Development Company (SADC)

The Province of North Holland, the City of Amsterdam, the Municipality of Haarlemmermeer, and the Schiphol Group established the Schiphol Area Development Company NV (SADC) in 1987 as a public-private company. SADC's objectives are to secure and improve the economic position of Amsterdam's Schiphol Airport and the surrounding areas through ongoing development of airport-related business parks and supportive infrastructure projects. Director Ruud Bergh is the former director of the development company Ontwikkelingsbedrijf in The Hague. During the coming years, Bergh will manage the further development of the Amsterdam Airport Area as one of the top regions for foreign investment in Europe.

David Blight
Member of the Executive Board
ING Real Estate Investments

Under the leadership of Australian David Blight, ING Real Estate Investments grew by €12 billion in 2005. The bank manages more than €42 billion of real estate investments around the world. ING Real Estate Investment Management works for those investors who want to spread their real estate investments among housing, retail, offices, logistics, business space, and parking facilities or a combination thereof. Investment Management operates in five regions around the world. The largest is in the United States with over €21.7 billion in assets. Here ING Clarion provides private-equity funds, REITs, fixed-income securities and property-management services.

Jaap Blokhuis
CEO
REDEVCO Europe

REDEVCO Europe, founded in 1999 as a limited European Real Estate Investment Company. REDEVCO Europe now handles a real estate portfolio of €6.5 billion and is active in 15 countries. REDEVCO Nederland has a real estate portfolio of €500 million invested in 90 properties which include prestigious high street shops, offices, and corporate buildings. The fund is privately owned by the Brenninkmeijer family, owners of the C&A department store chain. Blokhuis is following a strategy that will make REDEVCO more accessible to third parties in the future. REDEVCO is also active as developer and investor. "We have an ambitious growth objective," states Blokhuis. "We have a strong desire to put more money in the market." In 2006, he was selected as 'Man of the Year' by the Holland Real Estate jury.

Anne Bodzinga
General Director
BPF Bouwinvest

Pensioenfonds BPF has a special commitment to real estate. As a developer and administrator, CEO Anne Bodzinga controls a real estate portfolio worth some €4.8 billion. Over the past few years, his investment volume is some €350 million annually. Bodzinga placed that beside the development of large mixed-use complexes among which were a number of less-expensive homes. He is committed to investing in the social climate by paying particular attention to the long-term aspect of his investments. BPF is also engaged in developing its foreign portfolio, which is already good for some €312 million and within five years should be worth some €1.5 billion. BPF Bouwinvest currently has some 420,000 m^2 of commercial real estate in development.

Kees de Boo
CEO
NS Vastgoed

The upcoming renovations of the Hoog Catharijne in Utrecht provide director Kees de Boo with sufficient assurance that the NS Vastgoed order portfolio will be pretty full for the coming years. De Boo has already had an impressive career in real estate. He was involved in the establishment of AMVEST and then moved onto Rodamco Europe. NS Vastgoed owns some 4,800 hectares, mostly in areas near the Dutch railway network, but also in areas from where trains have long ago disappeared. It is here, mostly in urban downtown areas, that NS Vastgoed is working on projects that involve public transportation junctions.

Hein Brand
Member of the
Management Board
and CEO
ING Real Estate Finance

Hein Brand has in the name of ING Real Estate Finance overseen the financing of some €18.5 billion in real estate with a turnover of €4.5 billion. The company is shifting its real estate activities from local ING Bank branches to their Real Estate Finance Knowledge Center. The company's aim is "to be the leading provider of innovative real estate-based solutions, both locally and globally, which exceed our customers' performance expectations."

Onno Breur
*Member of the
Management Board*
Vesteda

Onno Breur joined the management of residential fund Vesteda per July 1, 2004. Onno Breur is Member of the Managing Board, dealing specifically with asset management (including disposition and product development), customer relations, facility management, and international orientation. Breur was trained as a real estate investor, and has worked with Achmea Vastgoed (real estate) and ING Vastgoed. Prior to this, he spent approximately 10 years in the United States working for Zadelhoff Makelaars and pension fund PGGM. Vesteda Group is a property fund focusing exclusively on residential property. With over 30,000 residential properties with a total value in excess of €4 billion. Vesteda concentrates on the higher-rent segment, with rents from €550 per month. As well as letting, Vesteda also develops higher-rent homes.

Hans ten Cate
Member of the Board
Rabobank

Rabobank, with Tjalling Halbertsma as their senior executive, has been able to build up its real estate branch. Hans ten Cate came from among the executive directors to actively oversee its early start-up phase. Rabobank is known for its decentralized structure, which meant that its prominent position in the investment, development and finance worlds was underexposed. But with the establishment of a more centralized real estate branch this will most certainly change. With more than 25 years experience and some 200 current projects under development (valued at €4 billion) in its portfolio, Rabo Vastgoed certainly belongs among the ranks of the largest housing developers in the Netherlands. Moreover, Rabo Vastgoed is also active in the (re)development of shopping centers and urban centers.

Erik Erenst
Director
Interpolis Vastgoed

Real estate investor, Interpolis, a subsidiary of Rabobank, manages assets valued at €3.5 billion, which is comprised of some 14 pension funds and makes it one of the largest real estate investors in the Netherlands. The total number of homes amounts to some 15,800. Its commercial portfolio also consists of roughly 900,000 m², mostly in the form of retail space and shopping centers. Interpolis Vastgoed is an independent subsidiary of Interpolis Pensioenen and was established solely to engage in real estate management for the pension funds clients. Erik Erenst was formerly employed at the Bedrijfspensioenfonds voor de Landbouw, Guo en Relan. At Interpolis Vastgoed, Erenst holds the position of Director.

Nico Eurlings
General Director
3W

3W has grown from a regional developer to one of the larger players in the Benelux region. Projects like Entre Deux, Mosae Forum, Belvédère and De Colonel in Maastricht are certainly proof of its growth. Nico Eurlings has transformed this former multifaceted company into one that now increasingly concentrates on its core activities. This shift in focus led to the takeover of Strienstra, which further strengthened its position in real estate development, and the selling off of its brokerage activities to Meeùs. 3W continues to expand beyond its Limburg roots with offices in Apeldoorn and Diemen as well as in Belgium.

DECISION MAKERS

Reinier van Gerrevink
CEO
VastNed

Reinier van Gerrevink shows remarkable calm as a real estate investor. VastNed manages to show positive results, even in a downward market. The VastNed Groep consists of two real estate funds quoted on the stock market: a store fund, and an office fund. Both funds are characterized by high dividend yields. The store portfolio consists of 600 objects worth a total of €1.36 billion. The office portfolio consists of almost 200 objects worth a total of €1.1 billion. Gerrevink, before assuming his position at VastNed in 2002, worked in management functions for ABN AMRO, Rodamco, and Robeco.

Chris Grongriep
Director
G&S Vastgoed

The preeminent developer of the Amsterdam-Zuidoost area has also garnered an important position at the Zuidas. Grongriep has always been prepared to take risks, but usually succeeds in profiting from his ventures. G&S specializes in the development and construction of flexible housing solutions and has realized office complexes for all of the major Dutch banks. Companies such as IBM, VNU, PricewaterhouseCoopers, and BP all turned to G&S for their turnkey headquarters.

Peter van Gool
Head of Real Estate/
Deputy Director
SPF Beheer

As Professor of Real Estate at the University of Amsterdam, Peter van Gool also contributes to the professionalization of the trade. Professor Van Gool studied general and monetary economy at the Vrije Universiteit (VU, Free University) in Amsterdam. For five years he served as head of investor relations and economic research at Wereldhave NV and then five years as financial assistant director and head of development and acquisitions at various corporations in the area of housing and living. Since 1998, Van Gool has served as head of real estate and assistant director of asset management at SPF Management (Spoorwegenpensionfonds, Railway Pension Fund) With investment assets worth €12 billion, SPF is one of the larger asset management firms in the Netherlands.

Gerard Groener
Managing Director
Corio Nederland Retail

At Corio, Gerard Groener is responsible for the development portfolio with a value of some €600 million in the Netherlands. Corio is one of the largest real estate funds quoted on the stock market, with a particular focus on European retail. The €3.9 billion portfolio mostly consists of shopping centers in the Netherlands, France, Italy, and Spain (approximately 175 objects and 4,300 rental agreements). Retail comprises roughly 75% of its portfolio. More than half of the Corio portfolio is located in the Netherlands. Corio has a goal to expand its retail section to approximately 80% of its portfolio. The figures for the first nine months of 2005 show an increase of €11.5 million to a total €151.6 million.

Arnold de Haan
CEO
Multi Development

In 2005, Arnold de Haan left his position at Commerz Grundbesitz Investmentgesellschaft (CGI) in Wiesbaden to take up a top position at AM, which was split apart at the end of January 2006. Arnold built up a broad range of international experience at his former employer, CGI, where he invested some €1.8 billion in the Netherlands. This experience will certainly come in handy in his new position as the CEO of Multi Development. Together with COO Hans van Veggel, he will certainly waste no time in expanding the international commercial activities of Multi Development.

Dick van Hal
Managing Director
Achmea Vastgoed

In 2005, Achmea Vastgoed grew to more than €7.3 billion for 60 clients; and Achmea Vastgoed will continue to grow even more. In 2006 more than €1 billion can be invested. This financial scale offers Achmea Vastgoed the power to use opportunities. The need for the right properties and good mortgage investments will continue. Since October 2004, Dick van Hal and Cor Worms fill the gap Onno Breur left behind at Achmea Vastgoed. Hailing from Levob Bank (director Fund Management, Treasury and Real Estate for six years) and Insurances in Leusden, Worms is coming from the outside to strengthen the real estate division. Working together with Worms Van Hal will try to put Achmea Vastgoed back on the map.

Pieter Hendrikse
General Manager
ING Real Estate Development

ING Real Estate is a market leader in the Netherlands in commercial real estate development, commercial real estate finance and real estate investment management. ING has a total business portfolio of more than €64 billion and offices in 15 countries. Pieter Hendrikse was appointed General Manager Development in March 2005. Hendrikse had previously served as Chairman of the European Board of ING Real Estate Investment Management, and has now made the switch from investment to development. In an additional function, Hendrikse serves as secretary of INREV, the European Association for Investors in Non-listed Real Estate Vehicles.

René Hogenboom
CEO
Altera Vastgoed

As an asset manager, Altera administers, among others, the pension funds of both KLM and the Hoogovens. Altera actually arose out of the Hoogovens pension fund. CEO René Hogenboom's intention is to convert Altera into a state-of-the-art investor. This will give it more disposable assets. Professionalism and transparency are the key words in Altera's approach. It currently manages assets of €1.4 billion. Pension funds can now participate in the newly established funds for housing, retail, offices, and business space. In December 2005, the pension funds of Stork and Media PNO both became clients of Altera. These funds brought 27 objects along with them worth some €90 million.

George van Hooydonk
Director Dutch Real Estate
Mn Services

Mn Services is the asset manager of the BPMT pension fund with a portfolio worth €4.8 billion. Mn's goal is to begin investing more for third parties. In the Netherlands, Mn invests directly (which is the responsibility of Van Hooydonk) and outside the Netherlands it participates in various real estate enterprises (Richard van Ovost). Mn Services has over 55 years of experience in pension administration, management support, and investment management. The client base, which includes leading pension funds and other institutions, has assets of €26.5 billion. The domestic real estate team currently manages over €1.3 billion, equally divided over residential, retail and office investments. The international real estate team actively manages assets of €2 billion.

Jacques van Hoven
Member of the Board
of Directors
Heijmans Vastgoed

In 2006, Heijmans employed approximately 9,600 people, who together realized a turnover of circa €2.6 billion and net earnings of circa €75 million. Jacques van Hoven is responsible for real estate development while Coen van Wichen is in charge of the real estate firm itself. Heijmans is a full-service construction and real estate enterprise that is involved in all real estate activities, from advice and design to maintenance and management. The goal for 2008 is to have 35% of company profits generated by advisory, design, and development activities, circa 45% generated by administrative functions, and circa 20% by maintenance and management activities. By 2008, some 20% of Heijman's activities will take place in countries outside the Netherlands.

Maarten Hulshoff
CEO
Rodamco Europe

With a portfolio worth some €8.7 billion, Rodamco Europe is the largest publicly listed property investment and management company in the retail sector in Europe. CEO Maarten Hulshoff saw his chance to transform Rodamco into a full-fledged real estate investment firm when at the end of January 2006 Rodamco received its official listing on the AEX (Amsterdam Stock Exchange). Investors value Hulshoff's reserved purchasing policy. Rodamco Europe ranks among the top in the Netherlands in both acquisitions and sales, with more than €150 million in transactions annually. In the third quarter of 2005, Rodamco Europe increased its pipeline portfolio to €2.4 billion.

George Jautze
CEO
ING Real Estate

With a total business portfolio of more than €64 billion and offices in 15 countries, ING Real Estate is also one of the strongest real estate companies worldwide. That makes chairman George Jautze one of the most important decision makers in the Netherlands. In 2006, ING Real Estate Development in Nederland (under the leadership of Jaco Meuwissen MRE) alone is worth some €4 to €5 billion with a turnover of some €500 million annually. In almost every other real estate sector – except the financing of housing— this bank and development firm sets the tone.

Rob de Jong
Chief Program Officer
TCN Property Projects

TCN is a European asset developer, with offices in the Netherlands, Germany, Portugal, Hungary, and Belgium. The company operates throughout Europe. TCN manages over 600,000 m² of European real estate with another 400,000 m² under development. CEO Rudy Stroink has distinguished himself as a modernizing developer, with original perspectives on concept, design, management, and financing. TCN's invests in its own projects with a commitment to the long-term. TCN management was further strengthened by the addition of Rob de Jong as Chief Program Officer (CPO). De Jong was hired away from BAM to help realize the expected increased growth in the coming years. The appointment in this newly created function left more room for the ever-expanding international acquisition efforts of Norbert Jansen (CIO) and Rudy Stroink (CEO).

Isaäc Kalisvaart
Member of the Executive Board
Bouwfonds MAB Ontwikkeling

Bouwfonds Property Development and MAB have been working together for over a year now. In the Netherlands it operates under the name Bouwfonds MAB Ontwikkeling, that is, as the big housing developer (of Zandvoort) and the innovative concept developer and retail specialist (in Kalisvaart). In 2005, they developed some 8,500 housing units and some 250,000 m² of commercial space. It has also managed to strengthen its position in a number of European countries by integrating its activities. Its main focus is on multifunctional projects, residential areas, and retail projects. For Bouwfonds, this means a shift from new residential developments to city center developments. Increased sales in 2005 ensured a larger turnover, which is mostly thanks to housing developments in the Netherlands and France.

Peter Keur
Chairman of the Board
FGH Bank

Since the end of October 2003, FGH Bank has been part of the Rabobank Group, the largest financial services provider in the Netherlands. Bying part of a highly formidable organization that boasts both private and commercial real estate finance among its core activities. The collaboration with Rabobank also provides access to an extensive national and international resource and knowledge network. FGH bank limits itselfs to the Dutch market, where in 2005, it realized a turnover of some €2.7 billion. Its headquarters is located in Utrecht plus it counts seven regional offices. FGH Bank employs a total of 215 people. The bank has grown significantly. "If you want to see increased growth, it's obvious that you start offering new product combinations", says Peter Keur who has been FGH's Chairman of the Board since 1995.

Pieter van de Kimmenade
Managing Director Netherlands
Aareal Bank

Aareal Bank AG, headquartered in Wiesbaden, Germany, is one of the leading international property banks listed on Deutsche Börse's MDAX index. Aareal Bank is active in three core business units: structured property financing, consulting/services, and property asset management. Aareal's lending activities in the Netherlands are mainly focused on commercial property markets. Clients include investors in shopping centers, retail parks, city and provincial offices, warehouses, and industrial parks. Van de Kimmenade is Aareal Bank AG's managing director in the Netherlands. He has found some market niches, including hotel financing. The Palace Promenade (Urban Entertainment Center along the Scheveningen boulevard) is also a client. Van de Kimmenade is also a board member of the Foreign Bankers Association.

DECISION MAKERS

Jean Klijnen
Chairman of the
Executive Board
Bouwfonds Asset
Management

Bouwfonds was bought out by ABN AMRO last year, and since then, Klijnen has provided excellent direction for Bouwfonds Asset Management. Bouwfonds Asset Management has successfully launched private funds for private investors with investments in the Netherlands, the US, and Germany (€350 million). It has created funds for institutional investors such as the fund that issued inflation contracts (€1.1 billion) and the Parking Fund (final total €300 million). The total market value of the assets under its management amount to €2 billion. The assets under its management are based in the Netherlands, the US (mainly residential), and Germany (offices).

Foppe Kooistra
Managing Director
Fortis Vastgoed
Ontwikkeling

Fortis Vastgoed Ontwikkeling is one of the large residential developers in the Netherlands, but is currently also making its presence known in the field of commercial real estate (with Provast in The Hague and with ING Real Estate and G&S at the Zuidas in Amsterdam). Its most renowned project is Leidsche Rijn, the largest new residential project in the Netherlands. Since 1999, when Kooistra first became its director, Fortis Vastgoed Ontwikkeling has weathered some turbulent times. Fortis Vastgoed Ontwikkeling develops some 800 to 1,000 residences annually in the Netherlands and currently has 260,000 m² of commercial real estate under development.

Jan de Kreij
CEO
Corio

The Corio portfolio in 2006 is valued at €4 billion. Corio has acquisition and sales transactions totaling circa €150 million annually. Corio invests 75% in retail, 20% in offices, and 5% in business space. Of this, 56% is invested in the Netherlands, 23% in France, 14% in Italy, and 7% in Spain. CEO Jan de Kreij employs a clear strategy: a goal of 80% of its capital invested in retail space, active 'hands-on' management of the Corio portfolio, and the stimulation of new home markets. A striking example of this is Corio's participation in Akmarez, an enormous shopping center in the suburbs of Istanbul, which, with its 16 million inhabitants, is now Europe's largest city. Besides being the CEO of Corio, Jan de Kreij is also chairman of ULI Europe (Urban Land Institute).

Karin Laglas
Managing Director
Rodamco Europe in the
Netherlands

Before Karin Laglas took up her position as director of Rodamco Europe in the Netherlands (July 2004), she had already experienced a long career at MAB. There she managed the French branch of MAB, and once back in the Netherlands, she became the director of MAB Nederland. Her most heroic feat to date is the development of Oosterdokseiland in Amsterdam. At Rodamco, Laglas is responsible for 40% of Rodamco Europe's total portfolio (€8.7 billion) in the Netherlands (approx. €3 billion). In keeping with its corporate strategy of 'Return on Retail', 86% of this total is invested in retail. Rodamco currently (co-)owns 26 shopping centers in the Netherlands. Rodamco also manages many of these shopping centers itself.

Jeremy Lewis
CEO
Eurocommercial Properties

Eurocommercial Properties invests for institutional investors in European retail, office, and warehouse properties. Its investment assets total €1.15 billion in retail, €1.15 billion in offices, and €1.3 billion in warehouses. The company strives to offer a diversified portfolio of properties in the European Union with an emphasis on modern shopping centers. It prefers existing buildings or those which, if constructed, are either pre-let or subject to development agreements minimizing vacancy risks. The fund remains one of the most transparent real estate funds in Amsterdam.

Tie Liebe
Director
William Properties

William Properties possesses a development portfolio worth some €1 billion, which consists mainly of multifunctional center projects. The company has been invited to participate in numerous competitions and has managed to realize a number of ambitious projects, including the Piazza in Eindhoven, which was nominated for the NRW Jaarprijs, and the Toren of Zuid in Rotterdam. In the mean time, the company now totals 35 employees. Besides Tie Liebe, Gerard de Greef (from AM) and Henk Jan Hollander (from Van Wijnen) have also recently joined the organization. The developer has, among others, the prestigious IJ-dock in Amsterdam in the pipeline. However, this project has recently been postponed.

Menno Maas
CEO
AMVEST

AMVEST has a housing portfolio worth €1.7 billion (18,000 rental units). The enterprise was founded by current chairman Menno Maas, together with Kees de Boo (now at NS Vastgoed) as a specialized and enterprising residential housing fund. With an annual 1,000 homes in development, AMVEST is one of the larger (rental unit) developers in the Netherlands. The focus runs the gamut from Vinex-neighborhoods to multifunctional city centers. AMVEST has developed on its own, which ensures that it only includes the types of housing units in its portfolio for which there is recognizable demand. Quality, sustainability, and adding value are its most important concerns. Although the fund's content is often compared to Vesteda, Vesteda is a bit larger and specializes in luxury rental units whereas AMVEST develops more total housing units and focuses more on middle-class rental units.

Adriaan Mast
Managing Director
Schiphol Real Estate

Ad Mast FRICS has brought leadership to Schiphol Real Estate (SRE). SRE manages six business parks at Schiphol, but it can also be found at other airports in Rotterdam, Eindhoven, Brisbane, Malpensa (Milan), and Hong Kong, all places where they either (partly) own or manage properties. As a real estate investor, SRE established its Acre Fund in 2006, valued at some €360 million. "The potential has increased dramatically," proposes Ad Mast, who has won much trust among colleagues in the real estate sector. "Schiphol Real Estate has managed to continue to grow over the past few years even in these times of slower economic growth." The company is one of the market leaders in the areas of development, management, and investments in commercial real estate at and around airports.

DECISION MAKERS

Jaco Meuwissen
General Manager
ING Real Estate
Development

Jaco Meuwissen and Hein van der Ploeg were both appointed General Managers at ING Real Estate Development in October 2005 and joined the Global Development Board as chaired by George Jautze. Meuwissen started his career at ING in 1997 as a developer. In 2000, he rose to Deputy Managing Director, in 2001, he was appointed Managing Director Development & Sales, and in 2002, he was made Chairman of Management. Before joining ING, Meuwissen was a consultant at Kolpron in Rotterdam. Meuwissen focuses mostly on development activities in the Netherlands, Belgium, France, Italy and its subsidiary 3W. Van der Ploeg, meanwhile, is responsible for development activities in Poland, Hungary, and the Czech Republic.

Roderick Munsters
CEO
ABP Vermogensbeheer

Roderick Munsters, previously at PGGM pension funds, is responsible for €160 billion in investments at ABP. Munsters is sure of the professionalization of real estate as an investment tool. He has also been involved in activities at EPRA. In 2005, ABP saw his real estate portfolio grow to €19 billion, partially thanks to substantial yields. (30 %). Because a real estate portfolio of 10% must be maintained against assets under management of €190 billion, ABP can once again take on a central role in global real estate.

Peter Noordanus
Chairman of the
Board of Directors
AM

Peter Noordanus is the CEO of BAM's holding, AM. Noordanus prepared the division of AM in the early part of 2006, while Hans van Veggel booked success on the operations side which was split off as MSREF. Since the takeover, Noordanus now works with Ruigrok, who used to manage AM Wonen. As a former Alderman of The Hague and chairman of the Neprom (Dutch sector association) Noordanus is a dedicated lobbyist, but an even more dedicated developer. Because of continued growth in housing development in the Netherlands, the company sold some 5,000 housing units in 2005.

Michiel Olland
Bouwfonds Property
Finance

Michiel Olland started with Bouwfonds in 2006 as Member of the Management Team of the business unit Property Finance International, responsible for the South of Europe and New Markets. Until the end of 2005, he worked as Chief Financial Officer at KFN. Olland previously worked at ABP Vermogensbeheer as the funds manager, responsible for all of ABP's real estate investments in Europe and Asia, at the Westland/Utrecht Hypotheekbank, where he served as Director Corporate Relationship Management, and at the merchant bank Banque de Suez Nederland. Michiel Olland also serves as the chairman of INREV (European Association for Investors in Non-listed Real Estate Vehicles).

Joop van Oosten
Chairman of the Executive Board
Koninklijke BAM/AM

BAM was already the largest construction company in the Netherlands. But it also belongs among the top nationally as a developer of commercial real estate. After it purchased AM Wonen, AM Grond, and AM Holding, BAM's position in the housing construction sector has only grown stronger than ever. Joop van Oosten took over the director's gavel from Klaas van Vonno, who will certainly enjoy his much-deserved retirement. The leadership of BAM Vastgoed is now in the hands of Henk Bree who, with the arrival of AM Peter Noordanus and Peter Ruigrok, is joined by highly valued colleagues.

Ton van Oosten
Director
Maeyveld

Ton van Oosten brought stability to IMCA Holding, after businessman Erik de Vlieger found himself in deep financial problems. In October 2005, IMCA was guided into a safe haven and renamed Maeyveld. Shortly thereafter, Joop Koster joined Maeyveld management. The company's real estate development department is expanding rapidly, with offices in a number of large cities. Maeyveld believes that the tenant is more important than the property. Maeyveld is currently striving to improve its position in the Netherlands as "the most conceptually creative innovator and co-creator, so that other parties can no longer avoid Maeyveld when they are looking for business or quality success." Moreover, Maeyveld is also focusing on downtown urban renewal projects.

Coen van Oostrom
CEO
OVG Projectontwikkeling

10 years ago, Coen van Oostrom founded OVG and he quickly rose to the top as an office developer. He has, in just a short period of time, managed to increase OVG's portfolio value to €1.1 billion. OVG Projectontwikkeling specializes in the (re)development of new and existing business-related real estate (offices, stores, and business space), high-quality residential construction projects and city center development. Van Oostrom distinguishes himself as a sharp, dynamic, and creative project developer, who is willing to stand in a client's shoes as the "service provider in meters." The most important element for Van Oostrom is not the location or the building but the end users. "Successful development focuses on people, not bricks," Van Oostrom observes.

Carel de Reus
Managing Director
Johan Matser Projectontwikkeling

Johan Matser Projectontwikkeling is the oldest developer in the Netherlands. The organization is known for its sustainable projects for which it regularly wins awards. In 2004, Carel de Reus received the first NEPROM Prize for a project in Arnhem and was nominated for another award by MIPIM. In 2003, De Reus himself received royal recognition for his social contributions, which include his former duties as chairman of NEPROM; as a board member at Nirov, at GIW and at Architectuur Lokaal; and as a member of the Kwaliteitsadviesraad at the Nationaal Dubo Centrum (Advisory Board on Quality at the National Dubo Center). "Founder Fred Matser was an anthroposophist," De Reus points out. "The roots of our commitment to sustainable projects stem from his early days." This, however, does not mean that this company does not have strong growth ambitions.

Anka Reijnen
CEO
Nieuwe Steen Investments

The Limburger Anka Reijen is the successor to Jo Zeeman as the manager of the Nieuwe Steen Investments fund. NSI is an investment fund that invests solely in Dutch property (offices, retail, housing, business buildings and large retail trade spaces). NSI has been registered at Euronext Amsterdam since 1998. Its investment returns increased to some €31 million in the first half of 2005, up from some €25 million for the first half of 2004. In the coming year, NSI will be focusing on the active management of its property portfolio and putting their efforts into quality and the optimizing of their various objects. Interest in NSI shares led to a record price of €19.10.

Michel Riaskoff
CEO
Foruminvest

The international expansion of retail developer Foruminvest has been impressive. The square meters available in the Netherlands may be modest, but outside the Netherlands, CEO Michel Riaskoff has managed to snatch some very big projects indeed. Foruminvest has offices in Naarden, Brussels, Paris, and Milan. In the years 1999, 2000, 2001 and 2002, Foruminvest received awards for the best developed shopping centers in the Netherlands and Europe from the ICSC (International Council of Shopping Centers). Foruminvest is one of the larger independent project developers in Europe. Riaskoff as an investor is increasingly interested in complete urban development projects.

Stan Roestenberg
General Director
Van Bohemen

Igo van Bohemen is one of the most renowned project developers in the Netherlands. He transferred his company over to Stan Roestenberg who has since pursued new initiatives. After Roestenberg took over as general director of Bohemen in 2000, he then acquired all of Igo van Bohemen's shares in 2003. Under the direction of Roestenberg, van Bohemen completely deals with all questions concerning space. Their main disciplines remain concept development, risk-taking project developments, and plan development for specific end users. The company has 15 employees.

Peter Ruigrok
Chairman of the
Board of Directors
AM

Since the takeover, the Board of Directors of BAM/AM Wonen and BAM/AM Grondbedrijf will include Peter Noordanus and Peter Ruigrok, who will both share the role of Chairman. Agreements have been made that AM Wonen will provide 35 to 40% of the construction production at BAM's construction company. AM Wonen/Grondbedrijf has approximately €10 billion in the pipeline on the basis of more than 40,000 residences.

Henk Rutgers
CEO
Bouwfonds Holding

After ABN AMRO took over Bouwfonds in 2001, Bouwfonds in 2005, turned around and bought out project developer MAB. With that purchase Bouwfonds now belongs among the largest developers of commercial real estate in the Netherlands. With the departure of Jaco Reijrink and Bart Bleker, the board of Directors was thinned out, following the Anglo-Saxon model, after which CEO Henk Rutgers is now the only one left waving the scepter. A series of takeovers really put him on the map. Internally, full attention is now being paid to the integration of MAB and the expansion of its asset management department. ABN AMRO wants to sell off Bouwfonds (total subsidiary) in 2006 because real estate (after the uncoupling of its mortgage portfolio to ABN AMRO) is no longer considered a core activity of the bank.

Jac Seelen
Director
Ballast Nedam
Ontwikkelingsmaatschappij

In 2005, Ballast Nedam saw the departure of two large shareholders, Project developer TCN Property Projects and investor Wedge. The shares were purchased by various institutional investors. TCN remains closely involved with Ballast Nedam, however. In 2005, they started a joint venture called Abl2, which was to focus on a new approach to integrated area development. This involves larger projects in which infrastructure and real estate are intertwined and are characterized by a managerial and financial complexity, with a diversity of interests. Seelen has also noticed another potential growth market: "The development, building, financing, exploiting of government buildings. We have the in-house expertise thanks to our learning experience gained in other countries."

Huub Smeets
Chairman of the Board
Vesteda

With a portfolio worth €4 billion, Vesteda belongs among the largest real estate funds not publicly traded on the stock market. It is also the most active with acquisitions of €247 million and sales of €291 million. Vesteda has made a special contribution to the professionalization of investment in homes both practice- and content-wise. Vesteda, emerging from the ABP pension fund, was successfully transformed into a truly independent fund with the spread ownership of shares by Huub Smeets's predecessor Hilverink. Smeets presents himself as a strong manager with a clear and consistent vision. He is well known for his involvement in a number of real estate plans and he has a great eye for urban architecture and landscape cohesion, as well as architectonic detail.

Ronald Smeets
General Manager
Fortis Vastgoed
Beleggingen

The Fortis Vastgoed real estate portfolio is comprised of investments totaling some €3.7 billion. Its international real estate portfolio totals more than €8 billion. Ronald Smeets is viewed as Fortis ASR's preeminent real estate leader by his colleagues. Smeets manages a diverse portfolio of real estate assets for Fortis and third parties. Fortis Vastgoed Beleggingen also serves as the real estate management team of Fortis. Smeets served as a promoter of Fortis's interests when he served as chairman of the Raad van Onroerende Zaken (Real Estate Council of the Netherlands) and was, until the spring of 2006, chairman of the IVBN (Vereniging van Institutionele Beleggers in Vastgoed, Nederland; Association of Institutional property investors in the Netherlands).

DECISION MAKERS

Rudy Stroink
CEO
TCN Property Projects

TCN is a European asset developer, with offices in the Netherlands, Germany, Portugal, Hungary, and Belgium. The company operates throughout Europe. TCN manages over 600,000 m² of European real estate with another 400,000 m² under development. CEO Rudy Stroink has distinguished himself as a modernizing developer, with original perspectives on concept, design, management, and financing. TCN's invests in its own projects with a commitment to the long-term. In 2004, Stroink formally vacated his position as a shareholder in Crow Holdings. That same year, TCN, along with investment partner Wedge, bought a 48% share of the Ballast Nedam construction company. TCN experienced rapid expansion, embarking on a number of exceptional projects such as Hilversum's Media Park and the redevelopment of the conference center in The Hague.

Nico Tates
Managing Director
Aberdeen Property Investors Europe

On a European level, Aberdeen Property Investors Europe manages more than €6 billion worth of capital which puts it in the ranks of the big players. In the Netherlands, Nico Tates manages investments worth more than €500 million for Aberdeen in the Netherlands. API has offices in Sweden, Norway, Finland, Denmark, the Netherlands, Belgium, Germany, Luxembourg and the United Kingdom. In 1998, Tates was asked to become managing director of Celexa Reim, which changed its name to Aberdeen Property Investors Continental Europe. Tates has also served as a member of the board of IVBN (Association of Institutional Property Investors in the Netherlands). In 1998, Tates became the founder, fundraiser, and manager of Celogix Property Fund, a European Logistics & Distribution Warehouse Fund.

Paul Trip
Director
IPMMC Vastgoed

Paul Trip was appointed Director of IPMMC Vastgoed in Utrecht, effective November 1, 2005. Trip is responsible for the expansion of IPMMC's real estate development activities. The IPMMC Board of Directors consists of Martin Verwoert, Jan Regterschot, and since November 1, Paul Trip. Trip worked for ING Real Estate for more than 15 years, the last three years of which he served as CEO of ING Real Estate Development.

Gijs Verweij
Chairman
Wereldhave

The real estate investment firm Wereldhave was founded in 1930 and continues to operate as an independent firm. Wereldhave invests in offices, shopping centers, business space, and housing in Belgium, Finland, France, the Netherlands, Spain, the United Kingdom and the United States. Its portfolio is worth approximately €2 billion, with its own assets totaling some €1.5 billion. After the return of director Rob de Ruijter in December 2005, Verweij was named Chairman of management for a term of four years. In 2002, Verweij won the Gouden Baksteen (Golden Brick) Award at the Troostwijk Convention, and research agency Rematch nominated him for the 2003 Investor Relations Award.

Paul Vismans
CEO
KFN

The real estate portfolio of KFN is currently worth some €2 billion. CEO Paul Vismans has worked hard to develop its international office portfolio. Office investor KFN was the first to make use of commercial mortgage backed security as a flexible financing tool in its European expansion activities. KFN, for the time being, still only has one shareholder, the ABP pension fund, from which the company initially arose. In setting up its international portfolio, the strategy of spread ownership of shares is high on Vismans's agenda. Vismans is the current chairman of ULI Nederland (Urban Land Institute) and a board member of the Steering Committee of ULI Europe.

Adriaan Visser
General Director
Development Corporation
Rotterdam (OBR)

Adriaan Visser (40) became the general director and head of services of Development Corporation Rotterdam (OBR) on February 1, 2006. The expansion of OBR's strategic skills is currently its most important task. Previous to this, Visser was working as a partner at Twynstra Gudde. Here he was very involved in the large-scale investment projects of public-private cooperation such as Maasvlakte 2. Visser was appointed by the state as project leader of the negotiations between the various ministries, the province of Zuid-Holland and the City of Rotterdam. Visser will serve as one of a trilateral directorship, together with Willem van Vliet, director of property affairs and real estate, and the as-yet to be appointed director of Economy.

DECISION MAKERS

Ward Vleugels
Chairman of the Board
Q-Park

Q-Park was initially a joint venture of ING Real Estate, but in the meantime, the shares were spread across numerous large institutional investors in the Netherlands. In 2005, Q-Park reached a net turnover of €250 million, compared to €200 million in 2004. In the parking market, Q-Park is ranked among the five largest parking companies, with activities in the Netherlands, Belgium, Denmark, Germany, France, England, and Ireland. Last year Vleugels decided to invest some €100 million in a 2,000 parking space parking garage in Amsterdam's Zuidas. Vleugels was the former director of the Ruijters Group and served as the chairman of the European Parking Association and the EPA Award for six years.

Ton van Vlimmeren
Director
Development Corporation
Utrecht (OGU)

Ton van Vlimmeren (51) was appointed director of Ontwikkelingsbedrijf Gemeente Utrecht (OGU). Van Vlimmeren was director of the Gemeentebibliotheek (city library) and succeeds Guus Verduijn who left the city of Utrecht in October 2005. The college considers Ton van Vlimmeren as the executive who in the coming years will reorient the OGU's tasks to become more result-oriented in order for it to realize some essential changes. Moreover, the naming of Van Vlimmeren fits into the college's career policies for the official top functions where mobility and flexibility function as examples.

Anneke de Vries
Country Manager
ING Real Estate
Development Nederland

ING Real Estate Development was very active in 2005 in the Netherlands, with projects such as the Spuimarkt in The Hague, the new Ernst & Young offices in de Zuidas, Montevideo in Rotterdam and the Cruquius Plaza in Hoofddorp. In 1995, Anneke de Vries started her career at ING Real Estate as a real estate developer. A year later, she was named the substitute head of the real estate development department, and shortly thereafter rose to assistant director and eventually to managing director of ING Real Estate Development. De Vries replaced Jaco Meuwissen as country manager of ING Real Estate Development Nederland in October 2005. Meuwissen is now responsible for Ontwikkeling Europa.

Jan Willem Wattel
Head of Amsterdam
Branche
Eurohypo

With total assets of €240 billion and a portfolio in real estate finance amounting to €100 billion, Eurohypo AG is Europe's leading specialized bank for real estate and public sector financing. An equity of €5.9 billion enables the bank to underwrite major exposures. In the first half of 2005, the bank achieved a return on equity of 9.1% after taxes. The short-term target is to increase the return to over 10% after taxes in 2007. Jan Willem Wattel is responsible for activities within the Netherlands, where Eurohypo has been operating since 1988. In the Netherlands, Eurohypo concentrates on the Randstad, the central business region between Amsterdam, Rotterdam and Utrecht.

Dietmar Werner
Director
VolkerWessels Vastgoed

With a turnover of approximately €3.75 billion, VolkerWessels ranks as the second largest contractor in the Netherlands, and with net assets of €450 million it is certainly the best capitalized. Its order portfolio increased to almost €4.5 billion in 2005. VolkerWessels is a building concern involved in the design, development, realization, and management of real estate. Operating from its strong position in its home market, the Netherlands, it strives for a good geographical dispersal of its activities in selected market segments in Europe and the Northwestern region of the United States. Furthermore, VolkerWessels tends to concentrate on housing, retail, and office development activities. Directeur of VolkerWessels Vastgoed, Dietmar Werner, also serves as the Chairman of Neprom.

Pieter Wetselaar
General Director
Rabo Vastgoed

Next to its dominant position in the Dutch mortgage market, Rabobank, with a realization of 40,000 homes per annum, also belongs among the ranks of the largest housing developers. Its real estate portfolio is worth some €3.4 billion. The company has through its various regional and concept development projects involving some 200 current projects become a seasoned partner in public-private cooperative ventures. And with almost 2,000 hectares of land it owns, Rabo Vastgoed will continue to play an increasingly important role in this sector. Because of its vast network of bank branches, Rabobank is able to focus on local market demands. Besides housing (80%), Rabobank Vastgoed is also increasingly involved in the development of shopping centers, offices, and business space. General director Pieter Wetselaar has been connected to the company since 1980.

Jaap Wolters
Director
Hanzevast

Jaap Wolters has booked numerous successes with various enterprises in Dutch real estate (MPC). Hanzevast, a subsidiary of MPC Capital, has €2.5 billion in investment assets connected with MPC funds. Wolters, director of both Hanzevast and MPC Capital NV, belongs not only among the ranks of the big salesmen in the Netherlands (€525 million), but is continuing to expand worldwide. Hanzevast develops, manages and invests. Hanzevast's transaction volume passed the €450 million per year mark in 2004. Its own assets increased from €25.7 million in 2003 to €37.5 million at the end of 2004. Erik Kremer was named director of investments at the beginning of 2006.

Cor Worms
Director
Achmea Vastgoed

In 2005, Achmea Vastgoed grew to more than €7.3 billion for 60 clients; and Achmea Vastgoed will continue to grow even more. In 2006 more than €1 billion can be invested. This financial scale offers Achmea Vastgoed the power to use opportunities. Since October 2004, Dick van Hal and Cor Worms fill the gap Onno Breur left behind at Achmea Vastgoed. Worms appears to be coming from the outside to strengthen the real estate division. He hails from Levob Bank (director Fund Management, Treasury and Real Estate for six years) and Insurances in Leusden. Working together with Van Hal, Worms will try to put Achmea Vastgoed back on the map. Worms RBA has been appointed as director of Achmea Vastgoed per October 1, 2004.

Henk van Zandvoort
Chairman of the
Executive Board
Bouwfonds MAB
Ontwikkeling

Bouwfonds Property Development and MAB have been working together for over a year now. In the Netherlands it operates under the name Bouwfonds MAB Ontwikkeling, that is, as the big housing developer (of Zandvoort) and the innovative concept developer and retail specialist (in Kalisvaart). In 2005, Bouwfonds MAB developed some 8,500 housing units and some 250,000 m² of commercial space. It has also managed to strengthen its position in a number of European countries by integrating its activities. Its main focus is on multi-functional projects, residential areas and retail projects. Increased sales in 2005 ensured a larger turnover, which is mostly thanks to housing developments in the Netherlands and France.

Ted Zwietering
Director
Development Corporation
The Hague

The municipality of The Hague is working on a Spatial Development Strategy. It is a vision of the future as related to the city's spatial structure and development. This strategy is meant to stimulate thought about the future of the city. Ted Zwietering has been the director of the Haags Ontwikkelingsbedrijf at the Dienst Stedelijke Ontwikkeling (DSO) for the city of The Hague since 2005. Zwietering is the former director of the Bouwen en Wonen service in Leiden, and he serves various functions in Amsterdam, among others, at the Project Management Bureau and at Volkshuisvesting (Public Housing Agency). Zwietering studied architecture in Eindhoven.

How passion becomes performance

Passion for quality drives excellent performance. That's why Achmea Vastgoed delivers higher returns on investments for its institutional clients. We focus on assets at the top of the real estate pyramid. And we have built a unique position in mortgage investments. How passion becomes performance: it's reflected in the value of your portfolio.

www.achmeavastgoed.com

achmea vastgoed

Quality & Performance

INDUSTRY TRENDS

VALUATION ACCURACY IN REAL ESTATE INDICES[1]

This is the first time that valuation accuracy has been studied in the Netherlands concerning commercial real estate held by institutional investors, using the unique ROZ/IPD Index valuation and sales data since the start of that index in 1995. The valuation method used is the market value according to the International Valuation Standards version 2 (IVS 2) and the American Institute for Management and Research (AIMR) standards as described in their Global International Performance Standards (Gips). Those standards have become even more important since the introduction of the International Accounting Standards (IAS) as of January 1st 2005.

By Aart Hordijk

The principle that freely traded assets in a competitive market provide a useful reference point for determining the value of other similar assets is widely adopted in real estate markets. Comparable sales evidence is frequently used as the basis for establishing the value of non-traded properties. This phenomenon is widely observed in appraisal-based real estate indices where the variability of returns is understated relative to the average return. However, a property index should reflect true market volatility as much as possible and valuations are the best estimate of a transaction price at a certain moment. Therefore, the aim of this chapter is to determine the accuracy of valuations, based on the latest valuation and the achieved selling price.

The main focus of this part of the study will be on valuation accuracy in commercial real estate, however residential is also a major investment category.

Methodology

The most obvious method of approaching the problem of valuation accuracy is to compare the actual appraised value and the subsequent achieved sale price, which is usually done by a total-variance and/or a partitioned variance test.

The total variance test involves computing the gap between each valuation and the achieved price, expressing this as a proportion of the valuation. The partitioned variance test takes the total variance test one step further by attempting to split the difference into systematic and random components. The systematic components are mainly caused by the lagging effect in two ways: the valuation being based on historic market evidence (information lag), and the varying period between the date of the latest valuation and the date of the sale transaction (time lag). The analysis is carried out on a yearly basis, allowing international comparison with the UK and the USA.

Systematic component of the appraisal error

The random appraisal error can also be divided into two components: a systematic lagging component and a random component. The systematic lagging component in the appraisal error exists as a result of the fact that appraisals are based on partially obsolete information and input, while market circumstances have in the meantime evolved. Using the quarterly return figures from the NCREIF index, Clayton et al (2001) discovered that on average, appraisers base their opinion on nine-month-old information. From a more theoretical point of view, the effect of the systematic lagging error due to market fluctuations on the interpolated monthly difference will be stable over time if it is accepted that annual capital movement in the ROZ/IPD Index shows a linear growth pattern over 12 months. Thus, to isolate the effect of the random appraisal error, the average monthly capital growth

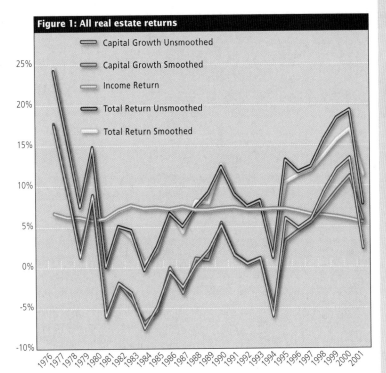

Figure 1: All real estate returns

- Capital Growth Unsmoothed
- Capital Growth Smoothed
- Income Return
- Total Return Unsmoothed
- Total Return Smoothed

Dr. A.C. Hordijk, MRICS
Director ROZ

Aart Hordijk studied economics at the Free University of Amsterdam. In 1995 the director of ROZ Real Estate Council of the Netherlands as well as the director of the Dutch real estate index organization, which cooperates with the IPD Investment Property Databank in London to produce the ROZ/IPD Real Estate Index. Internationally Hordijk is the representative for the Netherlands in the IVSC, the International Valuation Standards Committee and he is a member of the editorial board of the Journal of Real Estate Portfolio Management.

Valuation and Construction Issues in Real Estate Indices.
€22,- 165 pp, full color
Order on:
www.europe-re.com/
bookstore.
ISBN: 90-77997-01-6

This thesis concentrates on increasing the knowledge and transparency of real estate investments by institutional investors. Where possible the results have been placed in an international context, comparing them with similar figures, results and surveys, mainly from the UK and the US. It describes the development of a long-term time series for real estate returns and office market rental values. Unique databanks have been constructed going back to 1977. And the valuation consistency and accuracy of the valuations between 1995 and 2002. The last part of the thesis makes estimates of the real estate stock, the real estate investments by investors, and the potential investments in real estate in 11 European countries showing detailed information when possible and available.

over the year is used to correct the total difference per month.

Within this framework, the research has also adjusted for this systematic component in the appraisal error, but the average period used to look back on this aged information and input therefore needs to be approached. The nine-month-old information lag was also found in the Netherlands by major valuation firms like DTZ, Troostwijk and Jones Lang LaSalle, although recent observations show an improvement towards a six-month lag at the date of the appraisal.

Another lagging element occurs because of the fact that the ROZ/IPD Index requires many end of year valuations. The last figures show that around 4,000 external valuations were produced at the end of 2002. To schedule all this work, valuation firms will in practice start their work as early as October, which means another three months of information lag, if they don't make adjustments

for this (which is generally not done).

In addition to this systematic component of the appraisal error, it has to be realized that the final result of an appraisal is also influenced by the individual behavior and nature of the appraiser involved, which can be seen as a random residual. This residual is actually much harder to determine without information about the nature of the transactions used in the valuation process.

Remaining difference

Since this remaining difference is based on more behavioral elements of the appraiser, it is therefore also much more difficult to analyze.

However, Cullen (1994) examined the random error between 1982 and 1993 in order to find out whether random errors vary over time depending on the state of the real estate market.

But according to his findings, that did not appear to be the case. >>

ONLINE: www.holland-re.com/hordijk

Table 1: Total stock figures derived from property tax authorities (including all taxable real estate)

	NCREIF Index 1999	IPD UK Index 2002	ROZ/IPD Index 2002
Dated on			
Capital value (billion €) 2	52	200	38
No. of properties	2000	15200	6400
Inst. market coverage 3	37.5%	80%	85%
Inst. market coverage as % of total real estate stock	1-2%	3-4%	3-4%

Data

From the beginning of the ROZ/IPD Index in 1995, most institutional real estate investors were represented (directly or indirectly). As a result of the investors' commitment, the overall market coverage of the ROZ/IPD Netherlands Property Index was already extremely large, at 70% of institutional real estate investments undertaken by Dutch institutional investors in the Netherlands, and the coverage has grown towards 85% nowadays. Within the perspective of

investment markets' liquidity, the present coverage of the ROZ/IPD Index is compared with similar figures for the NCREIF and IPD UK Index (Table 1). Regarding market coverage corrected for market share, the real estate investments of institutional investors in the three countries represent approximately the same percentage of the total national real estate stock. The coverage of these institutional real estate markets is between 3% and 4% of the total real estate stock in each of

the countries. The capital value and number of properties covered by each of the indices indicate the average capital value per property. In the ROZ/IPD Netherlands Property Index, this is rather small compared with the average in the NCREIF Index and IPD UK Index. The index universe of the ROZ/IPD Netherlands Property Index has a significantly different market structure as a result of the large proportion of residential real estate investments, which generally have relatively smaller

Table 2: Number of properties sold and as % of the index universe

	NCREIF index		ROZ/IPD Index, ex. residentials		UK IPD Index	
	No. of sold properties	% of index universe	No. of sold properties	% of index universe	No. of sold properties	% of index universe
1982	10	3.0%			488	1.3%
1983	20	4.5%			596	2.4%
1984	42	8.7%			517	2.8%
1985	34	6.2%			601	4.0%
1986	58	10.1%			791	5.6%
1987	44	7.1%			1360	9.1%
1988	48	7.1%			1351	7.9%
1989	69	10.3%			1068	7.4%
1990	48	6.0%			606	5.2%
1991	47	5.3%			914	4.4%
1992	47	4.9%			723	4.8%
1993	71	7.4%			1283	7.4%
1994	61	7.0%			1367	7.7%
1995	84	7.6%	48	2.0%	1268	7.1%
1996	167	15.1%	126	4.9%	1329	7.6%
1997	209	18.1%	124	4.3%	1825	10.1%
1998	208	19.1%	71	1.9%	1605	7.3%
1999		13.9%	160	4.1%	1864	9.9%
2000		12.1%	109	2.7%	1258	8.2%
2001		10.4%	261	6.7%	1700	9.7%
2002		10.3%	237	6.2%	1406	11.9%

Note: NCREIF numbers of sold properties 1999 – 2003 were not available at the time

capital values compared with office investments. As far as retail investments are concerned, the average size per investment is also smaller in the Netherlands than in the UK and the USA, since investments in single shop unit represent a large portion of the retail universe in the ROZ/IPD Index.

The residential segment in the ROZ/IPD Netherlands Property Index has another particular feature: partial selling. During the last eight years in the Netherlands, part-selling of residential investments has been a widespread phenomenon and has turned out to be very beneficial for investors. Due to the popularity of part-selling in these years, it should be taken into consideration that the resulting reduction in the capital value of these properties could cause difficulties when the appraisals and subsequent sale prices are analyzed. Therefore, as mentioned before, the main research will be restricted to the commercial segments. Furthermore, in cases where there was no difference between the sale price and the previous valuation, this data was excluded, on the assumption that the sale price was already known at the date of valuation.

Due to the scale of the USA and UK real estate markets, one would expect higher liquidity than for the real estate market in the Netherlands, resulting in a more accurate price-fixing mechanism. With the release of more up-to-date and consistent transaction information, these Anglo-Saxon real estate investment markets should be considered more transparent and efficient than the comparable market in the Netherlands. As well as market capitalization, the counts of retail and office properties sold could be viewed as a proxy for the liquidity of a commercial market, as set out in Table 2. Although selling activity within the ROZ/IPD Index as a percentage of the total index universe is in the same order of magnitude as with the other indices, the numbers of properties sold for each index, related to market coverage and capitalization of each specific index, indicate roughly that a rather small sample of properties has been traded in the institutional real estate investment market in the Netherlands over the period under consideration. Obviously, the lack of a large number of transactions in the Netherlands can be expected to have repercussions on the price-fixing mechanism for this particular investment market, resulting in continuous smoothing of appraisals on the one hand due to lagging the underlying market and on the other, relating to the ability of the appraiser to do an appropriate appraisal.

In accordance with Brown (1995), Lizieri and Venmore Rowland (1991), Cullen (1994) and McAllister (1995), the application of the total variance test, which examines the difference between each valuation and the subsequent sale price, gives the following deviations per annum for each of the real estate markets studied, as shown in Table 3.

Although these three indices cover different cycles in their respective real estate markets, it should be noted that the average percentage difference between sale price and appraisal in the Netherlands is higher than in the USA and UK. This could be explained by the fact that UK and USA real estate markets have greater market depth, higher liquidity and a longer performance history. However the standard deviations don't vary too much; they are between 4.9% ands 5.9%. >>

Table 3:	Absolute mean difference by time period in % ((Price – Appraisal values) / Appraisal value)		
	NCREIF index	**ROZ/IPD Index**	**IPD UK Index**
1983			10.8%
1984			4.3%
1985	6.9%		8.3%
1986	0.1%		6.2%
1987	1.9%		14.7%
1988	-3.3%		15.1%
1989	-1.7%		20.6%
1990	-2.3%		-1.1%
1991	-13.4%		1.8%
1992	0.1%		1.2%
1993	-3.3%		4.4%
1994	-1.4%		4.5%
1995	0.9%	7.8%	-3.0%
1996	3.1%	4.6%	0.9%
1997	4.2%	4.3%	3.3%
1998	6.6%	15.3%	4.4%
1999	0.1%	14.3%	5.0%
2000	0.2%	10.1%	3.5%
2001	0.3%	2.5%	2.7%
2002	2.6%	4.2%	
Avg.	-0.1%	7.9%	5.7%
SD	5.1%	4.9%	5.9%

Source: ROZ-IPD Databank

Table 4: Distribution of deviation between sale and appraisal - absolute percent difference (%)			
	No. of properties	Percent	Cumulative
Less than -15%	30	2.6%	2.6%
Greater than −15% to -10%	31	2.7%	5.4%
Greater than −10% to -5%	33	2.9%	8.3%
Greater than −5% to -1%	129	11.4%	19.6%
Greater than −1% to 0%	86	7.6%	27.2%
Greater than 0% to 1%	65	5.7%	32.9%
Greater than 1% to 5%	193	17.0%	49.9%
Greater than 5% to 10%	204	18.0%	67.9%
Greater than 10% to 15%	121	10.7%	78.5%
Greater than 15% to 20%	73	6.4%	84.9%
Greater than 20% to 25%	61	5.4%	90.3%
Greater than 25%	110	9.6%	100.0%
Total	**1136**	**100%**	

Source: ROZ-IPD databank

Results

Many factors can be seen as causing the deviation between sale and appraisal found in inefficient real estate markets. However, if the results of the total variance test in the case of the ROZ/IPD Index are studied in more detail by analyzing the distribution of the overall price/valuation match for all of the sold properties recorded from 1995 - 2002, it becomes clear from Table 4 that right skewness occurs. More than 75% of the observed transactions have achieved a sale price higher than the appraisal.

Since the eight-year period covered involves a rising market, the findings concerning the skewness have to be put into perspective. This can be done by determining the percentage of the sale prices counts per year. They have an appraisal within the range of the standard error of the absolute difference calculated to give an indication of the spread of the observations, as shown in Figure 3. This gives a clear picture of variations over the eight-year period. In the case of the ROZ/IPD Index the percentage varies between 75% and 85% of the observations each

year; the average over the years was roughly 80%. Compared with similar research performed by Cullen (1994) for the UK real estate investment market, the percentages of the ROZ/IPD Index are slightly higher. This observation is, however, not very surprising in view of the fact that some extreme deviations will have a more substantial impact on average and standard error in the researched sample of the ROZ/IPD Index, than in the IPD UK sample which is based on a much larger count of transaction observations. This figure also indicates that evolving market circumstances can't be recognized in the pattern of the figure as it seems that variations in the ratios are modest.

As it is highly likely that many

of the sale decisions are based on a previous valuation, this confirms the hypothesis (Geltner and Fisher, 2000) that the distribution of sale prices would be partly truncated. This reflects the fact that in the bottom half of the distribution, prospective sales might be withdrawn from the (falling) market, so the observed sales are not always a representative sample of the market. Baum (2002) already suggested that valuations immediately before a sale tend to be on the low side, to make the sale more probable. Therefore, it has to be considered that in particular, random issues like remuneration schemes (managers will always be rewarded for realized profits and not for capital losses), have had a relevant impact on appraisal accuracy over the years.

A partitioned variance test was carried out on the ROZ/IPD Index in order to focus on the determination of the random appraisal error and its components. In relation to the previously discussed right skewed deviations and statements in the preceding paragraphs, the differences between appraisal and achieved sale price are explained by a systematic lagging error and a random appraisal error. It is known that market capital growth or decline occurs during

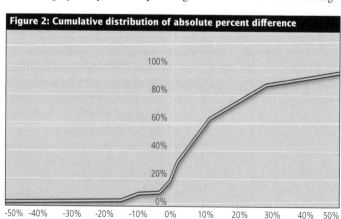

Figure 2: Cumulative distribution of absolute percent difference

Table 5: Break down of the difference between the latest appraisal and the sale price					
	Number	Average deviation	Market change between valuation and sale	Systematic info lagging	Random error appraisal
1995	48	7.8%	0.3%	0.2%	7.2%
1996	126	4.6%	0.2%	0.2%	4.2%
1997	124	4.3%	1.7%	1.5%	1.0%
1998	71	15.4%	3.0%	2.7%	9.7%
1999	160	14.3%	3.9%	3.4%	7.0%
2000	109	10.1%	3.6%	2.8%	3.7%
2001	261	2.5%	2.1%	1.6%	-1.1%
2002	237	4.2%	1.0%	1.0%	2.2%
Total	1136				
Average		7.9%	2.0%	1.7%	4.2%
St. dev.		4.9%	1.5%	1.0%	3.6%

Source: ROZ-IPD Databank

the period between the date of appraisal and the date of sale.

Table 5 shows the random appraisal error by correcting the total absolute difference compared with average growth rates for capital development in the observed years during the period between the appraisal and the actual sale, divided into a difference due to the time elapsing between the date of appraisal and date of sale as well as the so-called information lag, estimated at nine months for the Netherlands as previously argued.

Table 5 gives a clear picture of the effects of behavioral issues in the appraisal process during different time spans. It clearly indicates that in the case of the ROZ/IPD Netherlands Property Index, the random appraisal error as a percentage of the appraised value has three components, the systematic information lag, the time lag and the remaining random behavioral residual. These results obviously confirm the hypothesis that behavioral effects in the appraisal process have also had a significant impact on the appraisal process.

Conclusions

This study has analyzed the difference between the sale price and the previous valuation over the years 1995 - 2002, based on the ROZ/IPD Netherlands Property Index. During those years, an average of 7.9% was observed, based on the total vari-

ance test. The partitioned variance test was applied to correct for systematic errors, i.e. the time lag (the period between valuation date and sale date) as well as the information lag (the valuations are based on 'old' data). As far as the time lag is concerned, the correction leads to an average (random) appraisal error, which remains at 5.9%. This compares with previous studies in the UK (Cullen, 1994), showing an appraisal error of between 2% and 10%, and the USA (Clayton, Geltner et al), showing an appraisal error of between 6% and 13%, although these were based on different periods of time which also included a depressed market. After this, a correction for the information lag at the date of the valuation was calculated and this reduced the average appraisal error to a behavioral residual of 4.2 % on average.   «

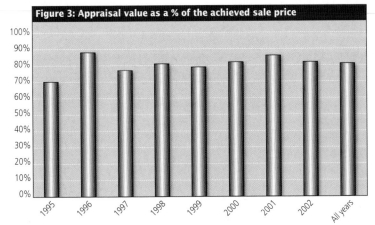

Figure 3: Appraisal value as a % of the achieved sale price

Note Hordijk: "In a few years' time this analysis should be repeated, since it is highly likely that if results under depressed market circumstances could be and were also included, the records would most probably be different."

PROF. DR. ED NOZEMAN

THE DUTCH DEVELOPMENT INDUSTRY: PROFILE AND MAIN TRENDS

The most self-evident questions are often the most difficult ones to answer. This also applies to an analysis of the Dutch real estate development industry. This article focuses on three issues: its economic importance, its main characteristics and the trends influencing its present and future functioning.

Development is an activity fundamental to the real estate market. It is defined as adding real estate to the existing stock, or redeveloping parts of that stock on the account and risk of the entrepreneur himself. Real estate is considered as comprising all buildings and the land on which they stand. A remarkable amount of information has been published on the process of development and its products. However, not much is known about real estate development as an economic activity. Apparently, that subject is not an easy one, impeded by a lack of public data. Based on the elaboration of various sources and on our own research, we are now able to reveal at least a part of it.

Economic importance

There are various ways to indicate or measure the importance of an industry. The easiest way is to focus on employment. For that aspect national statistics can be of some help. The Dutch Central Bureau of Statistics has been collecting employment data for the Dutch development industry since the early 90s. However, the way of collecting data has been changed during this time, which makes it impossible to present an extensive and reliable time series. Unfortunately, comparable data has only been produced since 2002 (see Table 1).

In spite of a decline in the total number of jobs, development jobs increased by 10% over the last three years. The total number

of companies increased by 4%, versus 17% for the number of development companies during the same period. The direct employment is rather modest when compared with the total national employment. Development employs a mere 0.08% of the total employment. However, it should be remembered that the spinoff, indirect employment, is considerably larger. This indirect employment affects not only other real estate activities such as property management, leasing and selling, but also influences industries outside the real estate sector, such as construction, consulting, financing and insurance. In 2000 the Dutch Association of Real Estate Developers (NEPROM) estimated that at least 10% of

Table 1: Number of companies and jobs in the Dutch real estate development industry compared with total national number of companies and jobs				
	1-1-2002	**1-1-2003**	**1-1-2004**	**1-1-2005**
Development companies	1,575	1,550	1,765	1,850
Jobs in development industry*	4,800 **	5,100 **	5,500**	5,300 **
Total number of companies	689,625	685,775	701,685	717,035
Total number of jobs*	6,998,600	7,055,600	6,994,700	6,929,400***

*except the self-employed **rounded up to thousands *** preliminary figure*

Source: www.statline.cbs.nl (Real estate development defined as SBI-code 7011)

The management of the industry is still a male stronghold.

Prof. dr. E.F. Nozeman
Professor of Real Estate
Development, University of
Groningen/Amsterdam School of
Real Estate

- **Ed Nozeman studied at the
  University of Utrecht and obtained
  his Ph.D. at the Free University
  Amsterdam.**
- **Former advisor to the Board of
  ING Real Estate Development, a
  company active worldwide in the
  field of integrated area develop-
  ment, shopping centers, offices and
  housing.**
- **Professor in Real Estate
  Development, University of
  Groningen/Amsterdam School of
  Real Estate.**
- **Independant consultant participant
  in various forums on real estate
  and urban planning issues.**

national employment was dependent on or the result of the development industry.

Keyrole

A second indicator is commissioning for construction of real
estate. Calculations based on
completions over the last five
years show an impressive performance. Between 2000 and 2004,
Dutch developers were responsible for the commissioning of
63% of newly-built housing
(yearly average 43,000 units),
76% of completed offices (yearly
average 990,000 m²), 94% of
new shopping centers (yearly
average 170,000 m²).
The obvious conclusion is that
Dutch developers play a key role
in the national economy.

Profile

From the national statistics it can
be concluded that most of the
development companies are
small: 91% have fewer than five
employees and the majority is
self-employed. The management
of the industry is still a male
stronghold, but 40% of the total
jobs are occupied by women

(compared to 42% for all services). Data on output, added
value and profitability for the
development industry are unfortunately not available, and performance indications can therefore not be presented.
We have created a list of the 118
most important Dutch developers
based on a portfolio ranking by
the review 'PropertyNL'. This
list formed a starting point for
the acquisition of relevant information through expert interviews
and websites on an interesting
number of aspects, viz: type of
affiliation ('blood group') or
independency, listed or non-
listed, location of headquarters/
office, market focus, and thematic focus.
Our analysis resulted in a remarkable picture of the Dutch development industry. Taking those
118 companies as a basis, the
industry is for a considerable part
independent (46%) and nearly
40% is affiliated with a financial
or construction company. Nearly
all companies are non-listed
(97%); volatility of the development business is not a stimulus to
be listed.   >>

MORE INFORMATION

**University of Groningen
Faculty of Spatial Sciences**

P.O. Box 800
9700 AV Groningen
The Netherlands
Tel.: +31 50 363 86 69
Fax: +31 50 363 39 01
E-mail: e.f.nozeman@rug.nl

ONLINE: www.holland-re.com/nozeman

INDUSTRY TRENDS

The number of development jobs increased by 10% over the last three years.

Opportunities

The development industry can also be approached by a SWOT-analysis. Socio-economic trends as modest economic growth, aging population and more households will influence the opportunities for the coming decades. Opportunities will arise from the recent move to a more market-oriented approach to physical planning by public bodies. On top of that, there is a lack of investment money in public bodies, which offers chances for the private side. It is inevitable that there will be progressive growth in public-private partnerships.

A shift from small-scale projects to large-scale area development will take place. That will imply long-term commitments with phased revenues for a decade or more. Private-private partnerships between developers or between developers and investors will be the answer to enable both parties to take advantage of each other's strengths.

In the meantime Mesopotamia will emerge. On one side scaling-up will continue for a part of the industry through mergers and take-overs, looking for opportunities abroad (Central and Eastern Europe) and developing new products (leisure, serviced housing and care). On the other side a downscaling process will take place; newcomers will arise with a different process approach and looking for untrodden niches.

Threats

A medal always has two sides. With the perspective of modest economic growth and a demographic slowdown or stabilization, the development industry will have to adapt to a replacement market instead of an expan-

Only 15% of the main offices of development companies are located in the capital, Amsterdam, but the lion's share are located in the Randstad, the urbanized western part of the country. Most firms have a national (48%) or international (24%) market orientation, which is both caused by the limited size and maturity of the Dutch market and the early orientation to foreign countries. There is not a very outspoken thematic specialization, 46% can be classified as all-round (residential, offices and retail), another 22% cover at least two categories (e.g. retail/offices). So 'omnivores' dominate the scene. Moreover, this industry shows a high level of professionalism, being well organized, highly skilled, well informed but moderately transparent.

Although an international comparison of profiles is not yet available, it is reasonably certain that the development industry in neighboring countries will show some differences owing to factors such as size and nature of the market, the degree of privatization and the importance of personal and political relations.

Dutch developers do not have a very outspoken thematic specialization, 46% can be classified as all-round (residential, offices and retail).

sion market in the Netherlands itself. New competitors have already entered that market. Former outsiders have and will prove to be capable colleagues. Housing corporations, fee developers and institutional investors show a tendency to participate in rewarding (and risk-bearing) developing activities.

Apart from increasing competition there is the increasing complexity and lengthening of projects. The national government has announced the abolition of red tape and superfluous regulations. But at the same time new rules are slipping in, partly originating in Brussels, partly from local governments. Operating in such a complicated world can only be successful when professionalization moves on. The industry will have to invest in continued training, expertise and strategic information.

Conclusion

The Dutch development industry, although a modest employer considering the number of firms and employees, is a key player when the spinoff from the industry is considered. Its profile is domi-

> DUTCH DEVELOPERS
> PLAY A KEY ROLE IN
> THE NATIONAL
> ECONOMY

nated by small independent companies, mainly non-listed, its location dispersed over the western part of the country, its geographical market focus is mainly international and considering its thematic focus most developers are 'omnivores', able to develop the whole array of real estate products. A fascinating period lies ahead. The matu-

rity of the market, economic perspective and demographic change will limit the opportunities. But at the same time aging and less public means will offer new perspectives. New competitors will enter and challenge the ruling players. A continued professionalization should be the adequate answer to a manifold and challenging future.　≪

J. Baptist M. Brayé MA, General Manager of Locatus

Ongoing increase in scale and reduced spread in the retail market

Traditional department stores: what's left to be said... Where in the past, these establishments were the anchors and consumer palaces of the Dutch city centers, today their role seems to be taken over by popular chain stores like H&M and Media Markt. How should we respond to this trend? Is it something to accept passively, or should we start thinking pro-actively about retail areas without department stores? And what would such a shopping environment look like... and what to do with the buildings?

Department stores were once the flagships of the retail trade. They were consumer palaces, where shoppers marveled at the opulence of their surroundings.
The building, its interior and the wares on display could only be described in superlatives. Nothing was held back in the attempt to impress the consumer,

Blob architecture in Cologne.

and the product range and the architectural setting worked in fine unison. This is truly a thing of the past. Today's department stores are democratic affairs, geared towards serving the entire population.

Reduced lines in functional shopping environments

The policies of today's department stores are determined by considerations of cost control and turnover rates rather than the wish to enchant the shopping audience. Professionalization and automatization enable a clear analysis of which segments of the product range yield the best returns. And it then becomes apparent that generally speaking, an exclusive product line, bulky articles – such as furniture and white goods – and perishable goods are less profitable stock. As a result, the stores' formerly sprawling array of products has been systematically reduced to strictly delineated ranges, pre-

sented in a primarily functional store interior. The magic is gone. What remains are prime retail locations.

Will the department store loose its role as a shopping attraction?

How long can this development continue? We cannot say precisely, but we do know that it is a finite process. After all, the more segments of the product range the department store rids itself of and the more volume reductions it carries out, the closer it gets to a point of no return. This is the point where the former shopping attraction is no longer able to attract an exceptional amount of people. At this point, the department store only draws the volume of shoppers that can be expected on the basis of its fair share. The store's added value for the surrounding retail area is no longer apparent, and there is no ground for its privileges. This question is a delicate point

Amazing interior of P&C in Cologne.

J. Baptist M. Brayé MA
General Manager

J. Baptist M. Brayé MA and Gerard Zandbergen MA together form the management of the Locatus retail planning information agency. Since 1994, Locatus has been gathering structural data regarding all sales outlets in the Netherlands. Locatus sells this valuable strategic information in the form of databases, publications, tailored information and web services.

To this end, Locatus employees visit each and every store in the Netherlands. This has proven the only way to gain a comprehensive overview of the complete Dutch retail offer. Locatus employees check information about the stores on the spot, and where necessary adapt the available floor plan accordingly. Following a sophisticated schedule, all retail outlets in the field are visited, and once we've brought this task to an end... we start all over again.

As of January 1, 2006, Locatus also started a retail planning information agency in Belgium.

within the retail planning process: when is an attraction still an attraction and when has it lost this role?

Increased scale and less spread

What will the retail landscape look like in the near future? Do we have prepare ourselves for a world without department stores? After all, a large volume of new retail space will be completed in the near future in the Netherlands. Furthermore, these new stores will be considerable larger than what was previously usual, and are meeting with increased interest on the part of the consumer. According to the current outlook, the Dutch retail offer will stabilize at around 100,000 outlets. In addition, the number of chain store branches will continue to grow. This development will concentrate in a diminishing number of large-scale retail areas that are characterized by either a large propor-

tion of fashion-related and luxury retail (particularly in the larger inner-city areas) or a combination of product range groups (white goods and audiovisual equipment, home accessories, DIY, sports equipment, home furnishing, household goods, etc). The range of nice little shops will also continue to be depleted – another process that has been going on for some years now. While the real specialized stores will probably carry on, their number will continue to fall and their critical customer base will grow. For some sectors, this base is already at 50,000 people per establishment.

In other words, the retail array will be thinned out from the bottom up. This means that it will not only increase in terms of scale, but it will also be less finely-meshed in terms of spread. The future will generally bring more floor space in bigger stores, but spread across fewer locations and in increasingly concentrated retail areas.   >>

MORE INFORMATION

Locatus
P.O. Box 139
3440 AC Woerden
The Netherlands
Tel: +31 348 49 02 77
Fax: +31 348 49 02 99
E-mail: baptist.braye@locatus .nl
Website: www.locatus.nl

ONLINE: www.holland-re.com/locatus

INDUSTRY TRENDS

The GRI is a global club of real estate industry investors, developers and lenders. Its mission is to help senior decision makers devise strategy and build relationships that make a difference.

If chairing a group discussion or any other involvement at future GRI events can be useful to you, we welcome your inquiries and invite you to contact us.

info@globalrealestate.org
Tel: +44. 20 8445 6757

GRI EVENTS

THE BRITISH GRI
London 30 March 2006

THE DEUTSCHE GRI
Frankfurt 8–9 May 2006

THE CHINA GRI
Shanghai 22–23 June 2006

THE GRI EUROPEAN SUMMIT
Paris 11–12 September 2006

THE INDIA GRI
Mumbai 13–14 November 2006

THE NEW EUROPE GRI
Budapest 27–28 November 2006

THE GRI CHAIRMEN'S RETREAT
St Moritz 18–21 January 2007

Ongoing updates at
www.globalrealestate.org

GLOBAL
REAL
ESTATE
INSTITUTE

Everything for sale everywhere

The retail trade has democratized and this is a good development. Today, nearly everyone has access to a large array of facilities, meaning that we have to get about to find something really special. And of course, this has always been the case! And these new special items require the development of new formats. Sometimes, an answer is found in increased scale (which brought us the department store, for instance), sometimes in the combination of retail and leisure functions, or attractive pricing (a factory outlet center as a kind of non-stop discounter of high-end equipment). Sometimes – fortunately – in the endeavor to create a sense of wonder with the consumer. The latest Sony Center, Apple design gadgets, the primarily brand-oriented flagship stores like that of Nike in London, the Armani department store in Milan, Rem Koolhaas' Prada outlet in New York are all examples that spring to mind. What is striking about these new 'anchors' is that they often revolve around on a single brand, which serves as the center of a world of wonder created through intensive marketing.

As it is, brands are steadily increasing their 'anchor' value, and this is hardly surprising. They are new promises wrapped up in old certainties, as can be observed in the glorious revival of brands like Burberry and Birkenstock.

Create a sense of wonder

So brands will be the anchors of the future. But they will require retail environments that reaffirm spending power. Whether standing in a stylish shopping street or surrounded by innovative

Department stores were the flagships of the retail trade.

modern architecture, stores need to be located in an area that creates a sense of wonder. Such locations will often need to be realized through redevelopment, for instance by breaking open old malls to create open air shopping environments. Developers need to create areas where the concept of public space is redefined. New environments where art, architecture, leisure and brands mutually enhance one another's experience.

Reallocating property

In the world of Dutch retail, the waning importance of the department store is an estab-

lished fact. Based on considerations of capital and profitability per square meter, the first reduction scenarios are already in play. Reduced scale, for example: abandoning product segments enable department stores to reallocate the property at their often desirable prime retail locations. Many redevelopment processes therefore include the downsizing of an existing department store. The space freed up by this measure is used to develop new retail units, which are subsequently successfully rented out to well-known and well-paying third-party retail formulas. ≪

IPD, Dr. Hans op 't Veld

The Dutch property investment market put in a European perspective

Real estate investment in recent years has increasingly become international investment. Investors have moved away from the traditional strategy of having a domestic portfolio and are now looking beyond their borders. This trend is highlighted by the growing share of indirect investments in portfolios and by the growth in the availability of investment performance indicators. The IPD European Index is an example of the latter. This article explores the position of the Dutch market in the European landscape and uses the IPD European Index publication to establish the relative importance of the Dutch real estate market within this landscape. The conclusion is that the market in Holland is poised to become more liquid.

Investors have increased foreign exposure

According to the Dutch Central Bureau of Statistics, the allocation to real estate of Dutch institutional investors has moved from some 10.8% in 1980 to

some 6.5% at the end of 2004. This trend is remarkable in view of the strong performance of real estate. Over the same period, the percentage of the portfolio invested outside Holland has gone up from 13.3% in 1980

to 23.9% in 2004. The trend towards foreign investment is quite clear over the long term. However, between 2002 and 2005, international holdings have fallen by about 5%, which might be explained by a sell-off in the

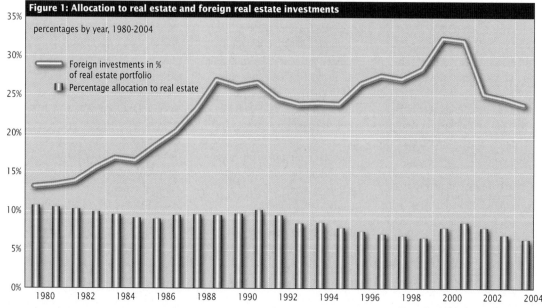

Figure 1: Allocation to real estate and foreign real estate investments

percentages by year, 1980-2004

— Foreign investments in % of real estate portfolio
▯ Percentage allocation to real estate

Source: Centraal Bureau voor de Statistiek

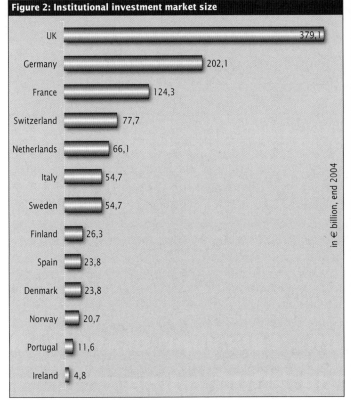

Figure 2: Institutional investment market size

Country	Value
UK	379,1
Germany	202,1
France	124,3
Switzerland	77,7
Netherlands	66,1
Italy	54,7
Sweden	54,7
Finland	26,3
Spain	23,8
Denmark	23,8
Norway	20,7
Portugal	11,6
Ireland	4,8

in € billion, end 2004

Source: IPD Pan-European property index 2004

more liquid international holdings coinciding with the drop in real estate allocation.

Whilst it is only logical to assume investors will continue to have a strong home bias, the likelihood of further movement away from Holland into Europe – and perhaps beyond - seems quite probable. Investors will look at the size of Holland in the European marketplace and the relative performance of markets to establish their long term exposure to different markets. Therefore, it is interesting to evaluate how the size of the market and performance have held up against the European universe. The IPD European Index facilitates such a comparison.

Netherlands make up about 6.2% of the European market

To get a view of how the (size of the) Dutch market relates to the European market, we are taking a look at the composiotion of the IPD European Index. This index describes the performance of (almost) all European property investment markets[1] and is based on the estimated investment size of the individual markets in this universe. Figure 2 illustrates the estimated size of the individual institutional property investment markets in Europe. From this figure, we learn that the investment market in the Netherlands actually ranks fifth on a European scale.

There is a marked difference between the three largest markets in Europe (i.e. UK, Germany and France) that together make up 65.9% of the total institutional universe and the remainder of the countries. The Dutch market has a 6.2% weight in the overall European market as presented »

[1] *Belgium and Austria are not included in the 2004 version of the IPD pan-European property index.*

IPD

IPD was established in the UK in 1985 by Rupert Nabarro and Ian Cullen.

IPD has been a market leader in property information services since 1985. Headquartered in London, we operate through subsidiaries and associate offices including France, Germany, Netherlands, Sweden, Denmark, South Africa, Canada, Portugal and Australia. That international network employs the world's largest team of specialists in the collection and analysis of property performance records, to give all those interested in property the reliable information needed to run their businesses. We use the latest technologies to collect information and deliver results accurately, quickly and efficiently.

MORE INFORMATION

IPD

1 St. John's Lane
London, EC1M 4BL
United Kingdom
E-mail: hans.op.veldt@ipdglobal.com
Tel.: +44 20 733 692 60
Fax: +44 20 733 693 99

ONLINE: www.holland-re.com/ipd

INDUSTRY TRENDS

PROVADA 2006

The Real Estate Meeting Point
13 t/m 15 juni RAI AMSTERDAM

Meld u nu aan en reserveer standruimte
voor de 2006 editie

Vraag de gratis nieuwsbrief aan
www.**PROVADA**.nl

info@provada.nl   030 - 605 14 24

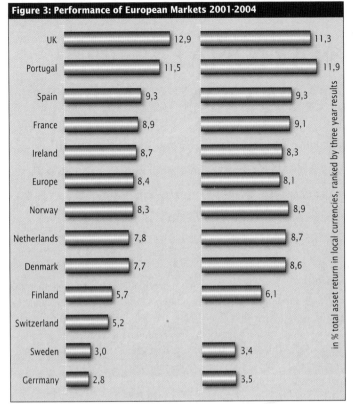

Figure 3: Performance of European Markets 2001-2004

	Three year total returns	Four year returns
UK	12,9	11,3
Portugal	11,5	11,9
Spain	9,3	9,3
France	8,9	9,1
Ireland	8,7	8,3
Europe	8,4	8,1
Norway	8,3	8,9
Netherlands	7,8	8,7
Denmark	7,7	8,6
Finland	5,7	6,1
Switzerland	5,2	
Sweden	3,0	3,4
Gerrmany	2,8	3,5

in % total asset return in local currencies, ranked by three year results

* Left hand graph shows three year total returns, right hand graph provides four year returns

in Figure 2. In terms of the percentage of weight in a European portfolio, the Dutch institutional investors therefore still seem substantially overweight in domestic investments.

The huge weight of domestic real estate is probably caused by a combination of factors. First of all, the presence of currency exchange rates limited the scope of investment portfolios to domestic investments. Secondly, there was limited data to substantiate the benefits of international investment and the information disadvantage of investing abroad was therefore substantial. And finally, the product to invest efficiently in foreign markets was lacking. Whilst most of these drawbacks of international investments no longer exist, it takes time to move from a domestic directly held portfolio

to international investments. It is therefore to be expected that a further shift in allocations is underway.

> ## THE INVESTMENT MARKET IN THE NETHERLANDS ACTUALLY RANKS FIFTH ON A EUROPEAN SCALE

Besides weight, performance determines investment volume. It is equally interesting to look at performance. Would a Dutch investor have been better off in

terms of returns by going abroad? Figure 3 provides the performance of the markets included in the IPD Pan-European Index. There are now four years of returns available to evaluate the performance of markets. This is not a long series to base allocation decisions on, but it illustrates the way in which returns have behaved.

The Dutch market exhibits results in line with the European average. The three year total return of 7.8% is 0.7% behind the European return, whereas the four year average return exceeds the European average by 0.6%. The British and Southern European markets did relatively well during the period for which the index is running whilst the German and Swedish markets were lagging. From the graphs, it is clear that the performance of European markets is quite different from country to country. This implies that diversification benefits are there and that a European strategy is potentially attractive.

Return differences and diversification will cause capital flows to increase

The message from the above is quite clear: the property investment market in the Netherlands is part of a European scene. This is both good and bad news: diversification will mean that capital continues to flow out of the country into other markets. At the same time, however, it is an opportunity as foreign capital flows into the Dutch market. Both of these trends imply that the capital flows will continue to increase over the foreseeable future. And increased liquidity is something all investors appreciate. ≪

The 2005 National Business Location Survey

The Dutch office market is ready for structural improvement. But national government and market parties hold remarkably different views with regard to its current situation and what could be done to improve it. This can be read in the report 'Nationaal vestigingsplaats onderzoek 2005' published by NVM Bedrijfs Onroerend Goed (BOG) in the fall of 2005.

A total of 70 Dutch municipal governments participated in the Nationaal vestigingsplaats onderzoek 2005 (2005 National Business Location Survey), as did the local NVM BOG realtors in the municipalities in question. The main conclusion of the study was that the market outlooks of the local government – which is responsible for the availability of office space – and the local business realtors – who are responsible for occupancy rates – are widely divergent.

Scarcity

An essential point of difference can be seen in the respondents' views with regard to scarcity in the market. While nearly half the municipalities are of the opinion that there is scarcity in the office market, the majority of the realtors find that there is a market surplus. A remarkable situation in this context is that in fact only those municipalities that have a large volume of office space (over 175,000 m²) have developed a policy outlook with respect to the office market. But

it remains to be seen whether this vision has sufficient relevance to the actual situation. A new plan is drawn up on average every five years – a long interlude in a rapidly changing market.

End users

Furthermore, the planners do not take sufficient account of the wishes of the end users when developing plans. Municipalities tend to outline impressive office complexes for large national and international end users, whereas a large majority of companies operate at regional or even local level (30.8 and 44% respectively).

Location factors

Local governments and market parties also disagree on the subject of location factors, particularly with regard to 'negative location factors'. Municipalities view limited possibilities for expansion or an unfavorable geographic location as possible reasons for a company to settle elsewhere. Business realtors are more concerned about poor accessibility and inadequate infrastructure – both issues to which they often feel local government does not pay sufficient attention.

Municipalities find that there is scarcity in the market while realtors find that there is a market surplus.

The development of office space in the Netherlands

Year	Total space	Available reserve	Rental sector
2000	38,455,000	21,534,800	56%
2004	43,337,000	26,252,200	61%
Increase:	13%	22%	

The available reserve of office space (i.e. the portion of the office market that is free for lease) has seen far stronger growth in recent years than the total reserve of office space. The free rental market is expected to increase further in the years to come. On the one hand this is due to a shift in emphasis towards the rental sector in the case of new construction projects. On the other hand there will be an increase in the number of sale and lease back constructions.

Oscar Smit
Chairman of the Board of NVM

NVM

The NVM is the largest association of real estate brokers and real estate experts in the Netherlands.
The housing supply from more than 3,600 NVM real estate brokers is updated daily and registered in the NVM network, using a nation wide computer network. This means your broker is able to announce that your home is for sale extremely quickly, to a massive market of potential buyers. In addition, he or she also has immediate access to a complete overview of all the homes for sale through his/her colleagues.
In order to guarantee a uniform high quality of service, NVM brokers have together drawn up the NVM Code of Practice. This concerns the level of expertise, objectivity and reliability of each and every individual NVM member. An NVM broker may not have any direct or indirect interest in immovable property, nor participate in unfair competition, and may never represent both the buyer and vendor in the same transaction in relation to conflict of interest.

Little regional coordination

Moreover, the survey indicates that plans are often spread out across various office locations and that there is little coordination at regional level. This last factor in particular is of vital importance if one plans to avoid the development of too many square meters.

'Hopeless' office space

Many realtors stress the importance of addressing rising vacancy rates, as well as redeveloping property, possibly for other functions such as living space. This is a particularly pressing issue in the case of the approx. 1 million m^2 of 'hopeless' office space – obsolete buildings that cannot be rented in their current state and that are therefore ripe for redevelopment.

Creating an attractive living-working environment

Piet Eichholtz, Professor of Real Estate Finance at the University of Maastricht, predicts a further increase in the structural offer. For years, the labor market drove up the demand for office space. Now that the labor market is stabilizing or even contracting, the demand for office space is also expected to diminish.
Furthermore, present development plans do not match the market's requirements. A lot of large-scale offices are on the drawing board, whereas the demand is primarily for small-scale office space. In Eichholtz' opinion, local governments think too much in terms of selling land and creating jobs, whereas they should sooner be concerned with how to create an attractive environment in which people can live and work.

Public-private collaboration

Improved collaboration between local government and market parties forms the foundation for the revival of the Dutch office market, and subsequent improvement of the Dutch competitive position in the international arena. Although government and market do not always see eye to eye, the National Business Location Survey 2005 shows that they do acknowledge the importance of closer collaboration, and have often already taken serious steps to this end – a conclusion that spells good news for the future.　≪

MORE INFORMATION

Nederlandse Vereniging van Makelaars en Vastgoeddeskundigen NVM

Fakkelstede 1
P.O. Box 2222
3430 DE Nieuwegein
The Netherlands
Tel.: +31 30 608 51 85
Website: www.nvm.nl

ONLINE: www.holland-re.com/nvm

INDUSTRY TRENDS

A.L.M. Vlak, LL.M, Board Member of Stichting Corporatie Vastgoedindex, Aedex and CEO of Aedex Databank Vastgoedtaxaties BV

Increased transparency in the Aedex/IPD Social Housing Property Index

For the first time ever, participants in an IPD-supported real estate index have given permission to publish the most important results figures of individual contributors. With this decision, the parties taking part in the Aedex/IPD Social Housing Property Index have made a major contribution towards increased transparency, with regard both to the individual company results and to the functioning of the real estate market in its entirety.

May 2005 saw the first publication of the individual financial results of housing corporations taking part in the Aedex/IPD Index. The index presented a ranking of the participants on the basis of their transformation activities: the level of investment and disinvestment activity of each corporation, expressed as a percentage of the investment value of the corporation's own property portfolio. Participants in the Aedex/IPD Social Housing Property Index subsequently decided to considerably expand the number of indicators determining the ranking of the individual corporations.

Returns

The corporation that produced the highest returns in 2004 was the Amsterdam-based Far West, with a result of 17.7% (see Table1). The lowest-scoring participant was housing corporation Trudo in Eindhoven, with 3.5%. In other words, all participants achieved a positive result in 2004. Return figures vary from year to year: a corporation that performs particularly well one year will not necessarily repeat this performance in every following year. Figures compiled over a three-year period will provide a more balanced picture, although it was not possible to produce three-year figures for all the participants in the index. Far West is one of the examples in this case.

However, figures are available for the corporation ranking second in the 2004 lineup: the Amsterdam-based Woonstichting De Key achieved a return of 15.1% in 2004, although its three-year average is significantly lower: 6.5%. Remarkably enough, Trudo, the corporation with the lowest result in 2004, has the same figure of 6.5% for its three-year average. It comes as no surprise that the differences between corporation returns are far less pronounced when compared on the basis of a three-year average.

2004 Aedex/IPD Index key data:		2004 Aedex/IPD Index 2004 key figures:	
Number of corporations	36	Total result	8.3%
Value of capital	€48.5 billion	Indirect returns	5.4%
Number of units (homes)	566,000	Direct returns	2.7%
Market share of 2004 Index	24%	Efficiency ratio	46.4%
Rental income in 2004	€2.4 billion	Primary policy result	1.8%
		Non-primary policy result	1.5%

The lowest three-year average return was 4.7% for Het Oosten, based in Amsterdam, and the highest was 10.9% for Corporatieholding Friesland. A remarkable fact in this context is that Het Oosten was the most active corporation with regard to the transformation of its portfolio, ranking first in that list.

> A CORPORATION THAT PERFORMS PARTICULARLY WELL ONE YEAR WILL NOT NECESSARILY REPEAT THIS PERFORMANCE IN EVERY FOLLOWING YEAR

Differences in ranking can primarily be attributed to variations in value development. The corporations with the highest total result also achieved the highest indirect returns. This applies to both the 2004 index year and the three-year average.

Efficiency

The Aedex/IPD Social Housing Property Index publishes the so-called efficiency ratio, just as other IPD indices do. This ratio expresses the operating costs as a percentage of gross income. The index average for this ratio in 2004 is 46.4%. This means that for every euro earned by the housing corporations, slightly less than half is spent on operating costs. These operating costs do not include overhead expenditure. A major portion of the operating costs is diverted to maintenance. Here, however, we can distin-

guish relatively large differences between the various housing corporations. This primarily has to do with varying maintenance duties, as well as the particular phase of the multi-year maintenance cycle that the individual corporation is in at the time of the measurement. The correlation between the efficiency ratio and direct returns can be very clearly determined (R=-0.6%).

Policy effect

One of the specific features of the Aedex/IPD Social Housing Property Index is the measurement of policy effect. A corporation's social responsibilities require it to make financial sacrifices, thus putting pressure on its total returns. It is therefore important that housing corporations present their social performance in quantitative terms. For this reason, the Aedex/IPD Social Housing Property Index also measures the effect of the corporations' specific social role on their returns. The participants in the index have therefore agreed to divide their housing portfolio into a section covered by their specific social policy (the primary portfolio) and a section where this is not the case (the non-primary portfolio). Both portfolios are appraised with respect to their market rent value. The actual yield of each home is subsequently calculated, as well the returns that would be achieved if the amount of rent received were determined by market levels rather than by a social-responsible lease contract. The latter figure is also called the estimated market-based yield. >>

A.L.M. Vlak, LL.M.
is a Board Member of Stichting Corporatie Vastgoedindex, Aedex, and CEO of Aedex Databank Vastgoedtaxaties BV.

Aedex

Stichting Corporatie Vastgoedindex, Aedex, is responsible for the Aedex/ IPD Social Housing Property Index, the annual financial performance survey of the Dutch housing corporations. This survey is conducted fully independent of government, financiers, supervisory bodies, individual participants and their collective interest groups. 58 corporations participated in the current publication, responsible for a total of 800,000 homes. This is equal to one third of the total housing portfolio operated by Dutch housing corporations.

MORE INFORMATION

Stichting Corporatie Vastgoedindex, Aedex

Olympia 1e
1213 NS Hilversum
The Netherlands
Tel.: +31 35 523 88 47
Fax: +31 35 523 82 19
E-mail: info@aedex.nl
Website: www.aedex.nl

ONLINE: www.holland-re.com/aedex

INDUSTRY TRENDS

The international market for retail real estate

Shopping
the world

- 7,208 participants
- 1,588 retailers
- 783 exhibiting companies
- 68 countries

To take part in MAPIC 2006:

Call your local representative to register or to reserve a stand.

Headquarters (Paris) tel.: +33 (0) 1 41 90 45 20

London tel.: +44 (0) 20 7528 0086

New York tel.: +1 (212) 284 5133

Tokyo tel.: +81 (3) 3542 3114

Reed MIDEM
A member of Reed Exhibitions

15-17 november 2006, Palais des Festivals, Cannes, France
www.mapic.com

		Total Returns		Indirect Returns		Direct Returns	
		2004	2002-2004	2004	2002-2004	2004	2002-2004
1	Far West, Amsterdam	17.7	-	13.9	-	3.4	-
2	Woonstichting De Key, Amsterdam	15.1	6.5	12.8	4.2	2.0	2.3
3	Stichting Nijestee, Groningen	13,4	9.1	10.8	6.4	2.3	2.5
4	Woonbron, Rotterdam (incl Delft)	12.9	9,5	9.3	6.2	3.3	3.1
5	Nieuw Wonen Friesland, Leeuwarden	11.8	-	7.7	-	3.8	-
6	Ymere, Amsterdam	11.2	5.8	7.7	2.8	3.2	3.0
7	Staedion, The Hague	9.9	7.6	7.2	4.6	2.5	2.9
8	Stichting Portaal, Baarn	9.8	8.1	7.2	5.5	2.4	2.5
9	Talis Woondiensten, Nijmegen	9.4	8.6	6.6	6.1	2.6	2.4
10	Het Oosten, Amsterdam	9.1	4.7	5.6	1.5	3.4	3.2
11	Singelveste, Breda	9.1	-	5.7	-	3.3	-
12	Woonunie, Deventer	8.6	5.8	5.8	3.3	2.7	2.5
13	Stichting In, Groningen	8.3	7.6	4.8	4.2	3.3	3.2
	Aedex/IPD Social Housing Property Index	**8.3**	**7.2**	**5.4**	**4.3**	**2.7**	**2.8**
14	Stichting Corporatieholding Friesland, Grou	8.1	10.9	4.0	6.3	4.0	4.4
15	Stichting Mitros, Utrecht	8.0	6.9	5.0	3.7	2.9	3.1
16	Wbv. Smallingerland, Drachten and Accolade	7.0	-	4.0	-	2.9	-
17	De Woonplaats, Enschede	6.9	7.5	4.3	4.7	2.5	2.6
18	Servatius Woningstichting, Maastricht (incl Eijsden)	6.9	-	4.1	-	2.7	-
19	SGBB, Hoofddorp	6.8	-	3.1	-	3.6	-
20	Stichting Casade Woondiensten, Waalwijk	6.6	6.7	3.2	3.4	3.3	3.2
21	Wbv. Eendracht Maakt Macht, Zandvoort	6.4	7.2	3.9	4.2	2.4	2.9
22	Aramis, Roosendaal (incl WSJ)	6.3	5.3	3.7	2.6	2.5	2.7
23	De Woonmaatschappij Haarlemmermeer, Hoofddorp	6.2	9.0	3.8	6.5	2.3	2.4
24	De Alliantie, Huizen	6.2	5.7	3.3	2.9	2.8	2.7
25	Woondrecht, Dordrecht	6.1	-	3.3	-	2.7	-
26	Oosterpoort Wooncombinatie, Groesbeek	6.1	-	3.6	-	2.5	-
27	Volksbelang, Raamsdonkveer	6.1	-	3.1	-	3.0	-
28	De Woningstichting, Wageningen	5.9	-	3.2	-	2.6	-
29	Wonen Limburg, Roermond	5.6	5.6	3.4	3.2	2.2	2.4
30	Stichting Wooncom, Emmen	5.0	-	2.1	-	2.8	-
31	WonenBreburg, Tilburg	4.8	5.5	2.5	2.5	2.2	3.0
32	Woonmaatschappij Maasland, Ravenstein	4.4	6.7	1.0	3.7	3.4	2.9
33	Wonen West Brabant, Bergen op Zoom	4.4	-	1.5	-	2.9	-
34	De Woonmaatschappij Haarlem, Haarlem	4.2	7.4	1.9	4.9	2.3	2.4
35	Woningstichting Leusden, Leusden	3.6	5.5	0.4	2.7	3.2	2.8
36	Stichting Trudo, Eindhoven	3.5	6.5	1.3	4.2	2.1	2.2

Social dividend

The policy effect figure is determined by calculating the difference between the market-based yield and the home's actual yield. In the case of the primary portfolio, this policy effect is also known as the social dividend.

The corporations' policy effect figures over 2004 range from 3.6% for Volksbelang, based in Raamsdonkveer, to 0.3% for the Groningen corporation Nijestee. The difference in figures can generally be explained by the fact that strong markets result in a

more pronounced policy effect than weaker markets. In contrast with the measured results, the difference between the three-year average social dividend of the corporations' primary portfolios and their 2004 policy effect figure is only a few tenths of a percent. ≪

STEC GROEP

ANTICIPATING AN AGEING POPULATION

The Dutch population is steadily growing older. Between now and 2040, the number of senior citizens in the Netherlands will increase from 2.3 to 4.1 million. This development will have far-reaching consequences for the real estate market. The residential, retail and office markets are already taking the rising proportion of over-65s into account, as can be read in the study 'Vastgoedmarkt en vergrijzing', carried out in 2005 by the Stec Groep by order of Vereniging van Institutionele Beleggers in Vastgoed, Nederland (IVBN).

By Ola Sinoo

In the Netherlands, the post-war baby boom generation is eagerly preparing for retirement, while average life expectancy is still increasing. Over the next few decades, these two factors will cause a strong increase in the number of senior citizens, not only those over 65 years of age but also the very elderly (over 75). This rapid ageing of the Dutch population is proportional as well as numerical. A decline in the birth rate has led to a decreased percentage of young people in the general make-up of the Dutch population. In 2040, the Netherlands is expected to have more than 4 million citizens over 65 years of age. This is roughly equivalent to a quarter of the total population at that time. With these figures, the over-65 age group is bound to make more and more of a mark on the Dutch residential, retail and office markets. This will create a range of opportunities for investors, provided they anticipate the specific needs and requirements of senior citizens with regard to their living environment.

Housing market

The ageing population will lead to an increased demand for homes adapted to the needs of senior citizens. This presents different requirements to those involved in the development of youth housing or family homes. The homes need to be safe, spacious and accessible by wheel chair, have all the modern conveniences as well as extensive sanitary facilities and user-friendly technology. Furthermore, the homes must have (health)care and other facilities like stores and public transport at close hand.

Graph 1 Growth of the over-65 age group between 2005 and 2040

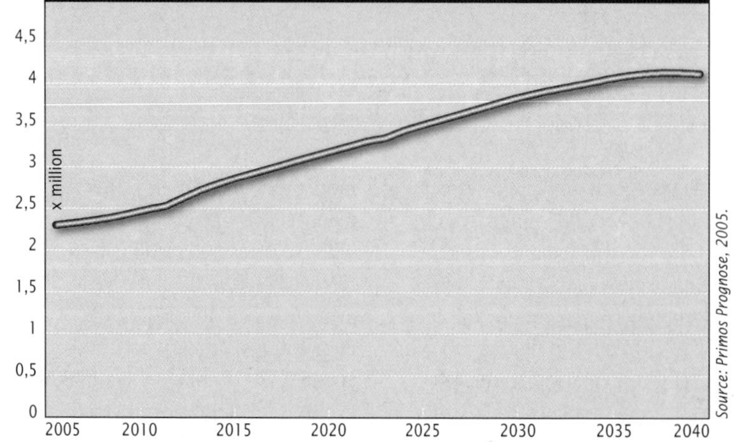

Source: Primos Prognose, 2005.

Population growth
The absolute size of the population plays a vital role in the demand for homes, retail space and office space. Between 2005 and 2030, the Dutch population will increase from 16.4 million to 17.6 million. After 2030, the Dutch population will remain stable according to current forecasts.

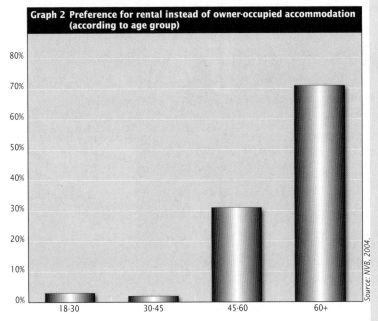

Graph 2 Preference for rental instead of owner-occupied accommodation (according to age group)

Source: NVB, 2004.

Y-axis: 0% to 80%
X-axis categories: 18-30, 30-45, 45-60, 60+

Stec Groep

Stec Groep is an international consultancy bureau specializing in location-choice, economic development and real estate investment and development. Typical clients are national investment companies, ministries and big municipalities, both in the Netherlands and abroad. The Stec Groep also provides consultancy services to individual companies, particularly project developers, investors and big companies.

Market Stec focuses on:

- Housing
- Commercial real estate (offices, industrials, retails)
- Industrial estates
- Site selection and investment promotion
- Economic development

INDUSTRY TRENDS

Many older people prefer a (more expensive) rental home to owner-occupied accommodation. This ensures that they need not worry about maintenance issues and often have direct access to care facilities – a reassuring thought. Moreover, moving into rental accommodation is a good way to release capital formerly 'tied up' in an owner-occupied home.

Senior-proof

Senior citizens form an increasingly important target group for the (upper-range) rental developments initiated by institutional investors. Adapting the portfolio strategy to this circumstance leads to the development of 'senior-proof' homes and the transformation of existing housing into homes for the elderly. After all, the demand for homes for senior citizens can only be partially met by new construction. Closer collaboration with healthcare organizations also offers various opportunities – for instance the development of healthcare boulevards or care hotels.

Retail market

In many cases, improved pension facilities and increased capital (thanks to owning their own homes for example) have increased senior citizens' purchasing power. Between 2005 and 2020, the difference in respective income positions between working people and pensioners will drop from approx. 25% to approx. 7%. As not only the number of senior citizens will increase, but also their personal disposable income, this age group will become increasingly important for retail turnover. This is why developers should focus generous attention on adapting shopping centers to the needs of the senior consumer. This can be achieved by improving accessibility (lifts, resting points, public transport connections), improving safety (cameras, lighting, homes above the stores for increased social control), creating more room for personal service and developing a product range more attuned to the elderly consumer. »

PHOTO: EUROPE REAL ESTATE PUBLISHERS

MORE INFORMATION

Stec Groep

P.O. Box 31210
6503 CE Nijmegen
The Netherlands
Tel.: +31 24 352 16 16
Fax: +31 24 352 16 10
E-mail: info@stec.nl
Website: www.stec.nl
Board of Directors: Duco Bodewes and Peter van Geffen

ONLINE: www.holland-re.com/stecgroep

CULTURE, CONVENIENCE, CHARACTER, IN ADDITION TO FEASIBILITY.

THE STEADY SUCCESS OF WILLIAM PROPERTIES CAN BE ATTRIBUTED

TO REALISM COMBINED WITH WIDE HORIZONS. COMPREHENSIVE

PROJECTS IN RESIDENTIAL, COMMERCIAL, RETAIL AND

RECREATIONAL DEVELOPMENT. THROUGHOUT THE NETHERLANDS

WE DEVELOP PROPERTY WITH A SENSE OF SUCCESS.

www.williamproperties.nl

William
Properties

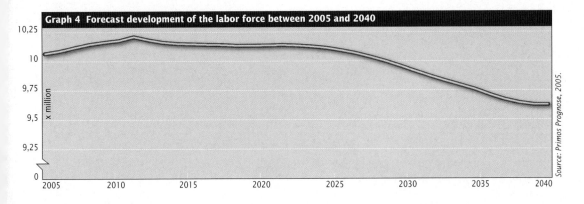

Graph 4 Forecast development of the labor force between 2005 and 2040

Source: Primos Prognose, 2005.

Focus on district and local shopping centers

For investors in retail real estate, the ageing of the population offers new opportunities. After charting the wishes and requirements of senior citizens with regard to various types of shopping centers, parties can make a study of how retail environments can be made more attractive for this growing target group. Senior citizens have a preference for easily accessible district and local shopping centers. These can be improved or added to the retail portfolio.

Office market

The demand for office space is expected to increase in the coming decades. Various trends play a role in this development. In the next few decades, the ageing of the population on the one hand and the decreased birth rate on the other will lead to a decline in the available labor

force. This will have a reducing effect on the demand for office space. As labor capacity becomes increasingly scarce, the cost of labor in the Netherlands will rise, leading more and more back office activities to be relocated to low-wage countries. In the Netherlands, the emphasis will shift towards knowledge-intensive sectors such as IT, consultancy and financial services. Population ageing will also lead to an increase in the number of healthcare institutes, insurance companies and welfare organizations. In the labor market, office space will become a term of employment, which is expected to lead to an increase in the number of square meters per employee. The market is also expected to place higher demands on the appearance and level of facilities of office property. In the coming years, the office market will remain extremely dynamic, for reasons including changing

quality requirements, corporate mergers, the amalgamation of company divisions and the dissolution of companies.

Quality office property

The next few years are expected to bring a modest increase in office-based employment, while market preferences with regard to regions, locations and accommodation are expected to undergo further development. For this reason, in the coming years there will still be sufficient development of new office real estate, with a focus on quality premises: spacious, well-equipped and with a pleasant ambiance. But each new office building will mean structural vacancy at other, older office locations. These obsolete buildings will either be torn down or redeveloped, requiring structural adaptations and more flexibility in local zoning schemes.   ≪

Graph 3 Retail space according to location type

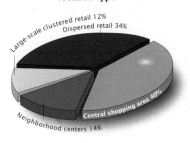

Large-scale clustered retail 12%
Dispersed retail 34%
Central shopping area 40%
Neighborhood centers 14%

Source: NVB, Thermometer Winkels (Den Haag, 2005).

Ageing in a European perspective
The Dutch demographic trend holds a middle position within the larger European framework. In 2005, 14% of the Dutch population was over 65 years of age. In various other European countries, the proportion of senior citizens was significantly higher: in France the over-65 age group made up 16.2% of the population, in Germany 16.9% and in Sweden 17.2%. In 2030, Italy and Germany will be at the forefront of European ageing, with approx. 27.5% of the population in both countries over the age of 65, versus approx. 23% in the Netherlands.

> **We make locations prosper**

Over a period of ten years NS Real Estate has been developing offices, homes, hotels, schools and stores.

In doing so NS Real Estate ensures an optimal set-up of public areas at railwaystations. Very accessible

and attractive. We are committed to high quality work.

NS Real Estate
PO Box 2319, 3500 GH Utrecht
The Netherlands
Telephone +31 (0)30 300 43 00
www.nsvastgoed.nl

NS Vastgoed

CORPORATE PAGES

PASSION BECOMES PERFORMANCE

Passion for quality drives excellent performance. That's why Achmea Vastgoed delivers higher returns on investments for its institutional clients. We focus on assets at the top of the real estate pyramid. And we have built a unique position in mortgage investments. How passion becomes performance: it's reflected in the value of the portfolio of our clients.

Achmea Vastgoed is an assets company in real estate and mortgages for institutional investors. Our assets under management are more than €7.3 billion for our 60 clients. And Achmea Vastgoed is growing. In 2006 more than €1 billion can be invested. This financial scale offers Achmea Vastgoed the power to use opportunities. The need for the right properties and good mortgage investments will continue. We are responsive and experienced; and at all times open to propositions.

Unique position

Achmea Vastgoed's acquisition and investment policies focus on growth and diversification. This means that properties are sought in different sub-sectors, types and price ranges. Mortgage lending means balancing the different risks: debtor risks, collateral risks

Dick van Hal,
Managing Director.

Cor Worms,
Managing Director.

A room with a view; The Pyramids in Amsterdam.

Westgate, Amsterdam.

Varrolaan 100, Utrecht.

and interest rate risks. This synergy between investments in real estate and mortgages makes Achmea Vastgoed unique. It enables investors to compose a well-balanced portfolio, yet accommodate it in one single service point. Another form of diversification is the supplementation of Dutch portfolios with investments in foreign real estate, increasing investment opportunities and improving the risk/return ratio of the total real estate portfolio.

International funds

Non-listed indirect real estate is leading the international real estate markets. In this respect Achmea Vastgoed has created two funds under the names AREA Fund Europe and AREA Fund North America. In collaboration with London based Property Market Analysis and Boston based Property & Portfolio Research, Achmea Vastgoed has devised international property allocations which seek to extend the range of opportunities for stable, high-single-digit returns for Dutch investors. Achmea Vastgoed, through the AREA

funds, participates in a variety of privately-placed property funds. With a clear demand from clients, we expect the number of participations to increase considerably in the near future. Property is a cyclical investment so by exposure to more than 20 domestic economies, including the new entrants to the European Union, we hope to smooth out the troughs which accompany single-country investing.

The capital of different investors is joined for a well-diversified portfolio of foreign property stocks. The investment philosophy is based on local expertise and the market position of local investment funds. The AREA Funds are limited to participations in unlisted funds because of their low volatility and low correlation with other investment categories. Foremost for us and our institutional clients are well-regulated and accessible markets. Europe and North America are the appropriate areas. We apply stringent selection criteria and do business with leading local partners only.

Organizational excellence

Achmea Vastgoed works hard to realize its objective: to be a market leader in property and mortgage investments for institutional clients. Our ambition defines our organization and our work methods. It calls for organizational excellence, professional and client-oriented. This is underlined by the SAS 70 Type I statement, which was put into effect in 2005. This guarantees to ourselves, our investors and commercial partners that our control mechanisms and control structure are sound. The focus of Achmea Vastgoed is our client; our style is based on integrity, professionalism, and enthusiasm. «

CORPORATE

MORE INFORMATION

Achmea Vastgoed B.V.

Gatwickstraat 1
P.O. Box 59347
1040 KH Amsterdam
The Netherlands
Tel.: +31 20 606 56 00
Fax: +31 20 606 56 09
E-mail: vastgoedinfo@achmea.nl
Website: www.achmeavastgoed.nl

BUILDING ON A SOLID FOUNDATION

In 1946, when Jacob Wiersema laid the foundation for what is now Bouwfonds, he could not possibly have envisaged what it would become. His initiative to bring home ownership within the reach of ordinary people is now a European, all-round property company, specializing in development, financing and asset management.

According to CEO Henk Rutgers, today's Bouwfonds can be characterized by an apparent contradiction in terms: dynamic and stable. "As a solid, realistic and dependable player in the property market, Bouwfonds is as dynamic as the markets in which it operates," he says. Bouwfonds is in the business of providing people with the space to live, work and shop and, thanks to its roots, it is keenly aware of its responsibilities in the social context in which it operates. "There's much more to property than just bricks and mortar,"

adds Rutgers. "At Bouwfonds we continuously strive to create added value for end-users." This is probably one of the few things that hasn't changed since Wiersma's time. Rutgers: "High quality, affordable accommodation is a bare necessity of regular and commercial life. The desire to provide this for our clients, on the basis of long-term partnerships, is a cornerstone of our enduring success."

International growth

During these past few years, this success has seen Bouwfonds outgrow its native Dutch market,

where it is one of the largest property organizations. Bouwfonds' ambition to become a leading European real estate player by 2010 is spearheaded by the growth of its main operating divisions: Bouwfonds Property Development, Bouwfonds Property Finance, and Bouwfonds Asset Management. Bouwfonds Property Development is an all-round developer of multifunctional projects in the residential, retail and office markets. During the coming years it will open more new offices in France and extend its activities with Scandinavian and Spanish

Henk Rutgers, CEO Bouwfonds.

Le Grand Angle, office with spacious parking facilities, Lille, France.

Haverleij, a prestigious residential development in Den Bosch, the Netherlands.

partners. Bouwfonds Property Finance, a project financer par excellence, has in-depth knowledge of the property market and the ability to see things from the developer's perspective. This division will strengthen its local presence in the most important European regions and place more emphasis on participations.

Meanwhile, Bouwfonds Asset Management – which focuses on initiating, structuring and managing real estate investment products – will roll out international property portfolios to be used as investment products.

Ingredients for success

Henk Rutgers is convinced that Bouwfonds has the ingredients for success to differentiate itself from its competitors and help it realize its ambitions. An in-depth knowledge of the industry gives Bouwfonds an intuitive ability to assess the projects, feasibility and identify risk potential. In fact, it often correctly sees potential where competitors are reluctant to look past the risk. Bouwfonds also has a strong preference for sustainable, mutually rewarding, long-term partnerships, as opposed to short-term hit-and-run affairs.

Furthermore, as its proven track record shows, Bouwfonds provides added value through quality not quantity, preferring to provide what clients really want, rather than low-cost mass production.

"Having separate divisions also gives substantial advantages," Rutgers assures. "It means that these divisions can benefit from one another's experience and expertise when they need to, yet operate autonomously to realize their respective goals.

All these qualities, and more, make Bouwfonds considerably more than the sum of its component parts and allow us to keep building on the foundation laid for us 60 years ago."   ≪

ODE, inner-city multifunctional project, Amsterdam, the Netherlands.

MORE INFORMATION

Bouwfonds

P.O. Box 15
3870 DA Hoevelaken
The Netherlands
Tel.: +31 33 253 91 11
Fax: +31 33 253 95 55
Website: www.bouwfonds.com

FOCUS ON MULTI-FUNCTIONAL PROJECTS AND CONCEPT DEVELOPMENT

The development of residential areas, integral areas and retail locations demands teamwork between the different professionals involved. Knowledge of the market, understanding the customer needs and a good sense of return and risk, together with technical and design know-how are all essential. Bouwfonds MAB Ontwikkeling is one of the largest developers of commercial real estate and the largest provider of open-market homes, which in 2005 meant some 250,000 m² of commercial space and some 8,500 housing units.

Multi-functional projects

Bouwfonds MAB Ontwikkeling is a very strong development organization with an outstanding market position. "The Bouwfonds portfolio currently consists of approximately 85% mono-functional and 15% multi-functional projects," states Henk van Zandvoort, Chairman of the Executive Board. "In both the Netherlands and in foreign countries we find increased talk of a dramatic rise in multi-functional projects. We have the know-how when it comes to complex city-center projects and how to give them a mixed-use character. The portion of multi-functional developments in our portfolio – including small-scale integral projects – will increase dramatically in the coming years. I expect that by the end of this decade some 70% of our projects will be mono-functional and 30% multi-functional."

Henk van Zandvoort, Chairman of the Executive Board

La Grande Cour on Westerdokseiland, Amsterdam.

Raaks, dynamic portal to the city of Haarlem.

Concept development

Our Studio Bouwfonds MAB in The Hague plays an important role in concept development. "The Studio Bouwfonds MAB combines urban and architectural design talent and market knowledge," says Van Zandvoort. Van Zandvoort expects that the importance of concept development for residential, work, and shopping will only continue to increase. "Governments have continued to withdraw ever further from involvement in these projects, which means that the responsibility for this kind of regional development falls increasingly more on the developers themselves. That means an increased demand for creativity, as well as a certain amount of stamina – including financial stamina. It is not just about large expenditures in these urban developments; it's also about long-term projects, which is why I expect that the market in this area will become increasingly limited to the big players. I see us playing a prominent role in all of this. ≪

Brandevoort, residential development in Helmond.

MORE INFORMATION

Bouwfonds MAB Ontwikkeling

P.O. Box 15
3870 DA Hoevelaken
The Netherlands
Tel.: +31 33 253 97 00
Fax: +31 33 253 96 85
E-mail: ontwikkeling@bouwfonds.nl
Website: www.bouwfonds.nl

CORPORATE

Room for entrepreneurs

Seeing opportunities and going for them. Creating openings and using them. Isn't that the essence of entrepreneurship, summed up in a few words? The entrepreneur who goes straight for his objective is looking for a financier who is a fellow entrepreneur. Like Bouwfonds Property Finance. A partner who lives and breathes tailor-made financing, based on a deep-seated know-ledge of the international real estate sector. Because entre-preneurs do not recognize borders.

Room for crossing borders

bouwfonds
property finance

BEST IN CLASS IN WHAT WE DO AND WHO WE WORK WITH...

Cushman & Wakefield (C&W) has been named European Commercial Agent of the Year at the 2005 European Property Awards held at the international property exposition ExpoReal in Munich, Germany.

The awards recognize the best examples of European property development, investment, innovation, management and consultancy and are judged by a panel of property professionals from across the continent. It is the first year the awards have been held and they are unique in recognizing success and innovation at a pan-European level.

C&W Managing Partner, Baldwin Poolman: "We have been building a truly European firm for well over 30 years. The award is a tribute to our people who operate as one team and not as a series of individual units."

Our services help clients turn fixed assets into dynamic assets, ready to make a significant contribution to overall corporate performance, regardless of the economy or business cycle. And it doesn't matter if our clients operate locally or internationally.

Worldwide activity

Poolman: "We see the real estate practice of our clients becoming more and more international. Our professionals are active in every major market worldwide, optimally positioning and marketing properties and uncovering hidden opportunities for clients. In the Netherlands we are supported by our local and worldwide research so we can provide clients with detailed market intelligence, making every

Baldwin Poolman,
Managing Partner.

Oosterdokseiland, the new heart of Amsterdam.

AMB Fokker Logistics Park, situated in the Amsterdam Airport Area.

recommendation a local one. We are proud that we are involved in some of the most prestigious internationally focused projects."

Our office agency department is leasing agent for The Atrium. The Atrium is one of the best known and most desirable office buildings in Amsterdam with a long history of satisfying the needs of even the most discerning tenants. It is situated within the heart of the prestigious Zuidas business district, home to many of the city's most respected companies. Impressive and contemporary, The Atrium offers an unrivalled blend of accessibility, style, service and flexibility; and the rents are highly competitive too. It is owned by Tishman Speyer, one of the leading owners, developers and operators of first-class real estate in the world.

Our industrial agency department is leasing agent for AMB Fokker Logistics Park. The park is situated at Schiphol-Oost, part of the main distribution and logistic area Amsterdam Airport Area. The property has excellent transport accessibility due to its close proximity to the A4 and A9 motorways. A large part of AMB Fokker Logistics Park is already leased by DHL.

And last but not least our retail department acts as an exclusive adviser for the approximately 24,000 m² retail and leisure facilities at Oosterdokseiland (ODE). ODE is situated on the banks of the IJ river, right next to Amsterdam Central Station. With ODE, 200,000 m² of metropolitan functions will be added to Amsterdam. The developer is Bouwfonds MAB Ontwikkeling and delivery is planned in phases from 2007-2009. ≪

The refurbished Atrium office building at the Zuidas, Amsterdam.

European Property Awards. **winner** 05

MORE INFORMATION

Cushman & Wakefield
Amstelveenseweg 760
P.O. Box 75456
1070 AL Amsterdam
The Netherlands
Tel.: +31 20 301 42 42
Fax: +31 20 301 42 19
Website: www.cushmanwakefield.com
Contact: Baldwin Poolman, Stephen Screene

CORPORATE

ING REAL ESTATE

CREATING VALUE

ING Real Estate is market leader in the Netherlands in commercial real estate development, commercial real estate finance and real estate investment management. With a total business portfolio of more than €64 billion and offices in 15 countries, ING Real Estate is also one of the strongest real estate companies worldwide. During 2005, the effectiveness of ING Real Estate's strategy to create value for its clients through the combination of development, investment management and finance was proven again and again.

ING Real Estate is an international network organization with offices in the Netherlands, Belgium, France, the United Kingdom, Spain, Germany, Italy, the Czech Republic, Poland, Hungary, the United States, Singapore, China, South Korea, and Australia.

Integrated real estate business ING Real Estate's mission is to be the leading provider of innovative real estate based solutions, both locally and globally, that exceed our customers' performance expectations.

The synergies and close collaboration between the business lines of ING Real Estate allow us to serve clients requiring services covering the entire value chain, with the exception of construction and brokerage.

Its extensive range of activities means that ING Real Estate is aware of the different angles of trends taking place at any particular time in the real estate market. The opportunities for cross-selling among the various core activities produce significant added value for an integrated real estate business.

Creating Value

ING Real Estate's primary aim is to make maximum use of our global expertise in the creation of valuable products, value for our clients, value for society and value for our employees.

Specialists in the fields of real estate development, finance and investment management work together to meet this objective.

G.J. Jautze, CEO.

Retail and residential center Stadshagen in Zwolle.

Overhoeks, Amsterdam.

When all participants work towards the creation of added value, projects and processes can run smoothly. With each discipline focused on making that extra effort, real estate products can be put together with intelligence. Clearly our broad range of knowledge and experience gives us a significant advantage in this area.

Within ING Real Estate and throughout the global network of ING Group there is a depth of expertise. Expertise that can be brought to bear on any particular situation through just a few phone calls, bringing clarity and perspective to every aspect of our work.

Real estate projects often become a part of our cultural heritage, examples of bold initiatives and sound investment decisions. In these instances we are no longer talking simply about added value, but of a timeless emotional value and, of course, significant economic value. We all work together to create this unique value. ≪

Montevideo in Rotterdam.

MORE INFORMATION

ING Real Estate

Schenkkade 65
P.O. Box 90463
2509 LL The Hague
The Netherlands
Tel.: +31 70 341 84 18
Fax: +31 70 341 84 19
E-mail: ingre.info@ingrealestate.com
Website: www.ingrealestate.com

"IT'S A MATTER OF DESIGN"

Multi Development (formerly AM Development) is quickly growing to become a pan-European investing developer. The Multi Development design & development formula combines architecture and urban development with high value in terms of use, experience and investment. This has enabled Multi Development to breathe new life into the Netherlands' inner cities, shopping centers and office parks time and time again.

Last year, Elsevier magazine voted the Papendorp office and business park in Utrecht the best business location in the Netherlands. "We set the tone here with our buildings for Cap Gemini, HP Netherlands and Atos Origin," says Ebbe van Wijngaarden, Director Office Development at Multi Development, currently involved in the development of buildings for KPN and CA (Computer Associates). Van Wijngaarden

states, "End users are taking advantage of the present supply situation in the office market to trade in out-of-date accommodation for new modern premises. Besides attractive price levels, they pay close attention to the quality of the building and its surroundings. It is generally easy for Multi Development to offer an attractive price-quality ratio, as we have extensive in-house design and development facilities at our disposal."

Creating identity

In Amsterdam, Multi Development has taken up a number of strategic development positions that enable it to offer its clients office accommodation in particularly attractive settings. "West of the Zuidas, on a former IBM site, we are developing a campus for offices with floor spaces ranging from 5,000 to 50,000 m², " says Sven Mathijssen, Director Multifunctional Developments of Multi Development.

Sven Mathijssen, Ebbe van Wijngaarden, Richard Reulink, and architect Willem Joost de Vries of T+T Design.

Zaanstad starts its long-awaited transformation of the city center.

The KPN Building strengthens Papendorp's popularity, Utrecht.   *The spectacular Musiskwartier in Arnhem will open this year.*

"At two locations on the Zuidas itself, we are developing integrated plans that combine offices and homes. We see opportunities to provide end users with individual office buildings that have their own distinct identities – something that many prospective clients are looking for in this area."

Combining functions

In Zaanstad, Mathijssen is working together with local government on an extensive transformation of the city center. "We are collaborating on an integrated project that will include stores, a cinema, homes and a parking garage. It will offer the environmental quality and retail variety that is so sorely missed in this area. Contracts have already

been signed for more than half of the area's 18,000 m² of retail space."

For consumers and retailers

Multi Development is also realizing large-scale inner-city projects in Maastricht, Arnhem and The Hague. In addition, Multi Development is renovating the city centers of smaller towns that have a strong regional service function like Woerden, Hardenberg and Ermelo. The company is involved in the development of shopping centers in the inner-city districts and suburbs of Almere, Enschede and Vleuten. In all of these retail projects, Director Retail Development Richard Reulink discerns a pressing need for

larger retail spaces, better parking facilities and a distinctive appearance and atmosphere. Reulink explains, "Consumers are demanding a more complete and varied picture. Multi Development's retail developments address this need and are set apart by their design quality. We strive to make an expansion of the town center in Hardenberg as distinctive and individual as the shopping center in the new city district of Vleuterweide, which takes rural living as its central theme. In Amersfoort the atmosphere of the Eemcenter area is heavily influenced by large-scale users. We aim to create locations that have a pleasant atmosphere."
IT'S A MATTER OF DESIGN.   ≪

Hardenberg provides an attractive centerpiece for the region.

MORE INFORMATION

Multi Development BV

P.O. Box 875
2800 AW Gouda
The Netherlands
Tel.: +31 182 69 09 00
Fax: +31 182 69 06 90
E-mail: info@multi-development.com
Website: www.multi-development.com

NS Vastgoed

DEVELOPING QUALITY REAL ESTATE IN THE STATION AREAS

As the owner of property in the areas surrounding the Dutch railway stations, NS Vastgoed is working towards the substantial improvement of these locations. Nothing must stand in the way of new economic and social impulses for the cities. Relying on its employees' specific knowledge and experience, NS Vastgoed works in close collaboration with the cities, companies and other involved parties to develop new locations for local government, schools, hotels and local and international companies. Setting up here, these organizations gain nothing less than a new calling card for the area.

In the direct vicinity of many Dutch station buildings, NS Vastgoed is currently developing projects of all sizes, in order to create more efficient, attractive and safe station areas. Besides regular quality office buildings, the locations accommodate council offices, educational complexes, homes, hotels and cinemas – making them attractive economic hotspots. The construction of the Dutch HSL high-speed rail link ensures that the five stations on the line will become even more attractive for international companies. For many of the travelers using this exclusive rail connection, the Amsterdam, Schiphol,

The Hague and Rotterdam station areas will be the first view they have of the Netherlands. There is only one opportunity to make a good first impression, so a lot of attention is being paid to the development of these areas.

New impulse

For years, companies have sought out quality accommodation in the vicinity of traffic junctions. A good example in the Netherlands is Schiphol, but the regional airports are also seeing an increase in commercial activity around the airport site. For these areas, this means a substantial new impulse to the local and regional economy.

Good accessibility

Commercial activity is really on the up and up in the direct surroundings of the railway stations. Thanks to the improvement of the road and rail connections leading to and from the area, these locations are eminently suited for companies that have many employees, guests or visitors. A good example is the increasing number of council offices realized by NS Vastgoed around railway stations. Due to the station's good connections, both council employees and visitors have a range of options by which to reach the council office building.

C.A.M. de Boo, CEO.

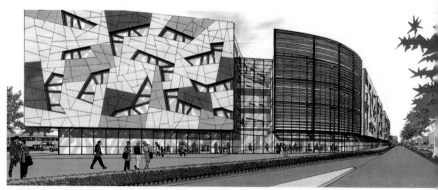

School (ROC) in Nijmegen, the Netherlands.

CORPORATE

Apartments Wijnhaeve, Rotterdam, the Netherlands.

HSL boost

NS Vastgoed is currently busily developing new projects in the areas surrounding the HSL stations – in The Hague for instance, where offices, apartments and stores are being constructed on Koningin Julianaplein. In Rotterdam, new office buildings are being realized in the direct vicinity of Rotterdam Central Station, and apartments and a hotel are being built near Rotterdam Blaak station.

In Breda, which is being developed into a new quality traffic hub with international connections, the area surrounding the station will gain new offices, stores, homes and an expansion of the already existing hotel.

Businesspark Cartesiusdriehoek, Utrecht.

Upgrading company grounds

Besides focusing on the locations adjacent to the railway, in the near future NS Vastgoed will also be making heavy investments in its company grounds. Due to the hiving off of various railway activities, these sites have been or will be assigned a new purpose. The Cartesiusdriehoek site in Utrecht, the former carriage workshop in Amersfoort and the Boezembocht business site in Rotterdam will all soon be upgraded. In these projects, NS Vastgoed will not only target the development of new property, but will also place considerable emphasis on the improvement of infrastructure and facilities. This will make the sites suitable for accommodating the local and regional business community in the coming decades.

NS Vastgoed is known as a developer with social commitment. We can rely on a staff of 125 professionals to bring inner-city locations to life, with buildings that both produce good returns and form an added value for their surroundings in economic and social terms. ≪

MORE INFORMATION

NS Vastgoed

P.O. Box 2319
3500 GH Utrecht
The Netherlands
Tel.: + 31 30 300 43 00
Fax: + 31 30 300 44 00
E-mail: nsv.info@ns.nl
Website: www.nsvastgoed.nl

'ASPIRE TO GROWTH WITH A MORE BALANCED PORTFOLIO'

Take a long-term vision and link it with taking advantage decisively of the opportunities offered by the real estate market. That's the foundation underpinning Redevco Nederland, the Dutch real estate organization of Redevco. Luuk Lantinga, Managing Director of Redevco Nederland, sees growth not as being the biggest player on the market, but as being a 'star performer' fulfilling that long-term vision. Redevco's history in retailing makes it clear where the focus lies, but offices and business premises also have to contribute to a balanced portfolio division.

Dynamics typify a market, and the real estate market – particularly today's real estate market – is no exception. If you want to strengthen your position, you need the agility of a smaller player and the strike power of a bigger player. Redevco Nederland fits that bill, as a part of the 'big' Redevco, one of the largest retail real estate companies in Europe with investments amounting to €6.5 billion. 'Seize the opportunities when they come' is Managing Director Luuk Lantinga's slogan. "We don't fit the image of the traditional investor, but on the contrary are very dynamic. We are very alert to opportunities on the market. We want to acquire projects that offer possibilities of (re)development. We're prepared to invest parts of the existing portfolio to achieve this aim.

We'll use different risk profiles to do this. The great advantage at Redevco is that we don't have a tax status that prohibits 'doing business', so we are in a position to run risks. This is an attractive perspective for municipalities, developers and retailers. In addition, because we are free to move, decision-making goes faster."

Luuk Lantinga, Managing Director of Redevco Nederland.

Roggestraat, Arnhem, the Netherlands.

Kalverstraat, Amsterdam, the Netherlands.

Decisive company

The fact that Redevco has easy access to capital contributes to its status of decisive investment company. "Tax regulations don't get in our way. That makes us the pre-eminent partner for parties that have been taking the initiative on the Dutch market for some time but that have more difficult recourse to the capital market. We can think and develop along with them, and don't have to own the entire development ourselves."

Diversifying the portfolio

As a European real estate investment company, Redevco's strongest position is in retail. The European branch has representation in 15 countries, especially on high street level. Redevco Nederland is also retail-driven, but Lantinga sees it as his task to introduce more diversification to the portfolio of around 100 objects. "We're coming from an investment mix of 92% retail and 8% other. In the coming period we have to achieve a more balanced division in the portfolio.

Apart from acquisitions in the office or logistics market, Redevco wants to strengthen its portfolio with retail projects outside of the town centers. Projects offering possibilities of (re)development are preferred." «

CORPORATE

Praxis, Assen, the Netherlands.

MORE INFORMATION

Redevco Nederland

P.O. Box 1340
1000 BH Amsterdam
The Netherlands
Tel.: +31 20 521 87 30
Fax: +31 20 521 87 40
E-mail: service@nl.redevco.com
Website: www.redevco.com

With Amvest you can live the way you want to live. Amvest realises rental homes through vision and daring. Location, quality and architecture take centre stage. Turn your house into a home. Because a newly built home from Amvest means you can even help decide on the layout and finishing. Your home is supplied to you in top condition, and we keep it that way. And our comprehensive service package lets you experience the true luxury of renting. For more information, go to www.amvest.nl or call +31 (0)20 430 12 12.

Amvest
My kind of living

WHO'S WHO

ACHMEA VASTGOED B.V.

Achmea Vastgoed B.V.
Gatwickstraat 1
P.O. Box 59347
1040 KH Amsterdam
The Netherlands
Tel.: +31 20 606 56 00
Fax: +31 20 606 56 09
E-mail: vastgoedinfo@achmea.nl
Website: www.achmeavastgoed.nl

Achmea Vastgoed grew in 2005 to more than €7.3 billion for our 60 clients; and Achmea Vastgoed will continue to grow even more. In 2006 more than €1 billion can be invested. This financial scale offers Achmea Vastgoed the power to use opportunities. The need for the right properties and good mortgage investments will continue. We are responsive and experienced, and at all times open to propositions.

Mission

Passion for quality drives excellent performance. That's why Achmea Vastgoed delivers better returns on investments for its institutional clients. We focus on assets at the top of the real estate pyramid. And we have built a unique position in mortgage investments. How passion becomes performance: it's reflected in the value of the portfolio of our clients.

Policy

The core /satellite investment policy enables us to respond flexibly to the different stages of the real estate cycle. This means that properties can be assessed in the overall context of the portfolio and in relation to market developments. Several factors play a role in composing portfolio: the current portfolio, prospects of the different real estate markets, desired risk profile and the benchmark. Portfolio's can be filled on a discretionary basis with units in real estate or mortgage funds, or a combination of the two. Internationally investments are possible in our AREA Fund Europe and AREA Fund North America. In 2006 we will modernize our property portfolios just as we have already started to do with our mortgage funds to achieve purchasing power.

People

Professionalism, team spirit and personal growth are key words for Achmea Vastgoed.
Our passion is real estate. Our focus is our client; our style is based on integrity, professionalism and enthusiasm.

D.J. van Hal
Managing Director

C. Worms
Managing Director

J.E.W. van der Bijl
Manager Client
Services &
Acquisition

G.J. Kertsholt
Manager Indirect
Real Estate
Investments

H. Ouwehand
Manager
Commercial Real
Estate Finance

E. Kok
Manager
Residential Real
Estate Finance

R. Vierkant
Manager Retail
Real Estate

A. van Spaandonk
Manager Residential
Real Estate

D. Gort
Manager Commercial
Real Estate

achmea vastgoed

ALTERA VASTGOED N.V.

Altera Vastgoed N.V.
Handelsweg 59F
P.O. Box 9220
1180 ME Amstelveen
The Netherlands
Tel.: +31 20 545 20 50
Fax: +31 20 545 20 60
E-mail: info@alteravastgoed.nl
Website: www.alteravastgoed.nl

Drs. R.J.M.
Hogenboom
CEO

Drs. C.J.M. van den
Hoogen RA MRE
CFO

Ing. R.Ch. Eujen
MRE Manager
Acquisitions

Altera Vastgoed N.V. is an independent, private real estate fund, open only to institutional investors. Pension funds are offered the opportunity to invest indirectly in four separate sector portfolios in the Netherlands: offices, industrial, retail and residential. The managed assets amount to around €1.4 billion.

The fund was created on January 1, 2000. Pension funds are able to participate by swapping their direct Dutch real estate portfolios for shares, and/or by investing cash. The pension funds are free to decide how much they want to invest in one or more sectors. Joining, leaving and switching sectors is flexible and can be done quarterly at competitive and low costs, with no fee increases.

Philosophy

Each sector has its own investment strategy and specific portfolio characteristics, based in part upon research. The returns targeted are benchmarked against the ROZ/IPD benchmark per sector, on a three-year basis. The management organization is integrated with the portfolios and delivers the performance within the proposed ratio for the general management costs. This should be equal to or less than 0.33% of the managed assets. From its inception, Altera Vastgoed has been one of the most cost-efficient real estate funds in the Netherlands. The property management is outsourced to specialist companies.

Procedures

Altera Vastgoed is characterized by a large degree of transparency. Its activities, responsibilities and the investment process are fully documented and accounted for in the 'Company Profile' (available upon request). Shareholders are directly involved in policymaking and are able to follow the progress of business on the basis of detailed quarterly reports.

People

Research and policy decisions, portfolio and asset management are carried out by a carefully-selected team of 22 highly-educated, seasoned professionals with experience in Dutch and international investment and real estate companies. Altera Vastgoed makes use of high quality management information systems.

Performance

The fund has the status of a fiscal investment institution, makes no use of leverage (up to 10% is permitted on a temporary basis) and pays a cash dividend each quarter.
Independent external parties value all objects in the four sector portfolios annually. The net asset value per sector portfolio is reported on a monthly basis. The performance is reported in detail quarterly and annually, and compared with the ROZ-IPD benchmark.

ALTERA
VASTGOED NV

sectoraal vastgoedfonds

AMSTERDAM SCHOOL OF REAL ESTATE

Amsterdam School of Real Estate
Wibautstraat 129
1091 GL Amsterdam
The Netherlands
Tel.: +31 20 668 11 29
Fax: +31 20 668 03 61
Website: www.asre.nl
      www.vastgoedkennis.nl
E-mail: info@asre.uva.nl
Contact: Drs. Leo B. Uittenbogaard

Ir. J.D. Doets
Chairman of
Amsterdam School
of Real Estate

Drs. L.B.
Uittenbogaard
Managing Director

Academic real estate institute

The Amsterdam School of Real Estate is a joint initiative of the Dutch Government, the real estate sector and the University of Amsterdam. The core objective is to collate, centralize and publicize national and international knowledge in the field of real estate. Thanks to the involvement of both the university and business, the Amsterdam School of Real Estate fulfills an interesting role bridging academic scholarship and industry practice.

The core activities

The Amsterdam School of Real Estate covers three core activities: education, research and information. From time immemorial these elements have been the foundations of knowledge and learning.

Education

The theme of the education program offered by the Amsterdam School of Real Estate is customized knowledge. Real estate professionals have a choice of two postgraduate programs: the executive course leading to the qualification of Master of Real Estate (MRE) and the specialists course, leading to Master of Science in Real Estate (MSRE).
The MRE is aimed at real estate specialists who want to move on from their specific, vocational job to a more general, strategically oriented management position. This intensive program has broad aims and focuses on strategic questions.
The MSRE (a modular based program) aims at real estate professionals in senior posts who want to enhance their professional specialization by further deepening their knowledge.

Research

The research activities undertaken by the Amsterdam School of Real Estate cover both policy-supporting research generally commissioned by third parties and applied academic research. Both forms of research concentrate on strategic questions that have a degree of social relevance. The research questions can be broad in scope, ranging from macroeconomic investigation to financial and technical policy matters. An independent approach and execution are guaranteed for every research project.

Information

The website www.vastgoedkennis.nl completes the range of knowledge-enhancing activities performed independently and with academic rigor by the Amsterdam School of Real Estate. It offers those with a professional interest rapid access to diverse sources of up-to-date information, including direct access to the Real Estate Information Center digital catalogue.

UNIVERSITEIT VAN AMSTERDAM

AMVEST

AMVEST
De Entree 43 - 8th floor
P.O. Box 12446
1100 AK Amsterdam ZO
The Netherlands
Tel.: +31 20 430 12 12
Fax: +31 20 430 12 13
E-mail: info@amvest.nl
Website: www.amvestwonen.nl

M.W.A. Maas
CEO

T.H. Lam
CFO

C.G.J.W. Martens
Deputy Director
Acquisition &
Developments

H. Touw
Deputy Director
Portfolio
Management

AMVEST is a trendsetting Dutch property company (with 65 employees) that develops, buys, exploits and sells housing projects. The housing portfolio has a value of over €2.6 billion with another €1.5 billion under development. The growing individualization of housing requirements and the desire for a freedom of choice keeps AMVEST focused on customer oriented property development. Because of our creativity and financial aims, AMVEST has become a trendsetter in the area of new products.

Strategy

In the coming years AMVEST's property portfolio will be modernized and expanded. Approximately 1,000 new rental houses are developed and realized annually for our own portfolio. At the same time approximately 500 houses are sold each year. Both activities shift the portfolio more to the economically stronger western and southern regions of the Netherlands. This portfolio policy focuses on providing an attractive long-term return in the context of an appropriate risk profile. AMVEST has beaten the ROZ/IPD benchmark for five years in a row.

Development

AMVEST's vision on the development of rental housing projects is based on intensive knowledge of the local market. Developing our own new investments enables us to focus on the actual wishes of consumers for their residential and living environments, while also providing greater levels of added value.

AMVEST is also involved in multi-segment housing projects. Through joint developments of rental and owner-occupied housing a well-focused housing supply can be offered to meet the real needs, both in expansion areas (VINEX-locations) and in urban regeneration locations.

Portfolio management

By renewing its portfolio every year, AMVEST improves the quality and the risk profile. Intensifying the customer focus and communicating with tenants at an early stage will lead to higher customer satisfaction.
New initiatives such as the AMVEST WoonPlusPunt meet new tenant's demands, especially those of the fast growing baby boom generation. The AMVEST WoonPlusPunt, located in areas with a dense supply of AMVEST houses, provides services including responsive maintenance, housekeeping, gardening, and food supply. In other areas tenants are facilitated with a virtual WoonPlusPunt (www.amvestwoonpluspunt.nl). A complete supply database of AMVEST housing can be found on the AMVEST website (www.amvestwonen.nl).

Zó wil ik wonen

AOS Nederland NV

AOS Nederland NV
Weena 272
P.O. Box 2016
3000 CA Rotterdam
The Netherlands
Tel.: + 31 10 412 00 35
Fax: + 31 10 412 00 49
E-mail: nederland@aosgroup.com
Website: www.aosgroup.com

Ing. Paul D. Trumpie
CFM
General Manager

Ir. Rogier Hageman
Business Unit
Manager, Real
Estate Consulting
& Accommodation
Management

Is your real estate meeting the demands of your organization?
Is your real estate performing according to international standards?
Do you need to increase efficiency in workspace use?
Are you facing the challenge of realizing a new building, renovation or moving project and lack the time or expertise?

AOS (formerly DBAssociates) offers dedicated solutions in the field of corporate real estate and facility management

Multinationals are less and less bound to their traditional residences and are increasingly managing their real estate and facilities on a global scale. In the Dutch market, sectors such as healthcare, education and energy are facing the liberalization of the market and upcoming competition. Focusing on costs and the identity of the real estate is essential to survive.

In this dynamic real estate market, AOS offers international expertise adapted to the demands of the local market. The international structure of AOS, with branches in Belgium, China, France, Luxembourg, the Netherlands, Spain, the US, the UK and Switzerland guarantees that we can meet your demands across the globe.

AOS is an independent consultancy and services organization focused on business-driven real estate and facilities management.
- Strategic accommodation management tunes the real estate strategy of a company to its strategic policy.
- Office innovation develops and implements workplace concepts that support the dynamic work processes in efficiency as well as in productivity.
- Accommodation management supports the organization in relocation projects with project management, space analysis, interior design, accommodation management and budget control.
- Corporate real estate and facility management services (FMIS) helps organizations with dedicated solutions to optimize the management of their real estate portfolio.

The added value of AOS helps our clients to increase the profitability and productivity of their real estate and to realize cost savings.

AOS as your solutions provider for real estate strategies and issues
AOS offers an independent alternative as solutions provider, working from the end user's perspective. Within this independent and entrepreneurial approach, our consultants provide services such as building selection, project development consultancy, due diligence for buildings and complete portfolios and development of real estate strategies.

Based on your corporate strategy, we develop real estate strategies which help you to find the best solution and will reduce investment and exploitation costs. In our consultancy we use the AOS Benchbase®, which is the biggest FM database of the Benelux with 2.5 million m^2 GLA and more than 400 buildings.

ARCADIS

ARCADIS
Utrechtseweg 68
P.O. Box 33
6800 LE Arnhem
The Netherlands
Tel.: +31 26 377 89 11
Fax: +31 26 443 83 81
Email: info@arcadis.nl
Website: www.arcadis.nl

drs. ing. D.J. Kras,
Managing Director
ARCADIS
The Netherlands

ir. C.T. Slingerland,
Managing Director
ARCADIS
The Netherlands

ir. T.F.M.
Steinebach,
Managing Director
Real Estate
ARCADIS
The Netherlands

In the field of Construction and Real Estate, ARCADIS can offer a complete service package for each phase of the development of property. We operate in the residential, health care, business-to-business, commercial, leisure and retail sectors, in which we provide services in the areas of project management, consultancy, design and engineering.

ARCADIS gets involved in many construction projects from the very outset, as the concept developer or as the initiator of a development project. This often entails cooperation in a consortium together with developers, users and investors in complex urban planning projects.

ARCADIS often performs the project management in such consortiums, while also getting involved in drawing up schedules of requirements and the complete architectural design. These projects combine various functions, thus integrating residential, business, retail and leisure premises. This yields a significant contribution to the continued amenability of towns and cities, thus enabling sustainable urban development.

In the field of business services and commercial property, we perform a vast range of assignments, from innovative office concepts to the entire engineering of business complexes, including the architectural design. ARCADIS' greatest strength in this field is that we seek specific solutions in close consultation with our clients, with a view to addressing the challenges they face. Even if a client wishes to award the contract for an entire construction project to a single party, ARCADIS can assume complete responsibility, including the finances.

One of our most outstanding qualities is technical expertise in the field of structural, mechanical, electrical and constructional engineering. Although these disciplines are often integral components of entire development projects, our clients also request them separately in the case of buildings that call for specialist knowledge due to their proportions, height, complexity or production process.

Thanks to ARCADIS' integrated approach and ability to control all disciplines, we can offer our clients the advantages of synergy manifest in the quality and swiftness of our work.
ARCADIS is a leading, global, knowledge-driven service provider, active in the fields of infrastructure, environment and buildings. With client success central to our total business approach, we fulfill project or program needs from concept to completion and beyond.

Our private and public sector clients call on us for a broad range of integrated services: feasibility studies, design, engineering, project management, implementation and facility management, plus related legal and financial services.

Together we generate €900 million in annual revenues. There are 10,000 of us, results-oriented people, continually investing in our skills to maximize client value while creating viable solutions.

WHO'S WHO

BAM Vastgoed

BAM Vastgoed
Regulierenring 35
P.O. Box 50
3980 CB Bunnik
The Netherlands
Tel.: +31 30 659 89 55
Fax: +31 30 659 82 80
E-mail: bunnik@bamvastgoed.nl
Website: www.bamvastgoed.nl

Drs. ing. R. Vollebregt
Chairman

Mr. H. Bree
Director

Ir. P. Esveld
Director

Development with a social context. That's our ethos. With only one objective: to offer market focused, spatial solutions that surprise and delight our clients.

BAM Vastgoed is active in all segments of the property market: multi-functional area development, shops, offices, housing of all types and in all price classes, museums, sports facilities, entertainment centers and inner-city redevelopment. With 25,000 homes and 2,000,000 m² of commercial properties in development, we are the main players in the Dutch property market. BAM is a national player operating close to the market, boasting five regional teams in the housing sector and three regional teams in the office space, retail and multifunctional development sectors.

We at BAM Vastgoed are eager to realize ambitious projects that contribute in a positive way to society. We work openly together with our customers and partners. It is how we work as a team at BAM that distinguishes us from the rest. Our enthusiasm and hunger to learn from our customers, project partners and from each other, determines the success of all our developments.

Amsterdam Offices
Residential
North-West Region
Elsrijkdreef 201
P.O. Box 22566
1100 DB Amsterdam
The Netherlands
Tel.: +31 20 569 47 77
Fax: +31 20 569 47 50

Capelle a/d IJssel Offices
Residential
West and South-West/
Southern Regions
Rivium Promenade 160
P.O. Box 8552
3009 AN Rotterdam
The Netherlands
Tel.: +31 10 266 31 00
Fax: +31 10 266 31 01

Zwolle Offices
Residential
North-East Region
Willemsvaart 21
P.O. Box 677
8000 AR Zwolle
The Netherlands
Tel.: +31 38 425 07 10
Fax: +31 38 425 07 50

Bunnik Head Office
Management, Staff and Services
Residential, Central/Eastern
Regions
Commercial Properties Northern,
Central and Southern Regions
Regulierenring 35
P.O. Box 50
3980 CB Bunnik
The Netherlands
Tel.: +31 30 659 89 55
Fax: +31 30 659 82 80

BESIX NEDERLAND B.V.

BESIX Nederland B.V.
Zuideinde 80
P.O. Box 8
2990 AA Barendrecht
The Netherlands
Tel.: +31 180 64 19 90
Fax: +31 180 64 19 91
E-mail: info@besix.com
Website: www.besix.com
Contact: hpost@besix.com

H.J.J. (Henk) Post
Commercial Manager

J. (Jean) Polet
Operations Manager

J.A. (Hans) Flierman
Manager General
Services

BESIX Nederland belongs to one of the larger building concerns in the Netherlands. With the motto 'BESIX builds up the Netherlands', the company has been realizing prestigious projects in the sectors of civil concrete construction, commercial and industrial building and maritime building for the past 15 years. A spearhead of this concern is the combination of ample experience and their engineering department's creativity. This way efficient solutions to complex problems continue to be found, often according to the 'design & construct' principle. BESIX continuously invests in its promise of quality. Therefore, values like creativity, dedication and perseverance form the basis of the project approach by BESIX.

As a part of the BESIX Group, with its main office in Brussels, BESIX Nederland is part of a healthy, substantial organization with returns of €857 million in 2004. Amongst other projects, the BESIX Group is well-known for receiving the commission to build the highest tower in the world - the more than 800-meter-high Burj Dubai in the Emirates. The BESIX Group has over 10,000 employees worldwide and boasts extensive constructing experience in 20 countries, both inside and outside of Europe. Its own equipment department provides all the tools, including ships, cranes and construction islands. Because of the support from the group there are almost no limits to the size of the projects BESIX Nederland can undertake.

Yearly, BESIX Nederland finalizes several large projects in various sectors. Exploits in the maritime sector are the construction of the Hoogwaterkering near Heusden, the tunnel elements of the second Benelux tunnel, and many kilometers of quay wall. In the civil concrete construction sector projects include the reconstruction of the Vaanplein, the train stations Amsterdam-Bijlmer and Barendrecht, and the tunnel underneath highway A12, just to name a few. Important projects in commercial and industrial building are the Sheraton Hotel at Schiphol and the drastic renovation and new developments at the main office of Shell Rijswijk. BESIX's current projects include the longest land tunnel in the Netherlands, the 2.4-km-long tunnel that is part of highway A73 near Roermond. The construction of the quay walls for Havenbedrijf Rotterdam and tower Montevideo in Rotterdam are in very advanced stages. Recently BESIX Nederland obtained the commission to construct the residential complex Schiecentrale in Rotterdam.

The force of impact of BESIX

The strength of BESIX is in its decisiveness. The level organizational structure is partially illustrated by the fact that the construction management for each project is located at the actual construction site. Decisions are made rapidly. That is why major local authorities, the industry and project developers regularly enlist BESIX to realize their challenges.

WHO'S WHO

BETTEN BEURSMEDIA NEWS

Betten Beursmedia News
Keizersgracht 424
1016 GC Amsterdam
The Netherlands
Tel.: +31 20 710 17 55
Fax: +31 20 710 18 75
E-mail:
bettenbeursmedia@tijdbeursmedia.nl
Website: www.bettenbeursmedia.nl

Herman Betten
Editor-in-Chief

Betten Beursmedia News and its Belgian subsidiary Tijd Nieuwslijn are the leading Dutch language financial wires in the Netherlands and Belgium respectively. The editorial teams of both news services offer on a daily basis a large stream of news reports aimed at professional and private investors. Speed, quality and reliability are the main characteristics of its products.

The news feed of Betten Beursmedia News in the Netherlands focuses on Dutch listed companies and market news. Betten Beursmedia news is widely known as the fastest and most complete financial newswire of the Netherlands. Tijd Nieuwslijn focuses on Belgian listed companies, market news and the large international companies, including the French blue chips.

Real estate coverage

Betten and Nieuwslijn include in their coverage all listed real estate companies, such as VastNed Offices/Industrial, DIM Vastgoed and Rodamco (the Netherlands) and Leasinvest, Befimmo and Cofinimmo (Belgium). In their coverage they include corporate results, M&A, new projects, press conferences, shareholder meetings and interviews. Also included are national and international analyst reports about those companies. In fact, the editorial teams report not only changes in recommendation and estimates, but also cover the argumentation used by the analysts and eventually confront the companies with those expert opinions.

Through data vendors such as MarketXXS, Reuters, Bloomberg, Tenfore and Thomson Financial, the news feeds of Betten Beursmedia News and Tijd Nieuwslijn reach most of the institutions active on Euronext Amsterdam and Euronext Brussels. Through data systems such as ERIS it reaches active private and semi-professional investors in the Benelux. Tijd Nieuwslijn is also available as a subscription service on the internet.

News by mobile phone

The internet news desk of Betten Beursmedia News delivers news and information to frequently visited websites such as Eurobench, Rabobank, SNS Bank, Robeco Group and Fortis Bank. Its news products are also available through mobile phones. Also media companies in and outside the Netherlands use Betten Beursmedia News, such as Het Financieele Dagblad (the leading business newspaper in the Netherlands), the news wire Novum and Eurobench.

Tijd Nieuwslijn is used on the leading Belgian financial and business website Tijdnet, the site of the Belgian business daily De Tijd. It also works for the business television channel KanaalZ, for the public television VRT, for De Standaard Online and the national news agency Belga and other websites and intranets. Recently Tijd Nieuwslijn started a French language service, part of which is published on the website of the French language business daily L'Echo. Betten Beursmedia News is a joint venture of Betten Financial News and Uitgeversbedrijf Tijd.

BETTEN BEURSMEDIA NEWS

BLAUWHOED

Blauwhoed B.V.
Lichtenauerlaan 80
P.O. Box 2552
3000 CN Rotterdam
The Netherlands
Tel.: +31 10 453 53 11
Fax: +31 10 452 63 53
Website: www.blauwhoed.nl

Blauwhoed specializes in complex projects in which knowledge, creativity and market sensitivity play decisive roles. Blauwhoed Vastgoed develops offices, retail/leisure centers and integral projects, while Blauwhoed Eurowoningen focuses on developing homes. Our changing society provides an important source of inspiration in these projects, and the knowledge and skill of the company's employees provides the instruments to give form to this change.

Blauwhoed considers it its responsibility to create living, working and shopping environments that are and remain attractive. The company has realized a wide range of projects, both in isolated locations and historic city centers. It has a strong preference for the integral approach, which includes the design of the public space surrounding the property. The 'Eurowoning' brand is a guarantee for exceptional quality and durability. At present, over 60,000 Eurowoningen houses have already been built in the Netherlands.

F.C.M. van Leeuwen
Chairman of the Board

R.J. van den Broek
MRE, Director of
Commercial Business

Blauwhoed regularly develops shopping centers in combination with homes, offices and leisure facilities. It realizes distinctive quality office environments at premium locations, often incorporating them within existing urban locations. These offices have excellent accessibility and ample parking facilities, and blend seamlessly with the surrounding area.

A.J.H. van Breukelen
Director of Development
and Realization

J.P. de Smeth
Director of Economic
and Legal Business

Blauwhoed also concentrates activities on locations that will eventually fulfill a new role: business parks that are transformed into residential areas, and neglected inner-city districts that are redesigned into top urban locations. The success of such projects depends on a multidisciplinary approach, working in partnership with government bodies, locals, builders and architects. It is this kind of collaboration that is Blauwhoed's forte.

Activities
- Integrated inner-city development/redevelopment
- Integrated zone developments
- Development/redevelopment of shopping centers
- Office development
- Housing development

WHO'S WHO

 BLAUWHOED

brengt wonen tot leven

BOUWFONDS HOLDING

Bouwfonds Holding
P.O. Box 15
3870 DA Hoevelaken
The Netherlands
Tel.: +31 33 253 91 11
Fax: +31 33 253 95 55
Website: www.bouwfonds.com
Contact: H.J. Rutgers

H.J. Rutgers
CEO

P.A. van der Harst
CFO

H.J.M. van Zandvoort
Member of
Management Team

J.L.M.J. Klijnen
Member of
Management Team

Bouwfonds is one of the largest property companies in the Netherlands and a key European player. Their vast property experience has become the basis for success in all property related fields: development of private housing and commercial real estate, property finance, asset management and managing property related public funds. Bouwfonds' ambition is to be a leading European property development, financing and asset management company in 2010. Bouwfonds has selected six main areas where the company wants to achieve a top-5 position with these three core activities: the Netherlands, Belgium, France, Germany, Spain and Scandinavia.

Bouwfonds, a brief history
The history of Bouwfonds is rooted in a commitment to the community. After the Second World War, Jacob Wiersema put forward an ambitious plan: a public savings bank to help low-income groups become homeowners. In partnership with local municipalities Bouwfonds succeeded in making newly built homes available for a €500 down payment and a weekly mortgage payment of €2. Almost six decades later, the brainchild of Jacob Wiersema has developed into a world-class enterprise. Social concern, social responsibility and integrity are, and will remain, the cornerstones of our business.

Bouwfonds in figures
At the moment Bouwfonds carries out its activities through a network of more than 40 offices in Belgium, Germany, France, Denmark, Spain, Sweden, Czech Republic, Slovakia, Hungary and the Netherlands. Moreover projects are undertaken in Portugal and various regions of the United States and Canada. Bouwfonds made a net profit of €314 million in 2005 with a balance sheet total of €43.5 billion. Bouwfonds employs around 1,900 people of which 300 are located outside the Netherlands.

Vision
Property should serve the needs of users, while also contributing to the quality of society as a whole. Users must be provided with an attractive domestic environment, as well as comfortable surroundings for working, shopping and leisure. These criteria form the basis for a sustainable return from investments in property.
In a changing world we constantly need new concepts and solutions for developing, financing and managing property. However, nobody can achieve this alone. Only when market players and public authorities cooperate effectively can the needs of both current and future users be optimally met.

Committed to partnership
The results we achieve as a company are the outcome of concerted efforts. We are first and foremost dedicated to engaging in constructive relationships with our business associates. Such partnership is founded on trust and entrepreneurship on both sides. Sharing a joint commitment to attain the aspired level of quality. The drive to succeed together is at the heart of everything we undertake.

BOUWFONDS MAB ONTWIKKELING

Bouwfonds MAB Ontwikkeling
Displayweg 8
3821 BT Amersfoort
P.O. Box 15
3870 DA Hoevelaken
The Netherlands
Tel.: +31 33 253 97 00
Fax: +31 33 253 97 77
E-mail: ontwikkeling@bouwfonds.nl
Website: www.bouwfonds.nl

Henk van Zandvoort
*Chairman of the
Executive Board*

Isaäc Kalisvaart
*Member of the
Executive Board*

Jos Franck
*Member of the
Executive Board*

Cees van Boven
*Managing Director
Bouwfonds MAB
Ontwikkeling CVG*

Jos Melchers
*Director
Bouwfonds MAB
Ontwikkeling CVG*

Ruud Berkhout
*Director
Bouwfonds MAB
Ontwikkeling CVG*

Friso de Zeeuw
*Director
New Markets*

Hans Rosenhart
*Director Special
Projects*

Bouwfonds MAB Ontwikkeling is your reliable and innovative partner in the Netherlands when it comes to the development of residential areas and multifunctional projects. Bouwfonds MAB is situated in the middle of society and, due to its years of experience, keeps an eye open for the desires of housing consumers and the end users. One of its main objectives is the realization of projects in existing urban areas. Furthermore, we work together with the public and private parties involved to come up with an integrated solution for these inner city projects where living, shopping and working are all interwoven. To this end, we call upon the expertise and creativity of our concept team Studio Bouwfonds MAB situated in our offices in The Hague.

The five regional offices of Bouwfonds MAB are each responsible for the realization of residential areas. Bouwfonds, along with local governments, develops integrated living concepts for suburbs and city centers alike. Multifunctional projects and commercial real estate projects are developed in our offices in The Hague. The Bouwfonds headquarters is located in Amersfoort. Bouwfonds MAB is one of the largest developers of private homes and commercial real estate in the Netherlands.

Bouwfonds MAB Ontwikkeling is a branch of Bouwfonds Property Development where all the development activities for France, Germany, Belgium, Luxembourg, the Czech Republic, Slovakia, Hungary, Spain, Denmark and Sweden take place. We make optimal use of the knowledge and skills learned elsewhere in Europe for our concept development activities in the Netherlands. Because of our healthy financial situation, Bouwfonds MAB Ontwikkeling can accommodate partners who need a long breath before making a decision.

At Bouwfonds MAB Ontwikkeling our starting point is the client's wishes. The client notices this in every aspect of our organization with its 60 years of experience. This experience allows us to find a balance between the client's wishes and what is realistically feasible like no other. This is how Bouwfonds MAB Ontwikkeling is able to contribute simultaneously to customer satisfaction and the success of cities, investors, local governments and commercial end users.

Bouwfonds MAB Ontwikkeling employs roughly 500 people. From its 12 offices, the organization sold some 8,000 homes and began construction on roughly 100,000 m^2 of commercial space in the Netherlands in 2005.

BOUWFONDS PROPERTY FINANCE

Bouwfonds Property Finance
P.O. Box 15
3870 DA Hoevelaken
The Netherlands
Tel.: +31 33 253 91 10
Fax: +31 33 253 91 09
E-mail: property.finance@bouwfonds.nl
Website: www.bouwfonds.nl

At Bouwfonds Property Finance (BPF), we specialize in financing a wide range of property development projects. What sets us apart as an international property finance organization is our comprehensive knowledge of real estate in the broadest sense. More than just financiers, we are a finance company focusing first and foremost on real estate. With our in-depth, in-house knowledge of real estate, we offer the advantage of expert property analysis, drawing on our vast knowledge of the world of property, real estate products and financing. Creatively, professionally, and skillfully.

J. Visscher
Director

R. Overbeek
Director BPF
Netherlands

Our way of doing business calls for a distinct approach. The professionals at BPF team up with their clients, emphasizing the mutual success that may be achieved through property financing. Regardless of whether we actively participate in a project or simply fund it, we can offer you a wide range of possibilities and will succeed where other companies fall short.

International

International expansion is Bouwfonds Property Finance's main ambition, and we have reaped great rewards so far. In the past few years, we have seen our funding activities in both Europe and the United States grow substantially. We have a clear mission: to be a trend-setting international property financier.

A.W. van Rijn
Director BPF
International

D.M. Melchiors
Director BPF
Special Projects

Organization

The financing activities are organized as follows:
- BPF Netherlands
- BPF International
- BPF Special Projects
- BPF Structured Finance & Distribution

Ch. de Koste
Director BPF
Structured Finance
& Distribution

Tailor-made solutions

BPF specializes in tailor-made solutions for its clients. We offer our national and international clients a broad suite of financing products. These include project financing, long-term investment financing, sale and lease-back arrangements (off-balance financing), long-term risk participation and structured finance solutions. If our client so desires, creative combinations of any of these products are also possible.

In 2005, the company's annual production was €3.7 billion and its financing portfolio was worth €10 billion. We currently employ about 250 people.

BOUWFONDS ASSET MANAGEMENT

Bouwfonds Asset Management
P.O. Box 15
3870 DA Hoevelaken
The Netherlands
Tel.: +31 33 750 47 50
Fax: +31 33 750 47 77
Website: www.bouwfonds.nl
Contact: J. Klijnen

J. Klijnen
Chairman of the
Executive Board

Bouwfonds Asset Management focuses on initiating and managing property investment products.

Core activities

Bouwfonds Asset Management focuses on initiating and managing property investment products. Bouwfonds Asset Management combines extensive knowledge of real estate and financial markets. Its four core activities consist of structuring funds, distribution (placement of own or outside property), acquisition of property and strategic management of property portfolios and funds.

Types of funds

- funds aimed at the private market, e.g. so-called 'Dutch funds' on behalf of German private investors and property partnerships on behalf of Dutch private investors;
- 'Institutional funds' aimed at specific sectors and specific areas, mainly for institutional investors;
- 'Structured products', tailor-made products linked to capital markets (securitizations), solving accounting issues (off-balance structures), etc.

Portfolio growth

Bouwfonds Asset Management has successfully launched private funds for private investors with investments in the Netherlands, USA and Germany (volume €350 million) and created funds for institutional investors, for example the fund that issued inflation contracts (volume €1.1 billion) and the Parking Fund (the final volume €300 million). Additionally, Bouwfonds Asset Management has entered into strategic partnerships with international property companies including ZOM Inc. which creates investment funds in the US-residential market and Polis AG, a German investor/asset manager.

The total market value of the assets under management amount to €2 million. The assets under management are based in the Netherlands, in the USA (mainly residential) and Germany (offices). The portfolio in the Netherlands consists of offices, retail and industrial warehouses.

bouwfonds
asset management

BUCK CONSULTANTS INTERNATIONAL

Buck Consultants International
P.O. Box 1456
6501 BL Nijmegen
The Netherlands
Tel.: +31 24 379 02 22
Fax: +31 24 379 01 20
E-mail: bci@bciglobal.com
Website: www.bciglobal.com
Contact: René Buck, Josephine
Glaudemans, Wim Pijpers

René Buck
President

Wim Pijpers
Partner

Josephine
Glaudemans
Partner

In the complex world of real estate Buck Consultants International seeks the combination of creativity, expertise, and ambition in offering a wide range of real estate consultancy services. Highly-trained and dedicated professionals continuously focus on developing optimal solutions and innovative visions for clients in both private and public sectors.
The Buck Consultants International approach includes applying in-depth knowledge of the needs of corporate end-users, a wide-spread expertise in the mechanisms of the real estate markets and an integrated vision on real estate, public policies, regional development and the spatial-economic and financial environment.

Research and analysis
Know-how leads to an advantage. The real estate markets are in continuous evolution. Recognizing the state of the world of tomorrow provides the basis for anticipating new trends and themes. We use modern and advanced techniques and models along with creative thinking.

Feasibility and development
Innovation is essential in real estate development and investment.
In our market and feasibility studies, site selection projects, concept development, and integrated area development, we provide not only crystal clear insight, but also match the ambitions and risk acceptance of users, developers, investors, and public authorities. In interaction with the client and its stakeholders we integrate principles that have proven to be successful, and pave new paths to feed the creative process of building and rebuilding space and buildings with future value.

Vision and Strategy
Real estate development, investment, and policy is a multidisciplinary process in uncertainty. It requires vision, a long-term scope and a well-founded strategy. The advice of Buck Consultants International is based on 20 years of experience in more than 1,000 assignments all over Europe. Our 70 professionals in Nijmegen, The Hague (both in the Netherlands), London, Paris, Brussels, Milan, Frankfurt, Madrid, New York and Shanghai are at your service.

**Buck
Consultants
International**

CONCIRE, CONCEPTS FOR URBAN AREAS

CONCIRE
'Willemswerf', Boompjes 40
P.O. Box 2325
3000 CH Rotterdam
The Netherlands
Tel.: +31 10 240 35 10
Fax: +31 10 240 35 25
E-mail: info@concire.nl
Website: www.concire.nl

Ir. Carol J. Hol
Director/Partner

Ing. Evert van der Hoek MBA
Director/Partner

Ing. Anne-Marie Godinho-Nunes
Area Developer

Drs. Jason A. Bell
Area Developer

CONCIRE
ONTWIKKELAAR VAN GEBIEDSCONCEPTEN

CONCIRE is both young and experienced, creative, and focused on results. CONCIRE is involved in the development of area concepts for urban areas in and around city and town centers. We create value for our customers. We enjoy our profession.

Our mission
CONCIRE was established to develop 'conceptional area development' as a new competence - in both a professional and a commercial sense. The innovative nature of conceptional area development is underlined by the fact that it does not necessarily have to be directed on the basis of an integral or a project/plan-based approach. Direction is based on thinking from and acting in accordance with area concepts. That is our mission.

Our inspiration
We take our inspiration from what we call 'the Pride of the Place' (Fierte van de Plek). In this process, individuality, honesty and emotion are the exponents of identity, authenticity and commitment. This leads to the development of areas with existing, renewed or newly created pride, which people can identify with and to which they will feel connected. This leads to the creation of maximum value development. That is our inspiration.

Our profession
The term 'conceptional' brings together the notions of 'conceptual' (conceiving and designing) and the 'conception' (the implementation) of an area concept at a particular location. To this end, we have developed a method that can be abbreviated with 'ADI^2': Analysis, Diagnosis, Idea, Intervention. We do not only focus on the physical column, but also view the assignment in its economic, social and cultural context, to the extent that this is required by the area-specific assignment. That is our profession.

Our services
At the core of our services lies a team-based endeavor to offer an area concept that is truly made to measure. The area concept comprises: the directional 'Idea', which is both durable and dynamic; the 'development strategy', which ensures that the idea is actually incorporated within a feasible realization process with a risk profile that's manageable and programmable for all parties involved; the 'marketing concept' and the 'marketing strategy', which target the positioning and presentation of the area in question.

Our clients
We work for all parties involved in area development. As an independent company, we can remain dedicated to serving our clients' best interests. We are competitive and motivated to enhance the competitive strength of our clients: the creation of maximum value. We are your partner in 'business as unusual'.

CUSHMAN & WAKEFIELD

Cushman & Wakefield
Amstelveenseweg 760
P.O. Box 75456
1070 AL Amsterdam
The Netherlands
Tel.: +31 20 301 42 42
Fax: +31 20 301 42 19
Website: www.cushmanwakefield.com
Contact: Baldwin Poolman

Baldwin Poolman
Managing Partner

Stephen Screene
Partner

Jan-Willem Bastijn
Partner

Paul Peeters
Partner

Cushman & Wakefield is the premier global real estate services provider with more than 11,500 employees in 57 countries. In the Netherlands we deliver comprehensive real estate solutions through four main business lines: Advisory Services, Agency Services, Client Solutions and Asset Services.

What makes Cushman & Wakefield the preferred choice? It's simple. Our extraordinarily talented and creative people deliver results worldwide for owners, occupiers, and investors.

Our people

We recruit, retain, and train the most experienced and talented professionals, then give them the flexibility and global platform needed to add value. Our employees, located throughout the world, assess each client's needs and implement solutions that fit the client's strategic, operational, and financial goals.

Our services

We assist clients in every stage of the real estate process, representing them in the buying, selling, financing, leasing, managing and valuing of assets, and providing strategic planning and research, portfolio analysis, site selection and space location, among many other advisory services.

Our results

By continually seeing past the immediate 'deal', and instead determining the highest and best use of property in every situation, in every corner of the world, we provide the greatest maximum opportunity for owners, occupiers, and investors, as well as our communities and society as a whole.

DE ALLIANTIE ONTWIKKELING B.V.

De Alliantie Ontwikkeling B.V.
P.O. Box 95
1270 AB Huizen
The Netherlands
Tel.: +31 35 528 07 00
Fax: +31 35 528 07 15
E-mail: info@de-alliantie.com
Website: www.de-alliantie.nl

Drs. D.A. (Dick)
Regenboog
General Director

J.W. (Jan) van
Barneveld
Director

A. (Ard) de Jong
Director

De Alliantie Ontwikkeling B.V. is an ambitious developer. With a staff of 50 professionals working from its main offices in Amersfoort and Huizen, the company realizes an annual production of 1,500 new homes in the Amsterdam, Almere, Hilversum and Amersfoort areas. But its ambition reaches beyond these borders. The company is also an enthusiastic participant in challenging development projects outside of the region. De Alliantie Ontwikkeling B.V. is an independent division of De Alliantie.

In these ventures, De Alliantie Ontwikkeling strives to develop a durable relationship with the other parties involved. It recognizes the long-term interests that are served by high-quality urban development, and is therefore willing to invest in lively new districts. De Alliantie Ontwikkeling is a loyal and reliable partner with an eye for the cultural and social aspects of the projects that it takes on. As a developer, it is characterized by commitment and by the active utilization of its extensive knowledge and experience.

De Alliantie Ontwikkeling primarily targets residential construction – with an emphasis on public housing, the combination of residential and care facilities, and the realization of social facilities within the framework of area development and urban restructuring. A substantial portion of this production is subsequently included in De Alliantie's real estate portfolio.

De Alliantie Ontwikkeling develops over 1,500 homes per year. However, it is not the sheer scale of the company's construction activities that sets it apart, but the value that it adds to its developments; for example by building a daycare center or neighborhood supermarket near the homes, or including a local elementary school and neighborhood facilities in the plans for a new district. In many cases, De Alliantie not only develops, but also participates as an investor. This offers clients the reassurance that De Alliantie is prepared to invest in a durable relationship in the most literal sense.

De Alliantie Ontwikkeling is particularly at home in urban restructuring projects. Indeed, the company's expertise in the field of restructuring can be considered one of its strongest competences. It is a question of exploring the urban development preconditions of a specific area and using them innovatively. And it is about taking a creative approach in the project's development stage towards the optimization of these preconditions. Working in close collaboration with the client, the specialists of De Alliantie Ontwikkeling do not shy away from these challenges, but take them on with confidence.

WHO'S WHO

de Alliantie
Ontwikkeling

DELTA ONTWIKKELINGSGROEP

Delta Ontwikkelingsgroep
Binnen Kalkhaven 39
P.O. Box 9
3300 AA Dordrecht
The Netherlands
Tel.: +31 078 614 08 44
Fax: +31 078 614 04 64
E-mail: info@deltaontwikkelingsgroep.nl
Website:
www.deltaontwikkelingsgroep.nl

Drs. C.C. Zachariasse RA   *Ing. K.M. Damstra*
General Director   *Commercial*
                               Director

Delta Ontwikkelingsgroep is a medium-sized real estate business with a contemporary vision towards the property market operating within the Netherlands, as well as in foreign real estate markets.

Delta is an active developer with young, dynamic people employing creativity as a 'key' in the development and realization of projects in virtually all sectors of the property market. Delta focuses particularly on the redevelopment of existing areas and complexes.

Europe and the United States
At present the activities are principally orientated towards the Dutch, American, French – and more recently – German market.
Alongside the challenges which are to a large extent present in these development areas, further international expansion is being looked at. Since its establishment in 1988 operations in the United States have gone under the name of Waterford Developments.

France
For a number of years in France – as well as in the Netherlands – projects have been developed and realized not only independently, but also in association with various partners. Delta Azur (a partnership with Bouwfonds Property Finance) is active in the South of France and ODB (Océanis Promotion, Bouwfonds Property Finance en Delta) is active in other parts of France with various developments on the market.
A large number of projects within the field of housing construction, shops and office/industrial buildings have been realized in the course of time.

Germany
Delta Immobiliënentwicklung Deutschland is the branch of Delta recently set-up in Germany, with an office in Düsseldorf. The work area of this establishment is mainly within the western corridor running from Hamburg, Bremen, the Rhine-Ruhr Area, Frankfurt, South Germany and Berlin.
Initially, the acquisition of projects within this part of Europe is orientated towards the development of logistics centers and production facilities, in which both redevelopment and new development are included in the possibilities.

EUROHYPO AG

Eurohypo Amsterdam Branch
Strawinskylaan 381
1077 XX Amsterdam
The Netherlands
Tel.: +31 20 799 36 00
Fax: +31 20 799 36 79
E-mail: amsterdam@eurohypo.com
Website: www.eurohypo.com

With total assets of €235 billion (2005) and a portfolio in Real Estate Finance of €97 billion and of €119 billion in Public Finance, Eurohypo AG is Europe's leading specialized bank for real estate and public sector financing. Eurohypo is part of Commerzbank Group. Eurohypo stands for a new type of bank: it is a universal specialist bank which focuses on its two target groups. Within this framework it offers a universal range of products across the entire value chain of real estate financing and public finance via a global sales network.

Jan Willem Wattel
Head of Corporate
Banking

Ina D. Füner-Rentrop
Head of Transaction
Management

Frank E. Fritsch
Deputy Head of
Corporate Banking

Commercial real estate finance is one of the Bank's core activities. Eurohypo has an excellent position in the global market. The Bank is the only real estate finance provider with a pan-European presence, the only German real estate finance provider with an established unit in the USA and the leader in European real estate investment banking.

In order to arrive at the optimal tailor-made solution, all state-of-the-art advisory and financing instruments are utilized. For professional clients Eurohypo offers the entire added value chain in complex real estate financing transactions, covering traditional business loans as well as real estate investment banking – e.g. securitization and mezzanine finance - in Europe and in the USA. Eurohypo's size facilitates the underwriting of large-volume loans enabling the bank to be one of the leading managers for syndicated loans in Europe.

In retail banking Eurohypo is also an important address for private customers in Germany. New commitments in this traditional private client business are focused on co-operation agreements with financial institutions with their own sales network (banks, insurance companies, home and savings associations). Another key competence of Eurohypo in this business is the loan servicing.

In public sector financing with tailor-made capital market products, structured loans and private placements, Eurohypo is an important partner for governments around the world. The Bank is also a major bond issuer and the market leader in the Pfandbrief segment. It has a wide range of refinancing options with worldwide access to the capital markets.

FAKTON

Fakton
World Trade Center
Beursplein 37
P.O. Box 30188
3001 DD Rotterdam
The Netherlands
Tel.: +31 10 205 62 10
Fax: +31 10 205 53 73
E-mail: info@fakton.nl
Website: www.fakton.nl

Lars Rompelberg
CEO

Joachim Blazer
CFO

Peter van Bosse
COO

Fakton financial property directors – a unique team

Over the past 20 years, Fakton has developed into a highly specialized consultancy firm that helps real estate parties to realize inner-city projects both efficiently and with solid financial returns. Our clients can rely on the experience of a team of real estate professionals. Within a range of activities, Fakton specializes in mediation, structured finance and risk management. In addition, the firm focuses on the development and dissemination of knowledge in the areas of financial programming and project management.

Whether it's a political ambition or a redevelopment project, there's something unique about any urban project; in its current form it may well be unfeasible, but it is desired nonetheless. The trick is to balance all the influencing factors (e.g. local circumstances, financial options) in such a way that a project can be realized without losing its 'soul'.

Unfortunately, it is also unique for all market parties involved – developers, investors, local government, corporations – to commit themselves to a unique result from the outset. Too often a party's individual interests prevail, and specific expertise is brought in too late – or with the wrong objectives. As a result, many real estate projects lose their momentum, and layer by layer the initial flair and profitability of a project is ground down.

Fakton anticipates these developments by acting as a partner in negotiations for all parties involved. Fakton's approach to this partnership is unique. In our view, the concept of 'teaming' plays a key role in effectively unleashing the potential of large-scale real estate projects. And so we negotiate, while bringing in knowledge and thinking along creatively, with regard to issues like environmental quality and process development. We offer solutions; for instance by developing new real estate products or financing constructions with a keen eye for timing and political prioritization.

This is the added value that sets Fakton apart from the competition and that serves as the cornerstone of our success. We know all the parties in the real estate market; we also have a firm understanding of their individual 'products'. This expertise allows us greater flexibility in the development of solutions in situations that others are ready to give up on. Our steadily increasing sales portfolio testifies to the value that the real estate community sets on our services. With several billion euro worth of real estate projects currently in our client portfolio, our six partners and 27 employees have more than enough reason to believe in our unique approach.

fakton

FGH BANK N.V.

FGH Bank N.V.
Leidseveer 50
3511 SB Utrecht
The Netherlands
Tel.: +31 30 232 39 11
Fax: +31 30 233 45 72
E-mail: info@fgh.nl
Website: www.fghbank.nl

P.C. Keur
Chairman of the
Board

F.B. Overdijk RA
Managing Director

P.H. Lubach
Regional Manager
South

Ir. F.H.P. Gielgens
MRE, Regional
Manager North

H. Dokter
Director
Syndications/
Structured Finance

Drs. F.P.M. Daemen
FGH Real Estate
Asset Management/
FGH Vastgoed
Expertise

FGH Bank, *the* **real estate bank, specializes in financing commercial real estate. Over the years it has become a leading authority in all aspects of the market. FGH Bank has extensive market knowledge at its disposal which it employs on a daily basis at both local and national levels. It is not only highly proficient in the areas of development, investment and unit sales, but has the additional advantage of possessing unmatched expertise in all other types of real estate transaction. As the real estate specialist, FGH Bank has all the requisite expertise available in-house, including legal and fiscal experts and its own Appraisal and Research Department with real estate market analysts, appraisers and structural engineers. The Client Relations Managers who are responsible for integrating all of these disciplines serve as the point of contact between the customer and the bank. The bank also has wide-ranging national network coverage, which is essential for closely monitoring regional market developments.**

Since the end of October 2003, FGH Bank has been part of the Rabobank Group, the largest financial services provider in the Netherlands. The bank is now part of a highly formidable organization that boasts both private and commercial real estate finance among its core activities. The collaboration with Rabobank also provides access to an extensive national and international resource and knowledge network.

As the real estate bank, FGH Bank has unique involvement with the commercial real estate market, which is in part demonstrated in the annual FGH Real Estate Bulletin. This publication reviews FGH Bank's market outlook along with trends in the various real estate market segments. A detailed description of regional and local market developments is an additional annual feature of the bulletin, which is published each year in March.

FGH Bank also awards the FGH Real Estate Award in alternate years. Since the award was instituted in 1989, it has developed into the most prestigious accolade for successful entrepreneurial endeavor in the Dutch real estate market. The award will be presented for the ninth time in November 2006.

Consultancy and Asset Management
Within the FGH Group, FGH Real Estate Asset Management is engaged in acquiring real estate and managing real estate funds and properties mainly on behalf of both domestic and foreign institutional investors. Clients can turn to FGH Real Estate Expertise for real estate consultancy, including appraisals, portfolio analyses, market research and fiscal and legal support. It also offers advice in the field of (re)accommodation and investment strategies.

FGH Real Estate	FGH Real Estate
Asset Management B.V.	**Expertise B.V.**
Van Eeghenstraat 82	Van Eeghenstraat 82
1071 GK Amsterdam	1071 GK Amsterdam
The Netherlands	The Netherlands
Tel.: +31 20 751 08 54	Tel.: +31 20 677 67 87
Fax: +31 20 677 67 80	Fax: +31 20 677 67 80
E-mail: assetmanagement@fgh.nl	E-mail: expertise@fgh.nl
Website: www.fgh-assetmanagement.nl	Website: www.vastgoedexpertise.nl

WHO'S WHO

FGHbank
DE VASTGOEDBANK

FORTIS VASTGOED BELEGGINGEN

Fortis Vastgoed Beleggingen
Archimedeslaan 6
P.O. Box 2008
3500 GA Utrecht
The Netherlands
Tel.: +31 30 257 23 80
Fax: +31 30 257 83 06
E-mail: info@fortisvastgoed.nl
Website:
www.fortisvastgoedbeleggingen.nl

Mr. R.W.M. Smeets
General Manager

Mr. L.J.M.G.
Hulsebosch MRE
Head Acquisition

Drs. E. Schrooten
MRE, Acquisition

C.J.A.M. Segeren
MRE, Head Property
Management

A.A. Jansen MRE
Acquisition

FORTIS

Vastgoed Beleggingen

we do mind

A stable yield that is much higher than the progressive average yield of the 10 year Euroswap rate, and of course out performance of the ROZ/IPD real estate index. That is the goal which Fortis Vastgoed Beleggingen is successfully pursuing. The organization is among the top of the real estate investors in the Netherlands.

A part of Fortis

Fortis is an integrated company offering services in the fields of banking and insurance. With a market capitalization of €31.4 billion (07/31/2005) and over 51,000 employees, Fortis ranks in the top 20 of European financial institutions. In its home market, the Benelux, Fortis occupies a leading position, which it aims to develop and bolster. Fortis is drawing on the expertise it has acquired in its home market to realize its European ambitions via growth platforms. Fortis also operates successfully worldwide in selected activities. In specific countries in Europe and Asia it effectively exploits its know-how and experience in bank assurance.

Fortis Insurance Netherlands is the country's second-largest insurer, offering non-life, life, pension healthcare, mortgage and other products. Fortis Vastgoed is the real estate investment company of Fortis in the Netherlands and is part of Fortis Insurance Netherlands. The investment portfolio includes residential properties, offices, car parks, as well as a large portfolio of prime retail properties and shopping centers. Fortis Vastgoed Beleggingen is active all over the Netherlands and provides tailor-made asset and property management services to private and institutional investors.
Fortis Vastgoed Beleggingen is not just an investor, but also a property manager, which allows the company to play an active role in the management of real estate projects. This provides Fortis with its own knowledge and expertise with respect to the leasing, maintenance and improvement of property. At Fortis Vastgoed Beleggingen asset management and property management go hand in hand.

Portfolio growth

Fortis is a real estate investor of large stature. Company-wide the total real estate portfolio amounts to more than €9 billion. In the Netherlands the assets under management at Fortis Vastgoed amount to €3.6 billion. Since 1999, nine real estate investment funds for private investors have been successfully launched. Furthermore, institutional investors can join in with Fortis Insurance Netherlands in retail, office and residential funds. Knowledge and expertise are not just slogans, but guarantee a full-service package and a stable performance for the long term.

WHO'S WHO

Fortis Vastgoed Ontwikkeling N.V.

Fortis Vastgoed Ontwikkeling N.V.
Archimedeslaan 6
P.O. Box 2009
3500 GA Utrecht
The Netherlands
Tel.: +31 30 257 35 12
Fax: +31 30 257 81 96
E-mail: info@fortisvastgoed.nl
Website:
www.fortisvastgoedontwikkeling.nl

Contact:
Managing Director:
F.H. (Foppe) Kooistra

F.H. (Foppe) Kooistra
Managing Director

Fortis Vastgoed Ontwikkeling is a fast growing, decisive and reliable real estate developer. Value for money is the basis of our formula, value that's attractive for the investor who is interested in a high return, as well as for the user for whom we provide ready-made accommodation. With a realistic view and an eye on the long-term, we take a good look at the market and the local situation; our projects fit in with social developments and contribute to the improvement of the living environment. We develop properties independently or in collaboration with various market segments. Knowledge of the field, financial decisiveness, creativity and personal involvement are the core elements in all aspects of our activities.

A part of Fortis

Large-scale and long-term responsibilities are no obstacle for durable developments: after all Fortis Vastgoed Ontwikkeling is part of the international Fortis Groep, an integrated company offering services in the fields of banking and insurance. With a market capitalization of €31.4 billion (07/31/2005) and more than 51,000 staff members, they belong to the 20 largest financial establishments in Europe. In its home market, the Benelux, Fortis is one of the largest financial service providers, offering a broad range of financial services for its private, business and institutional clients.

Partnerships

Fortis Vastgoed Ontwikkeling has a great deal of experience in location and area development. Large-scale expansion projects are often developed and realized in collaboration with various outside parties. Fortis Vastgoed Ontwikkeling also works closely together with city councils in which the complete development program and financing is often assumed by Fortis Vastgoed Ontwikkeling in order to limit the risk for the involved city council as much as possible.

Trendsetting developments

In the Netherlands the company constructs approximately 800-1,000 residences a year. This large-scale production is mainly thanks to the good position that the company has acquired through an active land policy. Among other things, Fortis Vastgoed Ontwikkeling is active at important VINEX locations such as Oosterheem in Zoetermeer and Leidsche Rijn in Utrecht.

FORTIS

Vastgoed Ontwikkeling

we do create

Additionally we focus on urban re(development) and large-scale office, retail and multifunctional projects. In total Fortis Vastgoed Ontwikkeling currently has 260,000 m^2 of commercial real estate in development or production. The largest project is Mahler4 along the Zuidas in Amsterdam. This mega-project, which consists of 160,000 m^2 of offices, 10,000 m^2 of facilities, and 200 residences in a residential tower, will be developed in different phases together with ING Real Estate and G&S Vastgoed. Our projects in The Hague include development of the Monarch together with Provastgoed Nederland, 75,000 m^2 of office space in the Beatrix quarter. Last year, the company also developed the 35,000 m^2 head office for T-Mobile in the Nieuw Laakhaven area of The Hague.

WHO'S WHO

HEIJMANS VASTGOED

Heijmans Vastgoed
Graafsebaan 65
P.O. Box 2
5240 BB Rosmalen
The Netherlands
Tel.: +31 73 543 51 11
Fax: +31 73 543 59 01
Website: www.heijmans.nl

C.A.M. (Coen) van Wichen, Chairman of the Board of Directors

Drs. W. (Willem) de Jager, Member of the Board of Directors

Ing. A.G.J. (Ton) Hillen, Member of the Board of Directors

Ir. M.T.A. (Max) Schep, Managing Director Commercial Property Development

Heijmans Vastgoed is one of the largest real estate developers in the Netherlands. The company is part of Heijmans N.V., a construction and development group with a turnover of some €2.6 billion that focuses on projects involving living, working, recreation, traffic, and transportation. Heijmans Vastgoed is a decisive partner in projects involving living, working and recreation in outlying areas, as well as those involving city center (restructuring) plans.

Nine regional branch offices and/or work organizations are responsible for the division called 'Living'. The development and sale of commercial property is managed centrally, just like that of the land bank company (the exploitation and management of land).

Development turnover in 2005 was some €800 million, of which €740 million in housing (3,700 housing units), €50 million in office space (22,000 m^2), and €10 million in retail (3,000 m^2). The 'Living' division is strongly focused on consumer-oriented development shaped by Heijmans' housebrand Wenswonen®. Heijmans Vastgoed plays a leading role in various cooperative projects (such as public-private collaborations) and finance construction.

Oostenburgereiland, developed by Heijmans, is expected to become a new and bubbling part of Amsterdam's center with some 100,000 m^2 of space developed on the old Stork site. It will consist of various clusters such as media & design, high-tech, public sector and education, leisure and culture, business services, special facilities, as well as urban living. As one of the former locations of the VOC (East India Company), it is a location steeped in history.

The inspiring environment of Oostenburgereiland has become the site of **INIT,** a unique and easily accessible business space constructed by Heijmans in Amsterdam's center. INIT consists of 33,000 m^2 of office space, a parking garage (216 spaces), and a car park for Stadsdeel Amsterdam Centrum, Werf Dienst Binnenstad.

Leerpark Dordrecht is an integral city center development consisting of an education center (60,000 m^2, 9,000 students), 450 housing units, 35,000 m^2 of business space, as well as offices, sports facilities, stores, and restaurants and cafés, all including infrastructure.

Heijmans is also a partner in the PPS-collaboration that realizes Vathorst Amersfoort. **Vathorst** is a new city quarter with some 11,000 housing units including services such as social services, education, sports, culture, a shopping center, and a national railway station, as well as 100,000 m^2 of office space and a 45-hectare business park.

Haverleij, a PPS-collaboration in 's-Hertogenbosch, is the result of a unique concept called 'country living'. Nine manors and one castle will become the location for some 1,000 homes and will include an 18-hole golf course also realized by Heijmans.

HOUTHOFF BURUMA

Houthoff Buruma

Office Amsterdam:
Gustav Mahlerplein 50
P.O. Box 75505
1070 AM Amsterdam
The Netherlands
Tel.: +31 20 605 60 00
Fax: +31 20 605 67 00

Office Rotterdam:
Weena 355
P.O. Box 1507
3000 BM Rotterdam
The Netherlands
Tel.: + 31 10 217 20 00
Fax: + 31 10 217 27 00

Website: www.houthoff.com

Onno de Bruijn
Notary

Robert Crince le Roy
Lawyer

Chris Goumans
Lawyer

Peter Habraken
Lawyer

Herman Lohman
Notary

Jaap Hoekstra
Lawyer

Aart Barkey Wolf
Notary

Jan Cees Kuiken
Notary

The Houthoff Buruma Mipim
delegation 2006.

HOUTHOFF BURUMA

The Houthoff Buruma Real Estate Department is a multidisciplinary team of about 90 lawyers and civil law notaries with vast experience in real estate transactions, project development, public-private partnerships, public-public partnerships and project finance. The Real Estate Department has at its disposal expertise in all relevant areas, including public procurement law, construction law, public law, leasing law, environmental law, etc. The Department is the largest of its kind in the Netherlands and is considered to be the market leader.

The development of new property projects is an especially complex process that involves many parties. This kind of development requires close interplay between project developers, government bodies, housing corporations, investors, lessees, buyers, estate agents, architects, consultants and builders. The essence of contracting in property development is the careful division of tasks, authorities and risks between all the parties involved in the project. Regardless of whether the property project concerns housing, recreation projects, shopping centers, hotels, parking garages or integrated projects, there always will be risks that need to be managed.

Our clients are contractors, investors, government bodies, housing corporations and major property developers. The high level of co-operation between the lawyers and civil law notaries within Houthoff Buruma produces the optimal legal result. The main areas of work are transactions, project development, public-private partnerships, public-public partnerships, construction (contracts and litigation), public procurement, public law and environmental law.

The Houthoff Buruma Real Estate Department is involved in almost every national or international property development or real estate transaction in the Netherlands.

ING REAL ESTATE

ING Real Estate
Schenkkade 65
P.O. Box 90463
2509 LL The Hague
The Netherlands
Tel.: +31 70 341 84 18
Fax: +31 70 341 84 19
E-mail: ingre.info@ingrealestate.com
Website: www.ingrealestate.com

Anneke de Vries
Development

Gerrit Beker
Development

Siebolt Bennema
Development

Dirk Jan v.d. Zeep
Development

Jan Vermaas
Investment
Management

Wim Wensing
Investment
Management

E.P. Bos
Investment
Management

Bert Kragtwijk
Finance

Jasper Klapwijk
Finance

ING Real Estate is a market leader in the Netherlands in commercial real estate development, commercial real estate finance and real estate investment management. With a total business portfolio of more than €64 billion and offices in 15 countries, ING Real Estate is also one of the strongest real estate companies worldwide. During 2005, the effectiveness of ING Real Estate's strategy to create value for its clients through the combination of development, investment management and finance was proven again and again.

Development

Creating value in real estate development means creating areas where people like to spend time – to live, work, shop and play. Projects are defined and designed in close cooperation with land-owners, investors, residents, entrepreneurs, retailers, and local governments. What we bring to the table are our 40 years of experience in urban planning, our research-based insights into retail, office and logistics trends, consumer behavior and lifestyles as well as an impressive track record of well-designed and skillfully executed projects.

Finance

Creating value in real estate means providing clients with flexible solutions based on extensive real estate expertise and state-of-the-art financial know-how. We are an international commercial real estate financier focusing on investors, developers and specific owner/user client groups. The possibilities are endless – fixed or floating rate, sale and leaseback, structured finance. Our mission is to add value by providing tailor-made financial solutions which exactly fit the clients' situations and demands.

Investment Management

Creating value in investment management is first and foremost realizing total returns that exceed or are at least equal to the targets that have been agreed with investors. We believe that excellence in investment management requires a skillful combination of product expertise, superior client service, local presence and in-depth research. Our aim is to provide all of these elements to all of our investors. ING Real Estate offers investors an extensive range of over 50 property funds, listed and non-listed, balanced and specialized with a regional, national and global focus. We also offer separate account management on both a direct and multi-manager basis.

ING
REAL ESTATE

IPMMC Vastgoed

IPMMC Vastgoed
Janssoniuslaan 80
P.O. Box 85457
3508 AL Utrecht
The Netherlands
Tel.: +31 30 281 73 00
Fax: +31 30 281 70 15
E-mail: info@ipmmc.nl
Website: www.ipmmc.nl
Contact: Tom Bleker, Thomas
Vambersky

Martin Verwoert   *Jan Regterschot*
Chairman   *Director*

Paul Trip
Director

Company information

IPMMC Vastgoed was founded in 1995, is based in Utrecht and employs around 45 highly qualified and experienced people, dealing with more than 25 complex real estate projects in the Netherlands.

IPMMC Vastgoed is a specialized real estate company, active in consultancy, management and the development of complex real estate projects.

IPMMC Vastgoed is characterized by its extensive knowledge of real estate, its focus on its customers' needs and a unique vision of 'the art of building'.

What we do:
- We advise on and develop complex property and accommodation projects
- We combine creativity with comprehensive knowledge concerning content, processes and marketing; and provide senior project management
- We position ourselves between the 'traditional' advisor, the construction manager, the estate agent and the developer
- We own a concept development group with architects and urban planning designers

Primarily involved in specialized projects frequently characterized by:
- Feasibility in complicated project environments
- Complex (inner) city problems and zoning procedures
- Customized solutions beyond the expected standards
- A high level of architectural and urban planning ambitions
- Complex (political/governmental) concerns and decision-making structures

Recent projects by IPMMC Vastgoed:
- Development of the Headquarters of DaimlerChrysler Services in Utrecht (23,500 m^2)
- Development of the Soccer Stadium with commercial spaces & leisure (40,000 m^2) in Zwolle
- Consulting services for the Municipality of Utrecht for their new City Hall
- Consulting services for the Ministry of Justice in The Hague (European Tender)
- The Project Management for ING-House in Amsterdam
- The Project & Process Management for the Van Den Ende Theatre in Amsterdam
- The renovation of the headquarters of Philips-Netherlands in Eindhoven

IPMMC
V A S T G O E D

WHO'S WHO

IVBN

**IVBN
Association of Institutional
Property Investors in the
Netherlands**
P.O. Box 620
2270 AP Voorburg
The Netherlands
Tel.: +31 70 300 03 71
Fax: +31 70 369 43 79
E-mail: info@ivbn.nl
Website: www.ivbn.nl

The IVBN (Association of Institutional Property Investors in the Netherlands) is a common interest organization representing the interests of institutional property investors in the Netherlands.

IVBN's members include pension funds, insurance companies and property funds (some of them listed at the Amsterdam Stock Exchange). Together the members represent investments of approximately €45 billion in Dutch real estate, which in turn covers about 90% of all Dutch institutional investments in real estate. IVBN members invest in residential property, offices and commercial real estate.

*R.W.M. (Ronald)
Smeets
President*

*M.W.A. (Menno)
Maas
Vice President*

The IVBN was incorporated in 1995 in order to represent the common interests of its members and in order to professionalize the sector. IVBN covers both direct and indirect property investments. The IVBN thereby sets the following goals:
- to stipulate the social context of property investments;
- to represent the common interests of property investors by providing insight into the consequences of both national and international market rules and regulations;
- to professionalize both people and means to the maximum;
- to publish and clarify background issues relating to performance optimization objectives of property investors.

*G.J. (George) Jautze
Treasurer*

*E.A. (Erik) Erenst
Secretary*

The IVBN wants to realize these objectives by:
- widely publishing its points of view;
- gathering information and putting this at the disposal of its members;
- stimulating the development of the profession of property investor, amongst others by promoting education;
- creating a venue for property investors in order to share knowledge;
- participating in discussions and issues relating to real estate.

J.J.M. (Anka) Reijnen

H. (Henk) de Bakker

Membership of the IVBN is open to institutional property investors who have invested at least €46 million in Dutch real estate.

Various study groups have been formed, such as Professionalization, Housing and Commercial Real Estate.

*R.J.M. (René)
Hogenboom*

*F.J.W. (Frank) van
Blokland
Director*

Vereniging van
Institutionele Beleggers
in Vastgoed Nederland

JOHAN MATSER PROJECTONTWIKKELING BV

Johan Matser
Projectontwikkeling bv
Ceintuurbaan 2
P.O. Box 334
1200 AH Hilversum
The Netherlands
Tel.: +31 35 626 00 00
Fax: +31 35 626 00 11
E-mail: info@johanmatser.nl
Website: www.johanmatser.nl

Ir. C.E.C. de Reus
Managing Director

Ir. J.C. Padberg
Managing Director

E. Zwaagman
Deputy Director
Realization &
Special Projects

Ing. H.E. Röling
MRE MRICS
Deputy Director
Retail

Drs. J.A. Posner
Deputy Director
Concepts &
Marketing

Ing. A.E. Bol
Director Urban
Redevelopment

Johan Matser Projectontwikkeling is an independent organization with over 65 years of experience in property development. Johan Matser concentrates on the development of residential projects as well as shopping centers, offices and industrial estates.

Mission statement

- Johan Matser is a leading and independent property development company focused on residential, commercial real estate and urban redevelopment projects.
- Johan Matser offers space solutions tailor-made to our customer's needs. We do this in a socially responsible and transparent manner.
- Johan Matser's concern for architectural and urban planning aspects is evidenced by our focus on the renewal and durability of our projects.
- Johan Matser's employees are enthusiastic and enjoy their work.

Independent with strong resources

Since July 1996, TBI Holdings BV has been the sole shareholder of Johan Matser. TBI, founded in 1981, is a financially strong holding company of mainly Dutch construction, engineering and utilities companies with a current total turnover of over €1.7 billion.
The financial strength of TBI, combined with the knowledge, alertness and independence of Johan Matser Projectontwikkeling ensures the organization's position as a strong and reliable player in the Dutch market.

Redevelopment

The redevelopment of inner-city areas and the renovation of post-war districts in the Netherlands will remain a major social task for years. Over the last decade, our business unit Stedelijke Herstructurering (Urban Redevelopment) has built up considerable experience in this area through close cooperation with municipalities and housing corporations. Within this long-term commitment we work to upgrade areas socially, economically and physically.

Built for the future

Johan Matser honors its social responsibilities by focusing on high caliber urban development projects of excellent architectural quality. This way the company focuses on a livable future that allows the client to realize all of their plans. A future recognized by a functional and pleasant environment of buildings and structures in which people live, work and play.

◘ JOHAN MATSER

JONES LANG LASALLE

Jones Lang LaSalle B.V.
Strawinskylaan 3103
1077 ZX Amsterdam
The Netherlands
Tel.: +31 20 540 54 05
Fax: +31 20 661 15 66
E-mail: infonl@eu.jll.com
Website: www.joneslanglasalle.nl
Contact: Mrs. M. Vuijk

Joost Captijn
Chairman

Eric de Clercq Zubli
Capital Markets

Eric Heijkoop
Agency Leasing &
Tenant Representation
the Netherlands

Jones Lang LaSalle is the global leader in real estate services and money management. We serve our clients' real estate needs locally, regionally and globally from offices in over 100 markets in 35 countries on five continents, with approximately 19,300 employees, including approximately 9,700 directly reimbursable property maintenance employees.

Our services include: outsourcing; space acquisition and disposition (tenant representation); facilities and property management; project and development management services; consulting; agency leasing; buying and selling properties; corporate finance; capital markets; hotel advisory; and valuations. We also provide real estate money management on a global basis for both public and private assets through LaSalle Investment Management.

Our services are enhanced by our integrated global business model, industry leading research capabilities, account management focus, operational excellence and strong brand.

Jones Lang LaSalle has grown by expanding both our client base and the range of our services and products, as well as through a series of strategic acquisitions and a merger. Our extensive global platform and in-depth knowledge of local real estate markets enable us to serve as a single source provider of solutions for our clients' full range of real estate needs. We solidified this network of services around the globe through the merger of the businesses of the Jones Lang Wootton companies (JLW) with those of LaSalle Partners Incorporated (LaSalle Partners), effective March 11, 1999.

Jones Lang LaSalle has five offices located in the Netherlands in Amsterdam, Rotterdam, The Hague, Utrecht and Eindhoven.

Jones Lang LaSalle B.V.
Strawinskylaan 3103
1077 ZX Amsterdam
Tel.: +31 20 540 54 05
Fax: +31 20 661 15 66

Jones Lang LaSalle B.V.
Weena 256
3011 NJ Rotterdam
Tel.: +31 10 411 04 40
Fax: +31 10 414 70 28

Jones Lang LaSalle B.V.
Alexanderveld 89
2585 DB The Hague
Tel.: +31 70 318 13 13
Fax: +31 70 364 39 08

Jones Lang LaSalle B.V.
Vivaldiplantsoen 260
3533 JE Utrecht
Tel.: +31 30 284 30 60
Fax: +31 30 294 32 95

Jones Lang LaSalle B.V.
Fellenoord 31
5612 AA Eindhoven
Tel.: +31 40 250 01 00
Fax: +31 40 250 01 25

LEXENCE

Lexence
Peter van Anrooystraat 7
P.O. Box 75999
1070 AZ Amsterdam
The Netherlands
Tel.: +31 20 573 67 36
Fax: +31 20 573 67 37
E-mail: info@lexence.com
Website: www.lexence.com

Attorneys:
S.H.J. Vissers
F.H.J. van Schoonhoven
T.H.G. Steenmetser
B.B. van Vliet
A. Kaspers
J. van Duijvendijk
W. Raas-de Lange
M.H.J. van Driel
E. van der Wiel
V. van Oijen

Civil-law notaries:
M. van Groningen
J. ten Have
J.W.A. Hockx
T.S. de Lange
R. Rietbroek

Lexence is a firm of attorneys and civil-law notaries specialized in Real Estate and Business Law, located in Amsterdam. Over recent years, our work for both Dutch and foreign companies has led to a healthy growth in our business. We base our success on enthusiasm and an unquenchable ambition to be the best. Lexence combines the advantages of being a compact organization with high-quality professional expertise.

The world never stops turning. Neither does the legal world. Lexence has the most up-to-date information at all times to satisfy our passion for new developments.

Real Estate Expertise
Lexence offers specialist legal support in the following areas of real estate and related matters:

- Real estate investments;
- Project development, purchase-contracting, turnkey;
- Project financing, secured loans, mortgage loans;
- Lease of commercial real estate (offices, shopping centers, logistics facilities, etc.), lease agreements, change in rent procedures;
- Real estate-related proceedings, arbitration and mediation;
- Construction licenses; planning regulations;
- Environmental permits, environmental liability and administrative fines;
- Administrative law proceedings.

International
Lexence can call on its partners in the Meritas Law Firms and Counselex Global Network. Our clients often find their legal way abroad through these independent, local and qualified law offices. Moreover, our vast and thorough knowledge of the Netherlands' real estate market and our international experience have proved very beneficial to international clients with interests abroad.

Partners Property Department: L-R (standing): Bas van Vliet, Menno van Groningen, Jelle ten Have, Stijn Vissers, Michiel van Driel, Wendela Raas-de Lange, Arthur Kaspers, Ferry van Schoonhoven, Jan Hockx, René Rietbroek. Front row: Taco de Lange, Tomas Steenmetser, Jan van Duijvendijk.

WHO'S WHO

MULTI DEVELOPMENT

Multi Development BV
P.O. Box 875
2800 AW Gouda
The Netherlands
Tel.: +31 182 69 09 00
Fax: +31 182 69 06 90
E-mail: info@multi-development.com
Website: www.multi-development.com

Hans van Veggel
Chairman of the
Board

Arnold de Haan
Chief Executive
Officer

Eric van Duren
Chief Investment
Officer

Nico Veldhuis
Member Executive
Committee

Marcel Kokkeel
Member Executive
Committee

Richard Reulink
Director Retail
Development
Netherlands

Heino Vink
Director Retail
Development
Nehterlands

Sven Mathijssen
Director
Multifunctional
Development
Netherlands

Ebbe van Wijngaarden
Director Office Develop-
ment Netherlands and
Technical Director

Bernd Haggenmüller
Director Asset
Management

Multi Development redefines the standards

Multi Development (formerly AM Development) never shies away from exploring new avenues. Stronger still: we believe our philosophy and actions have been and continue to be an inspiration for the entire real estate sector. For example, Multi Development's harmonious solutions for incorporating ultramodern shopping centers into century-old town centers are unique and have won many international awards. Today Multi Development takes a step further in redefining its standards...

Asset management

Multi Development is more than an investing developer. As past experience proves, the value of projects we have completed shows a steady growth over the years. And we like to keep that growth generated by the ideas we have within our own portfolio. Hence, following completion and delivery of our centers we, as Asset Managers, take care of this continuous growth in quality and value. Active and intensive Mall Management is an important instrument in that respect. We participate personally in the projects we develop which are financed by institutional investment structures.
Not only do we have the ability to initiate developments in real estate, we also participate in the increase in value. Our partner in this process of continued growth as an investing developer is one of the renowned Morgan Stanley Real Estate Funds.

What remains...

is a creative knowledge organization of experienced and inspiring professionals, which, if so instructed, does of course continue to develop as normal without participation. Our national organizations use regional markets as the basic principle for projects that respect and enhance local cultures and styles. This is how we develop projects in the Netherlands, Belgium, Germany, France, the United Kingdom, Portugal, Spain, Italy, Turkey, and in Central European countries such as the Czech Republic, Hungary, Poland, Slovenia and Slovakia. All projects are geared towards consumer preferences. Each time, our objective is to create an environment that captivates people. We add imaginative ingredients that in turn allow local people to take our projects to their hearts.

The pinnacle of partnership and commitment

The projects of Multi Development have reaped worldwide admiration. Inner city projects have won prestigious awards such as the MIPIM and ICSC. Shopping centers in Portugal (Forum Almada, Lisbon), the Czech Republic (Olympia Olomouc), Germany (Kamp Promenade, Osnabrück) and Spain (Espai Gironès, Gerona) have also recently won renowned real estate prizes. These projects have been realized through a combination of design, developments and the ability to invest. Our strategy is and continues to be aimed at developing these projects in a large number of countries and, in co-operation with a select number of financial parties, investing directly or indirectly into investment funds with new shopping centers in European regions where we anticipate significant growth.
MULTI IS ON THE MOVE.

ENTRE DEUX, MAASTRICHT

KPN, UTRECHT

MUSISKWARTIER, ARNHEM

HET NIEUWE RIJSWIJKSE BOS, RIJSWIJK

MULTI DEVELOPMENT

MULTI INVESTMENT

MULTI ASSET MANAGEMENT

THE NETHERLANDS | BELGIUM | BULGARIA | CZECH REPUBLIC | FRANCE | GERMANY | GREECE | HUNGARY | ITALY | POLAND | PORTUGAL | RUMANIA
SLOVAKIA | SPAIN | TURKEY | UKRAINE | UNITED KINGDOM

WHO'S WHO

INVERDAN, ZAANDAM

Mn Services

Mn Services
Burgemeester Elsenlaan 329
P.O. Box 5210
2280 HE Rijswijk (ZH)
The Netherlands
Tel.: +31 70 316 02 62
Fax: +31 70 316 05 05
E-mail: info@mn-services.nl
Website: www.mn-services.nl
Contact: Richard van Ovost,
George van Hooydonk

Richard van Ovost
Director International
Real Estate

George van Hooydonk
Director Dutch
Real Estate

Mn Services is an independent Dutch company that offers pension administration, management support and investment management services to pension funds and other institutional clients.
In total Mn Services has €30 billion in assets under management. €3.3 billion is committed to real estate on behalf of several institutions. Two specialized teams manage the Dutch and International Real Estate portfolios.

Dutch Real Estate
Mn Services is a major asset manager in the Dutch real estate market. The Dutch Real Estate team has currently more than €1.3 billion in assets under management. The investments are divided nearly equally among residential, retail and office. With over 40 years of experience and a team of dedicated and experienced real estate professionals, Mn Services is a well-known company with strong roots in the Dutch real estate market and has a strong track record within Dutch real estate. Since the introduction of the ROZ/IPD benchmark in 1995, Mn Services has beaten this benchmark many times.

International Real Estate
For well over 10 years, the International Real Estate team has built up a strong track record offering its clients exposure to real estate in Europe, North America and Asia.

The team offers tailor-made, research-driven solutions for the entire investment process from ALM and the optimal real estate allocation over regions, sectors and countries, to the selection and monitoring of the appropriate local partner (such as private fund managers and joint venture partners). According to our philosophy, the selection of the right local partner is crucial and over the years we have built an extensive network and database of these partners.

The International Real Estate team acts as a fund of funds manager on behalf of institutional clients, and is therefore able to take an independent position in selecting the 'best of the breed'.

Over the last few years the team has structured and closed well over 30 investments in private funds, co-investments, and joint ventures worldwide. The team actively manages listed and non-listed investments of over €2.1 billion.

NEPROM

Neprom
Westeinde 28
P.O. Box 620
2270 AP Voorburg
The Netherlands
Tel.: +31 70 386 62 64
Fax: +31 70 387 40 89
E-mail: bureau@neprom.nl
Website: www.neprom.nl
Contact: J. Fokkema

drs. ing. J. Fokkema   *drs. H. D. Werner*
Managing Director   *Chairman Neprom*

Neprom, the Association of Dutch Property Developers, was founded in 1974. The 67 member companies are active in various areas of the property market – including office buildings, retail and housing – and have a variety of backgrounds. Some are independent development companies, others are related to construction companies or financial institutions, whilst a third group comprises pension funds or insurance companies which develop property as part of their investment strategy.

The main goal of the Association is to encourage cooperation between public authorities and project developers. The Netherlands has a long-standing history with regard to planning. National, regional and local governments have a strong say in property development, brought about by planning regulations and licensing.

The following figures indicate the size of the Dutch property market: approximately 65,000 new houses are constructed annually, of which about 80% are in the private sector (where our members are active) and the other 20% consists of heavily subsidized housing for low-income groups. The amount of new office space is about 1.3 million m^2 per annum. New retail space varies considerably from year to year, and is an estimated average of 300,000 m^2 per annum.

Members of Neprom have a strong position within the Dutch property market. They are responsible for about 65% of new office buildings, 80% of new retail space and 50% of new housing in the private sector. Pension funds and insurance companies associated with Neprom hold about 80% of the institutional property investment capital in the Netherlands.

To become a member of Neprom, a company should have many years of experience in the property development business and must comply with strict financial, professional and moral standards. Owing to this market position and the high standards it sets, Neprom has become a valued partner for the Dutch authorities.

Vereniging van
Nederlandse
Projectontwikkeling
Maatschappijen

NRW-NEDERLANDSE RAAD VAN WINKELCENTRA

**NRW-Nederlandse Raad
van Winkelcentra**
Herculesplein 271
3584 AA Utrecht
The Netherlands
Tel.: +31 30 231 37 54
Fax: +31 30 234 12 87
E-mail: info@nrw.nl
Website: www.nrw.nl

*P.W. Affourtit
Chairman*

The NRW is a non-profit association for all enterprises and institutions that are professionally involved in shopping centers and the shopping center industry. The NRW's strength lies in their neutral and independent position within the shopping center property industry. The NRW is a member of the International Council of Shopping Centers, New York.

The NRW has over 200 company members and more than 400 personal members. Since the founding in 1986, NRW has become an authority in the areas of retail, real estate and town & country planning.

Throughout the year, the NRW organizes activities where members can meet one another, exchange information and discuss and learn about new national and international developments. Some of the activities are as follows:

- NRW annual award for the best shopping center (re-)developed in the past year. The winner of this highly appreciated award is announced at the annual meeting of the NRW;
- Study trips: every year the NRW organizes two study trips abroad. The keynote of these trips is to exhibit the most interesting developments in the shopping center business. During the study trips, interesting developments are seen and presentations are given about the culture, demographics and market developments in the countries visited;
- Lunch sessions: four times a year the members meet to be informed on recent developments, usually on location. Professionals, developers and the municipality are invited to give a presentation or take part in a discussion about current topics; the lunch sessions are usually combined with visits to a recently developed or renovated shopping center;
- NRW News: this quarterly news letter informs members about all of NRW's activities;
- NRW-register: this register gives a complete overview of all relevant data of more than 900 Dutch shopping centers. It is updated annually.

The Board:
P.W. Affourtit
H.F. Apon
prof. drs. ing. H.J. Gianotten
J.C.M.A. Gillis MBA MRICS
ing. G.H.W. Groener
ing. L. Lantinga
ing. W. Veldhuizen MRE
ing. J. Vermaas

Secretary General:
mrs. L.A. Kruit

NS VASTGOED

NS Vastgoed
Stationshal 17
P.O. Box 2319
3500 GH Utrecht
The Netherlands
Tel.: +31 30 300 43 00
Fax: +31 30 300 43 05
E-mail: nsv.info@ns.nl
Website: www.nsvastgoed.nl
Contact: Kees de Boo, Paul Rutte,
Bert Roterman

C.A.M. (Kees) de Boo
CEO NS Vastgoed

P. (Paul) Rutte
Director
NS Vastgoed
Development

B.H.P.T. (Bert) Roterman
Director Asset
Management
NS Vastgoed

NS Vastgoed (NS Real Estate) develops and manages property around stations as well as in other locations. Investing in station sites and developing them is its most obvious activity. These recognizable and easily-accessible locations are made more attractive and lively by the addition of features such as offices, housing, shops, hotels, schools and parking facilities.

In addition to large-scale and complex projects around larger stations, NS Vastgoed is developing housing, among other things, near smaller stations in more and more places.
As well as developing station sites, NS Vastgoed also manages property on former railway sites, often in town centers.
The company will be investing in increasing the value of these sites in the next few years.

NS Vastgoed does not restrict itself to just project development, however. As a shareholder in Vastgoedfonds Stationslocaties (Station Site Property Fund), it also plays a role in the management of station sites.

Projects under development
- City Hall – Gouda and Zaandam
- Student housing – The Hague
- Apartments Wijnhaeve – Rotterdam
- Apartments Amor Forte – Amersfoort
- Hotel – Amsterdam
- Hotel, offices – Breda
- School – Nijmegen
- Business park – Utrecht
- Parking facilities – nationwide

Exterior ROC (Regionaal Opleidingen Centrum),
Nijmegen.

Interior ROC, Nijmegen.

NVM

NVM – Dutch Association of Real Estate Brokers and Real Estate Experts
P.O. Box 2222
3430 DC Nieuwegein
The Netherlands
Tel.: +31 30 608 51 85
Fax: +31 30 603 54 68
E-mail: info@nvmorg.nl
Website: www.nvm.nl
Contact: G.A. Cremers

Oscar J. Smit
President

Wim. J. van Kampen
Vice President

Gerard. A. Cremers
Chief Executive

NVM is the foremost professional real estate association in the Netherlands. NVM stands for the Dutch Association of Real Estate Brokers and Real Estate Experts. This organization is made up of both real estate brokers (or real estate agents) and experts in the immovable property field. The NVM has now been in existence for more than 100 years (it was founded in 1898) and has more than 3,800 members, 3,000 of whom are residential real estate brokers. As an organization, we have set ourselves the task of monitoring and safeguarding quality levels within the sector.

Code of Ethics

To help us in this, we have drawn up an NVM Code of Ethics in which agreements on expertise, independence and reliability are enshrined. Every NVM member is obliged to adhere to this code. Failure to do so can result in a broker being called before the NVM's disciplinary committee. Furthermore, affiliated brokers must constantly prove that they are worthy of membership of the NVM. For example, we expect our members to regularly have customer satisfaction surveys performed by an independent research agency.

In the Netherlands a branch-coordinated system of certification is in place. All NVM-members are certified according to national professional criteria and registered as such.

Membership also involves the obligation to enter property portfolios into the NVM multi-listing system. This exchange system is operated nationwide and offers all affiliated brokers access to properties for rent or sale all over the Netherlands. The www.funda.nl site makes the complete NVM MLS-content available to consumers.

Organization

The NVM organization has been split up into separate branch and market organizations. The branch organization concerns itself with general matters of policy, such as national and international developments within the general professional field, public affairs and the provision of services to members in respect of legal affairs, public relations, research and development, automation, consumer support and quality care.

The market organization of NVM focuses on market developments within the real estate sector, and has been divided up into four specialist sections: NVM Residential Real Estate, NVM Commercial Real Estate, NVM Agrarian Real Estate and NVM Property Management. All NVM members belong to at least one of these four sections.

NVM

ORANJEWOUD BOUW & VASTGOED

Oranjewoud Bouw & Vastgoed
Rivium Westlaan 72
P.O. Box 8590
3009 AN Rotterdam
The Netherlands
Tel.: +31 10 235 18 34
Fax: +31 10 235 18 85
E-mail: info@oranjewoud.nl
Website: www.oranjewoud.nl
Contact: René Teunissen,
Arie Schippers, Geurt Breukink,
Peter Docters van Leeuwen

*Mr. R.J. (René)
Teunissen,
Director Oranjewoud
Bouw & Vastgoed*

*Mr. A.W. (Arie)
Schippers,
Business Manager*

*Ing. G.A. (Geurt)
Breukink,
Business Manager*

*Mr. P.B. (Peter)
Docters van
Leeuwen MBA,
Business Manager*

Oranjewoud Bouw & Vastgoed, a division of Oranjewoud Beheer, is a national consultancy and engineering organization in the Netherlands. We have high ambitions as far as shaping our living and working environment is concerned. Our goal in the field of real estate and building is to provide real solutions to questions, to create environments that are pleasant to live in, to develop a sustainable future, to seize every opportunity, to shape perspectives and to be at the cutting edge of our profession. We do this in a creative and constructive manner, while keeping in mind the interests of society, the financial possibilities, technological developments and the environment. In other words: we provide a clear vision without losing sight of reality.

Devising innovative proposals and coming up with creative solutions to complex questions is at the very core of our activities. Interaction is the key word. Looking beyond the boundaries of our profession is second nature to us and is reflected in the multidisciplinary nature of our real estate and building projects. We combine our own knowledge and expertise with the needs, opportunities, know-how and experience of our clients. The exchange of ideas and experiences leads to innovation. Partnership is the starting point.

Guide to project development
The life cycle of a building depends on the core business, identity, prospects and the employees. A building has to be the reflection of an organization at all times. Through the years several housing matters will occur (maintenance, alterations, development of a new building). For example, the development of a new building is characterized by many parties: the client, end-users, consultants and the architect. This development can take up a lot of time during a long period. Initially it seems to be a temporary project. But the core business of the company goes on and on, and in the meantime the process of the new building becomes a major, everyday item. That's when an independent experienced guide is the answer - a private consultant to look after the entire project.

Management and consultancy
Oranjewoud is the guide to real estate and building consultancy and management. Our consultancy is based on four pillars: organization, legislation, finance and engineering. Our real estate and building management extends to process and project management and the day-to-day running of things. We take care of the entire project, from the planning stage, advice, design and supervision, right through to realization. Naturally it is for the client to decide whether we will undertake the whole process or just a specific part of it. The combination of consulting and management, together with actual realization is our guarantee for feasible plans and high-quality work. A reassuring thought for our clients.

Real estate and building services
Our services within the field of real estate and building:
● Logistics concerns, Industrial plants, Office facilities, Retail stores
● Nursing homes
● (Primary) schools, City halls, Sports & leisure centers

PRICEWATERHOUSECOOPERS REAL ESTATE GROUP

PricewaterhouseCoopers
De Entree 201
P.O. Box 22735
1100 DE Amsterdam Southeast
The Netherlands
Tel.: +31 20 568 66 66
Fax: +31 20 568 68 88
Website: www.pwc.com/nl

*Drs. E. Hartkamp
RA MRE
Assurance Partner –
RE Leader
Netherlands*

*Drs. C.J. Hage RA
CPA
Assurance Partner –
Eurofirm RE
Assurance Leader*

*W.J.J. Verdegaal-
Ong RA
Assurance Director*

*Mr. F.M. van Zelst
Tax Partner – Global
and Eurofirm RE Tax
Leader*

*Drs. Chr. J.M.
Noordermeer Van Loo
Tax Partner –
Valuations*

*Mr. J.H. Elink
Schuurman MRE
Tax Partner*

*Mr. W.P. Otto
Tax Director*

*A. Mak van Waay
Advisory Partner –
Transactions*

*Ir. J. Manschot
Advisory Principal
Manager – Process
Improvement*

Whatever type of real estate challenge you're facing, our Real Estate Group's expert guidance and creative solutions will help you negotiate your way safely through any potential minefield. Combining in-depth technical expertise with extensive industry experience, the Group provides customized services and innovative solutions – from assurance and tax services to advisory services and valuations.

Assurance

Our assurance specialists can help you to improve your corporate reporting and provide assurance that your systems are operating effectively within a well-controlled environment. We can advise you on complex reporting issues involving IFRS and Sarbanes-Oxley and help you respond to the need for greater transparency and improved corporate governance.

Tax

Our dedicated real estate tax team can advise you on all property related tax issues, including the tax consequences of all types of transactions, such as asset acquisitions and sales, mergers and acquisitions, fund structuring, financing and corporate reorganizations. We also provide support and advice during tax audits and litigation, and offer compliance services for income and corporate income tax, as well as indirect taxes. The team includes specialists in local levies.

Advisory services and valuations

In every sector and for any type of property, we can advise on strategic issues (e.g., market analysis, mergers and acquisitions, and portfolio management) tactical issues (e.g., purchasing, risk management, valuations and portfolio management, organizational structure, and client satisfaction) and operational issues (e.g., process improvement and risk analysis). Our experienced appraisers provide a comprehensive range of valuation services.

In addition, we can assist you in evaluating in-house appraisal management functions, with particular emphasis on best practices and cost savings. Upon request, we review and evaluate existing policies, procedures and systems, and provide recommendations for improvements.

Connected Thinking

At PricewaterhouseCoopers in the Netherlands, over 4,000 professionals work together in 19 offices and from three different points of approach: Assurance, Tax and Human Resource Services, and Advisory. On the basis of our philosophy, Connected Thinking, we supply sector-specific services and seek surprising solutions – not only for large national and international companies, but also for government entities and non-profit organizations, as well as for medium-sized and smaller enterprises.

As an independent part of a worldwide network of more than 130,000 colleagues in 144 countries, we are able to draw upon a huge amount of knowledge and experience. We share this with each other, with our clients and with their stakeholders.

RABO VASTGOED B.V.

Rabo Vastgoed B.V.
Europalaan 40
P.O. Box 17100
3500 HG Utrecht
The Netherlands
Tel.: +31 30 216 17 19
Fax: +31 30 216 33 75
E-mail: rabovastgoed@rn.rabobank.nl
Website: www.rabovastgoed.nl

Ing. P. (Pieter)
Wetselaar

Drs. R.J.A.
(Robert Jan)
van Hamersveld RA

Ing. J. (Jan) Roelofs

Rabo Vastgoed is a large project developer in the Netherlands that co-ordinates and finances more than 200 real estate projects with a total value of €4 billion.
The company offers area and concept development and is therefore a well-known partner in not only private partnership but also in public-private-partnership. With a stock in hand of 40,000 houses, Rabo Vastgoed belongs to the largest project developers of the Netherlands.

The company develops and participates in commercial real estate with an order portfolio of 400,000 m^2 gross floor space.
The land portfolio comprises 1,940 hectares. Rabo Vastgoed works with capital cities, municipalities, architects and contractors.
The vast majority of projects are residential housing projects, ranging from a few dozen homes to entire suburbs. Local contractors are often partners in the projects. Most projects are budgeted at between €10 and €20 million, and up to over a €100 million in the case of the largest projects.

Rabo Vastgoed offers project management, financing and process management. Unlike most other project developers, Rabo Vastgoed organizes the various participation processes, not only co-ordinating the project but also providing tailor-made financial solutions.

As part of the Rabobank Group, the largest financial service provider of the Netherlands, Rabo Vastgoed is considered to be a reliable partner.

Rabo Vastgoed collaborates closely with partners who enjoy a good reputation. In all cases Rabo Vastgoed uses strict quality control measures to monitor the entire process. The project developer brings parties together and arranges co-operative links which bring out the best in all parties concerned, creating virtual organizations in which the partners can use their own particular expertise for the common good.

Eye for surroundings and environment
The philosophy of Rabo Vastgoed is clear and simple: project development must produce places where people gladly want to be. Places which are safe and interesting, where it is pleasant to live and work. Now, but also in the future.

Rabo Vastgoed always works closely with other, often regional, parties in the real estate sector. In order to be able to follow the regional market developments from close by, Rabo Vastgoed operates in five regions, and thereby profits from the unique knowledge of the 290 autonomous local co-operative Rabobanks spread throughout the Netherlands. This results in product market combinations that anticipate successfully on local interests and emotions. Rabo Vastgoed "develops with an eye for surroundings and environment." The result: new areas carefully embedded in existing structures, which are considered to be valuable for many years to come by users and visitors alike.

WHO'S WHO

REDEVCO NEDERLAND BV

Redevco Nederland BV
Rhijnspoorplein 26
P.O. Box 1340
1000 BH Amsterdam
The Netherlands
Tel.: +31 20 521 87 30
Fax: +31 20 521 87 40
E-mail: service@nl.redevco.com
Website: www.redevco.com

Luuk Lantinga
Managing Director

Jeroen Smit MRE
Portfolio manager

In 1999 Redevco Europe was founded as a European Real Estate Investment and Development Company. Redevco Europe now handles a real estate portfolio of €6.5 billion and is active in 15 countries. Redevco Nederland has a real estate portfolio of €500 million invested in 90 properties which precede shops at high-street level, offices and corporate buildings.

In the space of just six years, Redevco has become one of Europe's leading retail real estate companies. Its initial targets have largely been achieved. The organization is strong and well-established in many national markets; the portfolios have been restructured and expanded; the geographical and sector spread has been improved; and the tenant mix is now more balanced. New challenges await – we are aiming to expand further in the Dutch market and to optimize our portfolio.

Redevco Nederland
The activities of Redevco Nederland are focused on dynamically exploiting and redeveloping the properties held in portfolio. These are mainly individual downtown retail properties.

On the acquisition side, Redevco Nederland concentrates on out-of-town retail properties to create a more balanced portfolio structure. Redevco Nederland prefers properties offering development or redevelopment opportunities, and is willing to dispose of part of its existing portfolio in exchange for these.

The portfolio also embraces offices with development and redevelopment potential, and highly flexible logistics centers.

The various acquisitions and redevelopments planned and in the pipeline will grow the total portfolio value of Redevco Nederland from around €500 million currently to around €700 million in the year 2010.

Business philosophy
It is our people and our shared values that make Redevco what it is. A real estate company with high professional and ethical standards which achieves ambitious commercial targets by putting people at the center. Our company's mission is to professionally manage and develop a European real estate portfolio. We implement this mission by optimizing proceeds in terms of cash flow and value creation. We take market conditions and benchmarks into account, and use our existing European real estate portfolio as the basis for further development.

REDEVCO
business in balance

RODAMCO EUROPE IN THE NETHERLANDS

**Rodamco Europe
in the Netherlands**
Hoogoorddreef 11/2
P.O. Box 22816
1100 DH Amsterdam ZO
The Netherlands
Tel.: +31 20 312 01 20
Fax: +31 20 312 02 40
E-mail: info.nl@rodamco.com
Website: www.rodamco.com

*Ms. K. (Karin)
Laglas
Managing Director*

*Ms. H. (Hélène)
Pragt
Finance Director*

*Mr. B.J.G. (Bart)
van Rooijen
Asset Selection
Director*

*Mr. R.P. (Richard)
Dallinga
Retail Management
Director*

With an investment portfolio valued at €2.9 billion, Rodamco Europe in the Netherlands is the largest single market in the Rodamco Europe Group, and the leading listed retail property company in Europe (€8.7 billion). 86% of the portfolio of Rodamco Europe in the Netherlands is invested in prestigious retail projects.

Rodamco Europe in the Netherlands owns and manages top quality retail property in dominant locations in major Dutch cities. As owner/managers, the primary aim is customer satisfaction. By focusing on quality service to retail tenants and consumers, Rodamco Europe has been able to generate growth in shareholder and stakeholder value.

Over the past five years, and in line with the Return on Retail strategy, Rodamco Europe in the Netherlands has systematically divested office properties and invested in quality shopping centers. Every year, the share of retail in the portfolio has been increased. Currently, retail represents 86% of the total €2.9 billion in investments.

Managing Director Karin Laglas: "For us, investing in a shopping center is a long-term commitment. As we manage many of our shopping centers, and also handle leasing for all assets, we are actively involved with retailers and retail and tenant associations on a day-to-day basis. We are also a valued partner for regional and local authorities who play a key role in the retail environment in cities and towns. Local authorities are crucial to the management of high-street retail areas, where, with more than 300 shops throughout the country, we are also a significant owner."

On the asset selection side, Rodamco Europe is known for cherry-picking quality projects. The most recent example is the purchase of Stadshart Amstelveen in 2005. Laglas: "But we are also committed to growing the value of our assets through extension and refurbishment programs. We have an extensive pipeline portfolio (worth approximately €700 million of which approx. €300 million committed pipeline projects), working in close cooperation with some of the Netherlands' major developers. In 2005 this resulted in the opening of Shopping Center Vier Meren in Hoofddorp and Spazio in Zoetermeer.
In combination, our owner/manager roles give us a unique knowledge of and experience in all aspects of the retail property business. In our view, quality is the key to successful growth of both the portfolio and shareholder value. Our goal is quality in everything we do."

Rodamco Europe

ROTTERDAM AIRPORT VASTGOED

Rotterdam Airport Vastgoed B.V.
P.O. Box 12030
3004 GA Rotterdam
The Netherlands
Tel.: +31 10 446 35 78
Fax: +31 10 446 35 79
E-mail: vastgoed@rotterdam-airport.nl

Rotterdam Airport Vastgoed (RAV) is a joint venture between Schiphol Real Estate and Rotterdam Airport and a 100% subsidiary of Schiphol Group. Rotterdam Airport Vastgoed was set up for the purpose of redeveloping the area of Rotterdam Airport into a prestigious business location, named RTM Airpark. Plans involve the development of a total of 200,000 m^2 of office and business space. Schiphol Group and the Municipality of Rotterdam reached agreement in December 2000 on the allocation of areas on the airport site available for property development. Schiphol Group has leased the land for a term of 99 years.

A.A. (Ad) Mast
M.Sc. FRICS
Managing Director

Drs. Ir. J. (Jan)
Krijnen
Manager Real
Estate Investments

Ing. A.J. (Anton)
Koomen MRE
Real Estate
Developer

Drs. A.J.M. (Albert)
Kandelaar
Account Manager

Product

RAV manages the buildings at the airport commercially, administratively and technically on behalf of Rotterdam Airport. These buildings currently accommodate 40 business tenants in a total space of more than 18,800 m^2, excluding the Bel Air building which is also managed by RAV. There are also ground leases which together account for a ground area of 9,100 m^2.

Current developments

RAV is currently developing unique office and business spaces at Rotterdam Airport. Its ideal location in the southwest of the Randstad – just three kilometers from the center of Rotterdam, within the triangle linking Rotterdam, Delft and The Hague, and in the middle of the Delft-Rotterdam Kennisboulevard (Science Corridor) – together with excellent parking facilities and good accessibility, make Rotterdam Airport a unique business location.

Planning of RTM Airpark

The first phase of the master plan for the business park is the construction of a number of office villas and luxury pavilions of approximately 1,500 m^2 in the Entrance Area. The Entrance Area also offers excellent parking facilities on each individual plot, plus a spacious two-story parking garage built nearby offering 4,500 spaces for passengers and visitors. Grouped around the newly developed Rotterdam Airport Square you will find offices with approximately 55,000 m^2 of floor space and 30,000 m^2 of building space shared by several businesses. Around or close to the square there will be a wide range of cafes, restaurants and shops, creating a highly attractive recreational area within the dynamics of the international airport. Here too, an ample parking area is found beneath the buildings. There are plans to build a luxury business hotel at Rotterdam Airportplein close to all the amenities. This hotel will have about 400 rooms with conference facilities, and will be connected to the terminal. Naturally, short-term parking is available for passengers and visitors immediately in front of the terminal.

Between the airport aprons and the Randstad railway line, modern, flexible and attractive office spaces with a total floor area of around 100,000 m^2 will be developed and known as the business cluster. Rotterdam Airport is the ideal location voor internationally oriented businesses.

ROTTERDAM AIRPORT
VASTGOED BV

ROZ RAAD VOOR ONROERENDE ZAKEN

ROZ Raad voor Onroerende Zaken
Bezuidenhoutseweg 12
P.O. Box 93002
2509 AA The Hague
The Netherlands
Tel.: +31 70 349 01 95
Fax: +31 70 349 01 27
E-mail: info@roz.nl
Website: www.roz.nl
Contact: Dr. Aart C. Hordijk MRICS
Chairman: Prof. drs. P.P. Kohnstamm

Dr. A. C. Hordijk
MRICS
Director

The Real Estate Council of the Netherlands (ROZ) focuses on the interests of property owners and fulfils the role of 'watchdog' with regard to branch related subjects. This includes mortgage interest deduction. Every year, ROZ-IPD Property Index collaborates with IVBN to organize a seminar on relevant research subjects. In addition, ROZ provides rental contract frameworks, which are kept up-to-date by a commission of lawyers. These frameworks can be downloaded from the website.

Organization

ROZ is led by a board of directors, but day-to-day operations are done by a team of four people. When necessary, ad hoc committees are set up in order to lobby with regard to specific political issues. Depending on the subject, interested parties other than members may participate in the lobbying process.

Linked to ROZ is the ROZ-IPD Netherlands Property Index. This is a collaboration between the Investment Property Databank in London and ROZ. They publish the ROZ-IPD Index on a yearly, and since 2001, also quarterly basis. For added support, courses with respect to portfolio benchmarking and property valuations are provided.

Members

Aedes	Association of Housing Corporations
IVBN	Association of Institutional Investors in Real Estate
KNB	Royal Association of Notaries
Neprom	Association of Dutch Project Development
NVB	Association of Developers and Contractors
NVM	Dutch Association of Brokers
RVT	Real Estate Appraisal Association
VastgoedBelang	Real Estate Interests
VBO	Dutch Association of Estate Agents
VEH	Association of Private Home Owners
VVE Belang	Association of Common Ownership Interests

Publications

The most prominent ROZ publications are the rental contract frameworks and their translations. Updates of the models are announced on the website.

The ROZ-IPD Netherlands Property Index publishes quarterly performance figures and yearly performance figures of the property belonging to institutional investors and real estate funds. Although breakthrough research is also available, only a limited amount can be found on the website at this time. For more information please contact us via e-mail, info@roz.nl.

Raad voor
Onroerende Zaken

TCN Property Projects

TCN Property Projects
Symfonielaan 1
P.O. Box 7207
3430 JE Nieuwegein
The Netherlands
Tel.: +31 30 600 10 40
Fax: +31 30 630 01 22
E-mail: info@tcnpp.com
Website: www.tcnpp.com

TCN is a European asset developer, and with offices in the Netherlands, Germany, Portugal, Hungary and Belgium, the company operates all over Europe. TCN Property Projects is young and innovative and has a distinctive corporate culture.

TCN is growing fast to become one of the leading property companies in Europe. It distinguishes itself through innovative concepts, design and management. TCN uses an original and result-oriented approach to complex real estate projects. TCN has a workforce of more than 200 motivated employees, who project the company's image and relaxed atmosphere.

The Philosophy

TCN strives for a long-term involvement in all its projects and acts as investor, developer and manager. Value is created through the repositioning, redevelopment and trading of assets. The fastest-growing segment of TCN's business is in the privatization and re-development of existing real estate in cooperation with governments or semi-governments. TCN has proven to be a reliable partner in such processes whereby formerly state-owned assets are outsourced to private parties.

Think-Make-Do-Grow...

The core business departments of TCN are: Concepts, Development, Management and Assets. These units are in line with the entire life cycle of a property. TCN conceptualizes it, makes it and makes sure it is operated and owned effectively so that it can grow and mature.

TCN Programs

TCN Retail
TCN B2B
TCN@Work
TCN New Urban
TCN Cares

The TCN European Portfolio

TCN manages over 600,000 m^2 of real estate throughout Europe and has 400,000 m^2 under development. One of the largest projects in the Dutch portfolio is the Media Park in Hilversum. Examples of new activities in 2006 are: development study of AEP sites in and around Porto, Portugal; re-development of the Business Park Arnhem, the Netherlands; Public Private Partnership with the city of Muhlheim, Germany; development Retail Park Portimao, Portugal; purchase of the SIG Portfolio in Groningen, the Netherlands; and the development of two office complexes in Budapest, Hungary.

TCN is striving for further structural growth of its network in Europe, and is open to discuss this with potential local partners.

S. van Bohemen
TCN New Urban

R.F.C. Stroink
CEO

C. van Beurden
TCN International

E. Weimer
TCN Retail

N. Jansen
TCN Assets

G. Louwerse
TCN Concepts

R. de Jong
TCN Portugal

G. Simones
TCN Hungary

J. Reerink
TCN Germany

T. Weghorst
TCN Belgium

TWYNSTRA GUDDE CONSULTANTS AND MANAGERS

**Twynstra Gudde Consultants
and Managers**
Stationsplein 1
P.O. Box 907
3800 AX Amersfoort
The Netherlands
Tel.: +31 33 467 77 77
Fax: +31 33 467 76 66
E-mail: jgg@tg.nl
Website: www.twynstragudde.nl

Ir. J.L. Reijnen
*Urban and Regional
Development*

Ir. P.J. van Ruler
*Urban and Regional
Development*

Drs. W.E.M. Peper
*Urban and Regional
Development*

Mr. ing. M.E. Krul-
Seen
Land and Property

Ir. L.B. Scholte
*Real Estate Asset
Management*

Ir. P.P.G.M. Derks
*Accommodation
Development &
Consultancy*

Ing. C.E.M. Lemmens
*Accommodation
Management &
Consultancy*

Drs. H.L.M. van Lente
Urban Development

Drs. E. Koelé
Urban Development

E. van Savooyen
Parking Facilities

Twynstra Gudde

Twynstra Gudde Consultants and Managers is an independent Dutch management consultancy firm. For more than 40 years, Twynstra Gudde has operated as a network-company from its base in Amersfoort, where our professionals deliver appropriate and meaningful solutions to our clients. Our core competencies are project and program management, change management, management consulting and inter-organizational collaboration management.

Our aim is to provide solutions and deliver meaningful, measurable business benefits to our clients. We are convinced that sharing knowledge is key to our, and our clients' success. We do this by combining our visions and concepts with the latest scientific insights and developments, and by continuously bringing them into practice in cooperation with our clients.

Urban and Regional Development

Successful urban and regional development requires effective and close co-operation between those involved. Our consultants and (interim) managers operate successfully at different levels of urban and regional development. Our assignments come from local and regional authorities, central government, project developers, housing associations and health-care and education institutions.

We support our clients to form their goals and strategy. Moreover, we bring in process management and expertise from other fields of knowledge. The aim: achieving effective collaboration between public and private sectors. Not only do we support our clients in successful co-operation with other parties, we too regularly participate in networks and collaborate with a variety of players in specific projects, such as the Greenpark Project in Aalsmeer and Zuiderval in Enschede.

Our team is made up of specialists who cover strategic, urban and rural land-management, land and property financial-engineering and integrated parking policy.

Real Estate and Property Management

The success of an organization planning to relocate to new premises depends on the physical working environment and the facilities on offer. We recognize the significance of this by offering a pragmatic, result-oriented approach to facility and real estate issues. Our views on the development of property and accommodation are determined solely by the ambitions of the end users and the value to the owner. We believe that often, apparently conflicting interests can be dealt with harmoniously. Good property development is an attractive prospect for all concerned; it is a question of carefully coordinating the functional demands and the financial preconditions of all the parties involved. It's not only the physical end result that's important. The actual process of relocation has great significance for the end user. Relocation has the potential to be enormously symbolic and is also physically tangible.

VESTEDA GROUP

Vesteda Group
Plein 1992 1
P.O. Box 1211
6201 BE Maastricht
The Netherlands
Tel.: +31 43 329 66 66
Fax: +31 43 329 66 00
E-mail: info@vesteda.com
Website: www.vesteda.com

Mr. H.C.F. (Huub)
Smeets, Chairman
of the Board

F.H. (Frits) van der
Togt RA, Member of
the Board

O. (Onno) Breur
Member of the
Board

Ir. N. (Nico) Mol
Director Vesteda
Project BV

Ir. G.J.A.M. (Ger)
Römgens MRE
Director Strategy,
Asset Management &
Product Development

Mr. P. (Peter)
Keller MRE MRICS
Director Property
Management

Vesteda Group is a property fund focusing exclusively on residential property. With over 30,000 residential properties with a total value in excess of €4 billion, Vesteda is the largest residential property fund in the Netherlands. Vesteda concentrates on the higher-rent segment, with rents from €550 per month. As well as letting, Vesteda also develops higher-rent homes.

Vesteda is not listed on the stock exchange. Vesteda's shareholders are institutional investors: banks, insurance companies and pension funds. Investing in residential property offers these professional investors significant added value in the composition of their portfolios. Thanks in part to its size, Vesteda's invested capital is well diversified across geographical markets and price segments.

Vesteda focuses on modern and sustainable apartments and houses in the Dutch residential market, mainly for people over 50 and younger, single-person and dual-income households. These target groups are, like their homes, concentrated in and around large and medium-sized towns. Vesteda is the only property fund of its size in Europe that performs its own property letting and management. Vesteda offices in central locations in major urban areas, known as Woongaleries, handle the promotion of the brand, letting and personal customer contacts during the tenancy.

A key element of Vesteda's investment strategy is regular sales of a limited number of properties. Sales are linked to a similar number of residential properties being added to the portfolio each year. This structural renewal contributes to achieving and maintaining the desired geographical and qualitative composition of the portfolio, and consolidating capital gains.

The new, high-quality projects which are added to the investment portfolio are acquired and developed by Vesteda Project bv, Vesteda Group's in-house project development company. By participating in area developments Vesteda exercises influence on the quality of public spaces and urban development.

Vesteda Group employs over 300 people in a young and dynamic organization. Vesteda's size means it is able to maintain a cost-efficient, wide and deep professional organization where surveys and market research underlie the investment, sale and purchase policies.

La Fenêtre, CS-quadrant · The Hague, the Netherlands

Nieuw Park Leeuwensteijn, Sijtwende – Voorburg, the Netherlands

Boston, Oostelijk Havengebied – Amsterdam, the Netherlands

Montevideo, Wilhelminapier – Rotterdam, the Netherlands

Detroit, Oostelijk Havengebied – Amsterdam, the Netherlands

Vesteda-toren, Vestdijk – Eindhoven, the Netherlands

WHO'S WHO

VASLOC BEHEER

Vasloc Beheer
P.O. Box 2075
3500 GB Utrecht
The Netherlands
Tel: +31 232 67 50
Fax: +31 232 67 59
E-mail: info@vasloc.nl
Website: www.vasloc.nl
Contact: P.A.M. de Heer

P.A.M. de Heer
Managing Director

As manager of Basisfonds Stationslocaties, Vasloc Beheer invests and manages the assets of the two participation holders, NS Vastgoed and Vastgoedfonds Stationslocaties. Vastgoedfonds Stationslocaties is a closed-end investment company that offers institutional investors the opportunity to invest in real estate properties at public transport junctions with the objective of obtaining a yield in accordance with market conditions and with an acceptable risk profile.

Since the establishment of Basisfonds Stationslocaties in 1999, Vasloc Beheer has managed the Fund's real estate portfolio with the objective of expanding the Fund's investment portfolio to a value of €670 million within the first planning period. To realize growth, real estate located at public transport junctions is purchased from NS Vastgoed and other parties. This real estate can consist of a variety of properties, but for now, the emphasis is on office buildings.

Since Basisfonds Stationslocaties is directed toward portfolio growth, their core activity is the purchase, not sale, of real estate. In principle, this means a long-term investment. Because the real estate purchased will remain in their portfolio for a long period of time, Vasloc Beheer considers good location management to be of great importance in maintaining the quality – and value – of its real estate.

The financing of Vasloc Beheer's present and future real estate portfolio is handled by the two participation holders. Vastgoedfonds Stationlocaties' stock is distributed among a number of Dutch funds.

Pharos, Hoofddorp.

AMSTERDAM DEVELOPMENT CORPORATION

**Amsterdam Development
Corporation**
Weesperplein 8
P.O. Box 1104
1000 BC Amsterdam
The Netherlands
Tel.: +31 20 552 6111
Website: www.oga.amsterdam.nl

*Paul Cohen
Communications
Manager*

*Edo Arnoldussen
CEO*

*Hetty Vlug
Managing Director
Project Development*

*Bob van der Zande
Managing Director
Programming &
Coordination*

According to CEO Edo Arnoldussen, a key ambition of the Development Corporation (DC) is to "give regular new impetus to the city's development, by launching well thought-out projects that balance costs and gains. In addition the aim is to act as a knowledge center for area development." The DC concentrates on land development and housing expertise within its organization.

Introduction

The DC's core activity is the realization of the city's targets with regard to area and real estate development, working in conjunction with local district councils, other municipal services and market parties. This entails acquiring and preparing sites and/or areas for building, and creating conditions for the realization of real estate for living, working and facilities. In addition, the department manages the city's land on long lease. The City of Amsterdam holds no less than 80% of the land within the city limits. Moreover, the DC is responsible for guiding urban renewal and housing programs in the various city districts, as well as managing buildings and parking garages.

The organization has extensive expertise in the areas of contracts, planned economy, the formulation and calculation of building schemes and the restructuring of city areas. The DC has a good overview of market developments and makes strategic decisions accordingly.

Enterprising and encouraging

In Amsterdam, the DC has the central responsibility for the city's area and real estate development, acting in the capacity of project manager, advisor, negotiator, commissioner or fund manager. The most important clients are central city government and the local district councils of the City of Amsterdam. In addition, the department collaborates with market parties in various partnerships and a variety of capacities. The DC adopts an enterprising attitude, striving to initiate, stimulate and inspire developments. It identifies bottlenecks and obstacles, formulates solutions and, if necessary, is responsible for implementing the chosen solution.

One of the focal points in the development of new plans is the balancing of costs, gains, phasing and quality. In each stage of the urban planning process advice is given with regard to the feasibility of area and real estate concepts. The organization has thorough financial expertise within the town-planning sector, and this knowledge, in combination with the department's years of experience, supports its ambition to maximize the benefits for the community.

City of Amsterdam
Development Corporation

WHO'S WHO

CITY OF THE HAGUE

City of The Hague
Urban Development Department
P.O. Box 12655
2500 DP The Hague
The Netherlands
Tel.: +31 70 353 49 75 or
Tel.: +31 70 353 48 53
Fax: +31 70 353 47 03 or
Fax: +31 70 353 42 33
E-mail: b.kerner@dso.denhaag.nl
a.verwoest@dso.denhaag.nl
Website: www.denhaag.com

*Ted Zwietering
Director, The Hague
Development
Company*

*Bart Kerner
Department
Manager,
Process and Project
Management*

*Anita Verwoest
Communication
Adviser*

After New York, Vienna and Geneva, The Hague is the fourth largest United Nations city in the world. It is a gateway to Europe and the home of many headquarters and almost all the international organizations in the field of peace and the administration of justice. The Hague is international and prestigious, and exudes style on all fronts: in the spacious layout of the city, in the stately buildings and in the new architecture.

The Hague works

The Hague assumes a unique position in the fields of justice, politics and diplomacy. That success forms the basis of the strategy for the future. The policy is geared to providing high-quality accommodation and facilities to renowned organizations and companies. A city that creates the right set-up conditions has the best cards in its hand to attract organizations. All organizations, concerns and institutions that want to feel at home in Europe quickly and without any problems are attracted to The Hague, with its daring architecture and extensive facilities.

Global city by the sea

The municipality of The Hague is working on a Spatial Development Strategy: a vision of the future in terms of the city's spatial structure and development. In doing so we want to stimulate thought about the future of the city. A livable city and society – for us, our children, and our grandchildren. That's what it's all about.

We have identified three development zones: the coast and global city, the center zone, and the A4-zone. These developments offer the unique possibility for investors to establish their business in a renewing and international setting.

The Hague New Center

A stone's throw from the historical heart of the nation's politics, the city council and various market players are working together under the The Hague New Center flag (www.denhaagnieuwcentrum.nl) on a new and attractive part of the city. Nowhere else in Holland has an inner-city project of this size been realized in such a short time. In roughly 10 years the area between the Central Station and the Spui has undergone a real metamorphosis with an unusual mix of workplaces, homes and shops. The area is easily accessible from all sides.

Numerous developments

Besides The Hague New Center, the municipality of The Hague and various private parties have developed a large number of projects in the Laakhaven business park. The Hague's position as an international center of justice and peace is further enhanced by the development of the area surrounding the World Forum Convention Center with Europol and ICC. The Binckhorst area will also be provided with a new office site and the former Caballero factory site is set to be completely redeveloped with innovative facilities, cultural activities, offices, public space and catering facilities.

Gemeente Den Haag

ROTTERDAM DEVELOPMENT CORPORATION

**Rotterdam Development
Corporation (OBR)**

P.O. Box 6575
3002 AN Rotterdam
The Netherlands
Tel.: +31 10 489 36 85
Fax: +31 10 489 71 49
E-mail: r.jongste@obr.rotterdam.nl
Website: www.obr.rotterdam.nl
Contact: R. Jongste

R. Jongste
Co-ordinator
External Relations
Communication and
Public Affairs

Rotterdam is a city that has undergone massive change over the last ten years. From a traditional port – the second largest in the world today – to a city with a high quality and innovative (service) economy, with impressive architecture, an excellent supply of cultural and recreational facilities and an international population. As the economic and cultural center of the Rijnmond region (1.2 million inhabitants), Rotterdam (600,000 inhabitants) is an important front-runner of the Dutch economy. The city is working on a total renovation of its city center, the redevelopment of its old docks and the even further improvement of its cultural, recreational and tourist amenities.

City air provides air to breathe. That certainly applies to Rotterdam, the city of light, air and space. It's also a city where you will meet people of 160 different nationalities. The Maas river contributes to creating space, as a place where people can live, relax and enjoy water activities. Many old docks are being redeveloped, of which De Kop van Zuid is an excellent example. These areas will regain the attention of inhabitants, companies and visitors alike when houses, offices, shops and the hospitality trade are developed here, making the city even more attractive and more international. The redevelopment of the Central Station Area also contributes towards this goal.

It will undergo a massive metamorphosis as the new traffic junction for the High Speed Train (HSL), but also as a new central area for hotels, shops, offices and all kinds of other leisure amenities. In short, over the next few years Rotterdam will see a massive change.

It is justifiable to conclude that Rotterdam is an international city. And over the next few years even more projects will be on the way, such as the renovation of the Central Station Area and the urban redevelopment of certain city center locations, including a completely new medical center. Rotterdam is a city on the move!

UTRECHT, MEETING PLACE FOR TALENT

Real Estate Department
City of Utrecht
Vliegend Hertlaan 1-11
P.O. Box 8613
3503 RP Utrecht
The Netherlands
Tel.: +31 30 286 42 82
Fax: +31 30 286 71 40
E-mail: ogu.info@utrecht.nl
Websites: www.utrecht.nl
          www.leidscherijn.nl
          www.utrecht.nl/stationsgebied

Utrecht can be described as a meeting place for talent. The city is located centrally and strategically on the A2, A12 and A27 highways and has a highly-educated young labor force, an attractive investment climate and good infrastructure. The presence of the largest university in the Netherlands and various other research institutes contribute to Utrecht's profile as a center of knowledge. Additionally, many large businesses and financial services companies are headquartered here. Moreover, the historic, culturally-rich center makes the city a lovely place to live, visit and meet other people. Utrecht is also an ideal place for creative people to work and live. They comprise 33% of the Utrecht labor force, mainly working in media, arts and design: the highest percentage in the country.

Drs. Harm Janssen
Alderman of Real
Estate

Drs. Ton van
Vlimmeren
Director Real
Estate Department

Utrecht is under major redevelopment. Over the next ten years four large-area development projects will be in the works.

Leidsche Rijn, the construction of an urban district for 80,000 inhabitants
- 30,000 residences
- 720,000 m^2 of office space
- 270 hectares of business estate
- schools, shops, a hospital and many other facilities

Drs. Jo de Viet
Head Economic
Affairs Department

Ruud Nijveld
Executive Manager
Real Estate
Department

Utrecht Central Railway Station Area, the renovation and enhancement of the Central Station and its surrounding area
- a new central railway and bus station
- 2,320 residences
- 204,000 m^2 of office space
- 48,050 m^2 of shops, restaurants and cafes
- 33,500 m^2 of cultural facilities and 16,700 m^2 of hotel facilities
- 63,000 m^2 of leisure facilities

Drs. Nora Hugenholtz
Project Manager
Leidsche Rijn

Drs. Klaas Beerda
Office Consultant
Economic Affairs

Reconstruction of the existing city
- 10,000 new residences in repurposed locations
- 9,500 residences demolished and replaced with 9,000 new residential units
- 3,000 residences will be renovated

Drs. Ank Joosten
Marketing Manager
Economic Affairs

Aad Lafeber
Sales Manager
Real Estate
Department

Improvements to the main infrastructure
- 100% increase in railway tracks and creation of five new city stations
- construction of the HOV, a bus priority lane, to the university center
- widening of the A2 and peak traffic lanes on the A27 and A28
- improving accessibility to the city by altering traffic junctions

Gemeente Utrecht

development creates **space**

ace for others space for **motion** space for
space for yourself space for living space
r conversation space for beauty space for
ace for opinions space for business space for
space for **pleasure** space for motion
thoughts space for yourself space for
space for living space for
work space for opinions space for
space for pleasure space for others
motion space for thoughts space for
space for living space for **conversation**
ace for beauty space for work space for opinions
ace for business space for pleasure space for
hers space for motion space for thoughts
ace for **yourself** space for living space for
nversation space for beauty space for **opinions**
ace for business space for pleasure space
r work space for others space for conversation

MODULUS VASTGOED ONDERNEMINGEN

-*Architecture is a visual art,
and the buildings speak for themselves-*
(Julia Morgan)

It's the people working at REDEVCO who make this real estate company what it is today:
a highly professional organisation that works in accordance with standards and values that
it has set out for itself. An organisation that seeks to find a balance between its commercial
objectives and the social context it operates in. REDEVCO NEDERLAND in Amsterdam is
responsible for the management and further expansion of the Dutch portfolio. This portfolio consists of around 100 retail properties, mostly on A1 locations in major shopping
streets, as well as a number of office buildings and logistics centres. To achieve its growth
target REDEVCO NEDERLAND aims to invest primarily in retail real estate, both in city
centres and on the periphery.

REDEVCO
business in balance

www.redevco.com

Asset Managers

ABN AMRO Asset Management
P.O. Box 283
1000 EA AMSTERDAM
Tel.: +31 20 629 54 17
Fax: +31 20 628 42 26
E-mail: wouter.weijand@abnamro.com
www.abnamro.com
Contact: W. Weijand

• • • • • • • • • • • • • • • • • • •

Achmea Vastgoed B.V.
P.O. Box 59347
1040 KH AMSTERDAM
Tel.: +31 20 606 56 00
Fax: +31 20 606 56 09
E-mail: vastgoedinfo@achmea.nl
www.achmeavastgoed.nl

• • • • • • • • • • • • • • • • • • •

Aegon Asset Management
P.O. Box 202
2501 CE THE HAGUE
Tel.: +31 70 344 72 09
Fax: +31 70 344 87 06

• • • • • • • • • • • • • • • • • • •

AKRON Group
Hoofdweg Oostzijde 850-B
2132 MC HOOFDDORP
Tel.: +31 23 554 09 80
Fax: +31 23 554 09 88
www.akron-group.com
E-mail: p.ulm@akron-group.com
www.akron-group.com
Contact: P. Ulm, CEO

• • • • • • • • • • • • • • • • • • •

Annexum Invest
P.O. Box 75215
1070 AE AMSTERDAM
Tel.: +31 20 575 09 52
Fax: +31 20 557 09 51

• • • • • • • • • • • • • • • • • • •

Bouwfonds Asset Management
P.O. Box 15
3870 DA HOEVELAKEN
Tel.: +31 33 750 47 50
Fax: +31 33 750 47 77
www.bouwfonds.nl
Contact: J. Klijnen

• • • • • • • • • • • • • • • • • • •

Cristel Vastgoed
Wouburgseweg 9
2405 ED ALPHEN A/D RIJN
TEl.: +31 172 51 87 41
Fax: +31 172 51 80 83

• • • • • • • • • • • • • • • • • • •

Equity Estate B.V.
Kabelweg 37
1014 BA AMSTERDAM
Tel.: +31 20 488 14 42
Fax: +31 20 688 97 03
E-mail: vanerkelens@equityestate.nl
Contact: E. van Erkelens

FGH Real Estate Asset Management
Koningslaan 33
1075 AB AMSTERDAM
Tel.: +31 20 751 08 54
Fax: +31 20 677 67 80
www.fghbank.nl

• • • • • • • • • • • • • • • • • • •

ING Asset Management
P.O. Box 810
1000 AV AMSTERDAM
Tel.: +31 20 541 54 11
Fax: +31 20 541 54 12
www.ing.com
Contact: A.H. van Toorn

• • • • • • • • • • • • • • • • • • •

ING Real Estate Investment Management
P.O. Box 90463
2509 LL THE HAGUE
Tel.: +31 70 341 93 08
Fax: +31 70 341 94 18
www.ingrealestate.com

• • • • • • • • • • • • • • • • • • •

Mn Services
P.O. Box 5210
2280 HE RIJSWIJK ZH
Tel.: +31 70 316 02 62
Fax: +31 70 316 05 05
E-mail: info@mn-services.nl
www.mn-services.nl
Contact: Richard Th. van Ovost Msc. MRE MRICS

• • • • • • • • • • • • • • • • • • •

MPC Capital N.V.
P.O. Box 239
1200 AE HILVERSUM
Tel.: +31 35 523 24 00
Fax: +31 35 523 24 09

Banking & Financial Services

Aareal Bank AG
Stadhouderskade 14-E
1054 ES AMSTERDAM
Tel.: +31 20 589 86 60
Fax: +31 20 589 86 66
E-mail: infoamsterdam@aareal-bank.com
www.aareal-bank.com
Contact: P.W.H.M. van de Kimmenade,
Mr. J.M. Hendriks

ABN AMRO Bank N.V.
P.O. Box 283
1000 EA AMSTERDAM
Tel.: +31 20 628 89 00
Fax: +31 20 629 54 86
www.abnamro.com

• • • • • • • • • • • • • • • • • • •

Bouwfonds Property Finance
P.O. Box 15
3870 DA HOEVELAKEN
Tel.: +31 33 253 91 10
Fax: +31 33 253 91 09
E-mail: property.finance@bouwfonds.nl
www.bouwfonds.nl
Contact: J. Visscher,
R. Overbeek,
A.W. van Rijn,
D.M. Melchiors,
Ch. de Koste,

• • • • • • • • • • • • • • • • • • •

Deloitte Real Estate B.V.
P.O. Box 59156
1040 KD AMSTERDAM
Tel.: +31 20 582 50 61
Fax: +31 20 582 50 86

• • • • • • • • • • • • • • • • • • •

Van Doorn Securities
Dam 27
1012 JS AMSTERDAM
Tel.: +31 20 530 63 53
Fax: +31 20 530 63 50

• • • • • • • • • • • • • • • • • • •

Eurohypo
Strawinskylaan 381
1077 ZX AMSTERDAM
Tel.: +31 20 799 36 00
Fax: +31 20 799 36 79

• • • • • • • • • • • • • • • • • • •

FGH Bank N.V.
P.O. Box 2244
3500 GE UTRECHT
Tel.: +31 30 232 39 11
Fax: +31 30 233 45 72
E-mail: info@fgh.nl
www.fghbank.nl

• • • • • • • • • • • • • • • • • • •

ING Real Estate Finance
P.O. Box 90463
2509 LL THE HAGUE
Tel.: +31 70 341 94 70
Fax: +31 70 341 91 95
www.ingrealestate.com

• • • • • • • • • • • • • • • • • • •

ING Real Estate Finance East
P.O. Box 90153
5600 RE EINDHOVEN
Tel.: +31 40 203 41 00
Fax: +31 40 203 41 58
www.ingrealestate.com
Contact: R. Marx

• • • • • • • • • • • • • • • • • • •

ING Real Estate Finance North West
P.O. Box 23432
1100 DX AMSTERDAM
Tel.: +31 20 594 54 10
Fax: +31 20 594 56 04
www.ingrealestate.com
Contact: R. Zwager

• • • • • • • • • • • • • • • • • • •

ING Real Estate Finance South West
P.O. Box 2338
3000 CH ROTTERDAM
Tel.: +31 10 444 64 74
Fax: +31 10 444 64 84
www.ingrealestate.com
Contact:
L. van den Boogaard

• • • • • • • • • • • • • • • • • • •

Investate Financiering B.V.
P.O. Box 299
3000 AG ROTTERDAM
Tel.: +31 10 243 96 40
Fax: +31 10 243 96 45

• • • • • • • • • • • • • • • • • • •

Marsh B.V.
Insurance Brokers
P.O. Box 8900
3009 AX ROTTERDAM
Tel.: +31 10 406 09 22
Fax: +31 10 420 68 06

• • • • • • • • • • • • • • • • • • •

De Nederlandsche Bank
P.O. Box 98
1000 AB AMSTERDAM
Tel.: +31 20 524 91 11
Fax: +31 20 524 25 00

• • • • • • • • • • • • • • • • • • •

NIB Capital Bank N.V.
Corporate Finance
P.O. Box 75583
1070 AN AMSTERDAM
Tel.: +31 20 540 74 74
Fax: +31 20 540 74 00

• • • • • • • • • • • • • • • • • • •

Kempen & Co
P.O. Box 75666
1070 AR AMSTERDAM
Tel.: +31 20 348 80 00
Fax: +31 20 348 84 00
E-mail: mber@kempen.nl
www.kempen.nl
Contact: H. de Haan,
M. Berkelder,
P. Pruijmboom, P.H. Budde

• • • • • • • • • • • • • • • • • • •

PricewaterhouseCoopers Real Estate Group
P.O. Box 22735
1100 DE AMSTERDAM
Tel.: +31 20 568 66 66
Fax: +31 20 568 68 88
www.pwc.com/nl

• • • • • • • • • • • • • • • • • • •

Developers (1)

3W
P.O. Box 4525
6202 SB MAASTRICHT
Tel.: +31 43 366 77 00
Fax: +31 43 365 21 28
E-mail: info@3wvastgoed.nl
www.3winfo.nl
Contact: N.H.K.J. Eurlings

Alliantie Ontwikkeling bv
P.O. Box 95
1270 AB HUIZEN
Tel.: +31 35 528 07 00
Fax: +31 35 528 07 15
E-mail: info@de-alliantie.nl
www.de-alliantie.nl

AM NV
P.O. Box 520
3430 AM Nieuwegein
Tel.: + 31 30 609 72 22
Fax.: + 31 30 605 08 74
info@ameurope.nl
www.ameurope.com
Contact: P.G.A. Noordanus
P. Ruigrok

AMVEST
P.O. Box 12446
1100 AK AMSTERDAM ZO
Tel.: +31 20 430 12 12
Fax: +31 20 430 12 13
E-mail: info@amvest.nl
www.amvest.nl
Contact: Drs. M.W.A. Maas

Apron Development B.V.
P.O. Box 464
2980 AL RIDDERKERK
Tel.: +31 180 46 25 55
Fax: +31 180 41 72 77
E-mail: info@apron.nl
www.apron.nl

**Avantis European Science
and Business Park**
Snellius 8
6422 RM HEERLEN
Tel.: +31 45 568 81 10
Fax: +31 45 544 55 83
E-mail:
reneseijben@avantis.org
www.avantis.org
Contact: R. Seijben

BAA McArthur Glen
P.O. Box 219
6040 AE ROERMOND
Tel.: +31 475 31 58 75

BAM Vastgoed
P.O. Box 50
3980 CB BUNNIK
Tel.: +31 30 659 89 55
Fax: +31 30 659 82 80
E-mail:
bunnik@bamvastgoed.nl
www.bamvastgoed.nl
Contact: Ir. R. de Jong MBA

Besix
P.O. Box 8
2990 AA BARENDRECHT
Tel.: +31 180 64 19 90
Fax: +31 180 64 19 91
E-mail: hpost@besix.com
www.besix.com

Blauwhoed BV
P.O. Box 2552
3000 CN ROTTERDAM
Tel.: +31 10 453 53 11
Fax: +31 10 452 63 53
E-mail: info@blauwhoed.nl
www.blauwhoed.nl
Contact:
mr. drs. J.F.Ph. Houben

**Bouwfonds Property
Development / Bouwfonds
MAB Ontwikkeling**
P.O. Box 15
3870 DA HOEVELAKEN
Tel.: +31 33 253 97 00
Fax: +31 33 253 96 85
E-mail: ontwikkeling@
bouwfonds.nl
www.bouwfonds.nl
Contact:
H.J.M. van Zandvoort,
I.M. Kalisvaart, J.J.M. Franck

BPF Bouwinvest
P.O. Box 56045
1040 AA AMSTERDAM
Tel.: +31 20 583 16 00
Fax: +31 20 583 17 00
E-mail:
info@bpfbouwinvest.nl
www.bpfbouwinvest.nl

Van den Bruele Kaufman
Maliebaan 57
3581 CE UTRECHT
Tel.: +31 30 234 35 75
Fax: +31 30 236 47 06

Burgfonds B.V.
P.O. Box 130
5300 AC ZALTBOMMEL
Tel.: +31 418 68 11 33
Fax: +31 418 68 09 56
E-mail: info@burgfonds.nl
www.burgfonds.nl

Concire
'Willemswerf', Boompjes 40
P.O. Box 2325
3000 CH ROTTERDAM
Tel.: +31 10 240 35 10
Fax: +31 10 240 35 25
E-mail: info@concire.nl
www.concire.nl

**Crescendo Investment
Group B.V.**
P.O. Box 1208
5200 BG DEN BOSCH
Tel.: +31 73 614 22 11
Fax: +31 73 614 16 89

Delta Ontwikkelingsgroep
Binnen Kalkhaven 39
P.O. Box 9
3300 AA DORDRECHT
Tel.: +31 78 614 08 44
Fax: +31 78 614 04 64
E-mail: info@delta
ontwikkelingsgroep.nl
www.deltaontwikkelings
groep.nl

**Fortis Vastgoed
Ontwikkeling**
P.O. Box 2009
3500 GA UTRECHT
Tel.: +31 30 257 35 12
Fax: +31 30 257 81 96
E-mail:
info@fortisvastgoed.com
www.fortisvastgoed
ontwikkeling.nl
Contact: F.H. Kooistra,
H. van den Hoeven,
L.M. Visser

Foruminvest B.V.
P.O. Box 5169
1410 AD NAARDEN
Tel.: +31 35 695 60 60
Fax: +31 35 694 72 10
E-mail: info@foruminvest.nl
www.foruminvest.nl
Contact:
Drs. M.S. Riaskoff,
Drs. D. Ermia

**Gerard W. Bakker
Projektadviezen**
Beethovenstraat 89
1077 HS AMSTERDAM
Tel.: +31 20 670 26 41
Fax: +31 20 670 26 21

De Groene Groep
P.O. Box 23037
3001 KA ROTTERDAM
Tel.: +31 10 440 30 00
Fax: +31 10 440 30 01
info@degroenegroep.nl
www.degroenegroep.nl
Contact:
Ir. P.T.A.J. van Drunen

G&S Vastgoed B.V.
P.O. Box 75030
1070 AA AMSTERDAM
Tel.: +31 20 673 37 79
Fax: +31 20 679 91 72
E-mail: j.f.blackmore@
gensvastgoed.nl
www.gensvastgoed.nl
Contact: J.F. Blackmore

Heijmans Vastgoed
P.O. Box 2
5240 BB ROSMALEN
Tel.: +31 73 543 51 11
Fax: +31 73 543 53 00
www.heijmans.nl

**Heilijgers
Projectontwikkeling bv**
P.O. Box 340
3800 AH AMERSFOORT
Tel.: +31 33 454 57 00
Fax: +31 33 454 57 03
projectontwikkeling@
heilijgers.nl
www.heilijgers.nl
Contact: F.P. Lambert

Developers (2)

Hillen & Roosen Groep B.V.
P.O. Box 75950
1070 AZ AMSTERDAM
Tel.: +31 20 541 95 41
Fax: +31 20 541 95 42
E-mail:
info@hillen-roosen.nl
www.hillen-roosen.nl

Van Hoogevest Groep
P.O. Box 161
3800 AD AMERSFOORT
Tel.: +31 33 463 04 94
Fax: +31 33 465 03 32
E-mail: info@hoogevest.nl
www.hoogevest.nl
Contact:
Ir. M. van Hoogevest

**ING Real Estate
Development**
P.O. Box 90463
2509 LL THE HAGUE
Tel.: +31 70 341 93 19
Fax: +31 70 341 84 19
E-mail: ingreinfo@
ingrealestate.com
www.ingrealestate.com

IPMMC Vastgoed
Janssoniuslaan 80
P.O. Box 85457 UTRECHT
Tel.: +31 30 281 73 00
Fax: +31 30 281 70 15
www.ipmmc.nl

**Johan Matser
Projectontwikkeling B.V.**
P.O. Box 334
1200 AH HILVERSUM
Tel.: +31 35 626 00 00
Fax: +31 35 626 00 11
E-mail: info@johanmatser.nl
www.johanmatser.nl
Contact: Ir. J.C. Padberg,
Ir. C.E.C. de Reus

Kroon Vastgoed B.V.
Biltstraat 206
3572 BS UTRECHT
Tel.: +31 30 275 97 97
Fax: +31 30 275 97 98
info@kroonvastgoed.nl
www.kroonvastgoed.nl
Contact: Dhr. E. Kroon

Leyten en Partners B.V.
Westersingel 16
3014 GN ROTTERDAM
Tel.: +31 10 436 40 33
Fax: +31 10 436 62 25

**Lisman Inter Holding B.V.
Interprojekt Holding B.V.**
P.O. Box 3037
5203 DA DEN BOSCH
Tel.: +31 73 648 86 00
Fax: +31 73 644 99 79
E-mail: info@lih-vg.com
www.lih-vg.com
Contact: Ing. J.W.G. Sanders

LSI project investment nv
P.O. Box 30065
3001 DB ROTTERDAM
Tel.: +31 10 412 12 39
Fax: +31 10 412 14 36
www.lsi-nv.nl
Contact: L. Smits,
V. Ollefers, D. de Boer

**Maasstede Vastgoed
Ontwikkeling V.O.F.**
Wijnhaven 17
3011 WH ROTTERDAM
Tel.: +31 10 436 66 66
Fax: +31 10 266 24 43
info@maasstede.com
www.maasstede.com
Contact: Mr. R.A. Nederlof,
Drs. C.A. Kerkhoven

MEAC Vastgoed BV
Parklaan 38
1405 BUSSUM
Tel.: +31 35 698 47 41
Fax: +31 35 698 47 42
info@meacvastgoed.nl
www.meacvastgoed.nl
Contact: A.C. Groeneveld,
P.P.M. Fabriek

**Modulus Property
Development and
Investment**
Jan Thijssenweg 2
2289 AA RIJSWIJK (ZH)
Tel.: +31 70 307 00 03
Fax: +31 70 307 00 04
E-mail: info@mvgo.nl
www.mvgo.nl

Moes Projectontwikkeling BV
P.O. Box 127
8000 AC ZWOLLE
Tel.: +31 38 429 66 66
Fax: +31 38 429 66 90
E-mail: projectontw@
moesbouw.nl
www.moesbouw.nl

**Monteflore Vastgoed-
ontwikkelingen B.V.**
Naritaweg 108
1043 CA AMSTERDAM
Tel.: +31 20 419 31 70
Fax: +31 20 419 31 75
info@monteflore.com
www.monteflore.com
Contact: Ir. A. van Namen

Multi Development BV
Hanzeweg 16
P.O. Box 875
2800 AW GOUDA
Tel.: +31 182 690 900
Fax: +31 182 690 690
E-mail: info@multi-
development.com
www.multi-development.
com

**Van Namen + Partners
Vastgoedontwikkelingen B.V.**
Naritaweg 108
1043 CA AMSTERDAM
Tel.: +31 20 419 31 80
Fax: +31 20 419 31 85
E-mail: info@vannamen
partners.com
Contact: Ir. A. van Namen

Nemaco B.V.
P.O. Box 75267
1070 AG AMSTERDAM
Tel.: +31 20 570 38 90
Fax: +31 20 570 38 98
E-mail: email@nemaco-
development.nl
www.nemaco-
development.nl

**NHP Macobouw Project-
ontwikkeling B.V.**
P.O. Box 9445
1800 GK ALKMAAR
Tel.: +31 72 506 85 40
Fax: +31 72 506 85 41
E-mail:
info@nhpmacobouw.nl
www.nhpmacobouw.nl

NS Vastgoed
P.O. Box 2319
3500 GH UTRECHT
Tel.: +31 30 300 43 00
Fax: +31 30 300 44 00
E-mail: nsv.info@ns.nl
www.nsvastgoed.nl
Contact:
C.A.M. de Boo, P. Rutte

Óbidos Vastgoed B.V.
P.O. Box 75919
1070 AX AMSTERDAM
Tel.: +31 20 570 78 87
Fax: +31 20 570 78 88
E-mail: info@obidos.nl
www.obidos.nl
Contact:
Drs. R.J.T.M. Velthuyse

**Ontwikkelingsbedrijf
Vathorst Beheer B.V.**
Duisterweg 6
3829 MP
HOOGLANDERVEEN
Tel.: +31 33 451 10 10
Fax: +31 33 451 10 11
E-mail: info@vathorst.com
www.vathorst.com
Contact:
F.W.A. van der Horst

Provastgoed Nederland B.V.
P.O. Box 16395
2500 BJ THE HAGUE
Tel.: +31 70 308 10 30
Fax: +31 70 361 40 44

Rabo Vastgoed B.V.
P.O. Box 17100
3500 HG UTRECHT
Tel.: +31 30 216 17 19
Fax: +31 30 216 33 75
E-mail: rabovastgoed@
rn.rabobank.nl
www.rabovastgoed.nl
Contact: P. Wetselaar

Schiphol Real Estate B.V.
P.O. Box 75776
1118 ZX SCHIPHOL
Tel.: +31 20 601 28 88
Fax: +31 20 601 32 01
realestate@schiphol.nl
www.schiphol.com/realestate
Contact:
A.A. Mast M.Sc. FRICS

Sterner Groep B.V.
P.O. Box 8721
3009 AS ROTTERDAM
Tel.: +31 10 286 13 33
Fax: +31 10 251 89 90
E-mail: info@sterner.nl
www.sterner.nl

**STRABAG Bouw en
Ontwikkeling B.V.**
P.O. Box 3043
3301 DA DORDRECHT
Tel.: +31 78 654 77 66
Fax: +31 78 654 77 99
E-mail: info@strabag.nl
www.strabag.nl
Contact: J.M. Post

Takenaka Netherlands B.V.
P.O. Box 58024
1040 HA AMSTERDAM
Tel.: +31 20 686 61 01
Fax: +31 20 686 86 18

TCN Property Projects
P.O. Box 7207
3430 JE NIEUWEGEIN
Tel.: +31 30 600 10 40
Fax: +31 30 630 01 22
E-mail: info@tcnpp.com
www.tcnpp.com
Contact: C. van Beurden

**Trimp & van Tartwijk
Property Development NV**
Zuidplein 140
1077 XV AMSTERDAM
Tel.: +31 20 575 21 70
Fax: +31 20 575 21 69
E-mail: development@
trimpenvantartwijk.nl
www.trimpenvan
tartwijk.nl

Vesteda Group B.V.
P.O. Box 1211
6201 BE MAASTRICHT
Tel.: +31 43 329 66 66
Fax: +31 43 329 66 00
E-mail: info@vesteda.com
www.vesteda.com

Volker Wessels Vastgoed
P.O. Box 7317
2701 AH ZOETERMEER
Tel.: +31 79 368 06 80
Fax: +31 79 368 06 00

William Properties B.V.
P.O. Box 1012
3000 BA ROTTERDAM
Tel.: +31 10 206 46 46
Fax: +31 10 206 46 56
E-mail:
info@williamproperties.nl
www.williamproperties.nl

Federation / Association

Aedes, Vereniging van Woningcorporaties
P.O. Box 611
1200 AP HILVERSUM
Tel.: +31 35 626 82 00
Fax: +31 35 626 82 11
E-mail:
aedes@aedeswcp.nl
www.aedeswcp.nl

AVBB Algemeen Verbond van Bouwondernemingen
P.O. Box 90603
2509 LP THE HAGUE
Tel.: +31 70 328 62 00
Fax: +31 70 324 49 00
E-mail: avbb@avbb.nl
www.avbb.nl

Centraal Fonds Volkshuisvesting (CFV)
P.O. Box 5075
1410 AB NAARDEN
Tel.: +31 35 695 40 70
Fax: +31 35 695 40 80
E-mail: info@cfv.nl
www.cfv.nl

EIB Economisch Instituut voor de Bouwnijverheid
De Cuserstraat 89
1081 CN AMSTERDAM
Tel.: +31 20 642 93 42
Fax: +31 20 644 90 89
E-mail: eib@eib.nl
www.eib.nl

EPRA European Public Real Estate Association
Schiphol Boulevard 283
1118 BH SCHIPHOL
Tel.: +31 20 405 38 30
Fax: +31 20 405 38 40
E-mail: info@epra.com
www.epra.com
Contact:
N.J.M. van Ommen

IVBN
P.O. Box 620
2270 AP VOORBURG
Tel.: +31 70 300 03 71
Fax: +31 70 369 43 79
E-mail: info@ivbn.nl
www.ivbn.nl
Contact:
F.J.W. van Blokland

NEPROM
P.O. Box 620
2270 AP VOORBURG
Tel.: +31 70 386 62 64
Fax: +31 70 387 40 89
E-mail: bureau@neprom.nl
www.neprom.nl
Contact: J. Fokkema

NFIA Netherlands Foreign Investment Agency
P.O. Box 20101
2500 EC THE HAGUE
Tel.: +31 70 379 88 18
Fax: +31 70 379 63 22
E-mail: info@nfia.nl
www.nfia.nl

NRW Nederlandse Raad van Winkelcentra
Herculesplein 271
3584 AA UTRECHT
Tel.: +31 30 231 37 54
Fax: +31 30 234 12 87
E-mail: info@nrw.nl
www.nrw.nl
Contact: P.W. Affourtit

NVB (Association of Project Developers)
P.O. Box 620
2770 AP VOORBURG
Tel.: +31 70 386 02 04
Fax: +31 70 387 63 26
E-mail: info@nvb-bouw.nl
www.nvb-bouw.nl

NVM
P.O. Box 2222
3430 DC NIEUWEGEIN
Tel.: +31 30 608 51 85
Fax: +31 30 603 54 68
E-mail:
info@nvmorg.nl
www.nvm.nl

ROZ Raad voor Onroerende Zaken
P.O. Box 93002
2509 AA THE HAGUE
Tel.: +31 70 349 01 95
Fax: +31 70 349 01 27
E-mail: info@roz.nl
www.roz.nl
Contact:
Dr. A.C. Hordijk MRICS

Vereniging Eigen Huis (Association of Home Owners)
P.O. Box 735
3800 AS AMERSFOORT
Tel.: +31 33 450 77 52
Fax: +31 33 450 74 32
E-mail: veh@veh.nl
www.eigenhuis.nl

VNO-NCW
P.O. Box 93002
2509 AA THE HAGUE
Tel.: +31 70 349 03 49
Fax: +31 70 349 03 00
E-mail: informatie@
vno-ncw.nl
www.vno-ncw.nl

Funds

ABP Algemeen Burgerlijk Pensioenfonds
P.O. Box 4820
6401 JM HEERLEN
Tel.: +31 45 579 91 11

Altera Vastgoed N.V.
P.O. Box 9220
1180 ME AMSTELVEEN
Tel.: +31 20 545 20 50
Fax: +31 20 545 20 60
E-mail:
info@alteravastgoed.nl
www.alteravastgoed.nl
Contact:
Drs. R.J.M. Hogenboom

AMVEST
P.O. Box 12446
1100 AK AMSTERDAM ZO
Tel.: +31 20 430 12 12
Fax: +31 20 430 12 13
E-mail: info@amvest.nl
www.amvest.nl
Contact: Drs. M.W.A. Maas

Annexum Invest
P.O. Box 75215
1070 AE AMSTERDAM
Tel.: +31 20 575 09 52
Fax: +31 20 557 09 51

AZL Vastgoed
P.O. Box 4471
6401 CZ HEERLEN
Tel.: +31 45 576 33 27
Fax: +31 45 576 32 10
E-mail: azl-vastgoed@
azl-group.com
www.azl-group.com

Celogix Property Fund
P.O. Box 75035
1070 AA AMSTERDAM
Tel.: +31 20 577 76 66
Fax: +31 20 671 74 76
E-mail: general@celogix.nl
www.celogix.nl
Contact: Drs. B.Y. Reidsma
An Arlington Company

KFN
P.O. Box 2028
3500 GA UTRECHT
Tel.: +31 30 284 38 40
Fax: +31 30 284 38 45
E-mail: info@kfn.nl
www.kfn.nl
Contact: Paul Vismans,
Frank Hendriksen

Nieuwe Steen Investments N.V.
P.O. Box 4145
1620 HC HOORN NH
Tel.: +31 229 29 50 50
Fax: +31 229 23 13 72

PGGM
P.O. Box 117
3700 AC ZEIST
Tel.: +31 30 696 99 11

Renderend Bezit CV
P.O. Box 75035
1070 AA AMSTERDAM
Tel.: +31 20 577 76 06
Fax: +31 20 671 74 76
E-mail:
info@renderendbezit.nl
www.renderendbezit.nl
Contact:
Mr. H.J. Schutter MRE
An Arlington Company

Uni-Invest N.V.
Stadhouderskade 1
1054 ES AMSTERDAM
Tel.: +31 20 607 74 00
Fax: +31 20 607 74 40

VastNed Groep
P.O. Box 4444
3006 AK ROTTERDAM
Tel.: +31 10 242 43 00
Fax: +31 10 242 43 33

Wereldhave N.V.
P.O. Box 85660
2508 CJ THE HAGUE
Tel.: +31 70 346 93 25
Fax: +31 70 364 41 03

Vesteda Group B.V.
P.O. Box 1211
6201 BE MAASTRICHT
Tel.: +31 43 329 66 66
Fax: +31 43 329 66 00
E-mail: info@vesteda.com
www.vesteda.com
Contact: Mr. H.C.F. Smeets

Legal, Fiscal, Notary

Van Agt + Dussel Notarissen
P.O. Box 4121
3006 AC ROTTERDAM
Tel.: +31 10 242 54 00
Fax: +31 10 242 54 50
E-mail:
notaris.vanagt@vadnot.nl
Dussel.Margot@vadnot.nl
Hes.Maurits@vadnot.nl
www.vadnot.nl
Contact:
M.A.J.C.M. van Agt,
M.J. Dussel,
M.M. Hes

AKD Prinsen Van Wijmen
P.O. Box 666
5600 AR EINDHOVEN
Tel.: +31 40 234 56 00
Fax: +31 40 234 56 01
E-mail: marketing@akd.nl
www.akd.nl

Bartels Advocaten
P.O. Box 64
3500 AB UTRECHT
Tel.: +31 30 252 25 77
Fax: +31 30 252 39 43

Boekel De Nerée
P.O. Box 2508
1000 CM AMSTERDAM
Tel.: +31 20 431 31 31
Fax: +31 20 431 31 43

Bureau Breij B.V.
P.O. Box 15858
1001 NJ AMSTERDAM
Tel.: +31 20 471 19 49
Fax: +31 20 471 19 69
E-mail: info@breij.nl
www.breij.nl
www.debtcollection.nl
Contact: Mr. R.A.M. Breij

**CMS Derks Star
Busmann Hanotiau**
P.O. Box 85250
3508 AG UTRECHT
Tel.: +31 30 212 11 11
Fax: +31 30 212 13 33

**Hoogland C.S. Tax Lawyers
& Legal Counsels**
P.O. Box 424
3740 AK BAARN
Tel.: +31 35 548 90 00
Fax: +31 35 548 90 09
E-mail:info@hooglandcs.nl
www.hooglandcs.nl
Contact: Kees Hoogland

Houthoff Buruma
P.O. Box 1507
3000 BM ROTTERDAM
Tel.: +31 10 217 20 00
Fax: +31 10 217 27 00
E-mail: c.goumans@
houthoff.com
www.houthoff.com
Contact: C.M.F.M. Goumans

Lexence N.V.
P.O. Box 75999
1070 AZ AMSTERDAM
Tel.: +31 20 573 67 36
Fax: +31 20 573 67 37
E-mail: info@lexence.com
www.lexence.com
Contact: drs. M. Croon

NautaDutilh N.V.
P.O. Box 7113
1007 JC AMSTERDAM
Tel.: +31 20 717 10 00
Fax: +31 20 717 11 11
info@nautadutilh.com
www.nautadutilh.com
Contact: Kees Boodt

**Pels Rijcken &
Droogleever Fortuijn**
Koningin Julianaplein 30
2595 AA THE HAGUE
Tel.: +31 70 515 38 50
Fax: +31 70 515 31 24
ra.gallas@pelsrijcken.nl
www.pelsrijcken.nl
Contact: Rob Gallas,
Cees de Zeeuw,
Pim Huijgen, René Spit

Schaap & Partners
P.O. Box 23052
3001 KB ROTTERDAM
Tel.: +31 10 277 03 00
Fax: +31 10 436 49 77

Property Advisors (1)

**Amsterdam Airport Area
(AAA)**
P.O. Box 75700
1118 ZT SCHIPHOL
Tel.: +31 20 405 47 77
Fax: +31 20 653 18 94
E-mail: lc@aaarea.nl
www.aaarea.nl
Contact:
Drs. L.F. Kuijer-Campfens

Atisreal Netherlands B.V.
Concertgebouwplein 5
1071 LL AMSTERDAM
Tel.: +31 20 574 58 28
Fax: +31 20 574 58 29
E-mail: info@atisreal.nl
www.atisreal.nl
Contact: Ingmar Dirkse
van den Heuvel

**Catella Property
Consultants B.V.**
P.O. Box 56435
1040 AK AMSTERDAM
Tel.: +31 20 682 06 16
Fax: +31 20 684 42 91

CB Richard Ellis B.V.
Honthorststraat 19
1071 DC AMSTERDAM
Tel.: +31 20 626 26 91
Fax: +31 20 624 63 05

Colliers NMS
Titiaanstraat 13
1077 RC AMSTERDAM
Tel.: +31 20 675 75 00
Fax: +31 20 379 27 62
E-mail: info@colliers.nl
www.colliers.nl
Contact: N.J. ter Mors,
W.A.R. van der Noordaa

Cushman & Wakefield
P.O. Box 75456
1070 AL AMSTERDAM
Tel.: +31 20 301 42 42
Fax: +31 20 301 42 19
www.cushmanwakefield.com
Contact: Baldwin Poolman

**Van Dijk & Ten Cate
Real Estate Advisors**
Gebouw 'Officia 1'
De Boelelaan 7
1083 HJ AMSTERDAM
Tel.: +31 20 442 30 60
Fax: +31 20 404 93 56

DRS Makelaars
Amsteldijk 194
1070 AM AMSTERDAM
Tel.: +31 20 640 52 52
Fax: +31 20 641 52 25

DTZ Zadelhoff V.O.F.
P.O. Box 19125
3501 DC UTRECHT
Tel.: +31 30 233 25 52
Fax: +31 30 231 05 43

**Van Gool & Elburg
Vastgoedspecialisten**
Strawinskylaan 611
1077 XX AMSTERDAM
Tel.: +31 20 664 85 85
Fax: +31 20 675 02 59

Helm en Wesep
Mauritskade 33
2514 HD THE HAGUE
Tel.: +31 70 356 04 12
Fax: +31 70 356 12 90

Jacobus Recourt Makelaars
P.O. Box 17106
1001 JC AMSTERDAM
Tel.: +31 20 675 06 06
Fax: +31 20 675 03 77

Jones Lang LaSalle B.V.
Strawinskylaan 3103
1077 ZX AMSTERDAM
Tel.: +31 20 540 54 05
Fax: +31 20 661 15 66
E-mail: infonl@eu.jll.com
www.joneslanglasalle.nl
Contact: Mrs. M. Vuijk

**De Kousemaeker Vastgoed
Beleggingen & Consultancy
B.V.**
Koninginnegracht 52
2514 AE THE HAGUE
Tel.: +31 70 311 01 00
Fax: +31 70 311 01 09

Property Advisors (2)

Kroese & Paternotte
P.O. Box 75643
1070 AP AMSTERDAM
Tel.: +31 20 664 74 41
Fax: +31 20 679 35 22

Meeùs Bedrijfshuisvesting
Willemstraat 1-5
4811 AH BREDA
Tel.: +31 76 531 33 13
www.meeus.com

**De Mik Bedrijfs-
huisvesting B.V.**
Lichtenauerlaan 234
3062 ME ROTTERDAM
Tel.: +31 10 453 03 03
Fax: +31 10 453 23 13

MRE Vastgoed B.V.
P.O. Box 91
6865 ZH DOORWERTH
Tel.: +31 26 495 00 00
Fax: +31 26 495 00 01
info@mrevastgoed.nl
www.mrevastgoed.nl
Contact: J.G. Olthuis MRE

Nadorp Makelaars V.O.F.
P.O. Box 18590
2502 EN THE HAGUE
Tel.: +31 70 375 75 75
Fax: +31 70 375 75 44

Nelisse Makelaars O.G. B.V.
Statenlaan 128
2582 GW THE HAGUE
Tel.: +31 70 350 14 00
Fax: +31 70 350 66 86

Ooms Makelaars B.V.
P.O. Box 24040
3007 DA ROTTERDAM
Tel.: +31 10 424 88 88
Fax: +31 10 424 88 89

**Property Masters Europe
(PME) Group / European
Property Operations
Corporation (EPOC) N.V.**
P.O. Box 154
5240 AD ROSMALEN
Tel.: +31 73 528 67 30
Fax: +31 73 528 67 31

RSP Makelaars
P.O. Box 3617
5203 DP DEN BOSCH
Tel.: +31 73 648 87 50
Fax: +31 73 648 87 55

Savills Nederland B.V.
Gabriël Metsustraat 13
1071 DZ AMSTERDAM
Tel.: +31 20 672 22 11
Fax: +31 20 672 14 00

**Schoeman
Bedrijfshuisvesting**
P.O. Box 66
3900 AB VEENENDAAL
Tel.: +31 318 58 71 22
Fax: +31 318 58 71 18

**Trimp & van Tartwijk
Property Consultants NV**
Zuidplein 140
1077 XV AMSTERDAM
Tel.: +31 20 575 21 70
Fax: +31 20 575 21 69
E-mail: consultants@
trimpenvantartwijk.nl
www.trimpenvan
tartwijk.nl

**Troostwijk
Makelaars O.G. B.V.**
P.O. Box 9924
1006 AP AMSTERDAM
Tel.: +31 20 666 66 66
Fax: +31 20 666 66 62

**VEG Interior Building
Systems B.V.**
P.O. Box 6524
5600 HM EINDHOVEN
Tel.: +31 40 296 28 75
Fax: +31 40 244 98 90
E-mail: info@vegoffice.com
www.vegoffice.com
Contact: Ir. B. van Egmond

**Van der Vorm Vastgoed
B.V.**
P.O. Box 23313
3001 KH ROTTERDAM
Tel.: +31 10 436 92 18
Fax: +31 10 436 92 39

Property Investors (1)

**Aberdeen Property
Investors Europe B.V.**
P.O. Box 56435
1040 AK AMSTERDAM
Tel.: +31 20 687 05 53
Fax: +31 20 684 42 91
E-mail: nico.tates@
aberdeenproperty
investors.com
www.aberdeenproperty
investors.com
Contact: dhr. Nico Tates

Achmea Vastgoed B.V.
P.O. Box 59347
1040 KH AMSTERDAM
Tel.: +31 20 606 56 00
Fax: +31 20 606 56 09
www.achmeavastgoed.nl

**Arlington Property
Investors Europe B.V.**
P.O. Box 75035
1070 AA AMSTERDAM
Tel.: +31 20 577 76 66
Fax: +31 20 671 74 76
info@arlington.com
www.arlington.com
Contact: Drs. B.Y. Reidsma

Ahold Real Estate Europe
P.O. Box 3071
1500 HD ZAANDAM
Tel.: +31 75 659 54 20
Fax: +31 75 659 85 29
www.aholdrealestate
europe.com
Contact: Yvonne Koster

AKRON Group
Hoofdweg Oostzijde 850-B
2132 MC HOOFDDORP
Tel.: +31 23 554 09 80
Fax: +31 23 554 09 88
p.ulm@akron-group.com
www.akron-group.com
Contact: P. Ulm, CEO

Altera Vastgoed N.V.
P.O. Box 25
2000 AA HAARLEM
Tel.: +31 23 512 19 50
Fax: +31 23 512 19 60
E-mail: rene.hogenboom@
alteravastgoed.nl
www.alteravastgoed.nl
Contact:
Drs. R.J.M. Hogenboom

AZL Vastgoed
P.O. Box 4471
6401 CZ HEERLEN
Tel.: +31 45 576 33 27
Fax: +31 45 576 32 10
E-mail: azl-vastgoed@
azl-group.com
www.azl-group.com

Bouwfonds Holding
P.O. Box 15
3870 DA HOEVELAKEN
Tel.: +31 33 253 91 11
Fax: +31 33 253 95 55
www.bouwfonds.nl
Contact: H.J. Rutgers

Corio N.V.
P.O. Box 8243
3503 RE UTRECHT
Tel.: +31 30 282 93 00
Fax: +31 30 281 72 33
E-mail:
info@nl.corio-eu.com
www.corio-eu.com
Contact: J.A. de Kreij,
retail: ing. G. Groener,
offices: drs. J. Visser

Delta Lloyd Vastgoed
P.O. Box 1000
1000 BA AMSTERDAM
Tel.: +31 20 594 91 11
Fax: +31 20 594 38 10
E-mail:
vastgoed@deltalloyd.nl
www.deltalloydvastgoed.nl
Contact:
E.A. Dijkstra MRE MRICS

Property Investors (2)

Euro American Investors Group
Koninginnegracht 7
2514 AA THE HAGUE
Tel.: +31 70 364 73 00
Fax: +31 70 365 57 76
E-mail: info@eaig.nl
www.eaig.nl
Contact: J.P.M. Adema

Foram Management B.V.
Strawinskylaan 917
1077 XX AMSTERDAM
Tel.: +31 20 575 34 40
Fax: +31 20 575 34 46

Fortis Vastgoed Beleggingen
P.O. Box 2008
3500 GA UTRECHT
Tel.: +31 30 257 23 80
Fax: +31 30 257 83 06
E-mail:
info@fortisvastgoed.nl
www.fortisvastgoed
beleggingen.nl
Contact: Mr. R.W.M. Smeets

Fortis Vastgoed Landelijk
P.O. Box 2007
3500 GA UTRECHT
Tel.: +31 30 257 22 66
Fax: +31 30 257 81 94

Generali Vastgoed B.V.
P.O. Box 1888
1110 CL DIEMEN
Tel.: +31 20 660 16 20
Fax: +31 20 660 16 25
E-mail: rooms@generali.nl
www.generali.nl
Contact: R. Ooms

De Groene Groep
P.O. Box 23037
3001 KA ROTTERDAM
Tel.: +31 10 440 30 00
Fax: +31 10 440 30 01
E-mail:
info@degroenegroep.nl
www.degroenegroep.nl
Contact:
Mr. M.C. de Groene

Grouwels Vastgoed
Maasboulevard 5
P.O. Box 1292
MAASTRICHT
Tel.: +31 43 325 45 65
Fax: +31 43 325 26 99
E-mail: info@grouwels.nl
www.grouwels.nl
Contact: Jo Bastiaans,
Ir. Jort Bastiaans,
Piet Bougie

ING Real Estate Investment Management
P.O. Box 90463
2509 LL THE HAGUE
Tel.: +31 70 341 93 08
Fax: +31 70 341 94 18
www.ingrealestate.com

Insinger de Beaufort
P.O. Box 365
5600 AJ EINDHOVEN
Tel.: +31 40 265 52 55
Fax: +31 40 245 28 55

JBH Property Investments Finance & Consulting B.V.
P.O. Box 82412
2508 EK THE HAGUE
Tel.: +31 70 346 90 30
Fax: +31 70 354 00 82

Konre Groep B.V.
Baarnsche Dijk 21
3741 LP BAARN
Tel.: +31 35 548 58 50
Fax: +31 35 548 58 51

Kroonenberg Groep
P.O. Box 7538
1118 ZG SCHIPHOL
Tel.: +31 20 578 87 88
Fax: +31 20 675 04 30
E-mail:
info@kroonenberg.nl
www.kroonenberg.nl
Contact: L. Bamberger

Mubavi Vastgoed B.V.
P.O. Box 3230
5203 DE DEN BOSCH
Tel.: +31 73 624 02 15
Fax: +31 73 621 09 65

Óbidos Vastgoed B.V.
P.O. Box 75919
1070 AX AMSTERDAM
Tel.: +31 20 570 78 87
Fax: +31 20 570 78 88
E-mail: info@obidos.nl
www.obidos.nl
Contact:
Drs. R.J.T.M. Velthuyse

OVC Oosterbeekse Vastgoed Combinatie B.V.
Utrechtseweg 181
6862 AJ OOSTERBEEK
Tel.: +31 26 339 64 00
Fax: +31 26 339 64 09

Redevco Europe Services B.V.
P.O. Box 94277
1090 GG AMSTERDAM
Tel.: +31 20 599 62 62
Fax: +31 20 599 62 63
E-mail: eur@redevco.com
www.redevco.com
Contact: J.G. Blokhuis

Redevco Nederland B.V.
P.O. Box 1340
1000 BH AMSTERDAM
Tel.: +31 20 521 87 30
Fax: +31 20 521 87 40
E-mail:
service@nl.redevco.com
www.redevco.com

Rodamco Europe N.V.
P.O. Box 1233
3000 BE ROTTERDAM
Tel.: +31 10 217 64 00
Fax: +31 10 217 64 01
E-mail:
info@rodamco.com
www.rodamco.com
Contact: M.J. Hulshoff,
J.A. Bomhoff, K.W. Ledeboer

Rodamco Europe in the Netherlands
P.O. Box 22816
1100 DH AMSTERDAM ZO
Tel.: +31 20 312 01 20
Fax: +31 20 312 02 40
info.nl@rodamco.com
www.rodamco.com
Contact: Ir. K. Laglas

Schiphol Real Estate B.V.
P.O. Box 75776
1118 ZX SCHIPHOL
Tel.: +31 20 601 28 88
Fax: +31 20 601 32 01
realestate@schiphol.nl
www.schiphol.com/
realestate. Contact:
A.A. Mast M.Sc. FRICS

Stienstra Beleggingen B.V.
P.O. Box 79
6400 AB HEERLEN
Tel.: +31 45 563 81 00
Fax: +31 45 563 83 60
E-mail: jacques.verheijen@
stienstrab.nl
www.stienstra
beleggingen.nl
Contact: J.W.J. Verheijen

Vasloc Beheer B.V.
P.O. Box 2075
3500 GB UTRECHT
Tel.: +31 30 232 67 50
Fax: +31 30 232 67 59
E-mail:
info@vasloc.nl
www.vasloc.nl
Contact: P.A.M. de Heer

Vesteda
P.O. Box 1211
6201 BE MAASTRICHT
Tel.: +31 43 329 66 66
Fax: +31 43 329 66 00
E-mail: info@vesteda.com
www.vesteda.com
Contact: Mr. H.C.F.
Smeets

Property Managers

BPF Bouwinvest
P.O. Box 56045
1040 AA AMSTERDAM
Tel.: +31 20 583 16 00
Fax: +31 20 583 17 00
E-mail:
info@bpfbouwinvest.nl
www.bpfbouwinvest.nl
••••••••••••••••••••

**Dynamis ABC
Vastgoedmanagers B.V.**
P.O. Box 85348
3508 AH UTRECHT
Tel.: +31 30 256 51 51
Fax: +31 30 259 94 68
••••••••••••••••••••

**Dynamis P & A Retail
Vastgoedmanagers B.V.**
P.O. Box 85270
3508 AG UTRECHT
Tel.: +31 30 256 51 65
Fax: +31 30 265 51 66
••••••••••••••••••••

Hanze Vast Beheer B.V.
Verlengde Hereweg 174
9722 AM GRONINGEN
Tel.: +31 50 520 76 76
Fax: +31 50 520 76 77
••••••••••••••••••••

**Jacobus Recourt
Vastgoedmanagement**
P.O. Box 17106
1001 JC AMSTERDAM
Tel.: +31 20 521 72 17
Fax: +31 20 521 72 27
••••••••••••••••••••

**Jones Lang LaSalle
Vastgoed Management B.V.**
Weena 256
3012 NJ ROTTERDAM
Tel.: +31 10 411 04 40
Fax: +31 10 414 70 28
••••••••••••••••••••

Kats & Waalwijk Groep
P.O. Box 392
4200 AJ GORINCHEM
Tel.: +31 183 69 19 62
Fax: +31 183 66 19 24
E-mail: office@kw-groep.nl
www.kw-groep.nl
Contact: Ing. A. van Driel
MRE MRICS
••••••••••••••••••••

**K&O Property Management
BV**
P.O. Box 116
1170 AC BADHOEVEDORP
Tel.: +31 20 449 06 58
Fax: +31 20 449 06 78
www.knogroup.nl
••••••••••••••••••••

**Property Masters Europe
(PME) Group / European
Property Operations
Corporation (EPOC) N.V.**
P.O. Box 154
5240 AD ROSMALEN
Tel.: +31 73 528 67 30
Fax: +31 73 528 67 31
••••••••••••••••••••

**REBO Vastgoed
Management B.V.**
P.O. Box 111
7400 AC DEVENTER
Tel.: +31 570 61 27 52
Fax: +31 570 61 98 42
••••••••••••••••••••

**RVM Vastgoed-
management B.V.**
Wycker Grachtstraat 10k
6221 CW MAASTRICHT
Tel.: +31 43 351 55 00
Fax: +31 43 351 55 30
••••••••••••••••••••

**SCM, Shopping Center
Management B.V.**
P.O. Box 410
3990 GE HOUTEN
Tel.: +31 30 635 22 11
Fax: +31 30 635 30 34
E-mail: erooseboom@
scmeurope.com
info@scmeurope.com
www.scmeurope.com
••••••••••••••••••••

WPM Groep
P.O. Box 3478
5203 DL DEN BOSCH
Tel.: +31 73 649 14 00
Fax: +31 73 649 14 19
••••••••••••••••••••

Research & Consultancy

ABT bv
P.O. Box 82
6800 AB ARNHEM
Tel.: +31 26 368 31 11
Fax: +31 26 368 31 10
E-mail: abt@abt-consult.nl
www.abt-consult.nl
Contact: Ir. J.G. Hulsbergen
••••••••••••••••••••

Akro Consult
P.O. Box 97662
2509 GB THE HAGUE
Tel.: +31 70 326 26 23
Fax: +31 70 328 27 08
www.akroconsult.nl
••••••••••••••••••••

**Amsterdam School of
Real Estate**
Wibautstraat 129
1091 GL AMSTERDAM
Tel.: +31 20 668 11 29
Fax: +31 20 668 03 61
E-mail: info@asre.uva.nl
www.asre.nl
www.vastgoedkennis.nl
Contact:
Drs. L.B. Uittenboogaard
••••••••••••••••••••

AOS Nederland N.V.
Weena 272
3012 NJ ROTTERDAM
Tel.: +31 10 412 00 35
Fax: +31 10 412 00 49
E-mail:
nederland@aosgroup.com
www.aosgroup.com
Contact:
Ing. Paul D. Trumpie CFM,
Ir. Rogier Hageman
••••••••••••••••••••

ARCADIS
P.O.Box 220
3800 AE AMERSFOORT
Tel.: +33 477 10 00
Fax: +33 477 20 00
E-mail: info@arcadis.nl
www.arcadis.nl
••••••••••••••••••••

**BM Managers van het
Bouwproces B.V.**
P.O. Box 100
2130 AC HOOFDDORP
Tel.: +31 23 561 29 71
Fax: +31 23 563 26 76
E-mail: bm@bmadvies.nl
www.bmadvies.nl
Contact: Ir. R. Reedeker
••••••••••••••••••••

BOAG Bouw Advies Groep
P.O. Box 8595
3009 AN ROTTERDAM
Tel.: +31 10 209 35 35
Fax: +31 10 209 35 00
E-mail: info@boag.com
www.boag.com
Contact: C.A.G. Heijmans
••••••••••••••••••••

Brink Groep
P.O. Box 415
4000 AK TIEL
Tel.: +31 344 675 875
E-mail: info@brink.nl
www.brink.nl
••••••••••••••••••••

**Buck Consultants
International**
P.O. Box 1456
6501 BL NIJMEGEN
Tel.: +31 24 379 02 22
Fax: +31 24 379 01 20
E-mail: bci@bciglobal.com
www.bciglobal.com
Contact: Rene Buck,
Josephine Glaudemans,
Wim Pijpers
••••••••••••••••••••

**BV Technical
Management (TM)**
P.O. Box 68
3800 AB AMERSFOORT
Tel.: +31 33 451 14 11
Fax: +31 33 455 87 79
••••••••••••••••••••

**CBS Centraal Bureau voor
de Statistiek**
P.O. Box 4000
2270 JM VOORBURG
Tel.: +31 70 337 3800
Fax: +31 70 387 74 29
E-mail: infoservice@cbs.nl
www.cbs.nl
••••••••••••••••••••

MAPS & INDEX

Research & Consultancy (2)

Desenco Real Estate B.V.
P.O. Box 803
2700 AV ZOETERMEER
Tel.: +31 79 368 52 10
Fax: +31 79 361 55 31

ECORYS-Kolpron
Hoofdweg 330
3067 GK ROTTERDAM
Tel.: +31 10 453 84 00
Fax: +31 10 453 85 88

**Ernst & Young Real Estate
Hospitality & Construction
Group**
P.O. Box 3053
3502 GB UTRECHT
Tel.: +31 30 259 51 51
Fax: +31 30 259 23 50
www.ey.com
Contact: Ad Buisman,
Henk Wilbrink

Fakton
P.O. Box 30188
3001 DD ROTTERDAM
Tel.: +31 10 205 62 10
Fax: +31 10 205 53 73
E-mail: info@fakton.nl
www.fakton.nl

FGH Vastgoed Expertise
Koningslaan 33
1075 AB AMSTERDAM
Tel.: +31 20 677 67 87
Fax: +31 20 677 67 80
www.vastgoedexpertise.nl

**FMH Accommodation
Consultancy**
Hardwareweg 1
3821 BL AMERSFOORT
Tel.: +31 33 454 11 00
Fax: +31 33 454 11 11

Global Property Research
P.O. Box 75666
1070 AR AMSTERDAM
Tel.: +31 20 348 84 52
Fax: +31 20 348 89 62
E-mail: info@gpr.nl
www.propertyshares.com
Contact: F. Annokkee

**Jones Lang LaSalle
Research Consultancy B.V.**
P.O. Box 93020
2509 AA THE HAGUE
Tel.: +31 70 318 13 13
Fax: +31 70 634 39 08

Kotvis & Haksteen
P.O. Box 917
2800 AX GOUDA
Tel.: +31 182 52 64 25
Fax: +31 182 52 67 29

Maastricht University
P.O. Box 616
6200 MD MAASTRICHT
Tel.: +31 43 388 38 38
Fax: +31 43 388 48 75
E-mail: p.eichholtz@
berfin.unimaas.nl
www.unimaas.nl
Contact:
Prof. Dr. P.M.A. Eichholtz

**Oranjewoud
Bouw & Vastgoed**
P.O. Box 8590
3009 AN ROTTERDAM
Tel.: +31 10 235 18 34
Fax: +31 10 235 18 85
E-mail:
info@oranjewoud.nl
www.oranjewoud.nl
Contact: R.J. Teunissen,
A. Schippers, G.A. Breukink,
P.B. Docters van Leeuwen

PRC Bouwcentrum B.V.
P.O. Box 1051
2410 CB BODEGRAVEN
Tel.: +31 17 263 14 14
Fax: +31 17 261 19 02

Prins Development
Consultants Ned.
Driewegenweg 53
3881 EX PUTTEN
Tel.: +31 341 36 10 45
Fax: +31 341 36 06 88

Protocall B.V.
P.O. Box 16431
2500 BK THE HAGUE
Tel.: +31 70 380 81 78
Fax: +31 70 305 17 01

Regus Business Centres
Kingsfordweg 151
1043 GR AMSTERDAM
Tel.: +31 20 491 91 91
www.regus.com

Royal Haskoning
P.O. Box 151
6500 AD NIJMEGEN
Tel.: +31 24 328 42 84
Fax: +31 24 323 93 46

**Rijksuniversiteit
Groningen**
P.O. Box 800
9700 AV GRONINGEN
Tel.: +31 50 363 38 96
Fax: +31 50 363 3901
E-mail: e.j.prins@ frw.rug.nl
www.frw.rug.nl
Contact: Prof. Dr. E.J. Prins

Stec Groep B.V.
P.O. Box 31210
6503 CE NIJMEGEN
Tel.: +31 24 352 16 16
Fax: +31 24 352 16 10
E-mail: info@stec.nl
www.stec.nl
Contact: Duco Bodewes,
Peter van Geffen

Strabo B.V.
P.O. Box 15710
1001 NE AMSTERDAM
Tel.: +31 20 626 08 17
Fax: +31 20 623 68 07

**Technische Universiteit
Delft**
P.O. Box 5043
2600 GA DELFT
Tel.: +31 15 278 41 59
Fax: +31 15 278 31 71
E-mail: mvb@bk.tudelft.nl
www.tudelft.nl
Contact:
Prof. Ir. H. de Jonge

**Twynstra Gudde
Consultants and
Managers**
P.O. Box 907
3800 AX AMERSFOORT
Tel.: +31 33 467 77 77
Fax: +31 33 467 76 66
E-mail: info@tg.nl
www.twynstragudde.nl
Contact: mevrouw mr.
ing. M.E. Krul-Seen,
dhr. ing. C.E.M.
Lemmens

**University of
Amsterdam**
P.O. Box 19268
1000 GG AMSTERDAM
Tel.: +31 20 525 91 11
E-mail: info@uva.nl
www.uva.nl

**VEG Interior Building
Systems BV**
P.O. Box 6524
5600 HM EINDHOVEN
Tel.: +31 40 296 28 75
Fax: +31 40 244 98 90
E-mail: info@vegoffice.
com
www.vegoffice.com
Contact:
Ir. Berend van Egmond

Youropean Partners B.V.
P.O. Box 12516
1100 AM AMSTERDAM ZO
Tel.: +31 20 312 04 30
Fax: +31 20 312 04 44

Government & Authorities

City of Amsterdam

City of Amsterdam
P.O. Box 202, room 1365
1000 AE AMSTERDAM
Tel.: +31 20 552 32 46
Fax: +31 20 624 55 50
E-mail: kbuschman@
amsterdam.nl
www.amsterdam.nl
Contact: Karen Buschman

**City of Amsterdam
Development Corporation**
P.O. Box 1104
1000 BC AMSTERDAM
Tel.: +31 20 552 61 11
Fax: +31 20 552 60 06
E-mail: p.cohen@
oga.amsterdam.nl
www.oga.amsterdam.nl
Contact: Paul Cohen

**City of Amsterdam
Department of
Economic Development**
P.O. Box 2133
1000 CC AMSTERDAM
Tel.: +31 20 552 32 05
Fax: +31 20 552 28 60
E-mail:
sba@ez.amsterdam.nl
www.ez.amsterdam.nl

**Chamber of
Commerce Amsterdam**
P.O. Box 2852
1000 CW AMSTERDAM
Tel.: +31 20 531 40 00
Fax: +31 20 531 47 99
E-mail:
post@amsterdam.kvk.nl
www.amsterdam.kvk.nl

**Projectbureau Zuidas
WTC, Central Hall**
Strawinskylaan 59
1077 XW AMSTERDAM
Tel.: +31 20 575 21 11
Fax: +31 20 575 21 15
E-mail: info@zuidas.nl
www.zuidas.nl
Contact:
Frederijk Haentjens

Projectbureau IJ-burg
P.O. Box 1269
1000 BG AMSTERDAM
Tel.: +31 20 621 41 11
Fax: +31 20 621 41 70
E-mail: wkempes@pmb.nl
Contact: W. Kempes

Amsterdam Arena Area
Bijlmerplein 79
1102 BH AMSTERDAM ZO
Tel.: +31 20 311 84 44
Fax: +31 20 311 84 45
E-mail:
info@amsterdamarena.nl
www.amsterdamarena.nl

City of Rotterdam

City of Rotterdam
P.O. Box 70012
3000 KP ROTTERDAM
Tel.: +31 10 417 91 11
Fax: +31 10 417 93 82
E-mail: JKombrink@
stadhuis.rotterdam.nl
www.rotterdam.nl

**Rotterdam City Development
Corporation (OBR)**
P.O. Box 6575
3002 AN ROTTERDAM
Tel.: +31 10 489 36 85
Fax: +31 10 489 71 49
E-mail: r.jongste@
obr.rotterdam.nl
www.obr.rotterdam.nl
Contact: R. Jongste

**Directie Stedelijke
Ontwikkeling en Beheer
(SOB)**
P.O. Box 70012
3000 KP ROTTERDAM
Tel.: +31 10 417 25 14
Fax: +31 10 417 22 44
E-mail: rfa.bitterlich@
bsd.rotterdam.nl
www.rotterdam.nl

**Chamber of
Commerce Rotterdam**
P.O. Box 30025
3001 DA ROTTERDAM
Tel.: +31 10 405 77 77
Fax: +31 10 414 57 54
E-mail:
info@rotterdam.kvk.nl
www.rotterdam.kvk.nl

**Rotterdam Town Planning
and Housing Department**
P.O. Box 6699
3002 AR ROTTERDAM
Tel.: +31 10 489 69 66
Fax: +31 10 489 51 05
E-mail:
DSV@dsv.rotterdam.nl
www.dsv.rotterdam.nl

**Rotterdam Municipal
Port Management (GHR)**
P.O. Box 6622
3002 AP ROTTERDAM
Tel.: +31 10 252 10 10
Fax: +31 10 252 10 20
E-mail:
info@port.rotterdam.nl
www.port.rotterdam.nl

City of The Hague

City of The Hague
P.O. Box 12600
2500 DJ THE HAGUE
Tel.: +31 70 353 28 51
Fax: +31 70 353 36 15
E-mail: a.j.hilhorst@
bsd.denhaag.nl
www.denhaag.nl

**City of The Hague, Urban
Development Department**
P.O. Box 12655
2500 DP THE HAGUE
Tel.: +31 70 353 49 75
Fax: +31 70 353 47 03
E-mail: a.verwoest@
dso.denhaag.nl
www.denhaag.com
Contact:
A. Verwoest

**City of The Hague
Acquisitie- en
Relatiebeheer**
P.O. Box 12655
2500 DP THE HAGUE
Tel.: +31 70 353 46 11
Fax: +31 70 35 34 82
E-mail:
soverhg@dso.denhaag.nl
www.thehague.nl

**Chamber of
Commerce The Hague**
P.O. Box 29718
2502 LS THE HAGUE
Tel.: +31 70 328 71 00
Fax: +31 70 326 20 10
E-mail: vestdenhaag@
denhaag.kvk.nl
www.denhaag.kvk.nl

**Visitors Center
Urban Development**
Spui 70
2511 BT THE HAGUE
Tel.: +31 70 353 37 35
Fax: +31 70 353 42 33
E-mail:
dsobezoekerscentrum@
dso.denhaag.nl
www.denhaag.nl

RANDSTAD

**Holland Randstad
Rotterdam City Development
Corporation (OBR)**
P.O. Box 6575
3002 AN ROTTERDAM
Tel.: +31 10 489 36 85
Fax: +31 10 489 71 49
E-mail: r.jongste@
obr.rotterdam.nl
www.obr.rotterdam.nl
Contact: R. Jongste

City of Utrecht

City of Utrecht
P.O. Box 16200
3500 CE UTRECHT
Tel.: +31 30 286 10 00
Fax: +31 30 286 12 24
E-mail: info@utrecht.nl
www.utrecht.nl
Contact: L.J. Verhulst,
W. Lenting

**City of Utrecht
Department of City
Development**
P.O. Box 8406
3503 RK UTRECHT
Tel.: +31 30 286 40 73
Fax: +31 30 286 48 21
E-mail: ez@utrecht.nl
www.utrecht.nl
Contact: J. de Viet,
A. Joosten, K. Beerda

**City of Utrecht
Real Estate Department**
P.O. Box 8613
3503 RP UTRECHT
Tel.: +31 30 286 42 88
Fax: +31 30 286 71 40
E-mail: ogu.info@utrecht.nl
www.utrecht.nl
Contact:
A.G.J. van Vlimmeren,
R. Nijveld

**Chamber of
Commerce Utrecht**
P.O. Box 48
3500 AA UTRECHT
Tel.: +31 30 236 32 11
Fax: +31 30 231 28 04
E-mail:
info@utrecht.kvk.nl
www.utrecht.kvk.nl

**Projectbureau
Leidsche Rijn**
P.O. Box 8613
3503 RP UTRECHT
Tel.: +31 30 286 47 99
Fax: +31 30 286 48 14
E-mail: leidscherijn.
communicatie@utrecht.nl
www.leidscherijn.nl
Contact:
N. Hugenholtz

**Project Organization
Central Station Area**
P.O. Box 1273
3500 BG UTRECHT
Tel.: +31 30 286 96 00
Fax: +31 30 286 96 01
E-mail:
stationsgebied@utrecht.nl
www.utrecht.nl/
stationsgebied
Contact:
A. Hutschemaekers

DAILY NEWS

WHO'S WHO

FINANCIAL

TRENDS

COMPANIES

COUNTRIES

EDITORIAL

POLITICAL MAP

GERMANY

W a d d e n z e e

NORTH

SEA

Leeuwarden

Ten Boer *GRONINGEN*
Groningen

Dollart

Hoogezand
Sappemeer

F R I E S L A N D

Heerenveen

Assen

D R E N T H E

NOORD-HOLLAND

IJsselmeer

Hoogeveen

Alkmaar

Markermeer

Dronten
Lelystad

Zwolle

O V E R I J S S E L

Purmerend
Zaanstad
Haarlem **AMSTERDAM**

FLEVOLAND
Almere

Amstelveen
Hoofddorp

Hengelo
Enschede

Leiden

Apeldoorn

Amersfoort

UTRECHT
The Hague Alphen Utrecht
Rijswijk Zeist
Zoetermeer Nieuwegein Houten

G E L D E R L A N D

Delft
Schiedam
Rotterdam *ZUID-HOLLAND*

Arnhem

Dordrecht

Waal

Nijmegen

Grevelingen Krammt

's-Hertogenbosch

Oosterschelde

Breda
Etten-Leur
Roosendaal Tilburg

NOORD-BRABANT

Venray

Middelburg
ZEELAND
Bergen
op Zoom

Eindhoven

Helmond

Westerschelde

Venlo

GERMANY

LIMBURG

BELGIUM

Sittard
Geleen

Heerlen
Maastricht

0   30   60 km.

Amsterdam see page **116**	**Northern Region** (provinces of Groningen, Friesland, Drenthe) see page **228**
The Hague see page **142**	**Eastern Region** (provinces of Overijssel, Gelderland) see page **238**
Rotterdam see page **160**	**Central Region** (provinces of Flevoland, Utrecht) see page **216**
Utrecht see page **182**	**Western Region** (provinces of Noord-Holland, Zuid-Holland) see page **196**
	Southern Region (provinces of Noord-Brabant, Zeeland, Limburg) see page **248**

EDITORIAL · LOCATIONS · DECISION MAKERS · INDUSTRY TRENDS · CORPORATE · WHO'S WHO · MAPS & INDEX

URBAN NETWORKS

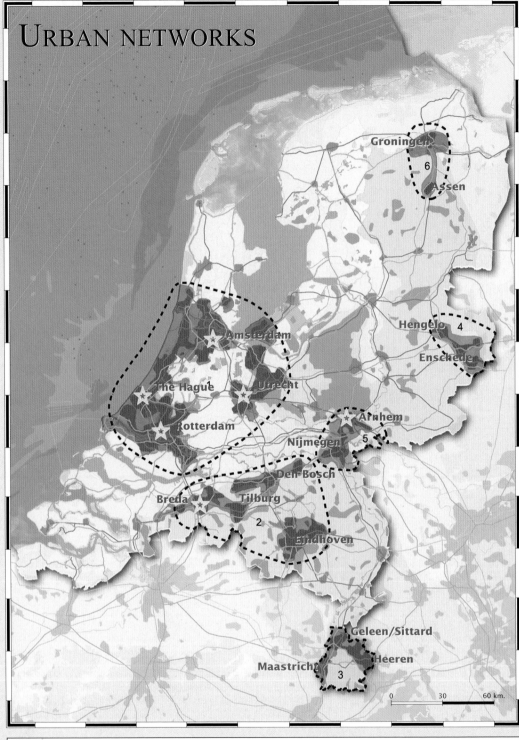

★	National Key Projects (see page 32)	
	National Urban Networks	
1 Randstad Holland		**4** Twente
2 BrabantStad		**5** Arnhem - Nijmegen
3 Zuid-Limburg		**6** Groningen - Assen

WATER-LEVEL MAP

0   30   60 km.

Coast basis

Primary dam

Open water (**1**-Waddenzee, **2**-IJsselmeer area, **3**-Southwest Delta)

Below sea level

EDITORIAL

LOCATIONS

DECISION MAKERS

INDUSTRY TRENDS

CORPORATE

WHO'S WHO

MAPS & INDEX

EDITORIAL · LOCATIONS · DECISION MAKERS · INDUSTRY TRENDS · CORPORATE · WHO'S WHO · MAPS & INDEX